KAPLAN

PUBLISHING

C000144864

NOW THIS EXAM KIT COMES WITH
FREE ONLINE ACCESS
TO EXTRA RESOURCES AIMED AT HELPING YOU PASS YOUR EXAMS

IN ADDITION TO THE OFFICIAL QUESTIONS AND ANSWERS IN THIS BOOK, GO ONLINE AND EN-gage WITH:

- Fixed Tests
- Interim Assessments
- Exam paper Guides
- Latest Official ACCA exam questions
- Answers updated to include legislation relevant to next exam
- Frequent and varied new additions to these resources – watch this space!

And you can access all of these extra resources anytime, anywhere using your EN-gage account.

How to access your online resources

If you are a Kaplan Financial tuition, full-time or distance learning student

You will already have an EN-gage account and these extra resources will be available to you online. You do not need to register again, as this process was completed when you enrolled. If having problems accessing online materials, please ask your course administrator.

If you purchased through Kaplan Flexible Learning or via the Kaplan Publishing website

You will automatically receive an e-mail invitation to EN-gage online. Please register your details using this e-mail to gain access to your content. If you do not receive the e-mail or book content, please contact Kaplan Flexible Learning.

If you are already a registered EN-gage user

Go to www.EN-gage.co.uk and log in. Select the 'add a book' feature and enter the ISBN number of this book and the unique pass key at the bottom of this card. Then click 'finished' or 'add another book'. You may add as many books as you have purchased from this screen.

If you are a new EN-gage user

Register at www.EN-gage.co.uk and click on the link contained in the e-mail we sent you to activate your account. Then select the 'add a book' feature, enter the ISBN number of this book and the unique pass key at the bottom of this card. Then click 'finished' or 'add another book'.

Your Code and Information

This code can only be used once for the registration of one book online. This registration will expire when the final sittings for the examination covered by this book have taken place. Please allow one hour from the time you submitted your book details for us to process your requ

ErT8-KDt9-Pl7y-hDF

For technical support, please visit www.EN-gage.co.uk

Professional Examinations

Paper F6

Taxation
(Finance Act 2009)

EXAM KIT

PUBLISHING

British Library Cataloguing-in-Publication Data

A catalogue record for this book is available from the British Library.

Published by:

Kaplan Publishing UK

Unit 2 The Business Centre

Molly Millar's Lane

Wokingham

Berkshire

RG41 2QZ

ISBN: 978 1 84710 771 8

© Kaplan Financial Limited, 2009.

Printed and bound in Great Britain.

Acknowledgements

The past ACCA examination questions are the copyright of the Association of Chartered Certified Accountants. The original answers to the questions from June 1994 onwards were produced by the examiners themselves and have been adapted by Kaplan Publishing.

We are grateful to the Chartered Institute of Management Accountants and the Institute of Chartered Accountants in England and Wales for permission to reproduce past examination questions. The answers have been prepared by Kaplan Publishing.

CONTENTS

 New features in this edition

In addition to providing a wide ranging bank of real past exam questions, we have also included in this edition:

- An analysis of all of the recent new syllabus examination papers.

- Paper specific information and advice on exam technique.

- Our recommended approach to make your revision for this particular subject as effective as possible.

  This includes step by step guidance on how best to use our Kaplan material (Complete text, pocket notes and exam kit) at this stage in your studies.

- Enhanced tutorial answers packed with specific key answer tips, technical tutorial notes and exam technique tips from our experienced tutors.

- Complementary online resources including full tutor debriefs and question assistance to point you in the right direction when you get stuck.

December 2009 – Real examination questions with enhanced tutorial answers

The real December 2009 exam questions with enhanced "walk through answers" and full "tutor debriefs", updated in line with legislation relevant to your exam sitting, is available on Kaplan EN-gage at:

www.EN-gage.co.uk

You will find a wealth of other resources to help you with your studies on the following sites:

www.EN-gage.co.uk

www.**acca**global.com/students/

INDEX TO QUESTIONS AND ANSWERS

INTRODUCTION

The style of current Paper F6 exam question is different to old syllabus Paper 2.3 questions and significant changes have had to be made to questions in light of the legislative changes in recent Finance Acts.

Accordingly, many of the old ACCA questions within this kit have been adapted to reflect the new style of paper and the new rules. If changed in any way from the original version, this is indicated in the end column of the index below with the mark *(A)*.

Note that the majority of the questions within the kit are past ACCA exam questions, the more recent questions (from 2005) are labelled as such in the index.

The pilot paper is included at the end of the kit.

KEY TO THE INDEX

PAPER ENHANCEMENTS

We have added the following enhancements to the answers in this exam kit:

Key answer tips

All answers include key answer tips to help your understanding of each question.

Tutorial note

All answers include more tutorial notes to explain some of the technical points in more detail.

Top tutor tips

For selected questions, we "walk through the answer" giving guidance on how to approach the questions with helpful 'tips from a top tutor', together with technical tutor notes.

These answers are indicated with the "footsteps" icon in the index.

ONLINE ENHANCEMENTS

 Timed question with Online tutor debrief

For selected questions, we recommend that they are to be completed in full exam conditions (i.e. properly timed in a closed book environment).

In addition to the examiner's technical answer, enhanced with key answer tips and tutorial notes in this exam kit, online you can find an answer debrief by a top tutor that:

- works through the question in full

- points out how to approach the question

- how to ensure that the easy marks are obtained as quickly as possible, and

- emphasises how to tackle exam questions and exam technique.

These questions are indicated with the "clock" icon in the index.

 Online question assistance

Have you ever looked at a question and not know where to start, or got stuck part way through?

For selected questions, we have produced "Online question assistance" offering different levels of guidance, such as:

- ensuring that you understand the question requirements fully, highlighting key terms and the meaning of the verbs used

- how to read the question proactively, with knowledge of the requirements, to identify the topic areas covered

- assessing the detail content of the question body, pointing out key information and explaining why it is important

- help in devising a plan of attack

With this assistance, you should then be able to attempt your answer confident that you know what is expected of you.

These questions are indicated with the "signpost" icon in the index.

Online question enhancements and answer debriefs will be available from Spring 2010 on Kaplan EN-gage at:

www.EN-gage.co.uk

INCOME TAX AND NATIONAL INSURANCE

CHARGEABLE GAINS

KAPLAN PUBLISHING

CORPORATION TAX

VALUE ADDED TAX

KAPLAN PUBLISHING

ANALYSIS OF PAST PAPERS

The table below summarises the key topics that have been tested in the new syllabus examinations to date.

Note that the references are to the number of the question in this edition of the exam kit, but the Pilot Paper is produced in its original form at the end of the kit and therefore these questions have retained their original numbering in the paper itself.

	Pilot 07	Dec 07	Jun 08	Dec 08	Jun 09
Income tax					
Exempt income	Q1	Q29		Q7	Q17
Basic income tax computation	Q1	Q29	Q16	Q7	Q17, Q18
Pension contributions		Q29			Q17
Gift Aid	Q1			Q7	Q17
Husband and wife			Q16		
Age allowance					Q17
Property income	Q1	Q6		Q7	
Furnished holiday lettings		Q6			
Rent-a-room relief		Q6			
ISAs			Q16		
Employed individual					
Factors indicating employment					Q18
Car and fuel benefit		Q29		Q7	
Living accommodation				Q7	
Beneficial loan	Q1		Q16		
Use of assets				Q7	
Mileage allowance	Q1		Q16		Q17
Self employed individual					
Adjustment to profits			Q16		
Capital allowances	Q1	Q29	Q16	Q27	Q17
Basis of assessment rules	Q4			Q27	
Change of accounting date	Q4			Q27	
Partnerships				Q27	
Pensions					
Basic relief				Q30	
Excess contributions charge				Q30	
No relevant earnings				Q30	
Income tax losses					
Factors influencing choice of loss relief		Q23			
Ongoing losses		Q23			
Relief against gains		Q23			

	Pilot 07	Dec 07	Jun 08	Dec 08	Jun 09
National insurance contributions					
Class 1		Q29		Q7	Q18
Class 1A				Q7	
Class 2		Q29			Q18
Class 4		Q29			Q18
Capital gains tax					
Residence / ordinary residence			Q38		
Exempt assets	Q3	Q37			
Chattels	Q3	Q37			Q39
Part disposal	Q3		Q38	Q42	
Shares	Q3	Q37	Q38	Q42	Q39
Takeover				Q42	
Wasting asset					Q39
Insurance for damaged assets			Q38		
Husband and wife	Q3	Q37			
Capital losses		Q23			Q39
Reliefs					
Entrepreneurs' relief	Q3		Q38		Q39
Principal private residence relief	Q3	Q37			Q39
Gift relief			Q38		
Rollover relief			Q38		
Incorporation relief			Q38		
Self assessment – individual					
Pay dates		Q29	Q32		
Payments on account		Q29	Q32		
Filing dates			Q32		Q17
HMRC enquiry			Q32		
Retention of records	Q1				Q17
Corporation tax					
Definition of accounting periods			Q54		
Adjustment to profits	Q2	Q56		Q57	Q50
Capital allowances – P & M	Q2	Q56	Q49, Q54	Q57	Q50
Industrial Buildings allowances	Q2		Q54	Q57	
Lease premiums	Q2				Q50
Basic PCTCT computation	Q2		Q54	Q42, Q57	
Property income	Q2			Q57	Q50
Overseas income			Q54		
Chargeable gains				Q42	
Long period of account			Q49		
Straddling 31 March liability comp			Q49		

	Pilot 07	Dec 07	Jun 08	Dec 08	Jun 09
Corporation tax losses					
Choice of loss relief – factors	Q5				
Trading losses	Q5	Q56		Q57	
Capital losses				Q42	
Groups					
Associated companies				Q57	Q50
Group relief		Q56			
Capital gains group					Q50
Self assessment – companies					
Due dates and interest					Q50
Penalties				Q57	
Value added tax					
Registration			Q54		
Pre-registration input VAT			Q54		
Deregistration					Q70
VAT return computation		Q29			Q70
Valid invoice			Q54		
Default surcharge	Q2			Q57	
Errors in a VAT return	Q2				
Transfer of going concern					Q70
Annual accounting scheme				Q57	
Cash accounting scheme					Q70
Flat rate scheme		Q29			

EXAM TECHNIQUE

- Use the allocated **15 minutes reading and planning time** at the beginning of the exam:
  - read the questions and examination requirements carefully, and
  - begin planning your answers.

  See the Paper Specific Information for advice on how to use this time for this paper.

- **Divide the time** you spend on questions in proportion to the marks on offer:
  - there are 1.8 minutes available per mark in the examination
  - within that, try to allow time at the end of each question to review your answer and address any obvious issues

  Whatever happens, always keep your eye on the clock and **do not over run on any part of any question!**

- Spend the last **five minutes** of the examination:
  - reading through your answers, and
  - **making any additions or corrections**.

- If you **get completely stuck** with a question:
  - leave space in your answer book, and
  - **return to it later.**

- Stick to the question and **tailor your answer** to what you are asked.
  - pay particular attention to the verbs in the question.

- If you do not understand what a question is asking, **state your assumptions**.

  Even if you do not answer in precisely the way the examiner hoped, you should be given some credit, if your assumptions are reasonable.

- You should do everything you can to make things easy for the marker.

  The marker will find it easier to identify the points you have made if your **answers are legible**.

- **Written questions**:

  Your answer should have:
  - a clear structure
  - a brief introduction, a main section and a conclusion.

  Be concise.

  It is better to write a little about a lot of different points than a great deal about one or two points.

- **Computations**:

  It is essential to include all your workings in your answers.

  Many computational questions require the use of a standard format:

  e.g. income tax computations, corporation tax computations and capital gains.

  Be sure you know these formats thoroughly before the exam and use the layouts that you see in the answers given in this book and in model answers.

- **Reports, memos and other documents**:

  Some questions ask you to present your answer in the form of a report, a memo, a letter or other document.

  Make sure that you use the correct format – there could be easy marks to gain here.

PAPER SPECIFIC INFORMATION

THE EXAM

FORMAT OF THE EXAM

Number of marks

5 compulsory questions which will be **predominantly computational**:

Question 1:	Income tax	25 or 30
Question 2:	Corporation tax	25 or 30
Question 3:	Chargeable gains (personal or corporate)	20
Question 4:	Any area of the syllabus	15
Question 5:	Any area of the syllabus	10
		100

Total time allowed: 3 hours plus 15 minutes reading and planning time.

Note that:

- Question 1 will focus on income tax and question 2 will focus on corporation tax. The two questions will be for a total of 55 marks, with one of the questions being for 30 marks and the other being for 25 marks.

- There will always be a minimum of 10 marks on VAT. These marks will normally be included within question 1 or 2, although there could be a separate question on value added tax.

- National Insurance Contributions will not be examined as a separate question, but may be examined in any question involving income tax or corporation tax.

- Groups and overseas aspects of corporation tax will only be examined in question 2, and will account for no more than one third of the marks available for that question.

- Questions 1 and 2 may include a small element of chargeable gains.

- Any of the five questions might include the consideration of issues relating to the minimisation or deferral of tax liabilities.

PASS MARK

The pass mark for all ACCA Qualification examination papers is 50%.

READING AND PLANNING TIME

Remember that all three hour paper based examinations have an additional 15 minutes reading and planning time.

ACCA GUIDANCE

ACCA guidance on the use of this time is as follows:

> This additional time is allowed at the beginning of the examination to allow candidates to read the questions and to begin planning their answers before they start to write in their answer books.
>
> This time should be used to ensure that all the information and, in particular, the exam requirements are properly read and understood.
>
> During this time, candidates may only annotate their question paper. They may not write anything in their answer booklets until told to do so by the invigilator.

KAPLAN GUIDANCE

As all questions are compulsory, there are no decisions to be made about choice of questions, other than in which order you would like to tackle them.

Therefore, in relation to F6, we recommend that you take the following approach with your reading and planning time:

- **Skim through the whole paper**, assessing the level of difficulty of each question.

- **Write down** on the question paper next to the mark allocation **the amount of time you should spend on each part.** Do this for each part of every question.

- **Decide the order** in which you think you will attempt each question:

  This is a personal choice and you have time on the revision phase to try out different approaches, for example, if you sit mock exams.

  A common approach is to tackle the question you think is the easiest and you are most comfortable with first.

  Others may prefer to tackle the longest questions first, or conversely leave them to the last.

  Psychologists believe that you usually perform at your best on the second and third question you attempt, once you have settled into the exam, so not tackling the bigger Section A questions first may be advisable.

  It is usual however that student tackle their least favourite topic and/or the most difficult question in their opinion last.

  Whatever you approach, you must make sure that you leave enough time to attempt all questions fully and be very strict with yourself in timing each question.

- **For each question** in turn, read the requirements and then the detail of the question carefully.

  Always read the requirement first as this enables you to **focus on the detail of the question with the specific task in mind.**

  For computational questions:

  Highlight key numbers / information and key words in the question, scribble notes to yourself on the question paper to remember key points in your answer.

  Jot down proformas required if applicable.

  For written questions:

  Take notice of the format required (e.g. letter, memo, notes) and identify the recipient of the answer . You need to do this to judge the level of financial sophistication required in your answer and whether the use of a formal reply or informal bullet points would be satisfactory.

  Plan your beginning, middle and end and the key areas to be addressed and your use of titles and sub-titles to enhance your answer.

  For all questions:

  Spot the easy marks to be gained in a question and parts which can be performed independently of the rest of the question. For example, writing down due dates of payment of tax, due dates for making elections, laying out basic proformas correctly.

  Make sure that you do these parts first when you tackle the question.

  Don't go overboard in terms of planning time on any one question – you need a good measure of the whole paper and a plan for all of the questions at the end of the 15 minutes.

  By covering all questions you can often help yourself as you may find that facts in one question may remind you of things you should put into your answer relating to a different question.

- With your plan of attack in mind, **start answering your chosen question** with your plan to hand, as soon as you are allowed to start.

 Always keep your eye on the clock and do not over run on any part of any question!

DETAILED SYLLABUS

The detailed syllabus and study guide written by the ACCA can be found at:

www.accaglobal.com/students/

KAPLAN'S RECOMMENDED REVISION APPROACH

QUESTION PRACTICE IS THE KEY TO SUCCESS

Success in professional examinations relies upon you acquiring a firm grasp of the required knowledge at the tuition phase. In order to be able to do the questions, knowledge is essential.

However, the difference between success and failure often hinges on your exam technique on the day and making the most of the revision phase of your studies.

The **Kaplan complete text** is the starting point, designed to provide the underpinning knowledge to tackle all questions. However, in the revision phase, pouring over text books is not the answer.

Kaplan Online fixed tests help you consolidate your knowledge and understanding and are a useful tool to check whether you can remember key topic areas.

Kaplan pocket notes are designed to help you quickly revise a topic area, however you then need to practice questions. There is a need to progress to full exam standard questions as soon as possible, and to tie your exam technique and technical knowledge together.

The importance of question practice cannot be over-emphasised.

The recommended approach below is designed by expert tutors in the field, in conjunction with their knowledge of the examiner and their recent real exams.

The approach taken for the fundamental papers is to revise by topic area. However, with the professional stage papers, a multi topic approach is required to answer the scenario based questions.

You need to practice as many questions as possible in the time you have left.

OUR AIM

Our aim is to get you to the stage where you can attempt exam standard questions confidently, to time, in a closed book environment, with no supplementary help (i.e. to simulate the real examination experience).

Practising your exam technique on real past examination questions, in timed conditions, is also vitally important for you to assess your progress and identify areas of weakness that may need more attention in the final run up to the examination.

In order to achieve this we recognise that initially you may feel the need to practice some questions with open book help and exceed the required time.

The approach below shows you which questions you should use to build up to coping with exam standard question practice, and references to the sources of information available should you need to revisit a topic area in more detail.

KAPLAN PUBLISHING

Remember that in the real examination, all you have to do is:

- attempt all questions required by the exam
- only spend the allotted time on each question, and
- get them at least 50% right!

Try and practice this approach on every question you attempt from now to the real exam.

EXAMINER COMMENTS

We have included the examiners comments to the specific new syllabus examination questions in this kit for you to see the main pitfalls that students fall into with regard to technical content.

However, too many times in the general section of the report, the examiner comments that students had failed due to:

- "misallocation of time"
- "running out of time" and
- showing signs of "spending too much time on an earlier questions and clearly rushing the answer to a subsequent question".

Good exam technique is vital.

THE KAPLAN PAPER F6 REVISION PLAN

Stage 1: Assess areas of strengths and weaknesses

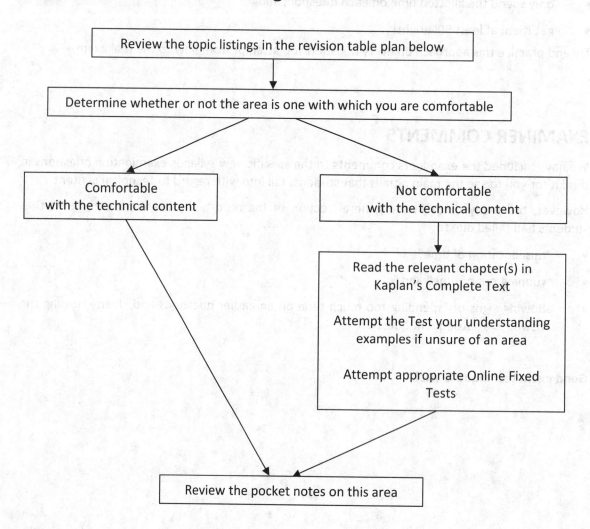

Stage 2: Practice questions

Follow the order of revision of topics as recommended in the revision table plan below and attempt the questions in the order suggested.

Try to avoid referring to text books and notes and the model answer until you have completed your attempt.

Try to answer the question in the allotted time.

Review your attempt with the model answer and assess how much of the answer you achieved in the allocated exam time.

KAPLAN PUBLISHING

Fill in the self-assessment box below and decide on your best course of action.

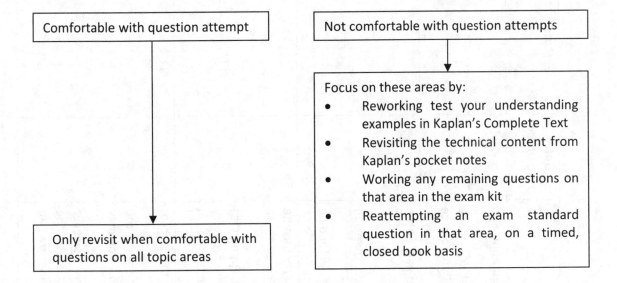

Note that :

 The "footsteps questions" give guidance on exam techniques and how you should have approached the question.

 The "clock questions" have an online debrief where a tutor talks you through the exam technique and approach to that question and works the question in full.

Stage 3: Final pre-exam revision

We recommend that you **attempt at least one three hour mock examination** containing a set of previously unseen exam standard questions.

It is important that you get a feel for the breadth of coverage of a real exam without advanced knowledge of the topic areas covered – just as you will expect to see on the real exam day.

Ideally this mock should be sat in timed, closed book, real exam conditions and could be:

- a mock examination offered by your tuition provider, and/or

- the pilot paper in the back of this exam kit, and/or

- the last real examination paper (available shortly afterwards on Kaplan EN-gage with "enhanced walk through answers" and a full "tutor debrief").

THE DETAILED REVISION PLAN

Topic	Complete Text Chapter	Pocket note Chapter	Questions to attempt	Tutor guidance	Date attempted	Self assessment
Personal income tax computation	2	1	1	Review the layout of an income tax computation and rates of tax. Question 1 in the exam will include at least one income tax computation, and it is crucial that you are comfortable with the proforma.		
– Employment income and assessable benefits	4	3	3 16 7	A popular exam topic, guaranteed to form part of the exam. There are many questions on this area. Start with Q3 which is a basic warm up question covering a number of employment benefits. Build up to Q16 and Q7 which are more demanding past exam questions on this area.		
– Property income	3	2	6	This is a detailed question solely on property income which is an excellent test of your retention of these rules. However, be aware that this topic often appears as part of a big income tax computation, where property is just one of a few sources of income for an individual.		
– Badges of trade	5	3	11	Revise the badges of trade rules from the pocket notes, before attempting this question. Note that although you are not required to apply the rules to a particular scenario in this question, you may be asked to do so in the exam. The consequences of the decision are however covered and this question demonstrates the importance of the badges of trade and how an individual is taxed as a consequence.		

KAPLAN PUBLISHING

Topic	Complete Text Chapter	Pocket note Chapter	Questions to attempt	Tutor guidance	Date attempted	Self assessment
– Adjusted trading profit, including capital allowances	5, 6 & 7	3 & 4	12 14 18	An adjustment of profits calculation is almost certain to be tested in the exam, although it may form part of question 1 for a sole trader/partnership or question 2 for a company. Q12 tests many of the typical adjustments you may see, and having practiced this question you can then attempt Q14 to time. Q14 has a small element of capital gains as well, which you could leave until you revise that area, or have a go and see what you remember! Q18 tests the rules for determining whether an individual is employed or self employed.		
– Basis of assessment	8	5	10 Pilot Q4	You may benefit from practicing the test your understandings from the complete text before attempting these questions. The opening year rules are commonly tested and Q10 provides good practice. Pilot paper Q4 tests the change of accounting date rules, which are not regularly examined, but many students find these difficult, and would benefit from practice here.		
– National insurance	12	8	29(a)	National insurance regularly forms part of a longer question, and can provide easy marks to a well-prepared student. This question covers NICs for both an employee and a self-employed individual.		

Topic	Complete Text Chapter	Pocket note Chapter	Questions to attempt	Tutor guidance	Date attempted	Self assessment
– Trading losses for individuals	10	7	23 22 19	These questions cover the range of ways losses can be tested – in an ongoing business, losses in the opening years and losses on cessation. In the current climate, losses are topical and it is important to be familiar with each of the reliefs.		
– Partnerships	9	6	25	The allocation of profits between partners is a relatively straightforward computation, but does require practice.		
– Pensions	11	8	28 30	Like National Insurance, pensions is a topic which is likely to form a small part of a longer question, however the two questions listed here provided excellent practice of the various ways this topic could be tested.		
– Tax admin for individuals	13	9	32 31	Administration is unlikely to appear as a standalone question; however, it is regularly tested at the end of a longer income tax question. It is very important to learn the dates for submission and payment as well as the potential penalties, surcharges and interest.		
Consolidation of personal tax			27	Having revised all of the above topics, attempt Q27 which is a recent question incorporating many aspects of the taxation of individuals.		
Corporation tax computation	18	13	–	Review the layout of a corporation tax computation and the rates of tax. Question 2 will include a corporation tax computation, and it is crucial that you are comfortable with the proforma.		

KAPLAN PUBLISHING

Topic	Complete Text Chapter	Pocket note Chapter	Questions to attempt	Tutor guidance	Date attempted	Self assessment
– Adjustment of profits and capital allowances	19	13	45 Pilot Q2a	It is important to be comfortable with the differences between sole traders and companies for adjustments to profits and capital allowances. Use Q45 to check that you are clear about these differences, then attempt pilot Q2(a), which is a more recent question on this topic.		
– Property income	19	13	47	There are minor but important differences between taxing property income for individuals and companies. This question is an unusually detailed property income question for a company, but provides good practice in this area.		
– Long periods of account	19	13	49 43	In order to deal with a long period of account, you need to learn the rules regarding apportioning different types of income between the two periods. Having revised these rules from the pocket notes, practice them using these questions.		
– Corporation tax losses	21	15	55	Many students are daunted by loss questions, however a systematic approach is all that is required and practice is key. Remind yourself of the layout required using the pocket notes, and practice the test your understandings from the complete text if you are not confident, before attempting Q55.		

Topic	Complete Text Chapter	Pocket note Chapter	Questions to attempt	Tutor guidance	Date attempted	Self assessment
– Groups	22	16	56 60	Groups and overseas aspects will only be tested in question 2 for no more than a third of the marks. The questions listed therefore only contain a small element in relation to groups. Q56 tests group relief, and Q60 covers both group relief and the capital gains aspects of groups		
– Overseas	23	17	52	As above, Q52 only contain a small element in relation to overseas issues. This question shows how the topic is likely to appear in the real exam.		
– Tax admin for a company	24	18	46	You are unlikely to see a standalone question on administration in the exam, however there are often easy marks available as part of other questions. It is therefore very important to learn the submission and payment dates as well as the penalty and interest rules.		
Chargeable gains for individuals	14	10	–	Chargeable gains will be tested in question 3 in the exam, and these questions will usually test a wide variety of the topics below. Revise the basic computation using the pocket notes before looking at the detailed areas.		
– Chattels, part disposals, shares, PPR, Entrepreneurs relief	15 & 17	11 & 12	37 Pilot Q3 39	These questions demonstrate how various aspects of capital gains will be tested in one question. Few of these areas are technically challenging, however, it is important that you can tackle them all.		

Topic	Complete Text Chapter	Pocket note Chapter	Questions to attempt	Tutor guidance	Date attempted	Self assessment
– Deferral reliefs	17	12	38	Recognising which deferral reliefs apply and whether they are available in full is an important aspect of capital gains. This question covers all of the deferral reliefs and provides excellent practice.		
Chargeable gains for companies	20	14	41	Remind yourself of the different gains rules for companies, and test your understanding using Q41.		
– Quoted shares	16 & 20	11 & 14	42	A brief revision of the share pool and matching rules from the pocket notes may be useful before attempting this question.		
Value added tax	25 & 26	19	70 29(b) 54(b) 57(b) Pilot Q2b	Start by reviewing the examiner's VAT article, which has been updated by Kaplan. VAT usually appears as part of question 1 or question 2 (for up to 10 marks); however Q70 is a standalone VAT question from the June 2009 exam. The remainder of the questions listed here contain VAT but are not included in the VAT section of the kit; however any of Qs 62-69 also provide further practice.		

Note that not all of the questions are referred to in the programme above.

We have recommended an approach to build up from the basic to exam standard questions.

The remaining questions are available in the kit for extra practice for those who require more questions on some areas.

TAX RATES AND ALLOWANCES

Throughout this exam kit:

1. You should assume that the tax rates and allowances for the tax year 2009/10 and for the Financial year to 31 March 2010 will continue to apply for the foreseeable future unless you are instructed otherwise.

2. Calculations and workings need only to be made to the nearest £.

3. All apportionments should be made to the nearest month.

Some tax rates and allowances will be reproduced in the examination paper for Paper F6. In addition, other specific information necessary for candidates to answer individual questions will be given as part of the question.

The following tax rates and allowances will be provided for the F6 examinations in the 2010 sittings:

INCOME TAX

		%
Basic rate	£1 – £37,400	20
Higher rate	£37,401 and above	40

A starting rate of 10% applies to savings income where it falls within the first £2,440 of taxable income.

Personal allowances

Personal allowance	Standard	£6,475
Personal allowance	65 – 74	£9,490
Personal allowance	75 and over	£9,640
Income limit for age related allowances		£22,900

Car benefit percentage

The base level of CO_2 emissions is 135 grams per kilometre.
A lower rate of 10% applies to petrol cars with CO_2 emissions of 120 grams per kilometre or less.

Car fuel benefit

The base figure for calculating the car fuel benefit is £16,900.

Pension scheme limits

Annual allowance	£245,000

The maximum contribution that can qualify for tax relief without any earnings is £3,600.

Authorised mileage allowance: cars

Up to 10,000 miles	40p
Over 10,000 miles	25p

Capital allowances

	Rate of allowance %
Plant and machinery	
General pool – First year allowance	40
– Writing-down allowance	20
Special rate pool	10

The first year allowance of 40% applies to expenditure during the period 6 April 2009 to 5 April 2010 (1 April 2009 to 31 March 2010 for limited companies).

Motor cars	
CO_2 emissions up to 110 grams per kilometre	100
CO_2 emissions between 111 and 160 grams per kilometre	20
CO_2 emissions above 160 grams per kilometre	10

Annual Investment Allowance	
First £50,000 of expenditure	100

Industrial buildings	
Writing-down allowance	2

CORPORATION TAX

Financial year

	2007	2008	2009
Small companies rate	20%	21%	21%
Full rate	30%	28%	28%
Lower limit	£300,000	£300,000	£300,000
Upper limit	£1,500,000	£1,500,000	£1,500,000
Marginal relief fraction	1/40	7/400	7/400

Marginal relief

$$(M - P) \times I/P \times \text{Marginal relief fraction}$$

Extended loss relief

Extended loss relief is capped at £50,000.

For limited companies it applies to loss making accounting periods ending between 24 November 2008 and 23 November 2010.

VALUE ADDED TAX

Standard rate of VAT	– Up to 31 December 2009	15.0%
	– From 1 January 2010 onwards	17.5%
Registration limit		£68,000
Deregistration limit		£66,000

CAPITAL GAINS TAX

Rate of CGT		18%
Annual exemption		£10,100
Entrepreneurs' relief	– Lifetime limit	£1,000,000
	– Relief factor	4/9 ths

NATIONAL INSURANCE CONTRIBUTIONS
(Not contracted out rates)

		%
Class 1 Employee	£1 – £5,715 per year	Nil
	£5,716 – £43,875 per year	11.0
	£43,876 and above per year	1.0
Class 1 Employer	£1 – £5,715 per year	Nil
	£5,716 and above per year	12.8
Class 1A		12.8
Class 2	£2.40 per week	
Class 4	£1 – £5,715 per year	Nil
	£5,716 – £43,875 per year	8.0
	£43,876 and above per year	1.0

RATES OF INTEREST

Official rate of interest:	4.75%
Rate of interest on underpaid tax:	2.50%
Rate of interest on overpaid tax:	Nil

TIME LIMITS AND ELECTION DATES

Income tax

Election / claim	Time limit	For 2009/10
Agree the amount of trading losses to carry forward	4 years from the end of the tax year in which the loss arose	5 April 2014
Current and prior year set-off of trading losses against total income (and chargeable gains)	12 months from 31 January following the end of the tax year in which the loss arose	31 January 2012
Three year carry back of trading losses in the opening years	12 months from 31 January following the end of the tax year in which the loss arose	31 January 2012
Three year carry back of terminal trading losses in the closing years	4 years from the end of the last tax year of trading	5 April 2014

National Insurance Contributions

Class 1 primary and secondary – pay days	14 days after the end of each tax month under PAYE system	19th of each month
Class 1 A NIC – pay day	19 July following end of tax year	19 July 2010
Class 2 NICs – pay days	Monthly direct debit or quarterly invoicing	
Class 4 NICs – pay days	Paid under self assessment with income tax	

Capital gains tax

Replacement of business asset relief for individuals (Rollover relief)	4 years from the end of the tax year in which the disposal occurred	5 April 2014
Holdover relief of gain on the gift of a business asset (Gift relief)	4 years from the end of the tax year in which the disposal occurred	5 April 2014
Entrepreneurs' relief	12 months from 31 January following the end of the tax year in which the disposal occurred	31 January 2012
Determination of principal private residence	2 years from the acquisition of the second property	

Self assessment – individuals

Election / claim	Time limit	For 2009/10
Pay days for income tax and Class 4 NIC	1st instalment: 31 January in the tax year 2nd instalment: 31 July following the end of tax year Balancing payment: 31 January following the end of tax year	31 January 2010 31 July 2010 31 January 2011
Pay day for CGT	31 January following the end of tax year	31 January 2011
Filing dates If return issued by 31 October in the tax year If return issued after 31 October in the tax year	Paper return: 31 October following end of tax year Electronic return: 31 January following end of tax year 3 months from the date of issue of the return	31 October 2010 31 January 2011
Retention of records Business records Personal records	5 years from 31 January following end of the tax year 12 months from 31 January following end of the tax year	31 January 2016 31 January 2012
HMRC right of repair	9 months from date the return was filed	
Taxpayers right to amend a return	12 months from 31 January following end of the tax year	31 January 2012
Taxpayers error or mistake claim	4 years from the end of the tax year	5 April 2014
HMRC can open an enquiry	12 months from submission of the return	
HMRC can raise a discovery assessment – No careless or deliberate behaviour – Tax lost due to careless behavior – Tax lost due to deliberate behaviour	4 years from the end of the tax year 6 years from the end of the tax year 20 years from the end of the tax year	5 April 2014 5 April 2016 5 April 2030
Taxpayers right of appeal against an assessment	30 days from the assessment – appeal in writing	

Corporation tax

Election / claim	Time limit
Replacement of business asset relief for companies (Rollover relief)	4 years from the end of the chargeable accounting period in which the disposal occurred
Agree the amount of trading losses to carry forward	4 years from the end of the chargeable accounting period in which the loss arose
Current year set-off of trading losses against total profits (income and gains), and 12 month carry back of trading losses against total profits (income and gains)	2 years from the end of the chargeable accounting period in which the loss arose
Surrender of current period trading losses to other group companies (Group relief)	2 years after the claimant company's chargeable accounting period
Election for transfer of capital gain or loss to another company within the gains group	2 years from the end of the chargeable accounting period in which the disposal occurred by the company actually making the disposal

Self assessment – companies

Election / claim	Time limit
Pay day for small and medium companies	9 months and one day after the end of the chargeable accounting period
Pay day for large companies	Instalments due on 14th day of: – Seventh, Tenth, Thirteenth, and Sixteenth month **after the start** of the chargeable accounting period
Filing dates	Later of: – 12 months from the end of the chargeable accounting period – 3 months form the issue of a notice to deliver a corporation tax return
Companies error or mistake claim	4 years from the end of the chargeable accounting period
HMRC can open an enquiry	12 months from the actual submission of the return
Retention of records	6 years from the end of the chargeable accounting period

Value added tax

Election / claim	Time limit
Compulsory registration Historic test: – Notify HMRC	30 days from end of the month in which the threshold was exceeded
– Charge VAT	Beginning of the month, one month after the month in which the threshold was exceeded
Future test: – Notify HMRC	30 days from the date it is anticipated that the threshold will be exceeded
– Charge VAT	the date it is anticipated that the threshold will be exceeded (i.e. the beginning of the 30 day period)
Compulsory deregistration	30 days from cessation
Filing of VAT return and payment of VAT	End of month following the return period

Section 1

PRACTICE QUESTIONS

INCOME TAX AND NATIONAL INSURANCE

INCOME TAX BASICS AND EMPLOYMENT INCOME

1   TOM AND MARY (ADAPTED)

Tom, aged 63, is married to Mary, aged 67. Tom is employed at an annual salary of £40,000 and is provided with a house which is owned by his employers. The house cost £120,000 and had a gross rateable value of £2,000. Tom had been provided with furniture for the house, costing £8,000 on 6 April 2008. On 5 April 2010 Tom bought the furniture from his employers for £2,000 when its market value was £4,000. Tom paid no rent for the accommodation and there was no business use. Tom was not required by his employers to occupy the house.

Tom received bank interest of £840 from HSBC on 30 June 2009.

Tom also owns an investment property which he rents out. The property is a furnished flat and was rented out at £800 per month, payable monthly in advance for the whole of 2009/10. Tom paid council tax of £1,500 and incurred interest charges of £800, on a loan he had taken out to acquire the property, during the year. He paid insurance premiums annually in advance of £500 on 1 May 2008 and £600 on 1 May 2009. Tom claims wear and tear allowance in respect of the property.

In the absence of a company pension scheme Tom had entered into a personal pension scheme with a UK insurance company and paid pension contributions (gross) of £18,660 into the scheme in 2009/10.

In January 2010, Tom's employer paid for each of its employees to visit an independent pensions advisor, at a cost of £100 per employee.

In 2009/10 Mary has the following income and capital gains:

	£
State retirement pension	4,500
Property business income	5,010
Dividends (amount received)	11,655
Capital gains	32,000

There are no allowable capital losses brought forward from earlier years.

In addition Tom and Mary had a joint building society account which was set up many years ago with £4,000 from Tom and £2,000 from Mary. Interest of £1,500 was credited to the account during 2009/10.

Mary won £500 on the Premium bonds during the year.

Required:

Calculate the 2009/10 taxation payable/repayable in respect of:

(a)   Tom   **(14 marks)**

(b)   Mary.   **(11 marks)**

Assume an official rate of interest of 4.75% pa.   **(Total: 25 marks)**

2   SALLY AND SANDRA BURTON

Sally and Sandra Burton, aged 66 and 76 respectively, are sisters.

The following information is available for 2009/10:

Sally Burton

(1)   Sally is employed by Burton plc as a part time manager working 3 days a week in one of the company's nationwide chain of retail clothing shops. She is paid a gross annual salary of £16,000 from which PAYE of £1,500 was deducted by her employer.

(2)   Sally was provided with a petrol powered motor car which has a list price of £17,118 on 6 June 2009. Sally made a capital contribution of £2,000 towards the cost of the motor car when it was first provided. The official CO_2 emission rate for the motor car is 197 grams per kilometre. Burton plc paid for all of the motor car's maintenance costs of £2,400 during 2009/10 as well as car parking costing £1,200. Her employer did not provide any fuel for private journeys.

(3)   Burton plc has provided Sally with living accommodation since 2008. The property was purchased in 2001 for £105,000, and was valued at £120,000 when first provided to Sally. It has an annual value of £1,294. Sally was not required by her job to live in the accommodation provided by her employer. Sally was required to reimburse her employer £75 each month for the use of the accommodation.

(4)   In addition to her employment income, Sally received interest of £1,000 on the maturity of a savings certificate from the National Savings & Investments bank during the tax year 2009/10. This was the actual cash amount received.

(5)   During 2009/10 Sally received building society interest of £1,800. This was the actual cash amount received.

Sandra Burton

(1)   Sandra is self-employed running a retail grocery shop. Her profit and loss account for the year ended 5 April 2010 is as follows:

	£	£
Gross profit		60,105
Depreciation	2,425	
Motor expenses (Note 2)	5,400	
Property expenses (Note 3)	9,600	
Other expenses (all allowable)	24,680	
		(42,105)
Net profit		18,000

(2)   During the year ended 5 April 2010 Sandra drove a total of 12,000 miles, of which 4,000 were for private journeys. Sandra's motor car originally cost £12,600, and at 6 April 2009 had a tax written down value of £9,600. She does not own any other assets that qualify for capital allowances.

(3)   Sandra purchased her grocery shop in 2001 for £105,000. She lives in a flat that is situated above the shop, and one-third of the total property expenses of £9,600 relate to this flat.

(4)   In addition to her self employed income, Sandra received £895 from an investment account at the National Savings & Investment bank during 2009/10. This was the actual cash amount received.

(5)   During 2009/10 Sandra received dividends of £900. This was the actual cash amount received.

Required:

(a)   Calculate Sally's income tax payable for 2009/10.   **(13 marks)**

(b)   Calculate Sandra's income tax payable for 2009/10.   **(12 marks)**

                                                                    (Total 25 marks)

 Online question assistance

3   VIGOROUS PLC

Vigorous plc runs a health club. The company has three employees who received benefits during 2009/10, and it therefore needs to prepare forms P11D for them. Each of the three employees is paid an annual salary of £35,000.

The following information is relevant:

Andrea Lean

(1)   Andrea was employed by Vigorous plc throughout 2009/10.

(2)   Throughout 2009/10 Vigorous plc provided Andrea with a 2200 cc petrol powered company motor car with a list price of £19,400. The official CO_2 emission rate for the motor car is 275 grams per kilometre. Vigorous plc paid for all of the motor car's running costs of £6,200 during 2009/10, including petrol used for private journeys. Andrea pays £150 per month to Vigorous plc for the use of the motor car.

(3)   Vigorous plc has provided Andrea with living accommodation since 1 November 2007. The property was purchased on 1 January 2005 for £130,000. The company spent £14,000 improving the property during March 2006, and a further £8,000 was spent on improvements during May 2009. The value of the property on 1 November 2007 was £170,000, and it has a rateable value of £7,000. The furniture in the property cost £6,000 during November 2007. Andrea personally pays for the annual running costs of the property amounting to £4,000.

(4)   Throughout 2009/10 Vigorous plc provided Andrea with a mobile telephone costing £500. The company paid for all business and private telephone calls.

Ben Slim

(1) Ben commenced employment with Vigorous plc on 1 July 2009.

(2) On 1 July 2009 Vigorous plc provided Ben with an interest free loan of £120,000 so that he could purchase a new main residence. He repaid £20,000 of the loan on 1 October 2009.

(3) During 2009/10 Vigorous plc paid £9,300 towards the cost of Ben's relocation. His previous main residence was 125 miles from his place of employment with the company. The £9,300 covered the cost of disposing of Ben's old property and of acquiring his new property.

(4) During the period from 1 October 2009 until 5 April 2010 Vigorous plc provided Ben with a new diesel powered company motor car which has a list price of £11,200. The official CO_2 emission rate for the motor car is 139 grams per kilometre. Ben reimburses Vigorous plc for all the diesel used for private journeys.

Chai Trim

(1) Chai was employed by Vigorous plc throughout 2009/10.

(2) During 2009/10 Vigorous plc provided Chai with a two-year old company van, which was available for private use. The van was unavailable during the period 1 August to 30 September 2009. Chai was also provided with private fuel for the van.

(3) Vigorous plc has provided Chai with a television for her personal use since 6 April 2007. The television cost Vigorous plc £800 in April 2007. On 6 April 2009 the company sold the television to Chai for £150, although its market value on that date was £250.

(4) Throughout 2009/10 Vigorous plc provided Chai with free membership of its health club. The normal annual cost of membership is £800. This figure is made up of direct costs of £150, fixed overhead costs of £400 and profit of £250. The budgeted membership for the year has been exceeded, but the health club has surplus capacity.

(5) On 1 January 2010 Vigorous plc provided Chai with a new computer costing £1,900. She uses the computer at home for personal study purposes.

Required:

(a) Explain what is meant by the term 'P11D employee'. **(3 marks)**

(b) Calculate the benefit figures that Vigorous plc will have to include on the forms P11D for Andrea, Ben, and Chai for 2009/10. **(19 marks)**

(c) Explain how the income tax liability in respect of benefits is collected by HM Revenue & Customs. **(3 marks)**

(Total: 25 marks)

4   JANE JONES

Jane Jones has the choice of two alternative offers of employment. Regardless of which alternative is chosen, she will commence employment on 6 April 2009 (you should assume that today's date is 15 March 2009) and will drive 12,000 miles during 2009/10 in the performance of her duties.

Aurora plc

Under the offer of employment from Aurora plc, Jane will receive a salary of £33,000. On 6 April 2009 Aurora plc will provide Jane with a new 1300cc motor car with a list price of £18,400 and a carbon dioxide emission rating of 118 gms/km. The company will pay for all running costs, including private petrol. Jane will pay Aurora plc £50 per month for the use of the motor car. Under this alternative Jane will not run a private motor car.

Zodiac plc

Under the offer of employment from Zodiac plc, Jane will receive a salary of £34,000. From 6 April 2009 she will use her private motor car for business mileage, for which Zodiac plc will pay an allowance of 20 pence per mile. The relevant HM Revenue & Customs authorised mileage rates are 40 pence per mile for the first 10,000 miles, and 25 pence per mile thereafter. Jane's total annual cost of running her private motor car, including leasing costs and fuel, will be £7,100.

Required:

(a) Calculate Jane's income tax liability for 2009/10 if she:

(i) accepts the offer of employment from Aurora plc; **(5 marks)**

(ii) accepts the offer of employment from Zodiac plc. **(5 marks)**

(b) Advise Jane as to which offer of employment is the more beneficial.

Your answer should be supported by a calculation of the amount of income, net of income tax, that she will receive for 2009/10 under each alternative offer of employment.

NIC should be ignored. **(5 marks)**

(Total: 15 marks)

5 **ALI PATEL** *Walk in the footsteps of a top tutor*

You should assume that today's date is 15 March 2009.

Ali Patel has been employed by Box plc since 1 January 2006, and is currently paid an annual salary of £29,000. On 6 April 2009 Ali is to be temporarily relocated for a period of 12 months from Box plc's head office to one of its branch offices. He has been offered two alternative remuneration packages:

First remuneration package

(1) Ali will continue to live near Box plc's head office, and will commute on a daily basis to the branch office using his private motor car.

(2) He will be paid additional salary of £500 per month.

(3) Box plc will pay Ali an allowance of 35 pence per mile for the 1,600 miles that Ali will drive each month commuting to the branch office.

The HM Revenue & Customs authorised mileage rates are 40 pence per mile for the first 10,000 business miles driven each year, and 25 pence per mile thereafter. Ali's additional cost of commuting for 2009/10 will be £1,800.

Second remuneration package

(1)   Box plc will provide Ali with rent-free living accommodation near the branch office.

(2)   The property will be rented by Box plc at a cost of £800 per month. The annual value of the property is £4,600.

(3)   Ali will rent out his main residence near Box plc's head office, and this will result in property business income of £6,000 for 2009/10.

Required:

(a)   **Calculate Ali's income tax liability and Class 1 national insurance contributions for 2009/10, if he:**

(i)   **accepts the first remuneration package offered by Box plc;**   **(6 marks)**

(ii)   **accepts the second remuneration package offered by Box plc.**   **(5 marks)**

(b)   **Advise Ali as to which remuneration package is the most beneficial from a financial perspective.**

Your answer should be supported by a calculation of the amount of income, net of income tax and Class 1 national insurance contributions, which he would receive for 2009/10 under each alternative.   **(4 marks)**

(Total: 15 marks)

6   **EDMOND BRICK**   *Walk in the footsteps of a top tutor*

Edmond Brick owns four properties which are let out.

The following information relates to the tax year 2009/10:

Property one

This is a freehold house that qualifies as a trade under the furnished holiday letting rules. The property was purchased on 6 April 2009. During the tax year 2009/10 the property was let for eighteen weeks at £370 per week. Edmond spent £5,700 on furniture and kitchen equipment during April 2009. Due to a serious flood £7,400 was spent on repairs during November 2009. The damage was not covered by insurance. The other expenditure on this property for the tax year 2009/10 amounted to £2,710, and this is all allowable.

Property two

This is a freehold house that is let out furnished. The property was let throughout the tax year 2009/10 at a monthly rent of £575, payable in advance. During the tax year 2009/10 Edmond paid council tax of £1,200 and insurance of £340 in respect of this property. He claims the wear and tear allowance for this property.

Property three

This is a freehold house that is let out unfurnished. The property was purchased on 6 April 2009, and it was empty until 30 June 2009. It was then let from 1 July 2009 to 31 January 2010 at a monthly rent of £710, payable in advance. On 31 January 2010 the tenant left owing three months rent which Edmond was unable to recover. The property was not re-let before 5 April 2010. During the tax year 2009/10 Edmond paid insurance of £290 for this property and spent £670 on advertising for tenants. He also paid loan interest of £6,700 in respect of a loan that was taken out to purchase this property.

Property four

This is a leasehold office building that is let out unfurnished. Edmond pays an annual rent of £6,800 for this property, but did not pay a premium when he acquired it. On 6 April 2009 the property was sub-let to a tenant, with Edmond receiving a premium of £15,000 for the grant of a five-year lease. He also received the annual rent of £4,600 which was payable in advance. During the tax year 2009/10 Edmond paid insurance of £360 in respect of this property.

Furnished room

During the tax year 2009/10 Edmond rented out one furnished room of his main residence. During the year he received rent of £5,040, and incurred allowable expenditure of £1,140 in respect of the room. Edmond always computes the taxable income for the furnished room on the most favourable basis.

Required:

(a) State the income tax advantages of property one being treated as a trade under the furnished holiday letting rules.   (3 marks)

(b) Calculate Edmond's furnished holiday letting loss in respect of property one for the tax year 2009/10.   (3 marks)

(c) Calculate Edmond's property business profit in respect of the other three properties and the furnished room for the tax year 2009/10.   (9 marks)

(Total: 15 marks)

7   **PETER CHIC**   *Walk in the footsteps of a top tutor*

Peter Chic is employed by Haute-Couture Ltd as a fashion designer. The following information is available for the tax year 2009/10:

Employment

(1) During the tax year 2009/10 Peter was paid a gross annual salary of £45,600 by Haute-Couture Ltd. Income tax of £14,286 was deducted from this figure under PAYE.

(2) In addition to his salary, Peter received two bonus payments from Haute-Couture Ltd during the tax year 2009/10. The first bonus of £4,300 was paid on 30 April 2009 and was in respect of the year ended 31 December 2008. Peter became entitled to this first bonus on 10 April 2009. The second bonus of £3,700 was paid on 31 March 2010 and was in respect of the year ended 31 December 2009. Peter became entitled to this second bonus on 25 March 2010.

(3) Throughout the tax year 2009/10 Haute-Couture Ltd provided Peter with a diesel powered motor car which has a list price of £22,500. The motor car cost Haute-Couture Ltd £21,200, and it has an official CO_2 emission rate of 232 grams per kilometre. Peter made a capital contribution of £2,000 towards the cost of the motor car when it was first provided to him. Haute-Couture Ltd also provided Peter with fuel for private journeys.

(4) Haute-Couture Ltd has provided Peter with living accommodation since 1 January 2007. The company had purchased the property in 2006 for £160,000, and it was valued at £185,000 on 1 January 2007. Improvements costing £13,000 were made to the property during June 2008. The annual value of the property is £9,100.

(5)   Throughout the tax year 2009/10 Haute-Couture Ltd provided Peter with two mobile telephones. The telephones had each cost £250 when purchased by the company in January 2009.

(6)   On 5 January 2010 Haute-Couture Ltd paid a health club membership fee of £510 for the benefit of Peter.

(7)   During February 2010 Peter spent five nights overseas on company business. Haute-Couture Ltd paid Peter a daily allowance of £10 to cover the cost of personal expenses such as telephone calls to his family.

Property income

(1)   Peter owns two properties, which are let out. Both properties are freehold houses, with the first property being let out furnished and the second property being let out unfurnished.

(2)   The first property was let from 6 April 2009 to 31 August 2009 at a monthly rent of £500, payable in advance. On 31 August 2009 the tenant left owing two months' rent which Peter was unable to recover. The property was not re-let before 5 April 2010. During March 2010 Peter spent £600 repairing the roof of this property.

(3)   The second property was purchased on 1 July 2009, and was then let from 1 August 2009 to 5 April 2010 at a monthly rent of £820, payable in advance. During July 2009 Peter spent £875 on advertising for tenants. For the period 1 July 2009 to 5 April 2010 he paid loan interest of £1,800 in respect of a loan that was taken out to purchase this property.

(4)   Peter insured both of his rental properties at a total cost of £660 for the year ended 30 June 2009, and £1,080 for the year ended 30 June 2010. The insurance is payable annually in advance.

(5)   Where possible, Peter claims the wear and tear allowance.

Other information

(1)   During the tax year 2009/10 Peter received building society interest of £1,760 and dividends of £720. These were the actual cash amounts received.

(2)   On 4 August 2009 Peter received a premium bond prize of £100.

(3)   During the tax year 2009/10 Peter made Gift Aid donations totalling £2,340 (net) to national charities.

Required:

(a)   **Calculate the income tax payable by Peter Chic for the tax year 2009/10. (21 marks)**

(b)   **Calculate the total amount of national insurance contributions that will have been paid by Peter Chic and Haute-Couture Ltd in respect of Peter's earnings and benefits for the tax year 2009/10.** **(4 marks)**

(Total: 25 marks)

INCOME TAX BASICS AND INCOME FROM SELF-EMPLOYMENT

8   CAROL COURIER

For the purposes of this question you should assume that today's date is 15 March 2009.

Carol Courier is employed by Quick-Speed plc as a delivery driver, and is paid a salary of £37,500 p.a. She contributes 5% of her gross salary into Quick-Speed plc's HM Revenue & Customs registered occupational pension scheme.

As an alternative to being employed, Quick-Speed plc have offered Carol the opportunity to work for the company on a self-employed basis. The details of the proposed arrangement for the year ended 5 April 2010 are as follows:

(1)   Carol will commence being self-employed on 6 April 2009.

(2)   Her income from Quick-Speed plc is expected to be £43,500.

(3)   When not working for Quick-Speed plc, Carol will be allowed to work for other clients. Her income from this work is expected to be £8,000.

(4)   Carol will lease a delivery van from Quick-Speed plc, and 100% of the mileage will be for business purposes. The cost of leasing and running the delivery van will be £4,400.

(5)   When she is unavailable Carol will have to provide a replacement driver to deliver for Quick-Speed plc. This will cost her £2,800.

(6)   Carol will contribute £2,000 (gross) into a personal pension scheme during 2009/10. This will provide her with the same benefits as the occupational pension scheme provided by Quick-Speed plc.

Required:

(a)   Assuming that Carol does not accept the offer from Quick-Speed plc and continues to be employed by the company, calculate her income tax and Class 1 NIC liability for 2009/10.   **(5 marks)**

(b)   Assuming that Carol accepts the offer to work for Quick-Speed plc on a self-employed basis from 6 April 2009 onwards, calculate her income tax, Class 2 NIC and Class 4 NIC liability for 2009/10.   **(6 marks)**

(c)   Advise Carol as to whether it will be beneficial to accept the offer to work for Quick-Speed plc on a self-employed basis.

Your answer should be supported by a calculation of the amount by which Carol's income for 2009/10 (net of outgoings, income tax and NIC) will increase or decrease if she accepts the offer.   **(4 marks)**

(Total: 15 marks)

9   CORDELIA

(a)   Which conditions must be met for a change of accounting date to be valid? **(3 marks)**

(b)   Cordelia, a sole trader commenced trading on 1 July 2002 and has always prepared her accounts to 30 June. She decides to change her accounting date to 30 September.

She is undecided whether to prepare accounts for the 3-month period to 30 September 2009 or for the 15-month period to 30 September 2010.

Cordelia's tax adjusted profits are as follows:

	£
Year ended 30 June 2009	48,000
Three months to 30 September 2009	15,000
Year ended 30 September 2010	60,000

Cordelia's overlap profits on commencement were	12,000

The overlap profits were for a period of 9 months.

Required:

Show Cordelia's trading income assessments for 2009/10 and 2010/11 on the assumption that:

(i)   she prepares accounts for 3 months to 30 September 2009;

(ii)   she prepares accounts for 15 months to 30 September 2010

and gives the appropriate notice to HM Revenue & Customs.   **(7 marks)**

(Total: 10 marks)

10   CHATRU (ADAPTED)

(1)   Chatru commenced trading on 1 November 2005. His first accounts were prepared to 30 April 2007 and thereafter to 30 April annually. He ceased trading on 31 March 2010.

His trading results, adjusted for income tax purposes were:

	£
1.11.05 – 30.4.07	40,500
Year ended 30.4.08	12,000
Year ended 30.4.09	24,000
Period to 31.3.10	50,000

Required:

(a)   Calculate the assessable income for all years in question.   **(8 marks)**

(b)   Calculate whether there would have been any income tax benefit in Chatru continuing to trade one extra month and preparing final accounts to his normal accounting date, on the assumption that his tax-adjusted profit for April 2010 was £4,200.   **(3 marks)**

(2)   Chatru, who is aged 63, had the following additional income and expenditure in 2009/10:

Investment income

(i)   He received dividends of £33,500, bank interest of £2,500 and interest from an Individual Savings Account of £1,500.

Property income

(i)   He rented out a room in his house to a student and charged rent of £150 per month.

(ii)   From 6 April 2009 he rented out a furnished property on which he received rent of £11,000. During the year he made payments on a loan which he had taken out to acquire the property of £5,000 of which £500 related to interest charges. He incurred allowable expenses of £1,500 which included £800 council tax and £200 water rates. He also spent £400 on a cooker for the property.

(iii)   Chatru and his wife, Sandra, jointly owned a piece of land in the ratio 25:75. They received rent of £4,000 per annum from renting the land to a local farmer.

Other information

(i)   On 1 March 2010 Chatru made a payment of £5,000 to a national charity under the Gift Aid scheme.

(ii)   Sandra works part-time earning £8,000 per annum and has no other income other than mentioned above.

(iii)   Chantru and Sandra have not made any elections in respect of their income.

For the purposes of this part assume that Chatru ceased to trade on 31 March 2010.

Required:

(a)   **Compute the income tax payable by Chatru for the tax year 2009/10.**

(15 marks)

(b)   **Advise Chatru and Sandra of two ways in which they may have reduced their joint income tax liability in 2009/10.**   **(4 marks)**

(Total: 30 marks)

11   ANDREW WALL (ADAPTED)

(1)   On 6 April 2009 Andrew Wall purchased a derelict freehold office building for £100,000. Legal fees of £800 were paid in respect of the purchase.

During 2009/10 Andrew renovated the office building at a cost of £60,000, with the renovation being completed on 15 January 2010. He immediately put the office building up for sale, and it was sold on 5 April 2010 for £225,000. Legal fees of £1,000 were paid in respect of the sale.

Andrew financed the transaction by a bank loan of £160,000 that was taken out on 6 April 2009 at an annual interest rate of 10%. The bank loan was repaid on 5 April 2010.

Andrew is employed as a doctor and his taxable income for 2009/10 (before taking account of the office building transaction) is £25,000. He has not disposed of any other assets during 2009/10.

Although Andrew purchased the office building with a view to making a profit, he believes that as an isolated transaction it should be treated as a capital gain rather than as a trade assessable to income tax.

Required:

(a)   **Briefly explain the criteria known as the 'badges of trade' that are used when determining whether a transaction constitutes the carrying on of a trade.**

You are not expected to quote from decided cases.   **(6 marks)**

(b) Calculate Andrew's additional 2009/10 tax liability in respect of the office building transaction if he is:

(i) treated as carrying on a trade; or

(ii) not treated as carrying on a trade.

You should ignore VAT and NIC. (9 marks)

(2) Andrew's brother, Bill owns a number of properties. Details of income and expenditure in respect of each of the properties in 2009/10 is as follows:

(i) Property 1:

An unfurnished house which was rented for £800 per month, payable quarterly in advance until 31 December 2009. The tenant left owing one month's rent which Bill was unable to recover.

The property remained empty until 1 April 2010 when it was rented for £1,100 per month, payable quarterly in advance.

Allowable expenses amounted to £500.

(ii) Property 2:

A furnished flat which Bill acquired on 1 June 2009. He paid mortgage interest of £700 on a loan which he took out to acquire the property.

On 1 June 2009 Bill incurred advertising fees of £500 and paid an insurance premium of £300 for the year to 31 May 2010. He paid decorating costs of £900 on 15 June 2009.

The flat remained empty until 1 December 2009 when it was rented for £500 per month, payable monthly in advance.

(iii) Property 3:

A retail shop which Bill rented for £1,000 per month payable quarterly in advance. On 1 January 2010 the tenant left the property and on 1 March 2010 Bill granted a 10 year lease to a new tenant for a premium of £12,000 and a monthly rent of £450 payable quarterly in advance.

Required:

Calculate Bill's property business income assessment for 2009/10. (10 marks)

(Total: 25 marks)

12   OLIVE GREEN (ADAPTED)

Olive Green is self-employed running a health food shop. Her profit and loss account for the year ended 31 March 2010 is as follows:

	£	£
Gross profit		130,750
Expenses		
Depreciation	2,350	
Light and heat (Note 1)	1,980	
Motor expenses (Note 2)	9,700	
Rent and rates (Note 1)	5,920	
Sundry expenses (Note 3)	2,230	
Wages and salaries (Note 4)	78,520	
		(100,700)
Net profit		30,050

Note 1 – Private accommodation

Olive lives in a flat that is situated above the health food shop. 30% of the expenditure included in the profit and loss account for light, heat, rent and rates relates to the flat.

Note 2 – Motor expenses

Motor expenses include £4,700 for the running of Olive's car. During the year ended 31 March 2010 Olive drove a total of 20,000 miles, of which 8,000 were for business purposes.

The motor expenses also include £3,000 leasing costs. This relates to the lease of a car with CO_2 emissions of 175 grams per kilometre which is used by the shop manager.

Note 3 – Sundry expenses

The figure of £2,230 for sundry expenses includes £220 for a fine in respect of health and safety regulations, £180 for the theft of cash by an employee, £100 for a donation to a political party, and £140 for a trade subscription to the Health and Organic Association.

Note 4 – Wages and salaries

The figure of £78,520 for wages and salaries includes an annual salary of £14,000 paid to Olive's daughter. She works in the health food shop as a sales assistant. The other sales assistants doing the same job are paid an annual salary of £10,500.

Note 5 – Goods for own use

Each week Olive takes health food from the shop for her personal use without paying for it. The weekly cost of this food is £30, and it has a selling price of £45.

Note 6 – Plant and machinery

The only item of plant and machinery is Olive's motor car. The tax written down value of this vehicle at 1 April 2009 was £15,800.

Note 7 – Patent royalties

Olive pays a patent royalty of £150 (gross) every quarter for the use of equipment that allows her to make her own organic breakfast cereal. This has not been accounted for in arriving at the net profit of £30,500.

Other income

(1) Olive has a part-time employment for which she was paid a salary of £6,000 during 2009/10. Income tax of £1,320 has been deducted from this figure under PAYE.

(2) During 2009/10 Olive received building society interest of £1,440 and dividends of £1,080. These were the actual cash amounts received.

(3) On 30 November 2009 Olive sold some investments, and this resulted in a capital gain of £12,300.

Other information

(1) During 2009/10 Olive paid interest of £220 (gross) on a loan taken out on 1 January 2008 to purchase equipment for use in her part-time employment.

(2) Olive contributed £2,600 (gross) into a personal pension scheme during 2009/10.

(3) Olive's payments on account of income tax in respect of 2009/10 totalled £4,900.

Required:

(a) Calculate Olive's tax adjusted trading profit for the year ended 31 March 2010.

Your computation should commence with the net profit figure of £30,050, and should list all of the items referred to in Notes (1) to (5) and (7), indicating by the use of zero (0) any items that do not require adjustment. **(8 marks)**

(b) (i) Calculate the income tax and capital gains tax payable by Olive for 2009/10;
(11 marks)

(ii) Calculate Olive's balancing payment for 2009/10 and her payments on account for 2010/11, stating the relevant due dates.

You should ignore national insurance contributions. **(3 marks)**

(c) Advise Olive of the consequences of not making the balancing payment for 2009/10 until 30 April 2011. **(3 marks)**

(Total: 25 marks)

13 SUE MACKER (ADAPTED)

(1) Sue Macker was made redundant from her employment on 15 March 2009. She is a vintage motor car enthusiast, and so decided to take this opportunity to indulge her hobby.

On 6 April 2009 Sue took out a bank loan of £75,000 at an annual interest rate of 10%, rented a workshop for twelve months at a rent of £400 per month, and purchased equipment at a cost of £13,500.

On 10 April 2009 Sue purchased four dilapidated vintage motor cars for £8,000 each. The restoration of the four motor cars was completed on 10 March 2010 at a cost of £12,000 per motor car. Sue immediately sold all of the motor cars for a total of £200,000.

Sue was then offered employment elsewhere in the country commencing on 6 April 2010. She therefore sold the equipment for £5,800 on 20 March 2010, and repaid the bank loan on 5 April 2010.

As she has just been indulging her hobby, Sue believes that the disposal of the vintage motor cars during the tax year 2009/10 should be exempt from tax.

She has done some research on the Internet and has discovered that whether or not she is treated as carrying on a trade will be determined according to the following six 'badges of trade':

(1)   The subject matter of the transaction.

(2)   The length of ownership.

(3)   Frequency of similar transactions.

(4)   Work done on the property.

(5)   Circumstances responsible for the realisation.

(6)   Motive.

Sue had no other income during the tax year 2009/10 except as indicated above.

Required:

(a)   **Briefly explain the meaning of each of the six 'badges of trade' listed in the question.**

        You are not expected to quote from decided cases.   **(3 marks)**

(b)   **Briefly explain why Sue is likely to be treated as carrying on a trade in respect of her vintage motor car activities.**   **(3 marks)**

(c)   **Calculate Sue's income tax liability and her Class 2 and Class 4 national insurance contributions for the tax year 2009/10, if she is treated as carrying on a trade in respect of her vintage motor car activities.**

        You should ignore VAT.   **(7 marks)**

(d)   **Explain why it would be beneficial if Sue were instead treated as not carrying on a trade in respect of her vintage motor car activities.**   **(2 marks)**

(2)   Mr Moeraki began trading as a computer consultant on 1 January 2010. His sales and expenses in the first six months, exclusive of VAT, are set out below.

All amounts shown are standard rated:

	Sales £	Expenses £
January	11,400	1,500
February	17,000	2,100
March	19,500	2,400
April	20,200	3,200
May	16,300	2,300
June	15,700	2,700
Total	100,100	14,200

The expenses relate to administration costs with the exception of £400 per month in respect of entertaining clients.

In June, Mr Moeraki incurred input tax of £2,900 in respect of computer equipment and £3,600 on the acquisition of a motor car. The car is used 80% for business purposes.

Required:

(a) State when a trader should notify HM Revenue & Customs that he is required to register for VAT and the date from which the registration will be effective.

(4 marks)

(b) State the date by which Mr Moeraki should notify HM Revenue & Customs that he is required to register for VAT and the date from which the registration will be effective.

(2 marks)

(c) Calculate the VAT payable or recoverable by Mr Moeraki for the period ended 30 June 2010 assuming he is registered from the compulsory registration date you determined in part (b).

(4 marks)

(Total: 25 marks)

14 TONY NOTE

Tony Note is self-employed running a music shop. His profit and loss account for the year ended 5 April 2010 is as follows:

	£	£
Gross profit		197,830
Expenses:		
Depreciation	2,640	
Motor expenses (Note 1)	9,800	
Professional fees (Note 2)	4,680	
Repairs and renewals (Note 3)	670	
Travelling and entertaining (Note 4)	4,630	
Wages and salaries (Note 5)	77,200	
Other expenses (Note 6)	78,780	
		(178,400)
Net profit		19,430

Note 1 – Motor expenses

During the year ended 5 April 2010 Tony drove a total of 20,000 miles, of which 2,500 were driven when he went on holiday to Europe. The balance of the mileage is 20% for private journeys and 80% for business journeys.

Note 2 – Professional fees

The figure for professional fees consists of £920 for accountancy, £620 for personal financial planning advice, £540 for debt collection, and £2,600 for fees in connection with an unsuccessful application for planning permission to enlarge Tony's freehold music shop.

Note 3 – Repairs and renewals

The figure for repairs and renewals consists of £270 for a replacement hard drive for the shop's computer, and £400 for a new printer for this computer.

Note 4 – Travelling and entertaining

The figure for travelling and entertaining consists of £3,680 for Tony's business travelling expenses, £480 for entertaining suppliers, and £470 for entertaining employees.

Note 5 – Wages and salaries

The figure for wages and salaries includes a salary of £16,000 paid to Tony's wife. She works in the music shop as a sales assistant. The other sales assistants doing the same job are paid a salary of £12,000 p.a.

Note 6 – Other expenses

The figure for other expenses includes £75 in respect of a wedding present to an employee, £710 for Tony's health club subscription, £60 for a donation to a political party, and £180 for a trade subscription to the Guild of Musical Instrument Retailers.

Note 7 – Use of office

Tony uses one of the six rooms in his private house as an office for when he works at home. The total running costs of the house for the year ended 5 April 2010 were £4,140.

Note 8 – Private telephone

Tony uses his private telephone to make business telephone calls. The total cost of the private telephone for the year ended 5 April 2010 was £680, and 25% of this related to business telephone calls. The cost of the private telephone is not included in the profit and loss account expenses of £178,400.

Note 9 – Goods for own use

During the year ended 5 April 2010 Tony took goods out of the music shop for his personal use without paying for them, and no entry has been made in the accounts to record this. The goods cost £600, and had a selling price of £950.

Note 10 – Plant and machinery

The tax written down values for capital allowances purposes at 6 April 2009 were:

General pool	£7,400
Expensive motor car	£16,200

The expensive motor car is used by Tony.

Disposal of freehold music shop

On 10 November 2009 Tony sold his freehold music shop for £320,000. The shop had been purchased on 8 August 2004 for £188,000, and was always used by Tony for business purposes. Tony has claimed to roll over the gain arising on the music shop against the cost of a new freehold music shop that he purchased on 4 October 2009 for £210,000.

Required:

(a) Calculate Tony's tax adjusted trading profit for the year ended 5 April 2010.

Your computation should commence with the net profit figure of **£19,430** and should list all the items referred to in Notes (1) to (9), indicating by the use of zero (0) any items that do not require adjustment. **(16 marks)**

(b) Calculate Tony's income tax and capital gains tax liabilities for the tax year 2009/10. **(6 marks)**

(c) Advise Tony as to how long he must retain the records used in preparing his tax return for 2008/09, and the potential consequences of not retaining the records for the required period. **(3 marks)**

(25 marks)

15   FOO DEE (ADAPTED)

On 31 December 2009 Foo Dee resigned as an employee of Gastronomic-Food plc. The company had employed her as a chef since 1999. On 1 January 2010 Foo commenced self-employment running her own restaurant, preparing accounts to 30 September.

The following information is available for 2009/10:

Employment

(1)   During the period 6 April 2009 to 31 December 2009 Foo's total gross salary from her employment with Gastronomic-Food plc was £38,000. Income tax of £8,609 was deducted from this figure under PAYE.

(2)   Foo used her private motor car for both business and private purposes during the period from 6 April 2009 to 31 December 2009. She received no reimbursement from Gastronomic-Food plc for any of the expenditure incurred.

Foo's total mileage during this period was 15,000 miles, made up as follows:

	miles
Normal daily travel between home and permanent workplace	4,650
Travel between home and permanent workplace in order to turn off a fire alarm	120
Travel between permanent workplace and Gastronomic-Food plc's suppliers	750
Travel between home and a temporary workplace for a period of two months	3,800
Private travel	5,680
	15,000

The relevant HM Revenue & Customs authorised mileage rates to be used as the basis of any expense claim are 40 pence per mile for the first 10,000 miles, and 25 pence per mile thereafter.

(3)   On 1 October 2009 Gastronomic-Food plc paid £12,900 towards Foo's removal expenses when she was permanently relocated to a different restaurant owned by the company. The £12,900 covered the cost of disposing of Foo's old property and of acquiring her new property.

(4)   Foo contributed 6% of her gross salary of £38,000 into Gastronomic-Food plc's HM Revenue & Customs' registered occupational pension scheme.

Self-employment

(1)   Foo's profit and loss account for her restaurant business for the nine-month period ended 30 September 2010 is as follows:

	£	£
Gross profit		159,980
Depreciation	3,500	
Motor expenses (Note 2)	4,200	
Property expenses (Note 3)	12,800	
Other expenses (all allowable)	50,700	
		71,200
Net profit		88,780

(2)   During the period 1 January 2010 to 30 September 2010 Foo drove a total of 6,000 miles, of which 2,000 were for private journeys.

(3)   Foo purchased her restaurant on 1 January 2010. She lives in a flat that is situated above the restaurant, and one-quarter of the total property expenses of £12,800 relate to this flat.

(4)   On 1 January 2010 Foo purchased a motor car with CO_2 emissions of 145 grams per kilometre for £14,600 (see note 2 above) and equipment for £41,200.

Other income

(1)   During the tax year 2009/10 Foo received building society interest of £640 and dividends of £360. These were the actual cash amounts received.

(2)   On 10 July 2009 Foo sold some investments, and this resulted in a capital gain of £17,100.

Other information

(1)   Foo contributed £1,600 (net) into a personal pension scheme during the period 1 January 2010 to 5 April 2010.

(2)   She did not make any payments on account of income tax in respect of the tax year 2009/10.

Required:

(a)   **Calculate Foo's tax adjusted trading profit for the nine-month period ended 30 September 2010.**   **(6 marks)**

(b)   (i)   **Calculate the income tax and capital gains tax payable by Foo for the tax year 2009/10.**   **(13 marks)**

        (ii)   **Calculate Foo's balancing payment for the tax year 2009/10 and her payments on account for the tax year 2010/11, stating the relevant due dates.**

                Ignore national insurance contributions.   **(3 marks)**

(c)   **Advise Foo of the consequences of not making the balancing payment for the tax year 2009/10 until 31 May 2011.**   **(3 marks)**

                                                                                      (Total: 25 marks)

16   SAM AND KIM WHITE   *Walk in the footsteps of a top tutor*

Sam and Kim White are a married couple. Sam is aged 46 and Kim is aged 51. The following information is available for the tax year 2009/10:

Sam White

(1)   Sam is self-employed running a retail clothing shop. His profit and loss account for the year ended 5 April 2010 is as follows:

	Note	£	£
Gross profit			140,300
Depreciation		7,600	
Motor expenses	2	8,800	
Patent royalties	3	700	
Professional fees	4	1,860	
Other expenses	5	71,340	
			(90,300)
Net profit			50,000

(2)   During the year ended 5 April 2010 Sam drove a total of 25,000 miles, of which 5,000 miles were driven when he visited his suppliers in Europe. The balance of the mileage is 25% for private journeys and 75% for business journeys in the United Kingdom.

(3)   During the year ended 5 April 2010 Sam paid patent royalties of £700 (gross) in respect of specialised technology that he uses when altering clothes for customers.

(4)   The figure for professional fees consists of £1,050 for legal fees in connection with an action brought against a supplier for breach of contract and £810 for accountancy. Included in the figure for accountancy is £320 in respect of personal capital gains tax advice for the tax year 2008/09.

(5)   The figure for other expenses of £71,340 includes £560 for gifts to customers of food hampers costing £35 each and £420 for gifts to customers of pens carrying an advertisement for the clothing shop costing £60 each.

(6)   Sam uses one of the eight rooms in the couple's private house as an office for when he works at home. The total running costs of the house for the year ended 5 April 2010 were £5,120. This cost is not included in the profit and loss account expenses of £90,300.

(7)   Sam uses his private telephone to make business telephone calls. The total cost of the private telephone for the year ended 5 April 2010 was £1,600, and 25% of this related to business telephone calls. The cost of the private telephone is not included in the profit and loss account expenses of £90,300.

(8)   During the year ended 5 April 2010 Sam took goods out of the clothing shop for his personal use without paying for them and no entry has been made in the accounts to record this. The goods cost £820, and had a selling price of £1,480.

(9)   The tax written down values for capital allowance purposes at 6 April 2009 were:

General pool	£14,800
Expensive motor car	£20,200

The expensive motor car is used by Sam.

Kim White

(1)   Kim is employed as a sales person by Sharp-Suit plc, a clothing manufacturing company. During the tax year 2009/10 she was paid a gross annual salary of £21,600.

(2)   On 1 June 2009 Sharp-Suit plc provided Kim with an interest free loan of £12,000 so that she could purchase a new motor car.

(3)   During the period from 1 June 2009 to 5 April 2010 Kim used her private motor car for business and private purposes. She received no reimbursement from Sharp-Suit plc for any of the expenditure incurred. Kim's mileage during this period included the following:

	Miles
Normal daily travel between home and permanent workplace	3,400
Travel between permanent workplace and Sharp-Suit plc's customers	11,200
Travel between home and a temporary workplace for a period of one month	1,300

(4)   During the tax year 2009/10 Kim paid interest of £140 (gross) on a personal loan taken out on 1 January 2008 to purchase a laptop computer for use in her employment with Sharp-Suit plc.

Joint income – Building society deposit account

The couple have savings of £25,000 in a building society deposit account which is in their joint names.

During the tax year 2009/10 Sam and Kim received building society interest totalling £1,200 from this joint account. This was the actual cash amount received.

Required:

(a)   **Calculate Sam's tax adjusted trading profit for the year ended 5 April 2010.**

   Your computation should start with the net profit of £50,000 and should list all the items referred to in Notes (1) to (8), indicating with a zero (0) any items that do not require adjustment.   **(11 marks)**

(b)   **Calculate Sam and Kim's respective income tax liabilities for the tax year 2009/10.**

   You should ignore any capital allowances that Kim might be entitled to.   (10 marks)

(c)   **Explain to Sam and Kim how their overall income tax liability could be reduced if they were to either:**

   (i)   **transfer their joint building society deposit account into individual savings accounts (ISAs); or**   **(2 marks)**

   (ii)   **transfer their joint building society deposit account into Kim's sole name.**
   (2 marks)

   Assume that 2009/10 rates and allowances continue to apply.

   (Total: 25 marks)

17 DOMINGO, ERIGO AND FARGO GOMEZ *Walk in the footsteps of a top tutor*

 Timed question with Online tutor debrief

Domingo, Erigo and Fargo Gomez are three brothers. The following information is available for the tax year 2009/10:

Domingo Gomez

(1)   Domingo is aged 67.

(2)   During the tax year 2009/10 he received the state pension of £4,500 and a private pension of £2,300.

(3)   In addition to his pension income Domingo received building society interest of £15,200 and interest of £600 on the maturity of a savings certificate from the National Savings and Investments Bank during the tax year 2009/10. These were the actual cash amounts received.

(4)   During the tax year 2009/10 Domingo made donations of £300 (gross) to local charities. These were not made under the gift aid scheme.

Erigo Gomez

(1)   Erigo is aged 56.

(2)   He is employed as a business journalist by Economical plc, a magazine publishing company. During the tax year 2009/10 Erigo was paid a gross annual salary of £36,000.

(3)   During the tax year 2009/10 Erigo used his private motor car for business purposes. He drove 18,000 miles in the performance of his duties for Economical plc, for which the company paid an allowance of 20 pence per mile.

(4)   During June 2008 Economical plc paid £11,400 towards the cost of Erigo's relocation when he was required to move his place of employment. Erigo's previous main residence was 140 miles from his new place of employment with the company. The £11,400 covered the cost of disposing of Erigo's old property and of acquiring a new property.

(5)   Erigo contributed 6% of his gross salary of £36,000 into Economical plc's HM Revenue and Customs' registered occupational pension scheme.

(6)   During the tax year 2009/10 Erigo donated £100 (gross) per month to charity under the payroll deduction scheme.

Fargo Gomez

(1)   Fargo is aged 53.

(2)   He commenced self-employment as a business consultant on 6 July 2009. Fargo's tax adjusted trading profit based on his draft accounts for the nine-month period ended 5 April 2010 is £64,800. This figure is before making any adjustments required for:

(i)   Advertising expenditure of £2,600 incurred during May 2009. This expenditure has not been deducted in calculating the profit of £64,800.

(ii)   Capital allowances.

(3)   The only item of plant and machinery owned by Fargo is his motor car. This cost £11,000 on 6 July 2009 and has CO_2 emissions of 152 g/km. During the nine-month period ended 5 April 2010 Fargo drove a total of 24,000 miles, of which 8,000 were for private journeys.

(4)   During the tax year 2009/10 Fargo contributed £5,200 (gross) into a personal pension scheme, and made gift aid donations totalling £2,400 (net) to national charities.

Tax returns

For the tax year 2009/10 Domingo wants to file a paper self-assessment tax return and have HM Revenue and Customs prepare a self-assessment on his behalf. Erigo also wants to file a paper tax return but will prepare his own self-assessment. Fargo wants to file his tax return online.

Required:

(a)   Calculate the respective income tax liabilities for the tax year 2009/10 of:

(i)   **Domingo Gomez;**   (6 marks)

(ii)   **Erigo Gomez;**   (6 marks)

(iii) **Fargo Gomez.**   (7 marks)

(b)   Advise Domingo, Erigo and Fargo Gomez of the latest dates by which their respective self-assessment tax returns for the tax year 2009/10 will have to be submitted given their stated filing preferences.   (3 marks)

(c)   Advise Domingo, Erigo and Fargo Gomez as to how long they must retain the records used in preparing their respective tax returns for the tax year 2009/10, and the potential consequences of not retaining the records for the required period.   (3 marks)

(Total: 25 marks)

 Calculate your allowed time, allocate the time to the separate parts......................

18   ANDREW ZOOM *Walk in the footsteps of a top tutor*

 Timed question with Online tutor debrief

Andrew Zoom is a cameraman who started working for Slick-Productions Ltd on 6 April 2009. The following information is available in respect of the year ended 5 April 2010:

(1)   Andrew received gross income of £50,000 from Slick-Productions Ltd.

He works a set number of hours each week and is paid an hourly rate for the work that he does.

When Andrew works more than the set number of hours he is paid overtime.

(2) Andrew is under an obligation to accept the work offered to him by Slick-Productions Ltd, and the work is carried out under the control of the company's production manager.

He is obliged to do the work personally, and this is all performed at Slick-Productions Ltd's premises.

(3) All of the equipment that Andrew uses is provided by Slick-Productions Ltd.

Andrew has several friends who are cameramen, and they are all treated as self-employed. He therefore considers that he should be treated as self-employed as well in relation to his work for Slick-Productions Ltd.

Required:

(a) **List those factors that indicate that Andrew Zoom should be treated as an employee in relation to his work for Slick-Productions Ltd rather than as self-employed.**

You should confine your answer to the information given in the question.

(4 marks)

(b) **Calculate Andrew Zoom's income tax liability and national insurance contributions for the tax year 2009/10 if he is treated:**

(i) **As an employee in respect of his work for Slick-Productions Ltd;**

You are not required to calculate the employers' national insurance contributions. **(3 marks)**

(ii) **As self-employed in respect of his work for Slick-Productions Ltd.** **(3 marks)**

(10 marks)

 Calculate your allowed time, allocate the time to the separate parts.....................

TRADING LOSSES

19 NORMA

Norma, who had been in business as a confectioner since 1 May 2005, disposed of the business and retired on 31 May 2009. She does not intend to start any other business, but will be employed part-time from 1 June 2009 on an annual salary of £8,000.

Her trading profits/(losses), as adjusted for taxation were:

	£	
Period ended 31.12.05	21,000	Profit
Year ended 31.12.06	17,000	Profit
Year ended 31.12.07	14,000	Profit
Year ended 31.12.08	5,000	Profit
Period ended 31.5.09	(10,000)	Loss

Norma has received bank interest of £2,000 (gross) each year since April 2005. In addition she realised a chargeable gain after the annual exemption, of £40,000 in June 2008.

Required:

Calculate Norma's taxable income and gains for each tax year that she was in business before any relief for the loss arising in the period ended 31 May 2009.

Explain the options available to Norma to utilise the loss and explain the effect on her tax liability of the loss relief claims identified.

Assume that rates and allowances for 2009/10 apply throughout. **(15 marks)**

20 MALCOLM (ADAPTED)

Malcolm started in business as a self-employed builder on 1 August 2008. His adjusted trading results, after capital allowances, were:

	£	
Period ended 30.11.08	(17,000)	Loss
Year ended 30.11.09	(30,000)	Loss
Year ended 30.11.10	24,000	Profit

Prior to being self-employed Malcolm was employed as a builder when his earnings were:

	£
2008/09 (to 31 July 2008)	15,000
2007/08	18,000

He received annual interest income of £3,000 (net) from 2007/08 onwards and in 2008/09 he realised a capital gain of £12,000.

Required:

Show how Malcolm's trading losses can be utilised most effectively, giving your reasoning.

You may assume the rates and allowances for 2009/10 apply to all years relevant to this question. All apportionments should be made in months. **(10 marks)**

21 LEONARDO

Leonardo, an art dealer commenced to trade on 1 September 2006. His trading results, adjusted for income tax, are:

	£	
1.9.06 to 31.5.07	40,500	Profit
1.6.07 to 31.5.08	(54,000)	Loss
1.6.08 to 31.5.09	(27,000)	Loss
1.6.09 to 31.5.10	9,000	Profit

Leonardo does not foresee making any appreciable profits in the next 2 or 3 years.

Leonardo has not had any other income in any of the years in question.

Required:

(a) Show how his trading loss can be utilised most effectively, giving your reasons.

(8 marks)

(b) State by what date(s) the claims you are proposing in part (a) should be submitted to HM Revenue & Customs. **(2 marks)**

(Total: 10 marks)

22   DEE ZYNE *Walk in the footsteps of a top tutor*

On 5 July 2009 Dee Zyne resigned as an employee of Trendy-Wear plc. The company had employed her as a fashion designer since 2001. On 6 July 2009 Dee commenced self-employment running her own clothing business, preparing accounts to 5 April.

The following information is available for 2009/10.

Employment

(1)   During the period 6 April 2009 to 5 July 2009 Dee's total gross salary from her employment with Trendy-Wear plc was £26,000. Income tax of £8,530 was deducted from this figure under PAYE.

(2)   During the period 6 April 2009 to 5 July 2009 Trendy-Wear plc provided Dee with a petrol-powered company motor car with a list price of £17,500. The official CO_2 emission rate for the motor car was 218 grams per kilometre. Trendy-Wear plc also provided Dee with fuel for private journeys. Dee paid £100 per month to Trendy-Wear plc for the use of the motor car, and she also made a capital contribution of £1,500 towards the cost of the motor car when it was first provided to her. The motor car was not available to Dee after 5 July 2009.

(3)   On 1 January 2008 Trendy-Wear plc had provided Dee with an interest-free loan of £60,000 so that she could purchase a yacht. Dee repaid £45,000 of the loan on 5 May 2009, and repaid the balance of the loan of £15,000 on 6 July 2009.

(4)   During the period from 6 April 2009 to 5 July 2009 Dee was provided with free meals in Trendy-Wear plc's staff canteen. The total cost of these meals to the company was £350.

Self-employment

(1)   Dee's tax adjusted trading loss for the period 6 July 2009 to 5 April 2010 was £11,440. This figure is before taking account of the information in note (2) and capital allowances.

(2)   During the period 6 July 2009 to 5 April 2010 Dee paid patent royalties of £500 (gross) in respect of specialised technology that she uses in her clothing business.

(3)   Dee purchased the following assets during the nine-month period ended 5 April 2010:

		£
10 July 2009	Computer	1,257
16 August 2009	Office furniture	2,175
13 November 2009	Motor car (1)	10,400
21 January 2010	Motor car (2)	17,800

Motor car (1) purchased on 13 November 2009 has CO_2 emissions of 135 grams per kilometre, is used by an employee, and 15% of the mileage is for private purposes.

Motor car (2) purchased on 21 January 2010 has CO_2 emissions of 165 grams per kilometre, is used by Dee, and 20% of the mileage is for private purposes.

Other information

(1)   During the period 6 April 2009 to 5 July 2009 Dee paid interest of £110 (gross) on a personal loan taken out on 1 August 2008 to purchase a computer for use in her employment with Trendy-Wear plc.

(2)   Dee's total income for each of the years 2003/04 to 2008/09 was £80,000.

Required:

(a)   Calculate Dee's tax adjusted trading loss for 2009/10.   **(6 marks)**

(b)   Assuming that Dee claims loss relief against her total income for 2009/10, calculate the income tax repayable to her for 2009/10.   **(15 marks)**

(c)   Describe the alternative ways in which Dee could have relieved her trading loss for 2009/10 against total income, and explain why these claims would have been more beneficial than the actual claim made in (b) above.

You should assume that the tax rates for 2009/10 apply throughout.   **(4 marks)**

(Total: 25 marks)

23   SAMANTHA FABRIQUE (ADAPTED)

Samantha Fabrique has been a self-employed manufacturer of clothing since 1994. She has the following gross income and chargeable gains for the tax years 2006/07 to 2010/11:

	2006/07	2007/08	2008/09	2009/10	2010/11
	£	£	£	£	£
Trading profit/(loss)	21,400	40,100	21,600	(84,000)	10,500
Building society interest	2,400	4,600	2,100	3,800	1,500
Chargeable gains/(loss)	10,400	18,800	23,300	(3,400)	11,000

Required:

(a)   State the factors that will influence an individual's choice of loss relief claims.

(3 marks)

(b)   Calculate Samantha's taxable income and taxable gains for each of the tax years 2006/07, 2007/08, 2008/09, 2009/10 and 2010/11 on the assumption that she relieves the trading loss of £84,000 for the tax year 2009/10 on the most favourable basis.

Explain your reasoning behind relieving the loss on the most favourable basis.

You should assume that the tax allowances for the tax year 2009/10 apply throughout.   **(12 marks)**

(Total: 15 marks)

PARTNERSHIPS

24 PETER, QUINTON AND ROGER (ADAPTED)

(1) Peter and Quinton commenced in partnership on 1 January 2007. Roger joined as a partner on 1 January 2008, and Peter resigned as a partner on 31 December 2009. Profits and losses have always been shared equally. The partnership's tax adjusted profits and losses are as follows:

	£	
Year ended 31 December 2007	40,000	Profit
Year ended 31 December 2008	90,000	Profit
Year ended 31 December 2009	(30,000)	Loss

All of the partners were in employment prior to becoming partners, and each of them has investment income. None of the partners has any capital gains.

Required:

(a) Briefly explain the basis by which trading profits are assessed on partners when they join a partnership. **(2 marks)**

(b) Calculate the trading income assessments of Peter, Quinton and Roger for 2006/07, 2007/08 and 2008/09. **(6 marks)**

(c) State the possible ways in which Peter, Quinton and Roger can relieve their share of the trading loss for 2009/10.

Your answer should include a calculation of the amount of loss relief available to each partner. **(7 marks)**

(2) Following Peter's retirement from the partnership Quinton has recently taken over responsibility for the partnership's Value Added Tax (VAT) affairs. He has contacted you with some queries regarding VAT interest charges and penalties.

Required:

(a) State when a VAT 'default surcharge' arises and for how long a 'default surcharge period' lasts **(3 marks)**

(b) State under what circumstances HM Revenue & Customs may raise assessments for VAT 'default interest' and the period for which interest is charged. **(3 marks)**

(c) Explain the consequences of Quentin finding an error on an earlier VAT return submitted by the partnership. **(4 marks)**

(Total: 25 marks)

25 XIO, YANA AND ZOE *Walk in the footsteps of a top tutor*

Xio, Yana and Zoe have been in partnership since 6 April 2001 as marketing consultants.

Until 30 June 2009 profits were shared 50% to Xio, 30% to Yana and 20% to Zoe. This was after paying an annual salary of £6,000 to Xio. On 30 June 2009 Zoe resigned as a partner, and from that date profits were shared equally between Xio and Yana. No salaries were paid after this date.

The partnership's profit and loss account for the year ended 5 April 2010 is as follows:

	£	£
Gross profit		200,600
Expenses:		
Depreciation	11,750	
Impaired debts (Note 1)	6,800	
Motor expenses (Note 2)	19,000	
Professional fees (Note 3)	5,300	
Repairs and renewals (Note 4)	7,500	
Other expenses (Note 5)	114,250	
	―――――	(164,600)
		―――――
Net profit		36,000
		―――――

Note 1 – Impaired debts

The figure for impaired debts consists of a loan to a supplier written off of £4,000, and an increase in an allowance for trade debtors of £2,800.

Note 2 – Motor expenses

The figure for motor expenses is in respect of mileage undertaken by the partners, of which 40% is for private purposes.

Note 3 – Professional fees

The figure for professional fees consists of £600 for accountancy, £2,600 for legal fees in connection with the defence of the partnership's internet domain name, and £2,100 for legal fees in connection with the grant of a new five-year lease of parking spaces for employees' motor cars.

Note 4 – Repairs and renewals

The figure for repairs and renewals consists of £2,800 for decorating the partnership offices, and £4,700 for constructing a new wall in order to split one large office room into two smaller rooms.

Note 5 – Other expenses

The figure of £114,250 for other expenses includes £1,060 for entertaining customers, £460 for entertaining employees, and £600 in respect of gifts to customers. The gifts were hampers of food costing £60 each. The remaining expenses are all allowable.

Note 6 – Plant and machinery

The tax written down values of the partnership's assets for capital allowances purposes at 6 April 2009 were as follows:

	£
General pool	17,000
Xio's motor car	16,500
Yana's motor car	8,750
Zoe's motor car	15,000

The partners' motor cars are all owned by the partnership, and in each case 40% of the mileage is for private purposes.

Zoe retained her motor car when she resigned from the partnership on 30 June 2009. On that date her motor car was valued at £12,400.

Other income

(1) Xio received building society interest of £800 during 2009/10. This was the actual cash amount received.

(2) Yana sold some investments during 2009/10, and this resulted in capital gains of £32,800.

(3) Zoe was appointed as the sales director of Aardvark plc on 1 July 2009, and was paid director's remuneration of £26,000 during 2009/10. She also received dividends of £10,800 during 2009/10. This was the actual cash amount received.

Required:

(a) Calculate the partnership's tax adjusted trading profit for the year ended 5 April 2010.
Your computation should start with the net profit figure of £36,000 and should list all the items referred to in Notes (1) to (5), indicating by the use of zero (0) any items that do not require adjustment. **(12 marks)**

(b) Calculate the trading income assessments of Xio, Yana and Zoe for 2009/10. **(4 marks)**

(c) Calculate the income tax and capital gains tax liabilities of Xio, Yana and Zoe for 2009/10. **(9 marks)**

(Total: 25 marks)

26 AMY BWALYA

(a) Amy Bwalya commenced in self-employment on 1 August 2007, preparing accounts to 31 May. Her trading profits for the first two periods of trading were as follows:

	£
Ten-month period ended 31 May 2008	38,500
Year ended 31 May 2009	52,800

Required:

Calculate the amount of trading profits that will have been assessed on Amy for the tax years 2007/08, 2008/09 and 2009/10.

Your answer should show the amount of overlap profits. **(5 marks)**

(b) Cedric Ding and Eli Fong commenced in partnership on 6 April 2005, preparing accounts to 5 April. Cedric resigned as a partner on 31 December 2009, and Gordon Hassan joined as a partner on 1 January 2010. The partnership's trading profit for the year ended 5 April 2010 is £90,000.

Profits were shared as follows:

(1) Eli was paid an annual salary of £6,000.

(2) Interest was paid at the rate of 10% on the partners' capital accounts, the balances on which were:

	£
Cedric	40,000
Eli	70,000
Gordon (from 1 January 2010)	20,000

Cedric's capital account was repaid to him on 31 December 2009.

(3) The balance of profits were shared:

	Cedric	Eli	Gordon
	%	%	%
6 April 2009 to 31 December 2009	60	40	
1 January 2010 to 5 April 2010		70	30

Required:

Calculate the trading income assessments of Cedric, Eli and Gordon for the tax year 2009/10. **(5 marks)**

(c) Ivan Jha ceased trading on 31 December 2009. He had commenced in self-employment on 1 October 2002, initially preparing accounts to 30 September. His overlap profits for the period 1 October 2002 to 5 April 2003 were £4,500.

Ivan subsequently changed his accounting date to 30 June by preparing accounts for the nine-month period to 30 June 2009. His trading profits for the final four periods of trading were as follows:

	£
Year ended 30 September 2007	36,000
Nine-month period ended 30 June 2008	23,400
Year ended 30 June 2009	28,800
Six-month period ended 31 December 2009	10,800

Required:

Calculate the amount of trading profits that will have been assessed on Ivan for the tax years 2007/08, 2008/09 and 2009/10. **(5 marks)**

(Total: 15 marks)

27 AE, BEE, CAE, DEE AND EUE (ADAPTED) *Walk in the footsteps of a top tutor*

(a) Ae and Bee commenced in partnership on 1 July 2007 preparing accounts to 30 June. Cae joined as a partner on 1 July 2009. Profits have always been shared equally.

The partnership's trading profits since the commencement of trading have been as follows:

	£
Year ended 30 June 2008	54,000
Year ended 30 June 2009	66,000
Year ended 30 June 2010	87,000

Required:

Calculate the trading income assessments of Ae, Bee and Cae for each of the tax years 2007/08, 2008/09 and 2009/10. **(5 marks)**

(b) Dee commenced in self-employment on 6 April 2006. She initially prepared accounts to 5 April, but changed her accounting date to 31 July by preparing accounts for the four-month period to 31 July 2008.

Dee's trading profits since she commenced trading have been as follows:

	£
Year ended 5 April 2007	35,160
Year ended 5 April 2008	32,880
Four-month period ended 31 July 2008	16,240
Year ended 31 July 2009	54,120

Required:

(i) Calculate the amount of trading profits that will have been assessed on Dee for each of the tax years 2007/08, 2008/09 and 2009/10; **(4 marks)**

(ii) State the amount of Dee's unrelieved overlap profits as at 5 April 2010.

(1 mark)

(c) Eue ceased trading on 30 September 2010, having been self-employed since 1 July 2001.

(1) Eue's trading profits for the final two periods of trading were as follows:

	£
Year ended 30 June 2009	61,200
Fifteen-month period ended 30 September 2010	72,000

Both these figures are before taking account of capital allowances.

(2) The capital allowances for the year ended 30 June 2009 were £2,100.

The tax written-down value of the capital allowances general pool at 1 July 2009 was £6,300. On 15 November 2009 Eue purchased a motor car with CO_2 emissions of 142 grams per kilometre for £2,400. All of the items included in the general pool were sold for £4,300 on 30 September 2010.

(3) Until the final period of trading Eue had always prepared accounts to 30 June. Her overlap profits for the period 1 July 2001 to 5 April 2002 were £19,800.

Required:

Calculate the amount of trading profits that will have been assessed on Eue for each of the tax years 2009/10 and 2010/11. **(5 marks)**

(Total: 15 marks)

PENSIONS AND NATIONAL INSURANCE

28   DUKE AND EARL UPPER-CRUST (ADAPTED)

Duke and Earl Upper-Crust, aged 44, are twin brothers.

Duke is employed by the High-Brow Bank plc as a financial adviser. During the tax year 2009/10 Duke was paid a gross salary of £120,000. He also received a bonus of £40,000 on 15 March 2010. On 31 March 2010 Duke made a contribution of £85,000 (gross) into a personal pension scheme. He is not a member of High-Brow Bank plc's occupational pension scheme.

Earl is self-employed as a financial consultant. His trading profit for the year ended 5 April 2010 was £34,000. On 31 March 2010 Earl made a contribution of £40,000 (gross) into a personal pension scheme.

Neither Duke nor Earl has any other income.

Required:

(a) **Calculate Duke and Earl's income tax liabilities for the tax year 2009/10, together with the actual net of tax amounts that Duke and Earl will have paid to their personal pension companies.** **(8 marks)**

(b) **Advise Duke and Earl of the maximum additional amounts that they could have contributed into personal pension schemes for the tax year 2009/10, whether or not such additional contributions would have qualified for tax relief, and the date by which any qualifying contributions would have had to have been paid.**

(4 marks)

(c) **Explain the effect of the pension scheme annual allowance limit of £245,000, and the tax implications if contributions are made in excess of this limit.** **(3 marks)**

(Total: 15 marks)

29 VANESSA SERVE AND SERENE VOLLEY *Walk in the footsteps of a top tutor*

(a) Vanessa Serve and Serene Volley, aged 32 and 35 years respectively, are sisters. The following information is available for the tax year 2009/10:

Vanessa Serve

(1) Vanessa is self-employed as a tennis coach. Her tax adjusted trading profit for the year ended 31 March 2010 is £52,400. However, this figure is before taking account of capital allowances.

(2) The only item of plant and machinery owned by Vanessa is her motor car. This originally cost £16,400, and at 1 April 2009 had a tax written down value of £10,400.

During the year ended 31 March 2010 Vanessa drove a total of 20,000 miles, of which 6,000 were for private journeys.

(3) Vanessa contributed £6,400 (gross) into a personal pension scheme during the tax year 2009/10.

(4) In addition to her self-employed income, Vanessa received interest of £1,100 from an investment account at the National Savings & Investments Bank during the tax year 2009/10. This was the actual cash amount received.

(5) Vanessa's payments on account in respect of the tax year 2009/10 totalled £8,705.

Serene Volley

(1) Serene is employed as a sports journalist by Backhand plc, a newspaper publishing company.

During the tax year 2009/10 she was paid a gross annual salary of £26,400. Income tax of £4,400 was deducted from this figure under PAYE.

(2) Throughout the tax year 2009/10 Backhand plc provided Serene with a petrol powered motor car which has a list price of £16,400. The official CO_2 emission rate for the motor car is 192 grams per kilometre.

The company did not provide Serene with any fuel for private journeys.

(3) Serene contributed 5% of her gross salary of £26,400 into Backhand plc's HM Revenue and Customs' registered occupational pension scheme.

(4) In addition to her employment income, Serene received interest of £1,200 on the maturity of a savings certificate from the National Savings & Investments Bank during the tax year 2009/10. This was the actual cash amount received.

(5) Serene did not make any payments on account in respect of the tax year 2009/10.

Required:

(i) **Calculate the income tax payable by Vanessa and Serene respectively for the tax year 2009/10.** **(11 marks)**

(ii) **Calculate the national insurance contributions payable by Vanessa and Serene respectively for the tax year 2009/10.** **(4 marks)**

(iii) **Calculate Vanessa and Serene's respective balancing payments for the tax year 2009/10 and their payments on account, if any, for the tax year 2010/11.**

You should state the relevant due dates. **(5 marks)**

(b) Note that in answering this part of the question you are not expected to take account of any of the information provided in part (a) above.

Unless stated otherwise all of the figures below are exclusive of VAT.

Vanessa Serve is registered for value added tax (VAT), and is in the process of completing her VAT return for the quarter ended 30 June 2010.

The following information is available:

(1) Sales invoices totalling £18,000 were issued in respect of standard rated sales. All of Vanessa's customers are members of the general public.

(2) During the quarter ended 30 June 2010 Vanessa spent £600 on mobile telephone calls, of which 40% related to private calls.

(3) On 3 April 2010 Vanessa purchased a motor car for £12,000. On 18 June 2010 £987 was spent on repairs to the motor car.

The motor car is used by Vanessa in her business, although approximately 10% of the mileage is for private journeys. Both figures are inclusive of VAT at the standard rate.

(4) On 29 June 2010 tennis coaching equipment was purchased for £1,760. Vanessa paid for the equipment on this date, but did not take delivery of the equipment or receive an invoice until 3 July 2010. This purchase was standard rated.

(5) In addition to the above, Vanessa also had other standard rated expenses amounting to £2,200 in the quarter ended 30 June 2010.

This figure includes £400 for entertaining customers.

Required:

(i)   Calculate the amount of VAT payable by Vanessa for the quarter ended 30 June 2010.   (5 marks)

(ii)   Advise Vanessa of the conditions that she must satisfy before being permitted to use the VAT flat rate scheme, and the advantages of joining the scheme.

        The relevant flat rate scheme percentage for Vanessa's trade as notified by HM Revenue and Customs is 6%.

        Your answer should be supported by appropriate calculations of the amount of tax saving if Vanessa had used the flat rate scheme to calculate the amount of VAT payable for the quarter ended 30 June 2010.   (5 marks)

                                                                   (Total: 30 marks)

30   ANN, BASIL AND CHLOE   *Walk in the footsteps of a top tutor*

You are a trainee accountant and your manager has asked for your help regarding three taxpayers who have all made personal pension contributions during the tax year 2009/10.

Ann Peach

Ann, aged 30, is self-employed as an estate agent. Her trading profit for the year ended 5 April 2010 was £48,000. Ann made contributions of £52,000 (gross) into a personal pension scheme during the tax year 2009/10.

Basil Plum

Basil, aged 42, is employed by the Banana Bank plc as a fund manager. During the tax year 2009/10 Basil was paid a gross salary of £320,000. Basil made contributions of £260,000 (gross) into a personal pension scheme during the tax year 2009/10. He is not a member of Banana Bank plc's occupational pension scheme.

Chloe Pear

Chloe, aged 54, lets out unfurnished property. For the tax year 2009/10 her property business profit was £23,900. Chloe made contributions of £8,200 (gross) into a personal pension scheme during the tax year 2009/10.

Neither Ann nor Basil nor Chloe has any other income.

Required:

For each of the three taxpayers Ann Peach, Basil Plum and Chloe Pear, state, giving reasons the amount of personal pension contributions that will have qualified for tax relief for the tax year 2009/10, and calculate their income tax liabilities for that year.

Marks are allocated as follows:

Ann Peach 3 marks; Basil Plum 5 marks; and Chloe Pear 2 marks.   (10 marks)

SELF ASSESSMENT

31   NICOLA (ADAPTED)

Nicola is 45 years old, single and a self-employed hairdresser. She submitted her income tax return to HM Revenue & Customs for 2008/09 on 15 September 2009 and her total income tax liability for 2008/09 under self-assessment was calculated at £7,500.

Payments on account for 2009/10 were accordingly set at:

31 January 2010	£3,750
31 July 2010	£3,750

On 15 December 2009, on the evidence of a profit forecast Nicola made a claim to reduce each of these payments on account to £2,500. These payments were made as follows:

31 January 2010	£2,500
31 October 2010	£2,500

Nicola's tax return for 2009/10 issued on 6 April 2010, was submitted to HM Revenue & Customs (HMRC) electronically on 28 February 2011 showing a total income tax liability for the year of £8,000.

On 31 March 2011 HMRC imposed a surcharge in respect of the 2009/10 income tax outstanding. On 31 May 2011 Nicola paid the balance of her 2009/10 liability and her first payment on account for 2010/11.

In view of the above recent events Nicola has been reviewing her tax affairs and in particular ways in which she may reduce her tax liability. Her friend has suggested a number of ways such as investing in an Individual Savings Account and increasing the level of expenses which she claims as deductible expenses through her business.

Required:

(1)   Calculate the following amounts payable by Nicola as a consequence of the above:

    (a)   the penalties due in respect of 2009/10   **(1 mark)**

    (b)   the surcharge due in respect of 2009/10   **(2 marks)**

    (c)   the interest payable in respect of 2009/10   **(7 marks)**

    (d)   the interest payable in respect of 2010/11.   **(1 mark)**

    Assume the rate of interest on unpaid tax is 2.5%.

(2)   Advise Nicola of the difference between tax avoidance and tax evasion, making reference to the suggestions made by her friend as ways of reducing her tax liability.   **(4 marks)**

                                                                 (Total: 15 marks)

32   PI CASSO

Pi Casso has been a self-employed artist since 1990, preparing her accounts to 30 June.

Pi's tax liabilities for the tax years 2007/08, 2008/09 and 2009/10 are as follows:

	2007/08	2008/09	2009/10
	£	£	£
Income tax liability	3,240	4,100	2,730
Class 2 national insurance contributions	114	120	125
Class 4 national insurance contributions	1,240	1,480	990
Capital gains tax liability	–	4,880	–

No income tax has been deducted at source.

Required:

(a)   **Prepare a schedule showing the payments on account and balancing payments that Pi will have made or will have to make during the period from 1 July 2009 to 31 March 2011, assuming that Pi makes any appropriate claims to reduce her payments on account.**

Your answer should clearly identify the relevant due date of each payment.

(7 marks)

(b)   **State the implications if Pi had made a claim to reduce her payments on account for the tax year 2009/10 to £Nil.** **(2 marks)**

(c)   **Advise Pi of the latest date by which her self-assessment tax return for the tax year 2009/10 should be submitted if she wants HM Revenue and Customs (HMRC) to prepare the self-assessment tax computation on her behalf.** **(3 marks)**

(d)   **State the date by which HMRC will have to notify Pi if they intend to enquire into her self-assessment tax return for the tax year 2009/10 and the possible reasons why such an enquiry would be made.** **(3 marks)**

(Total: 15 marks)

CHARGEABLE GAINS

INDIVIDUALS – CAPITAL GAINS TAX

33   CHANDRA KHAN (ADAPTED)

Chandra Khan disposed of the following assets during 2009/10:

(a)   On 15 June 2009 Chandra sold 10,000 £1 ordinary shares (a 30% shareholding) in Universal Ltd, an unquoted trading company, to her daughter for £75,000. The market value of the shares on this date was £110,000.

The shareholding was purchased on 10 July 1997 for £38,000. Chandra and her daughter have elected to hold over the gain as a gift of a business asset. Chandra is not employed by Universal Ltd.

(b)   On 8 November 2009 Chandra sold a freehold factory for £146,000. The factory was purchased on 3 January 1997 for £72,000.

75% of the factory has been used in a manufacturing business run by Chandra as a sole trader. However, the remaining 25% of the factory has never been used for business purposes.

Chandra has claimed to rollover the gain on the factory against the replacement cost of a new freehold factory that was purchased on 10 November 2009 for £156,000. The new factory is used 100% for business purposes by Chandra.

(c)   On 8 March 2010 Chandra incorporated a wholesale business that she has run as a sole trader since 1 May 2008. The market value of the business on 8 March 2010 was £250,000.

All of the business assets were transferred to a new limited company, with the consideration consisting of 200,000 £1 ordinary shares valued at £200,000 and £50,000 in cash. The only chargeable asset of the business was goodwill, and this was valued at £100,000 on 8 March 2010. The goodwill has a nil cost.

(d)   On 1 April 2010 Chandra sold a house for £350,000. She had purchased the house, as her main residence, for £75,000 on 1 April 2002.

Chandra occupied the house until 1 April 2006 when she went to live with a friend. She rented out the house until it was sold on 1 April 2010.

Required:

Calculate the chargeable gains, if any, arising from Chandra's disposals during 2009/10.

You should ignore the annual exemption and Entrepreneurs' relief.

Each of the four sections of this question carries equal marks (5 marks each).   (20 marks)

34   ALICE LIM (ADAPTED)

Alice Lim disposed of the following assets during 2009/10:

(a)   On 24 June 2009 Alice sold a freehold office building for £152,000. The office building had been purchased on 2 March 2008 for £134,000.

Prior to this on 15 April 2008 Alice had sold a freehold warehouse for £149,000 making a gain of £56,000. Alice made a claim to roll over the gain arising on the disposal of the warehouse against the cost of the office building.

Both the office building and the warehouse were used entirely for business purposes in a manufacturing business run by Alice as a sole trader.

(b)   On 9 January 2010 Alice sold 150,000 £1 ordinary shares in Alilim Ltd, an unquoted trading company, for £275,000.

Alilim Ltd had been formed on 17 October 2009 in order to incorporate a retail business that Alice had run as a sole trader since 18 May 1999. She became a director shareholder of the company and continued to run the business as a company.

All of the business assets were transferred to Alilim Ltd. The market value of the retail business on 17 October 2009 was £300,000. The consideration consisted of 200,000 £1 ordinary shares valued at £200,000, and £100,000 in cash.

The transfer of the business assets resulted in total chargeable gains of £120,000. This figure is before taking account of any rollover relief that was available upon incorporation.

(c)   On 27 February 2010 Alice sold 40,000 £1 ordinary shares (a 40% shareholding) in Family Ltd, an unquoted trading company, for £230,000. Alice had acquired the shares on 21 May 2009 when she purchased them from her mother for £120,000.

Alice's mother had originally purchased the shares on 19 December 2000 for £128,000. Alice and her mother elected to hold over the gain arising on 21 May 2009 as a gift of a business asset. The market value of the shares on that date was £168,000.

(d)   On 1 March 2010 Alice sold a house for £180,000. The property had originally been purchased on 1 April 2001 for £50,000 by Alice's husband. He transferred the property to Alice on 1 April 2005 when it was valued at £80,000. The house has always been rented out to tenants.

Required:

Calculate the chargeable gains arising from Alice's disposals during 2009/10, ignoring Entrepreneurs' relief and the annual exemption.

For part (b), also state the advice you would give to Alice to reduce her taxable gains. Calculations are not required, however you should consider Entrepreneurs' relief in your advice.

Marks for this question will be allocated on the basis of:

4 marks to (a), 7 marks to (b), 4 marks to (c) and 5 marks to part (d).   **(20 marks)**

35   MICHAEL CHIN (ADAPTED)

Michael Chin made the following gifts of assets to his daughter, Mika, during 2009/10:

(1)   On 30 June 2009 Michael gave Mika a business that he had run as a sole trader since 1 January 2005. The market value of the business on 30 June 2009 was £250,000, made up as follows:

	£
Goodwill	60,000
Freehold property	150,000
Net current assets	40,000
	250,000

The goodwill has been built up since 1 January 2005, and had a nil cost. The freehold property had cost £86,000 on 20 May 2007. Michael used 75% of this property for business purposes, but the other 25% has never been used for business purposes.

(2)   On 8 December 2009 Michael gave Mika his entire holding of 50,000 50p ordinary shares (a 60% holding) in Minnow Ltd, an unquoted trading company. The market value of the shares on that date was £180,000.

Michael had originally purchased the shares on 5 January 2009 for £87,500. On 8 December 2009 the market value of Minnow Ltd's chargeable assets was £250,000, of which £200,000 was in respect of chargeable business assets. Michael has never been employed by Minnow Ltd.

(3)   On 15 February 2010 Michael gave Mika 18,000 £1 ordinary shares in Whale plc, a quoted trading company. On that date the shares were quoted at £6.36 – £6.52.

Michael had originally purchased 15,000 shares in Whale plc on 7 December 2008 for £63,000, and he purchased a further 12,000 shares on 21 August 2009 for £26,400. The total shareholding was less than 1% of Whale plc's issued share capital.

(4) On 28 February 2010 Michael gave Mika a painting. On that date the painting was valued at £7,500. He had originally acquired the painting on 1 June 2008 for £4,000.

(5) On 2 March 2010 Michael gave Mika five acres of land attached to an investment property. He had acquired the property, together with the land for £500,000 in May 2009. The value of the land given to Mika on 2 March 2010 was £50,000 and the value of the investment property which Michael retained was £600,000.

(6) On 15 March 2010 Michael gave Mika an antique clock. On that date the clock was valued at £4,000. Michael had acquired the clock for £2,000 on 1 April 2008.

Where possible, Michael and Mika have elected to hold over any gains arising.

Michael incurred a capital loss of £17,300 during 2007/08, and made a capital gain of £11,800 during 2008/09.

Required:

Calculate Michael's capital gains tax liability for 2009/10, clearly showing the amount of any gains that can be held over. Ignore Entrepreneurs' relief.

You should assume that the rate of annual exemption for 2009/10 applies throughout.

(20 marks)

 Online question assistance

36 SOPHIA TANG (ADAPTED)

(1) Sophia Tang, aged 78, has been in business as a sole trader since 1 April 1985. On 31 March 2010 she transferred the business to her daughter Wong, at which time the following assets were sold to Wong:

(1) A freehold shop with a market value of £260,000. The shop had been purchased on 1 July 2004 for £113,000, and has always been used by Sophia for business purposes. Wong paid Sophia £160,000 for the shop.

(2) A freehold warehouse with a market value of £225,000. The warehouse had been purchased on 1 April 1986 for £70,000, and has never been used by Sophia for business purposes. Wong paid Sophia £100,000 for the warehouse.

Where possible, Sophia and Wong have elected to hold over any gains arising.

Sophia has made no other capital disposals in the tax year 2009/10.

Required:

(a) **Calculate Sophia's capital gains tax liability for the tax year 2009/10. Ignore Entrepreneurs' relief.** **(10 marks)**

(b) (i) **Explain why it would have been beneficial for capital gains tax purposes if Sophia had postponed the transfer of her business until 6 April 2010.** **(3 marks)**

(ii) **Explain the capital gains tax implications if Sophia had retained the business until her death, with the assets then passing to Wong under the terms of Sophia's will.** **(2 marks)**

(2)   Sophia acquired a house, as her main residence, on 6 April 2006 for £250,000.

Throughout her period of ownership she has used one of the eight rooms exclusively as an office for her business.

Required:

Assuming that Sophia were to sell the house for £400,000 on 6 April 2010, calculate Sophia's chargeable gain, if any, arising on the sale of the house, clearly showing the amount of any available reliefs. **(5 marks)**

Assume that the tax rates and allowances for 2009/10 continue into the future.

(Total: 20 marks)

37   DAVID AND ANGELA BROOK *Walk in the footsteps of a top tutor*

David and Angela Brook are a married couple. They disposed of the following assets during the tax year 2009/10:

Jointly owned property

(1)   On 29 July 2009 David and Angela sold a classic Ferrari motor car for £34,400. The motor car had been purchased on 17 January 2000 for £27,200.

(2)   On 30 September 2009 David and Angela sold a house for £381,900. The house had been purchased on 1 October 1989 for £86,000.

David and Angela occupied the house as their main residence from the date of purchase until 31 March 1993. The house was then unoccupied between 1 April 1993 and 31 December 1996 due to Angela being required by her employer to work elsewhere in the United Kingdom.

From 1 January 1997 until 31 December 2003 David and Angela again occupied the house as their main residence. The house was then unoccupied until it was sold on 30 September 2009.

Throughout the period 1 October 1989 to 30 September 2009 David and Angela did not have any other main residence.

David Brook

(1)   On 18 April 2009 David sold an antique table for £5,600. The antique table had been purchased on 27 May 2007 for £3,200.

(2)   On 5 May 2009 David transferred his entire shareholding of 20,000 £1 ordinary shares in Bend Ltd, an unquoted trading company, to Angela. On that date the shares were valued at £64,000. David's shareholding had been purchased on 21 June 2007 for £48,000.

(3)   On 14 February 2010 David made a gift of 15,000 £1 ordinary shares in Galatico plc to his son. On that date the shares were quoted on the Stock Exchange at £2.90 – £3.10. David had originally purchased 8,000 shares in Galatico plc on 15 June 2008 for £17,600, and he purchased a further 12,000 shares on 24 August 2008 for £21,600. David's total shareholding was less than 1% of Galatico plc's issued share capital.

Angela Brook

(1)   On 5 May 2009 Angela sold an antique clock for £7,200. The antique clock had been purchased on 14 June 2007 for £3,700.

(2)   On 7 July 2009 Angela sold 15,000 of the 20,000 £1 ordinary shares in Bend Ltd that had been transferred to her from David. The sale proceeds were £62,400.

Angela has taxable income of £40,000 for the tax year 2009/10. David does not have any taxable income.

Required:

Compute David and Angela's respective capital gains tax liabilities for the tax year 2009/10.   **(20 marks)**

38   WILSON BIAZMA (ADAPTED)

Wilson Biazma is resident and ordinarily resident in the United Kingdom for tax purposes. He disposed of the following assets during the tax year 2009/10:

(1)   On 21 April 2009 Wilson sold a freehold office building for £246,000. The office building had been purchased on 3 January 1991 for £104,000. Wilson has made a claim to rollover the gain on the office building against the replacement cost of a new freehold office building that was purchased on 14 January 2009 for £136,000. Both office buildings have always been used entirely for business purposes in a wholesale business run by Wilson as a sole trader.

(2)   On 26 May 2009 Wilson incorporated a retail business that he had run as a sole trader since 1 June 2006. The market value of the business on 26 May 2009 was £200,000. All of the business assets were transferred to a new limited company, with the consideration consisting of 140,000 £1 ordinary shares valued at £140,000 and £60,000 in cash. The only chargeable asset of the business was goodwill and this was valued at £120,000 on 26 May 2009. The goodwill has a nil cost. Wilson claimed Entrepreneurs' relief, but elected to disapply incorporation relief.

(3)   On 17 August 2009 Wilson made a gift of his entire holding of 10,000 £1 ordinary shares (a 100% holding) in Gandua Ltd, an unquoted trading company, to his daughter. The market value of the shares on that date was £160,000. The shares had been purchased on 8 January 2009 for £112,000. On 17 August 2009 the market value of Gandua Ltd's chargeable assets was £180,000, of which £150,000 was in respect of chargeable business assets. Wilson and his daughter have elected to hold over the gain on this gift of a business asset. Wilson has never worked for Gandua Ltd.

(4)   On 3 October 2009 an antique vase owned by Wilson was destroyed in a fire. The antique vase had been purchased on 7 November 2007 for £49,000. Wilson received insurance proceeds of £68,000 on 20 December 2009 and on 22 December 2009 he paid £69,500 for a replacement antique vase. Wilson has made a claim to defer the gain arising from the receipt of the insurance proceeds.

(5)   On 9 March 2010 Wilson sold ten acres of land for £85,000. He had originally purchased twenty acres of land on 29 June 2001 for £120,000. The market value of the unsold ten acres of land as at 9 March 2010 was £65,000. The land has never been used for business purposes.

Required:

(a)   Briefly explain when a person will be treated as resident or ordinarily resident in the United Kingdom for a particular tax year and state how a person's residence status establishes whether or not they are liable to capital gains tax.

You are not expected to explain the rules concerning people leaving or coming to the United Kingdom.   **(4 marks)**

(b)   Calculate Wilson's chargeable gains for the tax year 2009/10, clearly identifying the effects of the reliefs claimed in respect of disposals (1) to (4).   **(16 marks)**

(Total: 20 marks)

39   NIM AND MAE LOM *Walk in the footsteps of a top tutor*

 Timed question with Online tutor debrief

Nim and Mae Lom are a married couple. They disposed of the following assets during the tax year 2009/10:

Nim Lom

(1)   On 20 May 2009 Nim made a gift of 10,000 £1 ordinary shares in Kapook plc to his daughter. On that date the shares were quoted on the Stock Exchange at £3·70–£3·90, with recorded bargains of £3·60, £3·75 and £3·80. Nim has made the following purchases of shares in Kapook plc:

19 February 2001	8,000 shares for £16,200
6 June 2006	6,000 shares for £14,600
24 May 2009	2,000 shares for £5,800

Nim's total shareholding was less than 5% of Kapook plc, and so holdover relief is not available.

(2)   On 13 June 2009 Nim transferred his entire shareholding of 5,000 £1 ordinary shares in Jooba Ltd, an unquoted company, to his wife, Mae. On that date the shares were valued at £28,200. Nim's shareholding had been purchased on 11 January 2007 for £16,000.

(3)   On 26 November 2009 Nim sold an antique table for £8,700. The antique table had been purchased on 16 May 2006 for £5,200.

(4)   On 2 April 2010 Nim sold UK Government securities (Gilts) for £12,400. The securities had been purchased on 18 August 2008 for £10,100.

Mae Lom

(1)   On 28 August 2009 Mae sold 2,000 of the 5,000 £1 ordinary shares in Jooba Ltd that had been transferred to her from Nim (see (2) above). The sale proceeds were £30,400. Entrepreneurs' relief is not available in respect of this disposal.

(2)   On 30 September 2009 Mae sold a house for £186,000. The house had been purchased on 1 October 1999 for £122,000.

Throughout the period of ownership the house was occupied by Nim and Mae as their main residence, but one of the house's eight rooms was always used exclusively for business purposes by Mae.

Entrepreneurs' relief is not available in respect of this disposal.

(3) On 30 November 2009 Mae sold a business that she had run as a sole trader since 1 December 2001. The sale resulted in the following capital gains:

	£
Goodwill	80,000
Freehold office building	136,000
Investment property	34,000

The assets were all owned for more than one year prior to the date of disposal. The investment property has always been rented out.

Mae claimed Entrepreneurs' relief in respect of this disposal.

(4) On 31 March 2010 Mae sold a copyright for £9,600. The copyright had been purchased on 1 April 2005 for £10,000 when it had an unexpired life of 20 years.

Other information

Nim does not have any taxable income for the tax year 2009/10. He has unused capital losses of £16,700 brought forward from the tax year 2008/09.

Mae has taxable income of £50,000 for the tax year 2009/10. She has unused capital losses of £8,500 brought forward from the tax year 2008/09.

Required:

Compute Nim and Mae Lom's respective capital gains tax liabilities, if any, for the tax year 2009/10.

In each case, the amount of unused capital losses carried forward to future tax years, if any, should be clearly identified. (Total: 20 marks)

 Calculate your allowed time, allocate the time to the separate parts....................

COMPANIES – CHARGEABLE GAINS

40 SHREWD LTD (ADAPTED)

(1) Shrewd Ltd sold a factory on 15 February 2010 for £320,000. The factory was purchased on 24 October 1998 for £164,000, and was extended at a cost of £37,000 during March 2000. During May 2001 the roof of the factory was replaced at a cost of £24,000 following a fire. Shrewd Ltd incurred legal fees of £3,600 in connection with the purchase of the factory, and legal fees of £6,200 in connection with the disposal.

Assume indexation factors are as follows:

October 1998 to February 2010	0.298
March 2000 to February 2010	0.268
May 2001 to February 2010	0.226

Shrewd Ltd is considering the following alternative ways of reinvesting the proceeds from the sale of its factory:

(1)   A freehold warehouse can be purchased for £340,000.

(2)   A freehold office building can be purchased for £280,000.

(3)   A leasehold factory on a 40-year lease can be acquired for a premium of £350,000.

The reinvestment will take place during May 2011. All of the above buildings have been, or will be, used for business purposes.

Required:

(a)   **State the conditions that must be met in order that rollover relief can be claimed.**

You are not expected to list the categories of asset that qualify for rollover relief.   **(3 marks)**

(b)   **Before taking account of any available rollover relief, calculate Shrewd Ltd's chargeable gain in respect of the disposal of the factory.**   **(5 marks)**

(c)   **Advise Shrewd Ltd of the rollover relief that will be available in respect of each of the three alternative reinvestments.**

Your answer should include details of the base cost of the replacement asset for each alternative.   **(7 marks)**

(2)   Shrewd Ltd purchased a painting for the Board room on 1 June 1995 for £20,000. The painting was destroyed in a fire on 30 June 2009. The company received insurance proceeds of £30,000 on 1 September 2009 and purchased a new painting for £35,000 on 1 December 2009.

Assume the Retail Price indices are as follows:

June 1995	149.8
June 2009	211.9
September 2009	212.5

Required:

Advise Shrewd Ltd how the event will be treated for capital gains purposes.

Your answer should include advice on the availability of any beneficial elections and a calculation of the base cost of the new painting.   **(5 marks)**

(Total: 20 marks)

41   FORWARD LTD (ADAPTED)

(i)   Forward Ltd sold the following assets during the year ended 31 March 2010:

(1)   On 31 May 2009 Forward Ltd sold a freehold office building for £290,000. The office building had been purchased on 15 July 1991 for £148,000. The retail price index (RPI) for July 1991 was 133.8, and for May 2009 it was 211.7.

Forward Ltd purchased a replacement freehold office building on 1 June 2009 for £260,000.

(2) On 30 November 2009 Forward Ltd sold 5,000 £1 ordinary shares in Backward plc for £62,500. Forward Ltd had originally purchased 9,000 shares in Backward plc on 20 April 1986 for £18,000, and purchased a further 500 shares on 1 November 2009 for £6,500. Assume the retail price index for April 1986 was 97.7, and for November 2009 it was 212.9.

Forward Ltd purchased 10,000 £1 ordinary shares in Sideways plc on 1 December 2009 for £65,000.

(ii) On 1 May 1997 Forward Ltd had purchased a painting for the conference room for £15,000. On 1 December 2009, when it was worth £45,000, the painting was damaged. After the damage the painting was worth £20,000. Insurance proceeds of £22,000 were received on 1 February 2010. The proceeds were not used to repair the painting. Assume the retail price index for May 1997 was 156.9, for December 2009 was 213.1 and for February 2010 was 213.5.

Where possible, Forward Ltd has claimed to roll over any gains arising.

Forward Ltd's only other income for the year ended 31 March 2010 is its tax adjusted trading profit of £75,000. There are no associated companies.

Required:

(a) **Calculate Forward Ltd's corporation tax liability for the year ended 31 March 2010, and state by when this should be paid.**

Your answer should clearly identify the amount of any gains that have been rolled over. Capital allowances should be ignored. **(17 marks)**

(b) **Explain how Forward Ltd's rollover relief claim would have altered if on 1 June 2009 it had acquired a leasehold office building on a 15-year lease for £300,000, rather than purchasing the freehold office building for £260,000.** **(3 marks)**

(Total: 20 marks)

42   **HAWK LTD** *Walk in the footsteps of a top tutor*

Hawk Ltd sold the following assets during the year ended 31 March 2010:

(1) On 30 April 2009 a freehold office building was sold for £260,000. The office building had been purchased on 2 July 1990 for £81,000, and had been extended at a cost of £43,000 during May 2002. Hawk Ltd incurred legal fees of £3,200 in connection with the purchase of the office building, and legal fees of £3,840 in connection with the disposal. The office building has always been used by Hawk Ltd for business purposes.

The relevant retail prices indexes (RPIs) are as follows:

July 1990	126.8
May 2002	176.2
April 2009	211.5

(2) On 29 August 2009 5,000 £1 ordinary shares in Albatross plc were sold for £42,500. Hawk Ltd had purchased 6,000 shares in Albatross plc on 1 August 2009 for £18,600, and purchased a further 2,000 shares on 17 August 2009 for £9,400.

(3) On 27 October 2009 10,000 £1 preference shares in Cuckoo plc were sold for £32,000. Hawk Ltd had originally purchased 5,000 £1 ordinary shares in Cuckoo plc on 2 October 2009 for £60,000. On 18 October 2009 Cuckoo plc had a reorganisation whereby each £1 ordinary share was exchanged for three new £1 ordinary shares and two £1 preference shares. Immediately after the reorganisation each new £1 ordinary share was quoted at £4.50 and each £1 preference share was quoted at £2.25.

(4) On 28 March 2010 two acres of land were sold for £120,000. Hawk Ltd had originally purchased three acres of land on 1 March 2010 for £203,500. The market value of the unsold acre of land as at 28 March 2010 was £65,000.

Hawk Ltd's only other income for the year ended 31 March 2010 was a trading profit of £125,000.

Hawk Ltd does not have any associated companies.

Required:

(a) **Calculate Hawk Ltd's corporation tax liability for the year ended 31 March 2010.**

(16 marks)

(b) **Advise Hawk Ltd of:**

(i) **The minimum amount that will have to be reinvested in qualifying replacement business assets in order for the company to claim the maximum possible amount of rollover relief in respect of its chargeable gains for the year ended 31 March 2010.** **(2 marks)**

(ii) **The period during which the reinvestment must take place.** **(1 mark)**

(iii) **The amount of corporation tax that will be deferred if the maximum possible amount of rollover relief is claimed for the year ended 31 March 2010.** **(1 mark)**

(Total: 20 marks)

CORPORATION TAX

CORPORATION TAX BASICS AND ADMINISTRATION

43 ELONGATED LTD (ADAPTED)

(a) Elongated Ltd is a UK resident company that runs an advertising agency. The company commenced trading on 1 January 2008, and its results for the 15-month period ended 31 March 2009 are summarised as follows:

	£
Trading profit (note 1)	292,000
Property business income	70,250
Chargeable gain in respect of the disposal of a 1% shareholding on 20 March 2009	44,075
Gift Aid paid on 20 December 2008	(1,200)
Franked investment income received on 15 January 2009	40,000

Note 1 – Trading profit

The trading profit is adjusted for taxation. There are no capital allowances for the fifteen months to 31 March 2009.

Note 2 – Other information

Elongated Ltd has no associated companies.

Required:

(i)   Explain when an accounting period starts and when an accounting period finishes for corporation tax purposes. **(4 marks)**

(ii) Calculate Elongated Ltd's corporation tax liabilities in respect of the 15-month period ended 31 March 2009, and advise the company by when these should be paid. **(10 marks)**

(b)   Continuing with Elongated Ltd, the following information is relevant for the year ended 31 March 2010:

Trading profit

The trading profit as adjusted for taxation is £704,228. This figure is *before* taking account of capital allowances.

Plant and machinery

Elongated Ltd purchased the following assets during the year ended 31 March 2010:

		Cost
13 April 2009	Office furniture	£51,425
25 May 2009	Motor car (1)	£11,400
12 June 2009	Motor car (2)	£15,800
30 September 2009	Motor car (3)	£13,500

Motor car (1) purchased on 25 May 2009 for £11,400 has a CO_2 emission rate of 137 grams per kilometre. Motor car (2) purchased on 12 June 2009 for £15,800 has a CO_2 emission rate of 162 grams per kilometre. Motor car (3), purchased on 30 September 2009 for £13,500, has CO_2 emissions of 105 grams per kilometre.

Income from property

Elongated Ltd lets out two unfurnished office buildings that are surplus to requirements.

The first office building was let from 1 April 2009 until 31 December 2009 for an annual rent of £50,000. During January 2010 £9,600 was spent on decorating this office building. The office building was not re-let during the remainder of the year ended 31 March 2010.

The second office building was purchased on 1 June 2009. It was empty until 30 June 2009, but was let from 1 July 2009 until 31 March 2010. On 1 July 2009 the company received a premium of £70,000 for the grant of a ten-year lease, together with the annual rent of £34,000 which was payable in advance. During June 2009 Elongated Ltd spent £8,200 on advertisements in respect of the letting of this office building.

Other information

Elongated Ltd has no associated companies.

Required:

(i) Calculate Elongated Ltd's corporation tax liability for the year ended 31 March 2010. **(12 marks)**

(ii) State the date by which Elongated Ltd's self-assessment corporation tax return for the year ended 31 March 2010 should be submitted, and explain the penalty implications for the company if the return is submitted late.

(4 marks)

(Total: 30 marks)

44 ARABLE LTD

Arable Ltd commenced trading on 1 April 2009 as a manufacturer of farm equipment, preparing its first accounts for the nine-month period ended 31 December 2009. The following information is available:

Trading profit

The tax adjusted trading profit is £288,900. This figure is before taking account of capital allowances and any deduction arising from the premiums paid in respect of leasehold property.

Industrial building

Arable Ltd had a new factory constructed at a cost of £400,000 that the company brought into use on 1 May 2009. The cost was made up as follows:

	£
Land	120,000
Site preparation	14,000
Professional fees	6,000
Drawing office serving the factory	40,000
Showroom	74,000
Factory	146,000
	————
	400,000

Plant and machinery

Arable Ltd purchased the following assets in respect of the nine-month period ended 31 December 2009.

		£
15 February 2009	Machinery	31,000
18 February 2009	Building alterations necessary for the installation of the machinery	3,700
20 April 2009	Lorry	22,000
12 June 2009	Motor car (1)	11,200
14 June 2009	Motor car (2)	14,600
17 June 2009	Motor car (3)	13,000
29 October 2009	Computer	5,400

Motor car (1) purchased on 12 June 2009 for £11,200 has a CO_2 emission rate of 136 grams per kilometre. Motor car (2) purchased on 14 June 2009 for £14,600 has a CO_2 emission rate of 168 grams per kilometre. Motor car (3), purchased on 17 June 2009 for £13,000, has CO_2 emissions of 109 grams per kilometre.

The company will not make any short life asset elections.

Leasehold property

On 1 April 2009 Arable Ltd acquired two leasehold office buildings. In each case a premium of £75,000 was paid for the grant of a 15-year lease.

The first office building was used for business purposes by Arable Ltd throughout the period ended 31 December 2009.

The second office building was empty until 30 September 2009, and was then sub-let to a tenant. On that date Arable Ltd received a premium of £50,000 for the grant of a five-year lease, and annual rent of £14,800 which was payable in advance.

Loan interest received

Loan interest of £6,000 was received on 30 September 2009, and £3,000 was accrued at 31 December 2009. The loan was made for non-trading purposes.

Dividends received

During the period ended 31 December 2009 Arable Ltd received dividends of £18,000 from Ranch plc, an unconnected UK company. This figure was the actual cash amount received.

Profit on disposal of shares

On 5 December 2009 Arable Ltd sold 10,000 £1 ordinary shares in Ranch plc for £37,576. Arable Ltd had originally purchased 15,000 shares in Ranch plc on 10 May 2009 for £12,000. A further 5,000 shares were purchased on 20 August 2009 for £11,250. Arable Ltd's shareholding never represented more than a 1% interest in Ranch plc.

Assume that the relevant indexation factors are as follows:

May 2009	211.7
August 2009	212.3
December 2009	213.1

Other information

Arable Ltd has two associated companies.

Required:

(a) Calculate Arable Ltd's corporation tax liability for the nine-month period ended 31 December 2009. **(27 marks)**

(b) State the date by which Arable Ltd's self-assessment corporation tax return for the period ended 31 December 2009 should be submitted, and explain how the company can correct the return if it is subsequently found to contain an error or mistake. **(3 marks)**

(Total: 30 marks)

45   ZOOM PLC (ADAPTED)

Zoom plc is a manufacturer of photographic equipment. The company had profits chargeable to corporation tax of £820,840 for the year ended 31 December 2009.

The profit and loss account of Zoom plc for the year ended 31 December 2009 shows:

	£	£
Operating profit (Note 1)		812,500
Other operating income (Note 3)		16,400
Income from investments		
Bank interest (Note 4)	10,420	
Loan interest (Note 5)	22,500	
Income from property (Note 6)	44,680	
Dividends (Note 7)	49,500	
		127,100
		956,000
Interest payable (Note 8)		(46,000)
Profit before taxation		910,000

Note 1 – Operating profit

Depreciation of £48,100 has been deducted in arriving at the operating profit of £812,500.

Note 2 – Plant and machinery

On 1 January 2009 the tax written down values of plant and machinery were as follows:

	£
General pool	19,600
Expensive motor car	20,200

The following transactions took place during the year ended 31 December 2009:

		Cost/(Proceeds) £
15 January 2009	Purchased equipment	54,600
19 April 2009	Purchased a computer	12,300
29 April 2009	Sold the expensive motor car	(24,200)
30 April 2009	Purchased motor car (1)	16,600
3 May 2009	Sold a lorry	(9,800)
22 September 2009	Purchased motor car (2)	11,850
1 December 2009	Purchased motor car (3)	14,200
28 December 2009	Sold equipment (original cost £1,900)	(1,000)

Motor car (1) purchased on 30 April 2009 for £16,600 has a CO_2 emission rate of 170 grams per kilometre. Motor car (2) purchased on 22 September 2009 for £11,850 has a CO_2 emission rate of 156 grams per kilometre. Motor car (3), purchased on 1 December 2009 for £14,200, has CO_2 emissions of 106 grams per kilometre.

The expensive motor car sold on 29 April 2009 for £24,200 originally cost £23,200. The lorry sold on 3 May 2009 for £9,800 originally cost £17,200.

Note 3 – Other operating income

The other operating income consists of trade-related patent royalties that were received during the year ended 31 December 2009.

Note 4 – Bank interest received

The bank interest was received on 31 December 2009. The bank deposits are held for non-trading purposes.

Note 5 – Loan interest receivable

The loan was made for non-trading purposes on 1 April 2009. Loan interest of £15,000 was received on 30 September 2009, and interest of £7,500 was accrued at 31 December 2009.

Note 6 – Income from property

Zoom plc lets out two unfurnished office buildings that are surplus to requirements.

The first office building was let from 1 January 2009 until 31 October 2009 at a rent of £3,200 per month. On 31 October 2009 the tenant left owing two months' rent which Zoom plc was unable to recover. This office building was not re-let until February 2010.

The second office building was not let from 1 January 2009 to 30 April 2009. During this period Zoom plc spent £4,800 on advertising for new tenants, and £5,200 on decorating the office building. On 1 May 2009 the office building was let at an annual rent of £26,400, payable in advance.

Zoom plc insured its two office buildings at a total cost of £3,360 for the year ended 30 September 2009, and £3,720 for the year ended 30 September 2010. The insurance is payable annually in advance.

Note 7 – Dividends received

The dividends were all received from unconnected UK companies. The figure of £49,500 is the actual cash amount received.

Note 8 – Interest payable

The interest is in respect of a debenture loan that has been used for trading purposes. Interest of £23,000 was paid on 30 June 2009 and again on 31 December 2009.

Note 9 – Other information

Zoom plc made quarterly instalment payments in respect of its corporation tax liability for the year ended 31 December 2009.

Zoom plc has three associated companies.

For the year ended 31 December 2008 Zoom plc had PCTCT of £780,000.

Required:

(a) (i) Calculate the amount of capital allowances that Zoom plc can claim for the year ended 31 December 2009. **(12 marks)**

(ii) Prepare a computation for the year ended 31 December 2009 reconciling Zoom plc's profit before taxation with its profits chargeable to corporation tax.

Your reconciliation should commence with the profit before taxation figure of £910,000, clearly identify the tax adjusted trading profit and the amount of property business profit, and end with the figure of £820,840 for profits chargeable to corporation tax.

You should list all of the items referred to in Notes (1) and (3) to (8) that are relevant, indicating by use of zero (0) any items that do not require adjustment. **(8 marks)**

(b) Explain why Zoom plc was required to make quarterly instalment payments in respect of its corporation tax liability for the year ended 31 December 2009.

(3 marks)

(c) Calculate Zoom plc's corporation tax liability for the year ended 31 December 2009, and explain how and when this will have been paid.

You should assume that the company's profits chargeable to corporation tax of £820,840 accrued evenly throughout the year. (3 marks)

(d) Explain how your answer to part (c) above would differ if Zoom plc had no associated companies.

Your answer should include a calculation of the revised corporation tax liability for the year ended 31 December 2009. (4 marks)

(Total: 30 marks)

 Online question assistance

46 ALPHABETIC LTD (ADAPTED)

(a) Alphabetic Ltd prepares annual accounts to 31 July. It paid corporation tax of £100,000 on 1 June 2010 in respect of the accounting period to 31 July 2008. It subsequently transpired that the actual liability was £90,000 and £10,000 was repaid on 28 September 2010.

Required:

(i) Calculate the interest already charged on overdue tax which is now repayable to the company; and (1 mark)

(ii) State when interest accrues on overpaid tax payable to the company.

(1 mark)

Apportionments should be made in days and interest should be charged at 2.5% or paid at 0% pa.

(b) Betamatic Ltd initially estimates its chargeable profits for the year to 31 March 2010 will be £2,300,000. At the year end the estimate is reduced to £2,120,000 and, following the completion of the audit in June 2010, the final chargeable profits to show on the CT600 are £2,080,000.

Required:

Show the amounts of tax which Betamatic Ltd will pay and the pay days based on this information. (8 marks)

(Total: 10 marks)

47   REALITY LTD

Realty Ltd is in business providing property services to landlords. The company also lets out property which it owns itself, and during the year ended 31 March 2010 it let out four properties:

Property one

This is a freehold house that is let out unfurnished. The property was let out from 1 April 2009 to 31 December 2009 at a monthly rent of £750, payable in advance. On 31 December 2009 the tenant left owing two month's rent which Realty Ltd was unable to recover. The property was not re-let before 31 March 2010. During January 2010 the company spent £6,800 on repairing the roof of this property. During February and March 2010 £1,100 was spent on advertising for new tenants.

Property two

This is a freehold house that is let out furnished. The property was let out throughout the year ended 31 March 2010 at a monthly rent of £625, payable in advance. During July 2009 Realty Ltd spent £480 on replacement furniture.

The company claims the wear and tear allowance for this property.

Property three

This is a leasehold office building that is let out unfurnished. The property was acquired on 1 September 2009 when Realty Ltd paid a premium of £50,000 for the grant of a twenty-year lease. The property was immediately sub-let to a tenant, with Realty Ltd receiving a premium of £20,000 for the grant of a five-year lease. The company also received the annual rent of £6,600 which was payable in advance.

Property four

This is a freehold house that is let out unfurnished. The property was purchased on 1 October 2009 for £180,000, and was empty until 31 December 2009. During this period Realty Ltd spent £3,900 on decorating the property. The property was let out from 1 January 2010 to 31 March 2010 at a monthly rent of £800, payable in advance. During the year ended 31 March 2010 Realty Ltd paid interest of £5,600 in respect of the loan that was taken out to purchase this property.

Insurance

Realty Ltd insured all of its rental properties at a total cost of £5,040 for the year ended 31 December 2009, and £5,280 for the year ended 31 December 2010. The insurance is payable annually in advance.

Other information

For the year ended 31 March 2010 Realty Ltd has a trading profit of £84,000. The company also received loan interest of £9,600 in respect of a loan made for non-trading purposes.

Required:

(a)   Briefly explain the basis of assessment for property income.

      You are not expected to list the allowable deductions.   **(2 marks)**

(b)   Calculate Realty Ltd's property business profit for the year ended 31 March 2010.

                                                                              (10 marks)

(c)   Calculate Realty Ltd's corporation tax liability for the year ended 31 March 2010.

                                                                               (3 marks)

                                                                         (Total: 15 marks)

48 BALLPOINT LTD (ADAPTED) *Walk in the footsteps of a top tutor*

Ballpoint Ltd is a manufacturer of pens and other writing implements in the UK. The company is incorporated overseas, although its directors are based in the UK and hold their board meetings in the UK.

Ballpoint Ltd's summarised profit and loss account for the year ended 31 December 2009 is:

	£	£
Gross profit		956,800
Operating expenses:		
Depreciation	59,900	
Gifts and donations (Note 1)	4,100	
Repairs and renewals (Note 2)	40,800	
Professional fees (Note 3)	8,800	
Car lease costs (Note 4)	4,000	
Other expenses (Note 5)	330,000	
		(447,600)
Operating profit		509,200
Income from investments:		
Dividends (Note 6)		45,000
Profit from sale of fixed assets:		
Disposal of industrial building (Note 7)		60,000
		614,200
Interest payable (Note 8)		(94,200)
Profit before taxation		520,000

Note 1 – Gifts and donations

Gifts and donations are as follows:

	£
Gifts to customers (pens costing £20 each displaying Ballpoint Ltd's name)	2,040
Gifts to customers (food hampers costing £35 each)	770
Gifts to employees	270
Donation to a national charity (made under the Gift Aid scheme)	600
Donation to a local charity	
(Ballpoint Ltd received free advertising in the charity's magazine)	120
Donation to a political party	300
	4,100

Note 2 – Repairs and renewals

Ballpoint Ltd The figure of £40,800 for repairs and renewals includes £14,800 for replacing the roof of a warehouse, which was in a bad state of repair, and £13,900 for initial repairs to an office building that was acquired on 20 December 2008.

The office building was not usable until the repairs were carried out, and this fact was reflected by a reduced purchase price.

Note 3 – Professional fees

Professional fees are as follows:

	£
Accountancy and audit fee	2,300
Legal fees in connection with the issue of share capital	3,100
Legal fees in connection with the issue of a 4% debenture loan to purchase machinery that was subsequently cancelled	1,800
Legal fees in connection with the defence of the company's internet domain name	1,600
	8,800

Note 4 – Car lease costs

Ballpoint Ltd leases a car for its production manager at a cost of £4,000 p.a. The car has a CO_2 emission rate of 159 grams per kilometre.

Note 5 – Other expenses

The figure of £330,000 for other expenses includes £3,700 for entertaining customers, £1,700 for entertaining employees, £400 for counselling services provided to an employee who was made redundant, and a fine of £2,600 for publishing a misleading advertisement. The remaining expenses are all allowable.

Note 6 – Dividends received

During the year ended 31 December 2009 Ballpoint Ltd received dividends of £27,000 from Paper Ltd, an unconnected UK company, and dividends of £18,000 from Pencil Ltd, its 100% UK subsidiary company. Both figures are the actual cash amounts received.

Note 7 – Disposal of industrial building

The profit of £60,000 is in respect of a factory that was sold on 31 March 2009 for £300,000.

The factory had been purchased on 1 April 2003 for £240,000. The indexation allowance from April 2003 to March 2009 is £39,840.

The factory had originally been purchased new from a builder, and brought into use on 1 January 2004. It has always been used for industrial purposes.

The cost of £240,000 and the selling price of £300,000 are made up as follows:

	Cost £	Selling price £
Factory	145,000	180,000
Land	45,000	56,000
General offices	50,000	64,000
	240,000	300,000

Note 8 – Interest payable

The interest payable is in respect of the company's 6% debenture loan stock that was issued in the year 2004. The proceeds of the issue were used to finance the company's trading activities. Interest of £47,100 was paid on 30 June 2009 and again on 31 December 2009.

Note 9 – Plant and machinery

On 1 January 2009 the tax written down values of plant and machinery were as follows:

	£
General pool	8,200
Expensive motor car	9,800

The following transactions took place during the year ended 31 December 2009:

		Cost/ (Proceeds)
		£
2 February 2009	Purchased equipment	61,260
4 June 2009	Purchased motor car (1)	18,200
4 June 2009	Purchased motor car (2)	11,400
4 June 2009	Purchased motor car (3)	9,200
18 August 2009	Purchased equipment	4,300
12 November 2009	Sold equipment	(2,700)
20 December 2009	Sold motor car (2)	(10,110)

Motor car (1) purchased for £18,200 has a CO_2 emission rate of 164 grams per kilometre.
Motor car (2) purchased for £11,400 has a CO_2 emission rate of 149 grams per kilometre.
Motor car (3), purchased for £9,200, has CO_2 emissions of 102 grams per kilometre.

The equipment sold on 12 November 2009 for £2,700 was originally purchased for £13,800 on 10 April 2005.

Note 10 – Group relief

For the year ended 31 December 2009 Ballpoint Ltd has claimed group relief of £42,000 from its 100% subsidiary company, Pencil Ltd.

Note 11 – Other information

Ballpoint Ltd has only one associated company, Pencil Ltd.

Required:

(a) Explain why Ballpoint Ltd is treated as being resident in the United Kingdom, and state what difference it would make if the directors were based overseas and were to hold their board meetings overseas.   **(3 marks)**

(b) Calculate Ballpoint Ltd's tax adjusted trading profit for the year ended 31 December 2009.

Your computation should commence with the profit before taxation figure of £520,000, and should list all of the items referred to in Notes (1) to (8) indicating by the use of zero (0) any items that do not require adjustment.   **(20 marks)**

(c) Calculate Ballpoint Ltd's corporation tax liability for the year ended 31 December 2009.   **(7 marks)**

(Total: 30 marks)

49   DO-NOT-PANIC LTD (ADAPTED)

Do-Not-Panic Ltd is a United Kingdom resident company that installs burglar alarms.

The company commenced trading on 1 January 2009 and its results for the fifteen-month period ended 31 March 2010 are summarised as follows:

(1) The trading profit as adjusted for tax purposes is £315,000. This figure is before taking account of capital allowances.

(2) Do-Not-Panic Ltd purchased equipment for £24,000 on 20 February 2009.

(3) On 21 December 2009 Do-Not-Panic Ltd disposed of some investments and this resulted in a capital loss of £4,250. On 28 March 2010 the company made a further disposal and this resulted in a chargeable gain of £42,000.

(4) Franked investment income of £25,000 was received on 22 February 2010.

Do-Not-Panic Ltd has no associated companies.

Required:

Calculate Do-Not-Panic Ltd's corporation tax liabilities in respect of the fifteen-month period ended 31 March 2010 and advise the company by when these should be paid.

(10 marks)

50   GASTRON LTD *Walk in the footsteps of a top tutor*

 Timed question with Online tutor debrief

Gastron Ltd, a United Kingdom resident company, is a luxury food manufacturer.

Its summarised profit and loss account for the year ended 31 March 2010 is as follows:

	Note	£	£
Gross profit			876,500
Operating expenses			
Depreciation		85,660	
Amortisation of leasehold property	1	6,000	
Gift and donations	2	2,700	
Professional fees	3	18,800	
Other expenses	4	230,240	
			(343,400)
Operating profit			533,100
Income from investments			
Income from property	5	20,600	
Bank interest	6	12,400	
Dividends	7	54,000	
			87,000
Profit from sale of fixed assets			
Disposal of shares	8		80,700
			700,800
Interest payable	9		(60,800)
Profit before taxation			640,000

Note 1 – Leasehold property

On 1 April 2009 Gastron Ltd acquired a leasehold office building, paying a premium of £60,000 for the grant of a new ten-year lease. The office building was used for business purposes by Gastron Ltd throughout the year ended 31 March 2010. No legal costs were incurred by Gastron Ltd in respect of this lease.

Note 2 – Gifts and donations
Gifts and donations are as follows:

	£
Gifts to customers (pens costing £60 each and displaying Gastron Ltd's name)	1,200
Gifts to customers (hampers of food costing £25 each)	1,100
Donation to local charity (Gastron Ltd received free advertising in the charity's magazine)	400
	2,700

Note 3 – Professional fees

Professional fees are as follows:

	£
Legal fees in connection with the renewal of a 45-year property lease in respect of a warehouse	3,600
Legal fees in connection with the issue of debentures (see note 9)	15,200
	18,800

Note 4 – Other expenses

The figure of £230,240 for other expenses includes £1,300 for entertaining suppliers and £900 for entertaining employees.

Note 5 – Income from property

Gastron Ltd lets out the whole of an unfurnished freehold office building that is surplus to requirements. The office building was let from 1 April 2009 to 31 December 2009 at a monthly rent of £1,800, payable in advance. On 31 December 2009 the tenant left owing two months' rent which Gastron Ltd was unable to recover. During January 2010 the company spent £3,700 decorating the property. The office building was then re-let from 1 February 2010 at a monthly rent of £1,950, on which date the new tenant paid six months' rent in advance.

Note 6 – Bank interest received

The bank interest was received on 31 March 2010. The bank deposits are held for non-trading purposes.

Note 7 – Dividends received

During the year ended 31 March 2010 Gastron Ltd received dividends of £36,000 from Tasteless plc, an unconnected UK company, and dividends of £18,000 from Culinary Ltd, a 100% UK subsidiary company (see note 11). Both figures are the actual cash amounts received.

Note 8 – Profit on disposal of shares

The profit on disposal of shares is in respect of a 1% shareholding that was sold on 14 October 2009. The disposal resulted in a chargeable gain of £74,800. This figure is after taking account of indexation.

Note 9 – Interest payable

The interest payable is in respect of the company's 5% debenture loan stock that was issued on 1 April 2009. The proceeds of the issue were used to finance the company's trading activities. Interest of £30,400 was paid on 30 September 2009 and again on 31 March 2010.

Note 10 – Plant and machinery

On 1 April 2009 the tax written down values of plant and machinery were as follows:

	£
General pool	16,700
Expensive motor car	18,400

The following transactions took place during the year ended 31 March 2010:

		Cost/(Proceeds) £
19 May 2009	Purchased equipment	21,600
12 July 2009	Purchased motor car (1)	9,800
11 August 2009	Purchased motor car (2)	16,200
5 October 2009	Purchased a lorry	17,200
5 March 2010	Sold equipment	(3,300)

Motor car (1) purchased on 12 July 2009 for £9,800 has a CO_2 emission rate of 147 grams per kilometre. Motor car (2), purchased on 11 August 2009 for £16,200, has a CO_2 emission rate of 109 grams per kilometre. The equipment sold on 5 March 2010 for £3,300 was originally purchased in 2005 for £8,900.

Note 11 – Subsidiary company

Gastron Ltd owns 100% of the ordinary share capital of Culinary Ltd. On 13 February 2010 Culinary Ltd sold a freehold factory and this resulted in a capital loss of £66,000. For the year ended 31 March 2010 Culinary Ltd made no other disposals and paid corporation tax at the small company rate of 21%.

Required:

(a) Calculate Gastron Ltd's tax adjusted trading profit for the year ended 31 March 2010, after deducting capital allowances.

Your computation should commence with the profit before taxation figure of £640,000, and should list all of the items referred to in Notes (1) to (9) indicating by the use of zero (0) any items that do not require adjustment. **(15 marks)**

(b) Calculate Gastron Ltd's corporation tax liability for the year ended 31 March 2010, on the basis that no election is made between Gastron Ltd and Culinary Ltd in respect of capital gains. **(7 marks)**

(c) State the date by which Gastron Ltd's corporation tax liability for the year ended 31 March 2010 should be paid, and advise the company of the interest that will be due if the liability is not paid until 31 August 2011. **(3 marks)**

(d)   Explain the group relationship that must exist in order for two or more companies to form a group for capital gains purposes.   **(2 marks)**

(e)   State the time limit for Gastron Ltd and Culinary Ltd to make a joint election such that Culinary Ltd is treated as disposing of Gastron Ltd's shares (see Note 8), and explain why such an election will be beneficial.   **(3 marks)**

(Total: 30 marks)

 Calculate your allowed time, allocate the time to the separate parts....................

WITH OVERSEAS ASPECTS

51   ALBERT LTD (ADAPTED)

(a)   **Year ended 31 March 2010**

Albert Ltd is a UK resident trading company with no associated companies.

For the year ended 31 March 2010 it had an operating profit of £876,429. The following expenses have been deducted in calculating this figure:

	£
Depreciation	82,000
Donation under Gift Aid scheme	15,500
Donation to political party	48,000
Legal fees for collection of trade debts	3,500

Capital allowances

(1)   **Plant and machinery**

On 1 April 2009 the tax written down values of plant and machinery were as follows:

	£
General pool	45,200
Expensive motor car	22,400
Special rate pool	198,000

The following transactions took place during the year ended 31 March 2010:

		Cost/ (Proceeds) £
3 June 2009	Purchased machine	63,000
1 July 2009	Sold the expensive car	(18,200)
15 July 2009	Purchased a motor car	25,000

The motor car purchased on 15 July 2009 for £25,000 has a CO_2 emission rate of 107 grams per kilometre. The expensive motor car sold on 1 July 2009 was used by the finance director, and 60% of his mileage was for private journeys.

(2)   **Factory**

On 1 April 2009 Albert Ltd acquired a new factory for £380,000 (including land of £80,000) and immediately started to use it for industrial purposes.

Other information

In the year to 31 March 2010 Albert Ltd had interest income of £12,000 and realised a capital gain on the sale of an office building of £120,000. As at 1 April 2009 the company had trading losses brought forward of £25,000.

Required:

Calculate Albert Ltd's corporation tax liability for the year ended 31 March 2010.

In your adjustment of profits computation you should commence with operating profit of £876,429, and you should list all of the expenses deducted from operating profit referred to, indicating by the use of zero (0) any items that do not require adjustment. **(20 marks)**

(b) **Year ended 31 March 2011**

In the year ended 31 March 2011 Albert Ltd is forecasting to have a tax adjusted trading profit of £1,200,000. It will have no other income or gains.

Albert Ltd is planning to set up an overseas operation which is expected to make a trading profit of £180,000 in the year to 31 March 2011.

Albert Ltd is undecided as to whether the overseas operations should be set up as a branch of Albert Ltd or as a separate wholly owned overseas resident company. In either case the expected overseas profits would remain the same and the overseas tax payable on these profits would be £45,000.

If the operation is set up as an overseas subsidiary then gross dividends of £60,000 would be remitted to Albert Ltd in the year ending 31 March 2011. The overseas country withholds 10% withholding tax on dividends paid to overseas companies.

Required:

Calculate Albert Ltd's corporation tax liability for the year ended 31 March 2011 if the overseas operation is set up as:

(i) **a branch** **(3 marks)**

(ii) **a wholly owned overseas resident company.** **(2 marks)**

(Total: 25 marks)

52 **HELIUM LTD (ADAPTED)**

Helium Ltd is a large UK resident company. It owns 60% of the ordinary share capital of Argon Ltd and 5% of the ordinary share capital of Boron Ltd. Both of these companies are overseas resident companies.

Helium Ltd's tax-adjusted trading profit for the year ended 31 March 2010 was £175,810. This was before taking account of capital allowances and any deductions available in respect of the leasehold property.

Industrial buildings

Helium Ltd acquired a new factory from a builder for £450,000, which was brought into industrial use on 1 March 2010.

The cost was made up as follows:

	£
Land	95,000
Car park for customers and employees	15,000
Factory	220,000
Office	80,000
Air-conditioning unit (expected life 30 years)	40,000
	450,000

Plant and machinery

On 1 April 2009 the tax written down values of plant and machinery were as follows:

	£
General pool	13,100
Expensive motor car	25,400
Short-life asset (acquired 1 April 2006)	5,000

The following transactions took place during the year ended 31 March 2010:

		Cost/(Proceeds) £
1 May 2009	Purchased computer	21,000
1 June 2009	Sold the expensive car	(17,200)
5 June 2009	Sold machine (original cost £4,000)	(4,500)
18 June 2009	Purchased car	26,000

The motor car purchased on 18 June 2009 for £26,000 has a CO_2 emission rate of 172 grams per kilometre.

Leasehold property

On 1 August 2009 Helium Ltd paid a premium of £85,000 for the grant of a 20 year lease for an office building. The company also made three quarterly rental payments of £500 each during the year. The office building is used by the company for business purposes.

Other information

The company received net dividends of £10,000 and £9,000 from Argon Ltd and Boron Ltd respectively during this year, and overseas rental income of £110,500 (net). These amounts are stated after the deduction of 15% withholding tax.

The company made donations to charity of £30,000 under the Gift Aid scheme.

Required:

(a) Calculate Helium Ltd's tax adjusted trading profit for the year ended 31 March 2010.

Your computation should commence with £176,360 and should adjust for capital allowances and any deductions available in respect of the leasehold property.

(14 marks)

(b) Calculate Helium Ltd's corporation tax liability for the year ended 31 March 2010.

(9 marks)

(c) State when Helium Ltd's corporation tax liability for the year to 31 March 2010 is due for payment and the filing date for its tax return. **(2 marks)**

(Total: 25 marks)

WITH VAT ASPECTS

53 STRETCHED LTD (ADAPTED)

(1)   Stretched Ltd has always prepared its accounts to 31 December, but has decided to change its accounting date to 31 March. The company's results for the 15-month period ended 31 March 2010 are as follows:

(i)   The tax adjusted trading profit is £330,000. This figure is before taking account of capital allowances.

(ii)   Until January 2010 the company has never been entitled to capital allowances as all assets were leased. However, on 15 January 2010 the company bought a machine for £17,000.

(iii)   There is a property business profit of £45,000 for the 15-month period ended 31 March 2010.

(iv)   On 15 April 2009 the company disposed of some investments, and this resulted in a chargeable gain of £44,000. On 8 February 2010 the company made a further disposal, and this resulted in a capital loss of £6,700.

(v)   Franked investment income of £30,000 was received on 10 September 2009.

(vi)   A Gift Aid donation of £5,000 was made on 31 March 2010.

As at 1 January 2009 Stretched Ltd had unused trading losses of £23,000, and unused capital losses of £3,000.

Stretched Ltd has no associated companies.

Required:

(a)   Calculate Stretched Ltd's corporation tax liabilities in respect of the 15-month period ended 31 March 2010, and advise the company by when these should be paid.   (13 marks)

(b)   State the advantages for tax purposes of a company having an accounting date of 31 March instead of 31 December.   (2 marks)

(2)   Stretched Ltd is registered for VAT. The following information is available in respect of its VAT return for the quarter ended 30 June 2010.

(i)   On 10 June 2010 Stretched Ltd received an order for goods, together with a deposit of £5,000. It despatched the goods to the customer on 20 June 2010 and raised an invoice for the balance due of £25,000 on 1 July 2010. The invoice was paid on 30 July 2010.

(ii)   On 1 June 2010 Stretched Ltd received an invoice for £12,500 in respect of a new car for the sales director. On 1 June 2010 the director's old car was taken to auction and the company received a cheque for £7,000 in respect of the sale of the car. The private use of both cars by the sales director was 20%. In the quarter to 30 June 2010 the company paid fuel bills of £600 in respect of the sales director's cars.

(iii)   During the quarter ended 30 June 2010 the company incurred standard-rated costs of £1,000, in respect of the company's annual dinner dance for staff, and £500 on entertaining potential customers.

All figures are inclusive of VAT.

In the quarter to 30 September 2009 the company had submitted and paid its VAT liability late. The returns and payment for the quarters to 31 December 2009 and 31 March 2010 were submitted on time.

Required:

(a)   **Advise Stretched Ltd how the transactions in (i) to (iii) above should be dealt with in the VAT return for the quarter to 30 June 2010.**   **(7 marks)**

(b)   **Explain the implications if Stretched Ltd is two months late in submitting its VAT return and in paying the related VAT liability for the quarter ended 30 June 2010.**   **(3 marks)**

          (Total: 25 marks)

54   WIRELESS LTD *Walk in the footsteps of a top tutor*

(a)   Wireless Ltd, a United Kingdom resident company, commenced trading on 1 October 2009 as a manufacturer of computer routers. The company prepared its first accounts for the six-month period ended 31 March 2010.

The following information is available:

Trading profit

The tax adjusted trading profit based on the draft accounts for the six-month period ended 31 March 2010 is £68,400.

This figure is before making any adjustments required for:

(1)   Capital allowances.

(2)   Director's remuneration of £23,000 paid to the managing director of Wireless Ltd, together with the related employer's Class 1 national insurance contributions.

The remuneration is in respect of the period ended 31 March 2010 but was not paid until 5 April 2010. No accrual has been made for this remuneration in the draft accounts.

The managing director received no other remuneration from Wireless Ltd during the tax year 2009/10.

Plant and machinery

Wireless Ltd purchased the following assets in respect of the six-month period ended 31 March 2010:

		£
20 September 2009	Office equipment	10,400
5 October 2009	Machinery	10,200
11 October 2009	Building alterations necessary for the installation of the machinery	4,700
18 February 2010	Motor car	10,600

The motor car purchased on 18 February 2010 for £10,600 has a CO_2 emission rate of 136 grams per kilometre. It is used by the sales manager, and 15% of the mileage is for private journeys.

Construction of factory

Wireless Ltd had a new factory constructed at a cost of £200,000 that the company brought into use on 1 November 2009.

The cost was made up as follows:

	£
Land	60,000
Site preparation	8,000
Canteen for employees	22,000
General offices	42,000
Factory	68,000
	200,000

The factory is used for industrial purposes.

Loan interest received

Loan interest of £1,110 was received on 31 March 2010. The loan was made for non-trading purposes.

Overseas dividend

On 31 March 2010 Wireless Ltd received a dividend of £14,680 (net) from a 100% owned subsidiary company that is resident overseas. Withholding tax was withheld from the dividend at the rate of 25%.

Overseas branch profits

For the six-month period ended 31 March 2010, Wireless Ltd operated abroad through an overseas branch which made trading profits of £6,750 (net) after the deduction of withholding tax of 10%.

Donation

A donation to charity of £1,800 was paid on 20 March 2010. The donation was made under the Gift Aid scheme.

Required:

(i)   Explain when an accounting period starts for corporation tax purposes;
                                                                                                    (2 marks)

(ii)   Calculate Wireless Ltd's profits chargeable to corporation tax for the six-month period ended 31 March 2010.

        In your adjustment of profits computation you should commence with £68,400, and you should adjust for capital allowances and costs relating to the employment of the director.   **(14 marks)**

(b)   Note that in answering this part of the question you are not expected to take account of any of the information provided in part (a) above.

        Wireless Ltd's sales since the commencement of trading on 1 October 2009 have been:

		£
2009	October	9,700
	November	18,200
	December	21,100

		£
2010	January	14,800
	February	23,300
	March	24,600

The above figures are stated exclusive of value added tax (VAT).

The company's sales are all standard rated and are made to VAT registered businesses.

Wireless Ltd only sells goods and since registering for VAT has been issuing sales invoices to customers that show:

(1)   the invoice date and the tax point

(2)   Wireless Ltd's name and address

(3)   the VAT-exclusive amount for each supply

(4)   the total VAT-exclusive amount, and

(5)   the amount of VAT payable.

The company does not offer any discount for prompt payment.

Required:

(i)   **Explain from what date Wireless Ltd was required to compulsorily register for VAT and state what action the company then had to take as regards notifying HM Revenue and Customs (HMRC) of the registration.**   **(4 marks)**

(ii)   **Explain the circumstances in which Wireless Ltd would have been allowed to recover input VAT incurred on goods purchased and services incurred prior to the date of VAT registration.**   **(4 marks)**

(iii)   **Explain why it would have been beneficial for Wireless Ltd to have voluntarily registered for VAT from 1 October 2009.**   **(3 marks)**

(iv)   **State the additional information that Wireless Ltd must show on its sales invoices in order for them to be valid for VAT purposes.**   **(3 marks)**

(Total: 30 marks)

RELIEF FOR TRADING LOSSES

55   HALF-LIFE LTD

Half-Life Ltd commenced trading on 1 April 2006 and ceased trading on 30 June 2010.

The company's results for all its periods of trading are as follows:

	Year ended 31 March 2007 £	Year ended 31 March 2008 £	Year ended 31 March 2009 £	Period ended 30 June 2009 £	Year ended 30 June 2010 £
Tax adjusted profit/(loss)	224,000	67,400	38,200	(61,700)	(308,800)
Property business profit	8,200	12,200	6,500	4,400	–
Capital gains	–	–	5,600	–	23,700
Gift Aid	(1,200)	(1,000)	–	–	(700)

Half-Life Ltd does not have any associated companies.

Required:

(a) Assuming that Half-Life Ltd claims the maximum possible relief for its trading losses, calculate the company's profits chargeable to corporation tax for the years ended 31 March 2007, 2008 and 2009, the three-month period ended 30 June 2009, and the year ended 30 June 2010.

Your answer should clearly identify the amounts of any losses and Gift Aid payments that are unrelieved. (9 marks)

(b) State the dates by which Half-Life Ltd must make the loss relief claims in part (a). (2 marks)

(c) Calculate the amount of corporation tax that will be repaid to Half-Life Ltd as a result of making the loss relief claims in part (a).

Assume that the corporation tax rates for FY 2006 are the same as in FY 2007. (4 marks)

(Total: 15 marks)

56 SOFA LTD (ADAPTED)

(a) Sofa Ltd is a manufacturer of furniture. The company's summarised profit and loss account for the year ended 31 March 2010 is as follows:

	Note	£	£
Gross profit			272,300
Operating expenses			
Depreciation		87,100	
Professional fees	1	19,900	
Repairs and renewals	2	22,800	
Other expenses	3	364,000	
			(493,800)
Operating loss			(221,500)
Profit from sale of fixed assets			
Disposal of shares			4,300
Income from investments			
Bank interest	5		8,400
			(208,800)
Interest payable	6		(31,200)
Loss before taxation			(240,000)

Note 1 – Professional fees

Professional fees are as follows:

	£
Accountancy and audit fee	3,400
Legal fees in connection with the issue of share capital	7,800
Legal fees in connection with the renewal of a ten year property lease	2,900
Legal fees in connection with the issue of debentures (see Note 6)	5,800
	19,900

Note 2 – Repairs and renewals

The figure of £22,800 for repairs and renewals includes £9,700 for constructing a new wall around the company's premises and £3,900 for repairing the wall of an office building after it was damaged by a lorry. The remaining expenses are all fully allowable.

Note 3 – Other expenses

The figure of £364,000 for other expenses includes £1,360 for entertaining suppliers; £700 for entertaining employees; £370 for counselling services provided to an employee who was made redundant; and a fine of £420 for infringing health and safety regulations. The remaining expenses are all fully allowable.

Note 4 – Profit on disposal of shares

The profit on the disposal of shares of £4,300 is in respect of a shareholding that was sold on 29 October 2009.

Note 5 – Bank interest received

The bank interest was received on 31 March 2010. The bank deposits are held for non-trading purposes.

Note 6 – Interest payable

Sofa Ltd raised a debenture loan on 1 July 2009, and this was used for trading purposes. Interest of £20,800 was paid on 31 December 2009, and £10,400 was accrued at 31 March 2010.

Note 7 – Plant and machinery

On 1 April 2009 the tax written down values of plant and machinery were as follows:

	£
General pool	16,700
Expensive motor car	16,400

The following transactions took place during the year ended 31 March 2010:

		Cost/ (Proceeds) £
12 May 2009	Purchased equipment	11,400
8 June 2009	Sold the expensive motor car	(17,800)
8 June 2009	Purchased motor car (1)	22,200
2 August 2009	Purchased motor car (2)	10,900
19 October 2009	Purchased motor car (3)	13,800
8 January 2010	Sold a lorry	(7,600)
18 January 2010	Sold motor car (2)	(8,800)
10 February 2010	Purchased a second-hand freehold office building	280,000

Motor car (1) purchased on 8 June 2009 for £22,200 has a CO_2 emission rate of 162 grams per kilometre. Motor car (2) purchased on 2 August 2009 for £10,900, has CO_2 emissions of 157 grams per kilometre. Motor car (3) purchased on 19 October 2009 for £13,800 has CO_2 emissions of 108 grams per kilometre.

The expensive motor car sold on 8 June 2009 for £17,800 originally cost £26,800. The lorry sold on 8 January 2010 for £7,600 originally cost £24,400.

The cost of the second-hand office building purchased on 10 February 2010 for £280,000 includes fixtures qualifying as plant and machinery. £44,800 of the purchase price of the office relates to these fixtures.

Required:

Calculate Sofa Ltd's tax adjusted trading loss for the year ended 31 March 2010.

Your answer should commence with the loss before taxation figure of £240,000, and should list all of the items referred to in Notes (1) to (6) indicating by the use of zero (0) any items that do not require adjustment.

You should assume that the company claims the maximum available capital allowances. **(20 marks)**

(b)   Sofa Ltd has three subsidiary companies:

Settee Ltd

Sofa Ltd owns 100% of the ordinary share capital of Settee Ltd. For the year ended 30 June 2009 Settee Ltd had profits chargeable to corporation tax of £240,000, and for the year ended 30 June 2010 will have profits chargeable to corporation tax of £90,000.

Couch Ltd

Sofa Ltd owns 60% of the ordinary share capital of Couch Ltd. For the year ended 31 March 2010 Couch Ltd had profits chargeable to corporation tax of £64,000.

Futon Ltd

Sofa Ltd owns 80% of the ordinary share capital of Futon Ltd. Futon Ltd commenced trading on 1 January 2010, and for the three-month period ended 31 March 2010 had profits chargeable to corporation tax of £60,000.

Required:

Advise Sofa Ltd as to the maximum amount of group relief that can potentially be claimed by each of its three subsidiary companies in respect of its trading loss for the year ended 31 March 2010.

For the purposes of answering this part of the question, you should assume that Sofa Ltd's tax adjusted trading loss for the year ended 31 March 2010 is £200,000.

(5 marks)

(Total: 25 marks)

 Online question assistance

57   JOGGER LTD (ADAPTED) *Walk in the footsteps of a top tutor*

(a)   Jogger Ltd is a manufacturer of running shoes. The company's summarised profit and loss account for the year ended 31 March 2010 is as follows:

	Note	£	£
Operating loss	1		(56,400)
Income from investments			
Bank interest	4	8,460	
Loan interest	5	24,600	
Income from property	6	144,000	
Dividends	7	45,000	
			222,060
Profit from sale of fixed assets	8		
Disposal of shares			102,340
Profit before taxation			268,000

Note 1 – Operating profit

Depreciation of £12,340 has been deducted in arriving at the operating loss of £56,400.

Note 2 – Plant and machinery

On 1 April 2009 the tax written down values of plant and machinery were as follows:

	£
General pool	21,600
Expensive motor car	8,800

The following transactions took place during the year ended 31 March 2010:

		Cost/(proceeds) £
20 July 2009	Sold the expensive motor car	(11,700)
31 July 2009	Purchased motor car	11,800
14 March 2010	Sold a lorry	(8,600)

The motor car purchased on 31 July 2009 for £11,800 has a CO_2 emission rate of 153 grams per kilometre. The expensive motor car sold on 20 July 2009 for £11,700 originally cost £18,400. The lorry sold on 14 March 2010 for £8,600 originally cost £16,600.

Note 3 – Industrial building

On 15 June 2009 Jogger Ltd purchased a new factory for £340,000 (excluding the cost of land). Included within the above figure is an amount of £90,000 incurred in building general offices, and £50,000 in building a canteen for staff members. The factory was brought into use immediately.

Note 4 – Bank interest received

The bank interest was received on 31 March 2010. The bank deposits are held for non-trading purposes.

Note 5 – Loan interest receivable

The loan was made for non-trading purposes on 1 July 2009. Loan interest of £16,400 was received on 31 December 2009, and interest of £8,200 was accrued at 31 March 2010.

Note 6 – Income from property

Jogger Ltd lets out an unfurnished freehold office building that is surplus to requirements. The office building was let throughout the year ended 31 March 2010. On 1 April 2009 Jogger Ltd received a premium of £100,000 for the grant of a ten-year lease, and the annual rent of £44,000 which is payable in advance.

Note 7 – Dividends received

During the year ended 31 March 2010 Jogger Ltd received dividends of £45,000 from Sprinter plc, an unconnected UK company. This figure was the actual cash amount received.

Note 8 – Profit on disposal of shares

The profit on disposal of shares is in respect of a shareholding that was sold on 5 December 2009. The disposal resulted in a chargeable gain of £98,300. This figure is after taking account of indexation allowance.

Note 9 – Other information

Jogger Ltd has two associated companies.

Required:

(i)   Calculate Jogger Ltd's tax adjusted trading loss for the year ended 31 March 2010.

       Your computation should commence with the operating loss of £56,400, and should list all of the items referred to in Notes (1) and (4) to (8), indicating by the use of zero (0) any items that do not require adjustment.

       You should assume that the company claims the maximum available capital allowances.   **(7 marks)**

(ii)   Assuming that Jogger Ltd claims relief for its trading loss against total profits, calculate the company's corporation tax liability for the year ended 31 March 2010.   **(8 marks)**

(iii) State the date by which Jogger Ltd's self-assessment corporation tax return for the year ended 31 March 2010 should be submitted, and advise the company of the penalties that will be due if the return is submitted eight months late.

       You should assume that the company pays its corporation tax liability at the same time that the self-assessment tax return is submitted.   **(4 marks)**

(b)   *In answering this part of the question you are not expected to take account of any of the information provided in part (a) above.*

       Jogger Ltd has been registered for value added tax (VAT) since 1 April 2001.

       From that date until 30 June 2008 the company's VAT returns were all submitted on time. Since 1 July 2008 the company's VAT returns have been submitted as follows:

Quarter ended	VAT paid	Submitted
	£	
30 September 2008	42,700	One month late
31 December 2008	41,200	On time
31 March 2009	38,900	One month late
30 June 2009	28,300	On time
30 September 2009	49,100	On time
31 December 2009	63,800	On time
31 March 2010	89,100	Two months late

Jogger Ltd always pays any VAT that is due at the same time as the related return is submitted.

Required:

(i) State, giving appropriate reasons, the default surcharge consequences arising from Jogger Ltd's submission of its VAT returns for the quarter ended 30 September 2008 to the quarter ended 31 March 2010 inclusive, at the times stated. **(6 marks)**

(ii) Advise Jogger Ltd why it might be beneficial to use the VAT annual accounting scheme, and state the conditions that it will have to satisfy before being permitted to do so. **(5 marks)**

(Total: 30 marks)

WITH GROUP ASPECTS

58 STRAIGHT PLC (ADAPTED)

Straight plc is the holding company for a group of companies as follows.

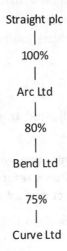

Straight plc
|
100%
|
Arc Ltd
|
80%
|
Bend Ltd
|
75%
|
Curve Ltd

All of the companies in the group have an accounting date of 31 March.

(a) **Straight plc**

For the year ended 31 March 2010 the following information is relevant:

Operating profit

The operating profit is £173,915.

The expenses that have been deducted in calculating this figure include the following:

	£
Depreciation	21,200
Car lease cost (Note 1)	8,500
Entertaining (Note 2)	12,000
Fine for breach of Health and Safety regulations	1,250

Notes

(1) On 1 April 2009 Straight plc entered into an agreement for the lease of a car for one of the company's salesmen. The car has CO_2 emissions of 162 grams per kilometre.

(2) Entertaining costs consist of £10,000 for entertaining potential overseas customers and £2,000 for a Christmas party for the company's ten staff.

(3) **Plant and machinery**

On 1 April 2009 the tax written down values of plant and machinery were as follows:

	£
General pool	31,200
Expensive motor car	18,400
Short-life asset	4,000

The following transactions took place during the year ended 31 March 2010:

		Cost/(Proceeds) £
3 April 2009	Purchased machinery	12,400
1 May 2009	Sold the expensive car	(15,200)

The expensive motor car sold on 1 May 2009 was used by a salesman, and 40% of his mileage was for private journeys. The short life asset had been acquired on 1 June 2004.

Required:

Calculate Straight plc's tax adjusted trading profit for the year ended 31 March 2010.

Your computation should commence with the operating profit of £173,915, and should list all of the relevant items referred to in part (a), indicating by the use of zero (0) any items that do not require adjustment.   **(10 marks)**

(b) As at 31 March 2009 Straight plc had unused trading losses of £15,000 and unused capital losses of £10,000.

Straight plc sold a freehold office building on 20 June 2009 for £350,000, and this resulted in a capital gain of £140,000. The company has made a rollover relief claim in respect of a replacement building purchased for £270,000.

During the year ended 31 March 2010 Straight plc received dividends of £18,000 from Arc Ltd, and dividends of £9,000 from Triangle plc, an unconnected company. These figures are the actual amounts received.

Arc Ltd sold a freehold warehouse on 10 March 2010, and this resulted in a capital loss of £40,000.

Required:

(i) Explain why Straight plc, Arc Ltd, Bend Ltd and Curve Ltd form a group for capital gains purposes, and why Curve Ltd would be excluded from the group if Straight plc's holding in Arc Ltd were only 80% instead of 100%.

(4 marks)

(ii) Before taking into account any transfer of capital gains or losses, calculate the corporation tax payable by Straight plc for the year ended 31 March 2010.

(8 marks)

(iii) State the time limit for Straight plc and Arc Ltd to make a joint election to transfer the capital gain arising on the disposal of Arc Ltd's freehold warehouse, and explain why such an election will be beneficial.

You are not expected to consider any alternative joint elections.   (3 marks)

(Total: 25 marks)

59   MEADOW LTD (ADAPTED)

(a)   Meadow Ltd is the holding company for a group of companies. The following information is relevant for the year ended 31 March 2010:

(1)   Operating profit

Meadow Ltd had an operating profit of £579,110. The following expenses have been deducted in calculating this figure:

	£
Depreciation	32,200
Donation to national charity under Gift Aid scheme	6,500
Gifts to customers (bottles of wine costing £8 each and bearing the company's name)	1,600
Legal fees re acquisition of factory	5,500
Interest paid on loan to acquire factory (see Note 2)	26,500

(2)   Purchase of factory

On 1 May 2009 Meadow Ltd acquired a new factory for £280,000 (including land of £50,000)

On 1 July 2009 Meadow Ltd installed a new central heating system in the factory which cost £40,000.

The company took out a bank loan on 1 May 2009 to partly finance the acquisition of the factory. There was no accrued interest payable at the year end.

(3)   Plant and machinery.

On 1 April 2009 the tax written down values of plant and machinery were:

	£
General pool	25,300
Expensive motor car	11,600

The following transactions took place during the year ended 31 March 2010:

		Cost/ (Proceeds) £
3 May 2009	Purchased a lorry	23,000
18 May 2009	Purchased Motor car (1)	14,400
12 June 2009	Purchased Motor car (2)	25,000

Motor car (1) purchased on 18 May 2009 for £14,400 has a CO_2 emission rate of 123 grams per kilometre. Motor car (2), purchased on 12 June 2009 for £25,000, has CO_2 emissions of 103 grams per kilometre.

The car acquired on 18 May 2009 is used by the quality control manager and 50% of his mileage is for private journeys.

(4)   Property income

In the year to 31 March 2010 Meadow Ltd had surplus office space in its freehold office building. On 1 July 2009 it therefore granted a 5 year lease to Woodland Ltd for a premium of £10,000 and an annual rent of £5,000 payable quarterly in advance.

(5)   Interest income

Meadow Ltd received interest of £500 in respect of a loan to an ex-employee. Interest of £200 was accrued in relation to this loan at 31 March 2010.

(6)   Chargeable gain

On 1 April 2009 Meadow Ltd sold its 5,000 ordinary shares in Grassland plc for £45,000. It had originally acquired 5,000 shares in Lawn Ltd for £12,000 on 1 May 2002. On 1 March 2006 Lawn Ltd was taken over by Grassland plc and Meadow Ltd received 1 ordinary share and 1 preference share in Grassland plc in exchange for its shares in Lawn Ltd.

Immediately after the takeover the ordinary shares and preference shares in Grassland plc were quoted at £5 and £2 per share respectively.

Meadow Ltd's shareholding in Grassland plc has never represented more than a 1% interest.

The indexation factor for May 2002 to April 2009 is 0.200.

Required:

Calculate Meadow Ltd's profits chargeable to corporation tax for the year ended 31 March 2010.

In your adjustment of profits computation you should commence with the operating profit of £579,110, and should list all of the items referred to in Note (1) and (2), indicating by the use of zero (0) any items that do not require adjustment.

(17 marks)

(b)   In the year ended 31 March 2010 the profits chargeable to corporation tax (PCTCT) of the Meadow Ltd group of companies were:

	£
Poppy Inc	250,000
Bluebell Ltd	50,000
Cowslip Ltd	190,000
Trefoil Ltd	350,000

Cornflower Ltd had a trading loss of £200,000 for the year ended 31 March 2010.

None of the companies have any other income or gains in the year to 31 March 2010.

Meadow Ltd owns:

–   100% of Poppy Inc, a company resident overseas,
–   80% of Cowslip Ltd
–   40% of Trefoil Ltd and
–   55% of Daisy Ltd (a dormant company).

Poppy Inc owns 80% of Cornflower Ltd and Cornflower Ltd owns 100% of Bluebell Ltd.

All companies are UK resident except for Poppy Inc.

Required:

(i)   **Explain why there are five associated companies in the Meadow Ltd group.**

   Your answer should identify the five associated companies.   (2 marks)

(ii)   **Explain which companies form a group for group relief purposes.**   (2 marks)

(iii) **Assuming that relief is claimed for Cornflower Ltd's trading loss of £200,000 in the most favourable manner, calculate the profits chargeable to UK corporation tax for all companies in the Meadow Ltd group for the year ended 31 March 2010.**   (4 marks)

(Total: 25 marks)

60   TOCK-TICK LTD (ADAPTED)

Tock-Tick Ltd is a clock manufacturer. The company's summarised profit and loss account for the year ended 31 March 2010 is as follows:

	£	£
Gross profit		825,020
Operating expenses		
Impaired debts (Note 1)	9,390	
Depreciation	99,890	
Gifts and donations (Note 2)	9,290	
Professional fees (Note 3)	12,400	
Repairs and renewals (Note 4)	128,200	
Other expenses (Note 5)	420,720	
		679,890
Operating profit		145,130
Profit from sale of fixed assets		
Disposal of office building (Note 6)		78,100
Income from investments		
Loan interest (Note 7)		12,330
		235,560
Interest payable (Note 8)		(48,600)
Profit before taxation		186,960

Note 1 – Impaired debts

Impaired debts are as follows:

	£
Trade debts recovered from previous years	(1,680)
Trade debts written off	7,970
Increase in allowance for trade debtors	3,100
	9,390

Note 2 – Gifts and donations

Gifts and donations are as follows:

	£
Gifts to customers (pens costing £45 each displaying Tock-Tick Ltd's name)	1,080
Gifts to customers (food hampers costing £30 each)	720
Donation to a recognised political party	6,200
Long service award to an employee	360
Donation to a national charity (made under the Gift Aid scheme)	600
Donation to a national charity (not made under the Gift Aid scheme)	250
Donation to a local charity (Tick-Tock Ltd received free advertising in the charity's magazine)	80
	9,290

Note 3 – Professional fees

Professional fees are as follows:

	£
Accountancy and audit fee	5,400
Legal fees in connection with the issue of share capital	2,900
The cost of registering the company's trademark	800
Legal fees in connection with the renewal of a 35-year property lease	1,300
Debt collection	1,100
Legal fees in connection with a court action for not complying with health and safety legislation	900
	12,400

Note 4 – Repairs and renewals

The figure of £128,200 for repairs and renewals includes £41,800 for replacing the roof of an office building, which was in a bad state of repair, and £53,300 for extending the office building.

Note 5 – Other expenses

Other expenses include £2,160 for entertaining suppliers; £880 for counselling services provided to two employees who were made redundant; and the cost of seconding an employee to a charity of £6,400. The remaining expenses are all fully allowable.

Note 6 – Disposal of office building

The profit of £78,100 is in respect of a freehold office building that was sold on 20 February 2010 for £276,000. The office building was purchased on 18 November 1997 for £197,900. Assume the indexation allowance from November 1997 to February 2010 is £66,900.

The building has always been used by Tock-Tick Ltd for trading purposes.

Note 7 – Loan interest received

The loan interest is in respect of a loan that was made on 1 July 2009. Interest of £8,280 was received on 31 December 2009, and interest of £4,050 was accrued at 31 March 2010. The loan was made for non-trading purposes.

Note 8 – Interest payable

The interest payable is in respect of a debenture loan that is used for trading purposes. Interest of £24,300 was paid on 30 September 2009 and again on 31 March 2010.

Note 9 – Plant and machinery

On 1 April 2009 the tax written down values of plant and machinery were:

	£
General pool	12,200
Expensive motor car	21,600
Short-life asset	2,300

The following transactions took place during the year ended 31 March 2010:

		Cost/ (Proceeds)
		£
28 May 2009	Sold the expensive motor car	(34,800)
7 June 2009	Purchased a motor car	14,400
1 August 2009	Sold the short-life asset	(460)
15 August 2009	Purchased equipment	6,700

The motor car purchased on 7 June 2009 has a CO_2 emission rate of 109 g/km.

The expensive motor car sold on 28 May 2009 for £34,800 originally cost £33,600.

Required:

(a) Calculate Tock-Tick Ltd's tax adjusted trading profit for the year ended 31 March 2010.

Your computation should commence with the profit before taxation figure of £186,960, and should list all of the items referred to in Note (1) and (8), indicating by the use of zero (0) any items that do not require adjustment.   **(19 marks)**

(b) Calculate Tock-Tick Ltd's profits chargeable to corporation tax for the year ended 31 March 2010.   **(5 marks)**

(c) It has now been discovered that Tock-Tick Ltd had acquired a 100% shareholding in Clock Ltd on 31 March 2009.

Clock Ltd made a tax adjusted trading loss of £62,400 for the year ended 31 December 2009 but was profitable in the following year.

On 15 March 2010 Clock Ltd purchased a new freehold office building for £270,000, that is to be used 100% for trading purposes.

(i) State the effect on Tock-Tick Ltd's profits chargeable to corporation tax for the year ended 31 March 2010 of the acquisition of Clock Ltd, assuming all beneficial elections and claims are made in respect of Clock Ltd's trading loss and its acquisition of the office building.   **(4 marks)**

(ii) Compute the corporation tax liability of Tock-Tick Ltd for the year ended 31 March 2010 assuming the beneficial claims and elections identified in (c)(i) above are made.   **(2 marks)**

(Total: 30 marks)

61   MUSIC PLC (ADAPTED)

Music plc is the holding company for a group of companies. The group structure is as follows:

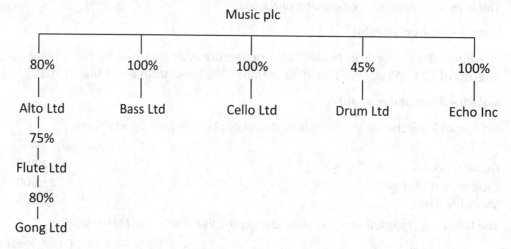

Music plc's shareholding in Bass Ltd was disposed of on 31 December 2009, and the shareholding in Cello Ltd was acquired on 1 January 2010. The other shareholdings were all held throughout the year ended 31 March 2010.

Echo Inc is resident overseas. The other companies are all resident in the United Kingdom.

For the year ended 31 March 2010 Music plc had a tax adjusted trading profit of £92,000. During the year Music plc received franked investment income of £15,000 from an unconnected company, bank interest of £12,000 and a dividend of £5,400 from Bass Ltd.

As at 31 March 2009 Music plc had unused capital losses of £32,000. On 5 January 2010 the company sold a freehold office building, and this resulted in a further capital loss of £65,000.

Alto Ltd sold a freehold warehouse on 10 March 2010, and this resulted in a capital gain of £120,000. An election has been made so that the gain is treated as Music plc's gain.

Music plc also owns a number of properties which it lets out. The following information relates to the properties let out during the year ended 31 March 2010. Music plc claims the wear and tear allowance on its properties, where appropriate.

Property one

Property one is a freehold house which is let out furnished. It was let out from 1 September 2009 at a quarterly rent of £2,500, payable in advance. In April 2009 Music plc incurred £2,500 on redecorating the house and £400 on a new dishwasher. During the year the company also incurred £1,500 on advertising for new tenants and agents fees, council tax of £1,200 and water rates of £600.

Property two

This is a freehold house which is let out unfurnished. It was let until 1 January 2010 at a monthly rent of £650, payable in advance. The tenants left owing the last month's rent, which the company never recovered.

New tenants occupied the house from 1 March 2010 at a rent of £700 per month. The tenants were unable to supply appropriate references and Music plc therefore required the tenants to pay the first six months rent up front.

On 10 April 2010 Music plc paid £500 in connection with repairs to the central heating system which had been carried out in March 2010.

Property three

This is a leasehold retail shop. On 1 June 2009 Music plc paid a premium of £60,000 for the grant of a 30 year lease. The property was sub-let to a tenant on 1 July 2009 in return for the payment of a premium of £45,000 for a 10 year lease and annual rent of £2,000 payable quarterly in advance.

Property four

Property four is a freehold apartment. It was acquired on 1 April 2009 in an uninhabitable condition. Music plc had to incur £4,000 on repairs to the roof and £2,000 on new decoration prior to renting the property. It incurred £250 on letting agency fees and rented the apartment from 1 July 2009 at a monthly rent of £500 payable in advance.

Year ending 31 March 2011

Music plc is considering either acquiring another property which it will rent out or investing in new plant and machinery in the year ending 31 March 2011. In either case it will take out a new bank loan of £100,000 at a 10% interest rate to partly fund the acquisition. Bank arrangement fees will be £300.

Required:

(a) State, giving appropriate reasons, which companies in the Music plc group of companies form a group for capital gains purposes. (5 marks)

(b) Explain why Music plc has six associated companies.

Your answer should identify the six associated companies. (4 marks)

(c) Calculate Music plc's property business profit for the year ended 31 March 2010. (8 marks)

(d) Calculate Music plc's corporation tax liability for the year ended 31 March 2010. (6 marks)

(e) Explain how the bank fees and interest costs will be treated for tax purposes if the company acquires another property or it acquires new plant and machinery in the year ended 31 March 2011. (2 marks)

(Total: 30 marks)

VALUE ADDED TAX

> The examiner has stated that there will be a minimum of 10 marks on VAT in the exam.
>
> These marks will often be in question one or two, and past exam questions where this has been the case are included in the kit under the heading of the primary tax being examined.
>
> However, the examiner sometimes sets a separate question on VAT, which could be worth up to 15 marks.

62 CONFUSED LTD

(a) Confused Ltd will commence trading in the near future. The company operates a small aeroplane, and is considering three alternative types of business. These are

(1) training, in which case all sales will be standard rated for VAT,

(2) transport, in which case all sales will be zero-rated for VAT, and

(3) an air ambulance service, in which case all sales will be exempt from VAT.

For each alternative Confused Ltd's sales will be £75,000 per month (exclusive of VAT), and standard rated expenses will be £10,000 per month (inclusive of VAT).

Required:

For each of the three alternative types of business

(i) **State whether Confused Ltd will be required or permitted to register for VAT when trading commences, and**

(ii) **Calculate the monthly amount of output VAT due and input VAT recoverable.**

Assume that the appropriate rate of VAT is 17.5% for this part. **(6 marks)**

(b) Puzzled Ltd has discovered that a number of errors have been made when preparing its VAT returns for the previous four quarters. As a result of the errors the company will have to make an additional payment of VAT to HM Revenue & Customs.

Required:

Explain how Puzzled Ltd can voluntarily disclose the errors that have been discovered, and when default interest will be due. **(3 marks)**

(c) Perplexed Ltd has been registered for VAT since 1994, but intends to cease trading on 31 December 2010. On the cessation of trading Perplexed Ltd can either sell its fixed assets on a piecemeal basis to individual purchasers, or it can sell its entire business as a going concern to a single purchaser.

Required:

Advise Perplexed Ltd as to what will happen to its VAT registration, and whether output VAT will be due, if the company ceases trading on 31 December 2010 and:

(i) **sells its fixed assets on a piecemeal basis, or**

(ii) **sells its entire business as a going concern.** **(6 marks)**

(Total: 15 marks)

63 ASTUTE LTD

(a)   Astute Ltd registered for VAT on 1 July 2009. The company has annual standard rated sales of £350,000. This figure is inclusive of VAT. As a result of bookkeeping problems Astute Ltd has been late in submitting its VAT returns to date.

Required:

Advise Astute Ltd of the conditions that it must satisfy before being permitted to use the VAT annual accounting scheme, and the advantages of joining the scheme.

(5 marks)

(b)   Bright Ltd registered for VAT on 1 January 2009. The company has annual standard rated sales of £75,000, and these are all made to the general public. The company has annual standard rated expenses of £10,000. Both figures are inclusive of VAT. The relevant flat rate scheme percentage for the company's trade is 9%.

Required:

Advise Bright Ltd of the conditions that it must satisfy before being permitted to use the VAT flat rate scheme, and the advantages of joining the scheme.

Your answer should be supported by appropriate calculations of the potential annual tax saving.

(5 marks)

(c)   Clever Ltd registered for VAT on 1 June 2009. The company has annual standard rated sales of £250,000. This figure is inclusive of VAT. The company pays its expenses on a cash basis, but allows customers three months' credit when paying for sales. Several of Clever Ltd's customers have recently defaulted on the payment of their debts.

Required:

Advise Clever Ltd of the conditions that it must satisfy before being permitted to use the VAT cash accounting scheme, and the advantages of joining the scheme.

(5 marks)

(Total: 15 marks)

64 ROCKING-HORSE LTD (ADAPTED)

Rocking-Horse Ltd commenced trading as a manufacturer of children's toys on 1 August 2009. Its outputs and inputs for each of the months from August to November 2009 are as follows:

	August	September	October	November
	£	£	£	£
Outputs				
Sales	4,500	5,800	24,800	70,800
Inputs				
Goods purchased	3,600	13,200	28,400	32,400
Services incurred	2,400	2,800	3,400	4,600
Fixed assets	62,000	–	–	–

The above figures are all exclusive of VAT.

Rocking-Horse Ltd's sales are all standard rated, and are made to VAT registered businesses. The inputs are all standard rated. The company has not disposed of any fixed assets.

On 1 November 2009 Rocking-Horse Ltd realised that its sales for November 2009 were going to be at least £69,000, and therefore immediately registered for VAT. On that date the company had a stock of goods that had cost £13,600 (exclusive of VAT).

Required:

(a) Explain why Rocking-Horse Ltd was required to compulsorily register for VAT from 1 November 2009, and state what action the company then had to take. **(3 marks)**

(b) Explain why Rocking-Horse Ltd was able to recover input VAT totalling £12,630 in respect of inputs incurred prior to registering for VAT on 1 November 2009.

(5 marks)

(c) Explain why it would have been beneficial for Rocking-Horse Ltd to have voluntarily registered for VAT from 1 August 2009. **(3 marks)**

(d) Explain HM Revenue & Customs' information and inspection powers and the purpose of a VAT control visit. **(4 marks)**

(e) Explain the unified tax appeal system. **(5 marks)**

(Total: 15 marks)

65 SANDY BRICK

Sandy Brick has been a self-employed builder since 2003. He registered for value added tax (VAT) on 1 January 2010, and is in the process of completing his VAT return for the quarter ended 31 March 2010.

The following information is relevant to the completion of this VAT return:

(1) Sales invoices totalling £44,000 (excluding VAT) were issued to VAT registered customers in respect of standard rated sales. Sandy offers his VAT registered customers a 5% discount for prompt payment.

(2) Sales invoices totalling £16,920 were issued to customers that were not registered for VAT. Of this figure, £5,170 was in respect of zero-rated sales with the balance being in respect of standard rated sales. Standard rated sales are inclusive of VAT.

(3) On 10 January 2010 Sandy received a payment on account of £5,000 in respect of a contract that was completed on 28 April 2010. The total value of the contract is £10,000. Both of these figures are inclusive of VAT at the standard rate.

(4) Standard rated materials amounted to £11,200, of which £800 were used in constructing Sandy's private residence.

(5) Since 1 December 2008 Sandy has paid £120 per month for the lease of office equipment. This expense is standard rated.

(6) During the quarter ended 31 March 2010 £400 was spent on mobile telephone calls, of which 30% relates to private calls. This expense is standard rated.

(7) On 20 February 2010 £920 was spent on repairs to a motor car. The motor car is used by Sandy in his business, although 20% of the mileage is for private journeys. This expense is standard rated.

(8) On 15 March 2010 equipment was purchased for £6,000. The purchase was partly financed by a bank loan of £5,000. This purchase is standard rated.

Unless stated otherwise all of the above figures are exclusive of VAT.

Required:

(a) State the VAT rules that determine the tax point in respect of a supply of services.

(3 marks)

(b) State the circumstances in which Sandy is required to issue a VAT invoice, and the period during which such an invoice should be issued. (2 marks)

(c) Calculate the amount of VAT payable by Sandy for the quarter ended 31 March 2010.

Assume that the rate of VAT is 17.5% throughout. (10 marks)

(Total: 15 marks)

66 VICTOR STYLE

Victor Style has been a self-employed hairdresser since 1 January 2007. His sales from the date of commencement of the business to 30 September 2009 were £5,300 per month. On 1 October 2009 Victor increased the prices that he charged customers, and from that date his sales have been £7,510 per month. Victor's sales are all standard rated.

As a result of the price increase, Victor was required to register for value added tax (VAT) and charge VAT on sales from 1 January 2010. As all of his customers are members of the general public, it was not possible to increase prices any further as a result of registering for VAT.

Victor's standard rated expenses are £400 per month.

Where applicable, the above figures are inclusive of VAT.

Assume that the VAT registration threshold for 2009/10 applied throughout.

Required:

(a) Explain why Victor was required to compulsorily register for VAT from 1 January 2010, and state what action he then had to take as regards notifying HM Revenue & Customs of the registration. (5 marks)

(b) Calculate the total amount of VAT payable by Victor during the year ended 31 December 2010.

You should ignore pre-registration input VAT. (3 marks)

(c) Advise Victor why it would have been beneficial to have used the VAT flat rate scheme from 1 January 2010.

Your answer should include a calculation of the amount of VAT that Victor would have saved for the year ended 31 December 2010 by joining the scheme.

The flat rate scheme percentage for hairdressing is 12%. (3 marks)

(d) Calculate the effect on Victor's net profit for the year ended 31 December 2010 as a consequence of the price increase and subsequent VAT registration. (4 marks)

(Total: 15 marks)

 Online question assistance

67   RAM-ROM LTD

Ram-Rom Ltd commenced trading as a manufacturer of computer equipment on 1 May 2009. The company registered for value added tax (VAT) on 1 January 2010.

Its inputs for each of the months from May 2009 to December 2009 are as follows:

		Goods purchased £	Services incurred £	Fixed assets £
2009	May	12,300	1,400	42,000
	June	11,200	5,100	–
	July	12,300	7,400	–
	August	16,400	6,300	14,400
	September	14,500	8,500	–
	October	18,800	9,000	–
	November	18,500	9,200	–
	December	23,400	8,200	66,600

During December 2009 Ram-Rom Ltd sold all of the fixed assets purchased during August 2009 for £12,000.

On 1 January 2010 £92,000 of the goods purchased were still in stock.

The above figures are all exclusive of VAT. Ram-Rom Ltd's sales are all standard rated.

A sample of the new sales invoice that Ram-Rom Ltd is going to issue to its customers is as follows:

SALES INVOICE

Ram-Rom Ltd
123 The High Street
London WC1 2AB
Telephone 0207 100 1234

Customer: XYZ Computers plc
Address: 99 The Low Road
                     Glasgow G1 2CD

Invoice Date and Tax Point: 1 January 2010

Item Description	Quantity	Price £
Hard Drives	5	220.00
Motherboards	2	100.00
Total Amount Payable (Including VAT)		320.00

Directors: Y Ram & Z Rom
Company Number: 1234567
Registered Office: 123 The High Street, London WC1 2AB

Ram-Rom Ltd pays for all of its inputs one month after receiving the purchase invoice. However, many customers are not paying Ram-Rom Ltd until four months after the date of the sales invoice. In addition, several customers have recently defaulted on the payment of their debts.

In order to encourage more prompt payment, Ram-Rom Ltd is considering offering all of its customers a 5% discount if they pay within one month of the date of the sales invoice. No discount is currently offered.

Required:

(a) Explain why Ram-Rom Ltd was able to recover input VAT totalling £37,380 in respect of inputs incurred prior to registering for VAT on 1 January 2010. **(5 marks)**

(b) State what alterations Ram-Rom Ltd will have to make to its new sales invoices in order for them to be valid for VAT purposes. **(3 marks)**

(c) Explain the VAT implications of Ram-Rom Ltd offering all of its customers a 5% discount for prompt payment. **(2 marks)**

(d) Advise Ram-Rom Ltd of the conditions that it must satisfy before being permitted to use the VAT cash accounting scheme, and the advantages of joining the scheme. **(5 marks)**

(Total: 15 marks)

68 LITHOGRAPH LTD (ADAPTED)

Lithograph Ltd runs a printing business, and is registered for VAT. Because its annual taxable turnover is only £250,000, the company uses the annual accounting scheme so that it only has to prepare one VAT return each year. The annual VAT period is the year ended 31 December.

Year ended 31 December 2008

The total amount of VAT payable by Lithograph Ltd for the year ended 31 December 2008 was £10,200.

Year ended 31 December 2009

The following information is available:

(1) Sales invoices totalling £250,000 were issued to VAT registered customers, of which £160,000 were for standard rated sales and £90,000 were for zero-rated sales.

(2) Purchase invoices totalling £45,000 were received from VAT registered suppliers, of which £38,000 were for standard rated purchases and £7,000 were for zero-rated purchases.

(3) Standard rated expenses amounted to £28,000. This includes £3,600 for entertaining customers.

(4) On 1 January 2009 Lithograph Ltd purchased a motor car costing £18,400 for the use of its managing director. The manager director is provided with free petrol for private mileage, and the cost of this is included in the standard rated expenses in Note (3). The car has CO_2 emissions of 210 g/km and the relevant annual scale charge is £1,660. Both figures are inclusive of VAT.

(5) During the year ended 31 December 2009 Lithograph Ltd purchased machinery for £24,000, and sold office equipment for £8,000. Input VAT had been claimed when the office equipment was originally purchased.

(6) On 31 December 2009 Lithograph Ltd wrote off £4,800 due from a customer as a bad debt. The debt was in respect of an invoice that was due for payment on 31 May 2009.

Unless stated otherwise all of the above figures are exclusive of VAT.

HM Revenue & Customs VAT control visit

On 4 June 2010 HM Revenue & Customs visited the business premises of Lithograph Ltd in order to carry out a VAT control visit. They discovered that for the year ended 31 December 2009 Lithograph Ltd had understated its output VAT because supplies classified as zero-rated should instead have been classified as standard rated.

Required:

(a)   Calculate the monthly payments on account of VAT that Lithograph Ltd will have made in respect of the year ended 31 December 2009, and state in which months these will have been paid.   **(2 marks)**

(b)   (i)   Calculate the total amount of VAT payable by Lithograph Ltd for the year ended 31 December 2009.

For this part of the question you should ignore the findings of the HM Revenue & Customs control visit.   **(6 marks)**

(ii)   Based on your answer to part (i) above, calculate the balancing payment that would have been paid with the annual VAT return, and state the date by which this return was due for submission.   **(2 marks)**

69   DENZIL DYER

Denzil Dyer has been a self-employed printer since 2005. He has recently registered for value added tax (VAT).

Denzil's sales consist of printed leaflets, some of which are standard rated and some of which are zero-rated. He sells to both VAT registered customers and to non-VAT registered customers.

For a typical printing contract, Denzil receives a 10% deposit at the time that the customer makes the order. The order normally takes fourteen days to complete, and Denzil issues the sales invoice three to five days after completion. Some customers pay immediately upon receiving the sales invoice, but many do not pay for up to two months.

Customers making an order of more than £500 are given a discount of 5% from the normal selling price. Denzil also offers a discount of 2.5% of the amount payable to those customers that pay within one month of the date of the sales invoice.

All of Denzil's printing supplies are purchased from a VAT registered supplier. He pays by credit card and receives a VAT invoice. However, Denzil also purchases various office supplies by cash without receiving any invoices.

Denzil does not use the annual accounting scheme, the cash accounting scheme or the flat rate scheme.

Required:

(a)   Explain why it is important for Denzil to correctly identify whether a sale is standard rated or whether it is zero-rated.   **(2 marks)**

(b)   Advise Denzil as to when he should account for the output VAT relating to a typical standard rated printing supply.   **(4 marks)**

(c)   Explain the VAT implications of the two types of discount that Denzil gives or offers to his customers.   **(3 marks)**

(d) Advise Denzil of the conditions that will have to be met in order for him to recover input VAT. You are not expected to list those goods and services for which input VAT is non-recoverable. **(3 marks)**

(e) State the circumstances in which Denzil is and is not required to issue a VAT invoice, and the period during which such an invoice should be issued. **(3 marks)**

(Total: 15 marks)

70 ANNE ATTIRE *Walk in the footsteps of a top tutor*

 Timed question with Online tutor debrief

Anne Attire runs a retail clothing shop. She is registered for value added tax (VAT), and is in the process of completing her VAT return for the quarter ended 30 November 2009.

The following information is available (all figures are exclusive of VAT):

(1) Cash sales amounted to £42,000, of which £28,000 was in respect of standard rated sales and £14,000 was in respect of zero-rated sales.

(2) Sales invoices totalling £12,000 were issued in respect of credit sales. These sales were all standard rated. Anne offers all of her credit sale customers a 5% discount for payment within one month of the date of the sales invoice, and 90% of the customers pay within this period. The sales figure of £12,000 is stated before any deduction for the 5% discount.

(3) Purchase and expense invoices totalling £19,200 were received from VAT registered suppliers. This figure is made up as follows:

	£
Standard rated purchases and expenses	11,200
Zero rated purchases	6,000
Exempt expenses	2,000
	19,200

Anne pays all of her purchase and expense invoices two months after receiving the invoice.

(4) On 30 November 2009 Anne wrote off two impairment losses (bad debts) that were in respect of standard rated credit sales. The first impairment loss was for £300, and was in respect of a sales invoice due for payment on 15 July 2009. The second impairment loss was for £800, and was in respect of a sales invoice due for payment on 10 April 2009.

Anne does not use the cash accounting scheme.

Anne will soon be 60 years old and is therefore considering retirement. On the cessation of trading Anne can either sell the fixed assets of her business on a piecemeal basis to individual VAT registered purchasers, or she can sell the entire business as a going concern to a single VAT registered purchaser.

Required:

(a) Calculate the amount of VAT payable by Anne Attire for the quarter ended 30 November 2009, and state the date by which the VAT return for this period was due for submission. (6 marks)

(b) State the conditions that Anne Attire must satisfy before she will be permitted to use the cash accounting scheme, and advise her of the implications of using the scheme. (5 marks)

(c) Advise Anne Attire as to what will happen to her VAT registration, and whether output VAT will be due in respect of the fixed assets, if she ceases trading and then:

(i) Sells her fixed assets on a piecemeal basis to individual VAT registered purchasers; (2 marks)

(ii) Sells her entire business as a going concern to a single VAT registered purchaser. (2 marks)

(15 marks)

 Calculate your allowed time, allocate the time to the separate parts....................

Section 2

ANSWERS TO PRACTICE QUESTIONS

INCOME TAX AND NATIONAL INSURANCE

INCOME TAX BASICS AND EMPLOYMENT INCOME

1   TOM AND MARY (ADAPTED)

Key answer tips

A classic husband and wife scenario requiring income tax computations for both individuals.

The detailed employment income computation should not have caused any problems but watch out for the age allowance and the extension of the basic rate band for pension contributions.

The wear and tear allowance is commonly forgotten, so make sure that when you spot the word 'furnished' in a question, you think 'wear and tear'!

(a)   **Tom**

Income tax computation – 2009/10

	Total	Other income	Savings
	£	£	£
Salary	40,000		
House benefit	2,000		
Additional charge on house (W1)	2,138		
Use of furniture (W2)	1,600		
Transfer of furniture (W3)	2,800		
	———		
Employment income	48,538	48,538	
Property business income (W4)	5,898	5,898	
BSI interest (£1,500 × 50% × 100/80)	937		937
Bank interest (£840 × 100/80)	1,050		1,050
	———	———	———
Total income	56,423	54,436	1,987
Less Personal allowance	(6,475)	(6,475)	
	———	———	———
Taxable income	49,948	47,961	1,987
	———	———	———

Income tax

£		£
47,961	at 20% (Other income)	9,592
1,987	at 20% (Savings)	397
49,948	Extended basic rate band (W5)	

Income tax liability	9,989
Less Tax credit: Interest (£1,987 × 20%)	(397)
Income tax payable	9,592

Tutorial notes:

1. *No benefit arises where an employer provides pensions advice for all its employees, provided the cost does not exceed £150 per employee.*

2. *Income from assets jointly held by husband and wife is split 50:50 between the spouses unless they have elected to have the income taxed in relation to their actual ownership proportions.*

   Tom and Mary have not made any elections in relation to their income, therefore the interest on a joint bank account will be split equally between them for tax purposes. The amount of capital contributed to the account by each spouse is therefore not relevant.

3. *As the pension contribution is less than 100% of Tom's earnings, the full amount will be eligible for tax relief.*

   Basic rate tax relief is given for personal pension contributions at source. Higher rate tax relief is given by extending the basic rate band by the gross amount of the pension contribution.

Workings

(W1) **Additional charge on house**

(£120,000 − £75,000) × 4.75% = £2,138

Tutorial note:

Where living accommodation provided cost in excess of £75,000 an additional benefit is levied on the employee, calculated as:

(excess of cost of house over £75,000 × official rate of interest)

(W2) Use of furniture

Benefit = 20% x M.V. of asset when it is first made available to the employee

= (20% × £8,000) = £1,600

(W3) Transfer of furniture

Greater of:

			£
(i)	MV at date of transfer		4,000
	Less: Amount paid		(2,000)
	Excess		2,000
(ii)	Original cost		8,000
	Less: Annual value for 2008/09 and 2009/10		
	(20% × £8,000 × 2 years)		(3,200)
			4,800
	Less: Amount paid		(2,000)
	Excess		2,800

(W4) Property business income

	£
Rent (£800 × 12)	9,600
Less: Council tax	(1,500)
Mortgage interest	(800)
Insurance (£500 × 1/12) + (£600 × 11/12)	(592)
Wear and tear allowance (10% × (£9,600 − £1,500)	(810)
Property business income	5,898

(W5) Extension of basic rate band

	£
Basic rate band threshold	37,400
Plus Personal pension contribution (gross)	18,660
Extended basic rate band	56,060

Tutorial note:

The total taxable income of £49,948 is less than the extended basic rate band threshold of £56,060, therefore all of the income falls into the basic rate band.

(b)   **Mary**

Income tax computation – 2009/10

	Total	Other income	Savings	Dividends
	£	£	£	£
Pension	4,500	4,500		
Property income	5,010	5,010		
BSI interest				
(£1,500 × 50% × 100/80)	937		937	
Premium bonds	Exempt			
Dividends (£11,655 × 100/90)	12,950			12,950
Total income	23,397	9,510	937	12,950
Less Age allowance (W)	(9,242)	(9,242)		–
Taxable income	14,155	268	937	12,950

Income tax

		£
£		
268 at 20% (Other income)		54
937 at 10% (Savings) (Note)		94
12,950 at 10% (Dividends)		1,295
14,155		
Income tax liability		1,443
Less Tax credits:		
Dividends		(1,295)
Interest (£937 × 20%)		(187)
Repayment due		(39)

Tutorial notes:

1.   *Premium bonds are exempt income.*

2.   *Where 'other income' is less than £2,440, any 'savings income' falling into the first £2,440 of taxable income is taxed at 10%.*

3.   *There is no repayment in respect of the tax credit attaching to the dividends. They are therefore offset in priority to the tax credit on interest, which is repayable.*

Working: Personal age allowance

		£	£
PAA (aged 67)			9,490
Less Abatement:	Total income	23,397	
	Income limit	(22,900)	
Excess		497 x ½	(248)
Reduced PAA			9,242

Capital gains tax computation – 2009/10

	£
Capital gain	32,000
Less Annual exemption	(10,100)
Taxable gain	21,900
Capital gains tax (£21,900 x 18%)	3,942

2   SALLY AND SANDRA BURTON *Online question assistance*

Key answer tips

Two income tax computations required for taxpayers entitled to a personal age allowance. However, due to the level of income, abatement of the allowance is necessary.

One sister is employed, the other self-employed, allowing the examiner to test a wide range of the personal tax syllabus.

Always watch out for exempt income and consider whether income is received gross or net.

(a)   **Sally Burton**

Income tax computation – 2009/10

	Total	Other income	Savings income
	£	£	£
Salary	16,000		
Car benefit (W1)	3,402		
Living accommodation (W2)	2,532		
Employment income	21,934	21,934	
NS&I Savings Certificate interest	Exempt		
Building society interest (£1,800 × 100/80)	2,250		2,250
Total income	24,184	21,934	2,250
Less Personal Age Allowance (W3)	(8,848)	(8,848)	
Taxable income	15,336	13,086	2,250

Income tax

£		£
13,086 x 20% (Other income)		2,617
2,250 x 20% (Savings income)		450
15,336		
Income tax liability		3,067
Less Tax suffered at source:		
PAYE		(1,500)
Building society interest (£2,250 x 20%)		(450)
Income tax payable		1,117

Tutorial note:

NS&I Savings Certificate income is exempt from income tax.

NS&I Investment account interest is taxable and received gross.

(b) **Sandra Burton**

Income tax computation – 2009/10

	Total	Other income	Savings income	Dividend income
	£	£	£	£
Trading income (W4)	24,145	24,145		
NS&I Investment account interest (received gross)	895		895	
Dividends (£900 × 100/90)	1,000			1,000
Total income	26,040	24,145	895	1,000
Less Personal Age Allowance (W3)	(8,070)	(8,070)		
Taxable income	17,970	16,075	895	1,000

Income tax

£		£
16,075 x 20% (Other income)		3,215
895 x 20% (Savings income)		179
1,000 x 10% (Dividend income)		100
17,970		
Income tax liability		3,494
Less Tax credit: Dividends (£1,000 x 10%)		(100)
Income tax payable		3,394

Workings

(W1) **Car Benefit**

CO_2 emissions = 197 g/km, available all year

	%
Petrol	15
Plus (195 − 135) × $^1/_5$	12
	——
Appropriate percentage	27
	——

	£
List price of car	17,118
Less Capital contributions	(2,000)
	——————
Appropriate percentage	15,118
	——————
Car benefit (£15,118 x 27% x 10/12)	3,402
	——————

Tutorial note:

The maintenance costs are ignored as they are covered in the car benefit percentage. The car parking cost is exempt

(W2) **Living accommodation**

	£
Annual value	1,294
Additional benefit for expensive accommodation:	
(£120,000 (Note) − £75,000) x 4.75%	2,138
	——————
	3,432
Less: Contributions to employer (£75 × 12 months)	(900)
	——————
	2,532
	——————

Tutorial note:

The property was bought in 2001, which is more than 6 years before it was made available to Sally. Therefore in the additional benefit computation the cost must be replaced with the market value of the accommodation when the property was made available.

(W3) **Personal age allowance**

			£	£
Sally				
PAA (aged 66)				9,490
Less Abatement:	Total income		24,184	
	Income limit		(22,900)	
Excess			1,284 x ½	(642)
Reduced PAA				8,848
Sandra				
PAA (aged 76)				9,640
Less Abatement:	Total income		26,040	
	Income limit		(22,900)	
Excess			3,140 x ½	(1,570)
Reduced PAA				8,070

(W4) **Computation of tax adjusted trading profit**

	£
Net profit as per accounts	18,000
Add: Depreciation	2,425
Motor expenses (£5,400 × 4,000/12,000)	1,800
Private accommodation (£9,600 × 1/3)	3,200
Adjusted trading profit	25,425
Less: Capital allowances (W5)	(1,280)
Tax adjusted trading profit	24,145

(W5) **Capital allowances**

	Expensive car £	Business use	Allowances £
TWDV b/f	9,600		
WDA (20%)	(1,920)	x (8,000/12,000)	1,280
TWDV c/f	7,680		

Key answer tips

A familiar full blown capital allowances computation is given in the workings to this answer to show how the allowances are calculated.

However, where there are not many transactions it is perfectly acceptable to do one or two lines and just calculate the allowances available on each asset acquired rather than a full computation.

If you do this however, be careful and make sure you explain your calculations clearly.

3   VIGOROUS PLC

Key answer tips

This question required the calculation of three benefit packages for three higher paid employees. All of the key benefits that you need to be able to deal with appear in this question!

Easy marks were available in parts (a) and (c) for explaining the term P11D and how benefits are assessed.

However, careful calculation is required for the benefits as there are many places where calculations can go wrong. Remember to time apportion the calculation where the benefit is not available all year, and don't forget to deduct any employee contributions paid.

(a)   **P11D employees**

- Employees earning at a rate of £8,500 a year or more, and most directors (irrespective of earnings), are P11D employees.

- Benefits must be included when calculating the figure of £8,500, and these are calculated as if they were received by a P11D employee.

- Full-time working directors are excluded if they earn less than £8,500 a year and do not own more than 5% of their company's ordinary share capital.

(b)   **Assessable benefits – 2009/10**

Andrea Lean

	£
Car benefit (W1)	4,990
Fuel benefit (W1)	5,915
Living accommodation	
– Rateable value	7,000
– Additional benefit (W2)	3,277
– Furniture (£6,000 at 20%)	1,200
Mobile telephone	Nil

Tutorial notes:

1.   *The living accommodation cost in excess of £75,000 so there will be an additional benefit.*

Since the property was purchased within six years of first being provided, the benefit is based on the cost of the property plus improvements prior to 6 April 2009 (see W2).

2.   *The provision of one mobile telephone does not give rise to a taxable benefit, even if there is private use.*

Workings

(W1) **Car and fuel benefits**

CO_2 emissions = 275 g/km, available all year

	%	
Petrol	15	
Plus $(275 - 135) \times {}^1/_5$	28	
Appropriate percentage	43	Restricted to 35%

	£
Car benefit (£19,400 x 35%)	6,790
Less Contributions (£150 x 12)	(1,800)
	4,990
Fuel benefit (£16,900 x 35%)	5,915

(W2) **Additional benefit for expensive accommodation**

	£	
Cost of property (January 2005)	130,000	
Improvements before 6 April 2009	14,000	
	144,000	
Less Limit	(75,000)	
	69,000	
Additional benefit	x 4.75%	£3,277

Tutorial note:

Improvements in May 2009 are not taken into account in calculating the benefit for 2009/10, as only improvements up to the start of the tax year are included.

However, they will be taken into account next year in calculating the benefit for 2010/11.

Ben Slim

	£
Beneficial loan (W1)	3,800
Relocation costs (£9,300 – £8,000)	1,300
Car benefit (W2)	1,008

Tutorial notes:

1. *Only £8,000 of relocation costs are exempt.*

2. *There is no fuel benefit as Ben reimburses the company for the full cost of private diesel.*

Workings

(W1) Beneficial loan

	£
Average method	
Loan at start of year	120,000
Loan at end of year	100,000
	220,000
Average loan (£220,000 ÷ 2)	110,000

		£
Assessable benefit (£110,000 × 4.75% × 9/12)		£3,919

Precise method		
(£120,000 x 4.75% x 3/12)	1,425	
(£100,000 x 4.75% x 6/12)	2,375	
		£3,800

Ben will elect for the precise method and the benefit will therefore be £3,800.

(W2) Car benefits

CO_2 emissions = 139 g/km, available 6 months

	%
Petrol	18
Plus (135 – 135) × $^1/_5$	Nil
Appropriate percentage	18
Car benefit (£11,200 x 18% x 6/12)	£1,008

Chai Trim

	£
Van benefit (£3,000 x 10/12)	2,500
Fuel benefit (£500 x 10/12)	417
Television (W)	330
Health club membership	150
Computer (£1,900 x 20% x 3/12)	95

Tutorial notes:

1. The van was only available for ten months of 2009/10 so the fixed annual £3,000 benefit is time apportioned.

2. Private fuel for the van was provided for ten months of 2009/10 so the benefit is time apportioned.

3. In-house benefits are valued according to the marginal cost. The taxable benefit in relation to the health club membership is therefore the direct costs of £150.

4. The computer was only available for 3 months so the benefit is time apportioned.

Working: Sale of television

Greater of

		£	
(i)	MV at date of transfer	250	
	Less Amount paid	(150)	
		——	
			£100
(ii)	Original cost	800	
	Less Annual value for 2007/08 and 2008/09		
	(20% x £800 x 2 years)	(320)	
		——	
		480	
	Less Amount paid	(150)	
		——	
			£330

(c) **Income tax liability in respect of assessable benefits**

- The income tax on recurring benefits, such as company motor cars, will normally be collected through the PAYE system by a reduction in the employee's tax coding.

- Tax not collected on this basis will be due under the self-assessment system.

- However, tax of less than £2,000 can be collected by an adjustment to an employee's tax coding for a subsequent tax year, whilst tax on minor benefits may be paid under an employer's PAYE settlement agreement.

4 JANE JONES

Key answer tips

A purely computational question requiring consideration of the benefits of having a company car versus claiming a mileage allowance.

In part (c) a decision should be made on which offer to accept based on the net cash flow consequences.

(a) **Income tax liability – 2009/10**

(i) **Offer of employment from Aurora plc**

	£
Salary	33,000
Car benefit (W)	1,240
Fuel benefit (W)	1,690
	——
Employment income	35,930
Less Personal allowance	(6,475)
	——
Taxable income	29,455
	——
Income tax liability (£29,455 x 20%)	5,891
	——

Working: Car and fuel benefit

CO_2 emissions = 118 g/km, available all year

Appropriate % = 10% (emissions below 120 g/km)

	£
Car benefit (10% × £18,400)	1,840
Less Contributions (12 × £50)	(600)
	1,240
Fuel benefit (10% × £16,900)	1,690

(ii)   **Offer of employment from Zodiac plc**

	£
Salary	34,000
Less Expense claim (W)	(2,100)
Employment income	31,900
Less Personal allowance	(6,475)
Taxable income	25,425
Income tax liability (£25,425 x 20%)	5,085

Working: Expense claim

The mileage allowance received will be tax-free.

Jane can make the following expense claim:

	£
10,000 miles at 40p	4,000
2,000 miles at 25p	500
	4,500
Mileage allowance received (12,000 at 20p)	(2,400)
Allowance deduction	2,100

(b)   **Most beneficial offer of employment**

	Aurora £	Zodiac £
Salary	33,000	34,000
Mileage allowance received	–	2,400
Car running costs	–	(7,100)
Contribution	(600)	–
Income tax	(5,891)	(5,085)
Net disposable income	26,509	24,215

If she accepts the offer from Aurora, Jane will be £2,294 (£26,509 – £24,215) better off.

Tutorial note:

When calculating the net disposable income think just in terms of cash and identify all cash coming in and all cash payments going out.

Cash payments out obviously include the tax liabilities but also includes other expenses such as the running costs of the car or the contribution made for the provision of the car.

5   ALI PATEL   *Walk in the footsteps of a top tutor*

Key answer tips

A common style question requiring the comparison of two remuneration packages and the impact on the income tax computation and national insurance liabilities.

Part (b) requires a decision to be made based on the net cash flow position after taking account of all costs including income tax and national insurance.

Tutor's top tips:

Part (a) of this question involves some fairly straightforward income tax computations.

Don't forget that there will be no car benefit if Ali uses his own car for business purposes!

You also need to calculate Class 1 NICs. Remember that for the employee, only cash earnings are subject to national insurance.

(a)   **Income tax and Class 1 NICs**

    (i)   **First remuneration package**

	£
Ali's income tax liability – 2009/10	
Salary (£29,000 + (£500 × 12))	35,000
Mileage allowance (W)	420
	———
Employment income	35,420
Less Personal allowance	(6,475)
	———
Taxable income	28,945
	———
Income tax liability (£28,945 × 20%)	5,789
	———
Class 1 primary NIC – 2009/10	
(£35,000 – £5,715) × 11%	3,221
	———

Working: Mileage allowance

The relocation is not expected to last for more than 24 months, so the branch office will be treated as a temporary workplace.

Mileage for the year = (1,600 x 12) = 19,200 miles

Ali will therefore be taxed on the mileage allowance paid by Box plc as follows:

	£	£
Mileage allowance (19,200 at 35p)		6,720
Authorised mileage allowance:		
10,000 miles at 40p	4,000	
9,200 miles at 25p	2,300	
		(6,300)
Taxable income		420

Tutorial note:

For NIC purposes only the excess mileage allowance above 40p per mile is subject to NIC. As Ali will be paid 35p per mile none of the mileage allowance is charged to NIC

(ii) **Second remuneration package**

Ali's income tax liability – 2009/10

	£
Salary	29,000
Living accommodation (W)	9,600
Property business profit	6,000
Total income	44,600
Less Personal allowance	(6,475)
Taxable income	38,125

Income tax:

£	
37,400 at 20%	7,480
725 at 40%	290
38,125	
Income tax liability	7,770

Class 1 primary NIC – 2009/10

(£29,000 – £5,715) × 11%	2,561

Working: Living accommodation

The benefit of living accommodation will be the greater of:

(i)	Annual value	£4,600
(ii)	Rent paid by the employer (£800 x 12)	£9,600

(b)   **Most beneficial remuneration package**

Tutor's top tip:

When calculating the net disposable income think just in terms of cash and identify all cash coming in and all cash payments going out. Cash payments out obviously include the tax liabilities but also includes other expenses such as commuting costs.

Even if you made some mistakes in part (a), as long as you include your tax figures here in this part you will be awarded full marks.

The question specifically asks you to advise Ali as to which remuneration package is most beneficial, so make sure that you do this. A statement of which package should be accepted is therefore needed.

You will be given full marks here if your advice is consistent with your analysis, even if it is wrong!

	Package (1) £	Package (2) £
Salary	35,000	29,000
Property business income	Nil	6,000
Mileage allowance received	6,720	Nil
Commuting costs	(1,800)	Nil
Class 1 NIC	(3,221)	(2,561)
Income tax	(5,789)	(7,770)
Net disposable income	30,910	24,669

If he chooses the first remuneration package, Ali will be £6,241 (£30,910 − £24,669) better off.

6   **EDMOND BRICK**   *Walk in the footsteps of a top tutor*

Key answer tips

A tricky question, exclusively on property income, covering virtually the whole syllabus on this area.

Detailed working knowledge is required however, there are still a lot of easy marks to be gained.

Tutor's top tips:

Part (a) is a classic written part of a question on furnished holiday lettings and should have provided easy marks.

However, be careful, this question only required the income tax advantages of furnished holiday lettings – not any other tax advantages.

So, ensure that you read the question carefully, and do not waste time giving information that scores no marks

(a)   **Income tax advantages of furnished holiday lettings**

- Capital allowances are available on plant and machinery instead of the 10% wear and tear allowance.

- Loss relief is available against total income instead of just against property business profits.

- The income qualifies as relevant earnings for pension tax relief purposes.

Tutorial note:

A furnished holiday letting property is also treated as a business property for capital gains tax purposes and consequently has the advantage of being eligible for gift relief, rollover relief and Entrepreneurs' relief.

However, remember that mentioning the other tax advantages was not required and gained no marks.

(b)   **Furnished holiday letting loss – 2009/10**

Tutor's top tips:

Having read the question requirement first, you will have seen that the question clearly requires you to prepare a property income computation.

Therefore, when reading the body of the question, be sure to identify which properties are let furnished and which are let unfurnished (if any). In addition, which of the furnished properties are likely to satisfy the conditions to be treated as furnished holiday lettings (FHL).

Highlight the information on the question paper, keeping the FHL information separately from the other properties which are pooled together.

	£	£
Rent receivable (£370 × 18)		6,660
Repairs	7,400	
Other expenses:	2,710	
Capital allowances (£5,700 × 100% AIA)	5,700	
		(15,810)
Furnished holiday letting loss		(9,150)

Tutorial note:

Remember that furnished holiday lettings are treated as profits of a separate trade and therefore the trading income rules are followed.

In particular, capital allowances are given on plant and machinery, furnishings etc – instead of the wear and tear allowance. The annual investment allowance is therefore available on the first £50,000 of expenditure.

(c)   **Property business profit – 2009/10**

Tutor's top tips:

There are several properties to deal with in this question. However, only one computation is required.

There is no need to do separate computations to calculate a profit or loss for each property. Edmond will be assessed on the net property income for the year.

Set up your answer with subheadings "income" and "allowable expenses" and leave space underneath to insert the relevant information. Then go through the information in the question about each property in turn and extract the points to go straight into the answer in a logical order.

Note that on your first reading of the question you should already have highlighted the key information. You should have identified which properties are let unfurnished and furnished, and therefore which are eligible for the wear and tear allowance.

The most common mistakes made in exams on questions like this are either to forget the allowance completely, or to incorrectly apply it to all properties.

In addition, watch out for the rent-a-room relief if the owner rents out any part of his own property. Often the rent is below the deminimis limit of £4,250 and is therefore exempt. However, this is not always the case.

	£	£
Income		
Rent receivable – Property 2 (£575 × 12)		6,900
– Property 3 (£710 × 7)		4,970
– Property 4		4,600
Furnished room – Own property(W2)		790
		——
		17,260
Premium received for sub-lease – Property 4	15,000	
Less: £15,000 × 2% × (5 – 1)	(1,200)	
	——	13,800
		——
		31,060
		——
Allowable expenses		
Council tax	1,200	
Wear and tear allowance (W1)	570	
Irrecoverable rent (£710 × 3) (Note)	2,130	
Advertising	670	
Loan interest (Note)	6,700	
Rent paid	6,800	
Insurance (£340 + £290 + £360)	990	
	——	(19,060)
		——
Property business profit		12,000
		——

Tutorial note:

All rents accrued must be included in the computation. However, where all attempts have been made to collect the rent from the tenant, but it is not recoverable, relief is available by deducting the irrecoverable amount as an allowable deduction.

For individuals, interest payable on a loan taken out to purchase a property which is let out to tenants, is an allowable deduction against rental income. Note that for companies, such interest is not allowable against rental income. Instead, it is allowable against other interest income.

Workings

(W1) **Wear and tear allowance – Property 2**

	£
Rent receivable	6,900
Less Council tax	(1,200)
	——
	5,700
	——
Wear and tear allowance (£5,700 x 10%)	570
	——

(W2) **Rent-a-Room Relief**

Claiming rent-a-room relief in respect of the furnished room is more beneficial than the normal basis of assessment as shown below:

		£	
(i)	*Normal assessment*		
	Rents	5,040	
	Less Expenses	(1,140)	
		——	£3,900
(ii)	*Claiming rent-a-room relief*		
	Rents	5,040	
	Less Rent-a-room limit	(4,250)	
		——	£790

Examiner's report

In part (a) some candidates discussed the qualifying conditions for a furnished holiday letting rather than the advantages of a property being so treated.

Parts (b) and (c) presented few problems.

The only aspects that consistently caused difficulty were the capital allowances for the furnished holiday letting (candidates either claimed wear and tear allowance or deducted the full cost of the capital expenditure) and the furnished room (candidates did not appreciate that rent-a-room relief could be claimed).

ACCA marking scheme		
		Marks
(a)	Capital allowances	1.0
	Loss relief	1.0
	Relevant earnings for pension purposes	1.0
		———
		3.0
(b)	Rent receivable	0.5
	Repairs	1.0
	Other expenses	0.5
	Capital allowances	1.0
		———
		3.0
(c)	Lease premium received	1.5
	Rent receivable	1.5
	Furnished room	1.0
	Council tax	0.5
	Wear and tear allowance	1.0
	Impairment losses	0.5
	Advertising	0.5
	Loan interest	1.0
	Rent paid	0.5
	Insurance	1.0
		———
		9.0
Total		15.0

7   PETER CHIC *Walk in the footsteps of a top tutor*

Key answer tips

A classic individual income tax computation, covering several aspects of employment income, together with a small element of other types of income.

Initially, due to the amount of information given in the scenario, this question looks very daunting. However, there was nothing that should have caused significant problems.

Tutor's top tips:

Part (a) of this question was straight forward if approached logically. Remember to run down each line of the question in turn and consider the implications of each piece of information. Remember not to get held up on any one calculation.

Always ensure that you read the question carefully. The requirement is to calculate income tax payable. Ensure you do not drop easy marks by only calculating the income tax liability.

Make the marker your friend, if you keep your calculations clear and easy to read you will score much higher marks. Always ensure your workings are clearly labelled.

(a)   Peter

Income tax computation – for 2009/10

	Total income £	Other income £	Savings income £	Dividend income £
Employment income (W1)	81,005	81,005		
Property income (W4)	3,660	3,660		
Building Society interest (£1,760 x 100/80)	2,200		2,200	
Dividends (£720 x 100/90)	800			800
Total income	87,665	87,665	2,200	800
Less Personal Allowance	(6,475)	(6,475)		
Taxable income	81,190	78,190	2,200	800

Tutorial note:

The premium bond prize is exempt from income tax.

Income tax:	£		£
Other income – Basic rate (W5)	40,325	x 20%	8,065
Other income – Higher rate	37,865	x 40%	15,146
	78,190		
Savings income – Higher rate	2,200	x 40%	880
Dividends – Higher rate	800	x 32.5%	260
	81,190		

Income tax liability		24,351
Less Tax deducted at source:		
Dividends (£800 x 10%)		(80)
Building society interest (£2,200 x 20%)		(440)
PAYE		(14,286)
Income tax payable		9,545

Workings

(W1) Employment income

	£	£
Salary		45,600
Bonus – Paid 30 April 2009		4,300
Bonus – Paid 31 March 2010		3,700
		53,600
Assessable benefits:		
Car Benefit (W2)	7,175	
Fuel Benefit (W2)	5,915	
Living accommodation		
– Annual value	9,100	
– Additional benefit (W3)	4,655	
Mobile phone (£250 x 20%) (Note)	50	
Health Club membership (Note)	510	
Overnight allowance	Nil	
		27,405
Employment income		81,005

Tutorial note:

1. *The exemption for mobile telephones does not apply to the second telephone. The normal 20% use of assets benefit applies.*

2. *The membership of the health club is assessed at the cost to the employer.*

3. *Payments for private incidental expenses are exempt up to £10 per night when spent outside the UK.*

(W2) **Car and fuel benefit**

CO_2 emissions = 232 g/km, available all year

	%	
Diesel	18	
Plus (230 – 135) × $^1/_5$	19	
Appropriate percentage	37	Restricted to 35%

	£	£
List price	22,500	
Less Capital contribution	(2,000)	
	20,500	
Car benefit (£20,500 x 35%)		7,175
Fuel benefit (£16,900 x 35%)		5,915

(W3) **Living accommodation – Additional benefit**

The living accommodation cost is in excess of £75,000 so there will be an additional benefit.

Since the property was not purchased more than six years before first being provided to Peter, the benefit is based on the cost of the property plus subsequent improvements.

The additional benefit is therefore:

(£160,000 + £13,000 – £75,000) x 4.75% = £4,655

(W4) **Property income**

	£	£
Income		
Rent receivable– Property 1 (£500 × 5)		2,500
– Property 2 (£820 × 8)		6,560
		9,060
Allowable expenses		
Irrecoverable rent (£500 × 2) (Note)	1,000	
Repairs	600	
Advertising	875	
Loan interest	1,800	
Insurance ((£660 x 3/12) + (£1,080 x 9/12))	975	
Wear and tear allowance		
(£1,500 x 10%) (Note)	150	
		(5,400)
Property business profit		3,660

Tutorial note:

1. *All rents accrued must be included in the computation. However, where all attempts have been made to collect the rent from the tenant, but it is not recoverable, relief is available by deducting the irrecoverable amount as an allowable deduction.*

2. *The wear and tear allowance can only be claimed in respect of the first property since the second property is not let out furnished.*

    The wear and tear allowance on Property 1 is based on the rents actually received of £1,500 (£2,500 rents receivable – £1,000 irrecoverable debts).

    *Note that on the subject of the calculation of the wear and tear allowance, HMRC manuals refer to "net rents" as the start position and this has been interpreted to mean "rents receivable **after** irrecoverable debts have been deducted".*

    However, credit was also given in the exam if the allowance was calculated based on the rents receivable without a deduction for irrecoverable debts.

(W5) Extension of basic rate band

	£
Basic rate band threshold	37,400
Plus Gross gift aid donation (£2,340 x 100/80)	2,925
	———
Extended basic rate band	40,325
	———

(b)   National Insurance Contributions

Tutor's top tips:

Part (b) required a little care, but as long as you remember that NIC is payable on cash earnings only by the employee, and on both the cash earnings by the employer (Class 1 secondary) and assessable benefits (Class 1A), then there should not be too many problems.

Note that it does not matter if you have calculated the employment income incorrectly in part (a) as long as you calculate the NIC correctly on whatever figure you have, you will still score maximum marks on this part.

Payable by Peter

	£
(£43,875 – £5,715) x 11%	4,198
(£53,600 – £43,875) x 1%	97
	———
Class 1 Primary NICs	4,295
	———

Payable by Haute-Couture Ltd

	£
Class 1 Secondary NIC	
(£53,600 – £5,715) x 12.8%	6,129
Class 1A NICs	
(£27,405 (part (a) (W1)) x 12.8%)	3,508
	———
	9,637
	———

Examiner's report

This question was very well answered by the majority of candidates.

In part (a) a few candidates did not appreciate that both bonuses were to be treated as earnings, whilst the basis of assessing the second mobile telephone was not always known. Some candidates deducted the gift aid donation rather than extending the basic rate tax band.

In part (b) the most common mistake was to include taxable benefits when calculating Class 1 National Insurance contributions.

ACCA marking scheme			Marks
(a)	Salary		0.5
	Bonus payments		1.0
	Car benefit – Relevant percentage		1.0
	– Capital contribution		0.5
	– Calculation		0.5
	Fuel benefit		1.0
	Living accommodation – Annual value		1.0
	– Additional benefit		2.0
	Mobile telephone		1.0
	Health club membership		0.5
	Overseas allowance		0.5
	Property business profit – Rent receivable		1.0
	– Impairment losses		0.5
	– Repairs		0.5
	– Advertising		0.5
	– Loan interest		1.0
	– Insurance		1.0
	– Wear and tear allowance		1.0
	Building society interest		0.5
	Dividends		0.5
	Premium bond prize		0.5
	Personal allowance		0.5
	Extension of basic rate band		1.0
	Income tax		1.5
	Tax suffered at source		1.5
			———
			21.0
			———
(b)	Employee Class 1 NIC		1.5
	Employer Class 1 NIC		1.5
	Employer Class 1A NIC		1.0
			———
			4.0
			———
Total			25.0
			———

INCOME TAX BASICS AND FROM SELF-EMPLOYMENT

8   CAROL COURIER

Key answer tips

A straight forward purely computational question dealing with the income tax and national insurance consequences of being self-employed.

Part (c) requires a comparison of the net disposable income arising from the two options.

(a)   **Carol continues to be employed**

Carol's income tax liability – 2009/10

	£
Salary	37,500
Less Pension contributions (£37,500 x 5%)	(1,875)
Employment income	35,625
Less Personal allowance	(6,475)
Taxable income	29,150
Income tax liability (£29,150 x 20%)	5,830

Class 1 NICs – Primary contributions

(£37,500 – £5,715) × 11%	3,496

(b)   **Carol accepts self-employed contract**

Carol's income tax liability – 2009/10

	£
Income (£43,500 + £8,000)	51,500
Less Expenses (£4,400 + £2,800)	(7,200)
Trading income	44,300
Less Personal allowance	(6,475)
Taxable income	37,825
Income tax liability (£37,825 x 20%) (Working)	7,565

Working: Extension of the basic rate band

The personal pension contribution results in Carol's basic rate tax band threshold being extended as follows:

	£
Basic rate band	37,400
Plus Gross pension contributions	2,000
Extended basic rate band	39,400

All of Carol's taxable income of £37,825 falls into this extended basic rate band and is therefore taxed at 20%.

Class NICs	£
(£43,875 – £5,715) × 8%	3,053
(£44,300 – £43,875) × 1%	4
	3,057

Class 2 NICs	
(£2.40 for 52 weeks)	125

(c) **Benefit of accepting self-employed contract**

	Employed £	Self employed £
Salary	37,500	Nil
Trading income	Nil	44,300
Pension contributions paid (Note)	(1,875)	(1,600)
NIC – Class 1 and Class 4	(3,496)	(3,057)
NIC – Class 2	Nil	(125)
Income tax	(5,830)	(7,565)
Net disposable income	26,299	31,953

It is therefore beneficial for Carol to accept the offer to work on a self-employed basis as her net income will increase by £5,654 (£31,953 – £26,299).

Tutorial note:

Carol will pay personal pension contributions net of basic rate tax. If self-employed she will therefore pay £1,600 (£2,000 × 80%).

Key answer tips

When calculating the net disposable income think just in terms of cash and identify all cash coming in and all cash payments going out.

Cash payments out obviously include the tax liabilities but also includes other expenses such as pension contributions

9 CORDELIA

Key answer tips

This question is exclusively on the change of accounting date rules.

Part (a) gives easy marks in asking for the conditions that must be satisfied for a valid change.

Part (b) covers the two different basis of assessment rules depending on whether a short or long accounting period is produced in order to change the accounting date of the business.

(a) **Conditions to be met for valid change of accounting date**

- The change of accounting date must be notified to HM Revenue & Customs (HMRC) on or before 31 January following the tax year in which the change is to be made.

- The first accounts to the new accounting date must not exceed 18 months in length.

  If the period of account between the old accounting date and the proposed new accounting date is longer than 18 months, then two sets of accounts will have to be prepared.

- There must not have been another change of accounting date during the previous five tax years.

  This condition may be ignored if HMRC accepts that the present change is made for genuine commercial reasons.

(b) **Trading income assessments**

(i) **Preparing accounts for 3 months to 30 September 2009**

Tax year	Basis of assessment	£
2009/10	Year to 30.6.09	48,000
	3 months to 30.9.09	15,000
		63,000
	Less: 3 months of overlap relief (£12,000 x 3/9)	(4,000)
		59,000
2010/11	Year to 30.9.10 (CYB)	60,000

Overlap relief to carry forward (6 months) = £8,000

(ii) **Preparing accounts for 15 months to 30 September 2010**

Tax year	Basis of assessment	£
2009/10	Year to 30.6.09 (CYB)	48,000
2010/11	15-month period to 30.9.10	75,000
	Less: 3 months of overlap relief (as above)	(4,000)
		71,000

Tutorial note:

As the accounting year end is moving to a date later in the tax year, the basis period for the year of change will be the period ending with the new accounting date.

In the tax year of change, profits for 15 months are assessed. The normal basis of assessment is 12 months.

Accordingly, 3 months of the overlap profits that arose on commencement may be offset.

Note that the same total profits are assessed in total over the two years; the second option gives the longer delay before the profits are taxed.

10   CHATRU

Key answer tips

A question in three parts but the parts are not independent.

In part (a) you have to apply the opening and closing year rules to calculate the trading income assessments.

The 2009/10 assessment is then needed in the income tax computation in part (b), which is a straight forward 'bread and butter' computation that should not have caused problems.

Part (c) requires some thought into tax planning advice for a husband and wife. Typically the solution is to recommend the transfer of some assets generating income from the higher rate taxpayer to the lower rate taxpayer. However, there are other valid points that could have been made.

(1)   (a)   **Assessable income**

Tax year	Basis of assessment		£
2005/06	Actual basis (1.11.05 – 5.4.06)		
	£40,500 × 5/18		11,250
2006/07	Actual basis (6.4.06 – 5.4.07)		
	£40,500 × 12/18		27,000
2007/08	12 months ended 30.4.07		
	£40,500 × 12/18		27,000
2008/09	CYB (y/e 30.4.08)		12,000
2009/10	Year of cessation – 1.5.08 to 31.3.10		
	(£24,000 + £50,000)	74,000	
	Less: Overlap profits (1.5.06 – 5.4.07)		
	£40,500 × 11/18	(24,750)	
			49,250
	Total assessable income		126,500

Tutorial note:

Check that total assessments = total tax adjusted profits of the business:

(£40,500 + £12,000 + £24,000 + £50,000) = £126,500

(b) **Assessments (cessation 30.4.10)**

Tax year	Basis of assessment	£	£
2005/06	(as above)		11,250
2006/07	(as above)		27,000
2007/08	(as above)		27,000
2008/09	(as above)		12,000
2009/10	CYB (y/e 30.4.09)		24,000
2010/11	Year of cessation – 1.5.09 to 30.4.10		
	(£50,000 + £4,200)	54,200	
	Less: Overlap profits (as above)	(24,750)	
			29,450
			130,700

Tutorial note:

Check that total assessments = total tax adjusted profits of the business:

(£126,500 + £4,200) = £130,700

Assessments under the current year basis ensure that all profits earned are assessed. If Chatru continues to trade for one extra month, earning an additional £4,200 his total assessments will increase by £4,200.

However, by trading for one extra month, the amount assessed in 2009/10 is reduced from £49,250 to £24,000. This may be an income tax benefit if Chatru has little or no other income, as profits are now covered by the basic rate band.

Tutorial note:

The taxpayer can choose his date of cessation. The choice of date is important as there is an opportunity to alter the timing of assessments over the final years. This may change the rate of tax at which the profits are assessed and the due date of payment.

In practice this is an important tax planning consideration in the closing years of a business.

Key answer tips

Strictly there is no need, in parts (a) and (b), to provide a proof that total profits earned equals total profits assessed but it is good practice and will uncover any arithmetic mistakes for you to go back and correct.

However, only go back and correct an answer if you have time. Normally it is better to move on and finish the question.

(2)   (a)   **Income tax computation – 2009/10**

	Total	Other	Savings	Dividends
	£	£	£	£
Trading income (part 1 (a))	49,250	49,250		
Property business income (W1)	10,000	10,000		
Bank interest (£2,500 × 100/80)	3,125		3,125	
ISA interest (Exempt)	Nil			
Dividends (£33,500 × 100/90)	37,222			37,222
Total income	99,597	59,250	3,125	37,222
Less Personal allowance	(6,475)	(6,475)		
Taxable income	93,122	52,775	3,125	37,222

Income tax		£
£		
43,650	at 20% (W2) (Other income)	8,730
9,125	at 40% (Other income)	3,650
52,775		
3,125	at 40% (Savings)	1,250
37,222	at 32.5% (Dividends)	12,097
93,122		

	£
Income tax liability	25,727
Less Tax suffered at source	
Dividends (£37,222 at 10%)	(3,722)
Bank interest (£3,125 at 20%)	(625)
Income tax payable	21,380

Key answer tips

The trading income figure in the income tax computation comes from part (1) (a).

Remember that even if you got that part wrong, you can get all of the marks in part (2) (a) for following through your computation in the correct way using your trading income figure – so keep going!

Workings

(W1) **Property business income**

(i) **Rent from the room in house**

The rental income is less than £4,250 per annum and is therefore exempt from income tax under the rent a room scheme.

(ii) **Property business profit**

Furnished property	£
Rent received	11,000
Less: Interest paid	(500)
Allowable expenses	(1,500)
Cooker – capital – not allowable	–
Wear & tear allowance	
(10% × (£11,000 – £800 – £200))	(1,000)
	8,000
Land (£4,000 × 50%) (Note 2)	2,000
Property business profit	10,000

Tutorial note:

1. *The purchase of the cooker is capital expenditure.*

2. *Income from assets jointly held by husband and wife is split 50:50 between the spouses unless they have elected to have the income taxed in relation to their actual ownership proportions.*

The question states that Chatru and Sandra have not made any elections in relation to their income.

The rental income will therefore be split equally between them for tax purposes.

(W2) **Extended basic rate band**

	£
Basic rate band	37,400
Plus Gross Gift Aid donation (£5,000 x 100/80)	6,250
Extended basic rate band	43,650

(b)   **Chatru and Sandra – Ways to reduce joint income tax liability**

Sandra's only taxable income is from her part-time earnings of £8,000 and rental income from the land of £2,000 per annum. She is therefore a basic rate taxpayer.

Chatru was a higher rate taxpayer in 2009/10 and if the level of his dividend income remains the same he is likely to continue to be so in future years.

Chatru has suffered tax on his property income and savings income at 40% and on his dividend income at 32.5%.

Sandra has an unused basic rate band of £33,875 (W). She would therefore only pay tax at 20% on this income up to the level of her remaining basic rate band.

Chatru and Sandra should therefore have considered the following to reduce their income tax liability:

(1)   Electing for the rental income from the land to be taxed in accordance with their actual ownership proportions of 25:75. This would have reduced their joint tax liability by £200 (£1,000 × (40% – 20%)).

(2)   Transferring income generating assets such as the shares and the bank account into Sandra's name in order to produce income to fully utilise her basic rate band.

(3)   Transferring funds from either the bank account or the shareholdings into an Individual Savings Account in Sandra's name in order to generate tax free income.

Key answer tips

The question only required two ways in which the couple could have saved tax. The full answer above is produced for tutorial purposes.

Working: Remaining basic rate band

	£	£
Basic rate band		37,400
Earnings	8,000	
Property income	2,000	
	–––––	
	10,000	
Less Personal allowance	(6,475)	
	–––––	
Taxable income		(3,525)
		–––––
Remaining basic rate band		33,875
		–––––

Tutorial note:

Remember that to calculate the remaining basic rate band you need to compare £37,400 to Sandra's taxable income which is after deducting her personal allowance.

11   ANDREW WALL

Key answer tips

The first part of the question involves the disposal of a property and consideration of the badges of trade to decide whether the disposal of a property should be assessed to income tax or capital gains tax.

Computations for both possibilities are required and care should be taken with the treatment of the interest on the loan taken out to purchase the property.

Part (2) is an independent part requiring a detailed property income computation. There is no particular point of difficulty here but don't forget the wear and tear allowance on the furnished property!

(1)   (a)   **Badges of trade**

(1)   *The subject matter of the transaction.*

Trading is indicated where property does not yield an ongoing income or give personal enjoyment to its owner.

(2)   *The length of ownership.*

The sale of property within a short time of its acquisition is an indication of trading.

(3)   *Frequency of similar transactions.*

Trading is indicated by repeated transactions in the same subject matter.

(4)   *Work done on the property.*

A trading motive is indicated where work is carried out to property to make it more marketable, or where steps are taken to find purchasers.

(5)   *Circumstances responsible for the realisation.*

A forced sale to raise cash for an emergency indicates that the transaction is not trading in nature.

(6)   *Motive.*

If a transaction is undertaken with the motive of realising a profit, this is a strong indication of trading.

(b) **Andrew**

Additional tax liability – 2009/10

(i) **Carrying on a trade**

	£	£
Income		225,000
Cost of property	100,000	
Renovation costs	60,000	
Loan interest (£160,000 x 10%)	16,000	
Legal fees (£800 + £1,000)	1,800	
		(177,800)
Taxable profit		47,200

Income tax		
£		
12,400 at 20% (W)		2,480
34,800 at 40%		13,920
47,200		
Additional income tax		16,400

Tutorial note:

1. *If Andrew is treated as carrying on a trade the income will be subject to income tax as trading income.*

2. *All of the expenses incurred in purchasing, renovating and selling the office building are deductible, including the interest on the loan.*

(ii) **Not carrying on a trade**

	£
Proceeds	225,000
Less Incidental costs of disposal	(1,000)
	224,000
Less Cost of property (£100,000 + £800)	(100,800)
Renovation costs	(60,000)
Chargeable gain	63,200
Less Annual exemption	(10,000)
Taxable gain	53,100
Capital gains tax (£53,100 x 18%)	9,558

Tutorial note:

1. If Andrew is not treated as carrying on a trade the office building transaction will be subject to capital gains tax.

2. No relief is available for the interest on the loan used to finance the transaction.

3. Entrepreneurs' relief is not available as Andrew is not disposing of all or part of a business. There is no relief for the disposal of isolated assets.

Working: Remaining basic rate band

	£
Basic rate band	37,400
Taxable income	(25,000)
Remaining basic rate band	12,400

(2) **Bill**

Property business income assessment – 2009/10

	£	£
Income		
Rent receivable – Property 1 (£800 × 9)		7,200
– Property 2 (£500 × 4)		2,000
– Property 3 ((£1,000 × 9) + £450)		9,450
		18,650
Lease premium – Property 3 (Note)		
Premium received	12,000	
Less: £12,000 × 2% × (10 – 1)	(2,160)	
		9,840
		28,490
Allowable expenses		
Irrecoverable rent – Property 1	800	
Allowable expenses – Property 1	500	
Mortgage interest – Property 2	700	
Advertising – Property 2	500	
Insurance (£300 × 10/12) – Property 2	250	
Decoration – Property 2	900	
Wear and tear allowance (£2,000 × 10%)	200	
		(3,850)
Property business profit		24,640

Tutorial note:

1. *Property business income is assessed on the accruals basis. The date that rent is received is irrelevant.*

2. *Relief is available for irrecoverable rents as an allowable expense.*

3. *The receipt of a premium on the grant of a short lease (≤ 50 years) gives rise to taxable property income on the landlord in the year of receipt of the premium.*

4. *Decoration costs and repairs for newly purchased properties are allowed as revenue expenditure unless the property was purchased in an unuseable state. In this case, any repairs and decoration necessary to make the property useable would be deemed to be part of the capital cost of the property.*

    As there is no indication in the question as to the state of the property when purchased, it is assumed that it was in a useable state and therefore the repair costs are allowable as revenue expenditure.

Key answer tips

It is not necessary to prepare a calculation of the profit or loss for each property separately. Only one computation is required bringing in all of the income and deducting all of the allowable deductions for all of the properties.

Bill will be assessed on the net profits from all properties in the tax year.

Don't forget the wear and tear allowance on the furnished property!

12   OLIVE GREEN

Key answer tips

A classic, straightforward income tax computation for a self-employed individual with some self-assessment points at the end.

The adjustment of profit should not have caused problems. Remember to read the private use / business use proportion of Olive's car carefully and adjust both the profits figure and the capital allowances.

The income tax computation was not difficult; the only area of concern may have been the relief for interest on the loan taken out to purchase an asset for use in Olive's employment.

Calculating balancing payments, payments on account and interest for late payment of tax are commonly examined and should not have been problematic.

(a)   **Tax adjusted trading profit – year ended 31 March 2010**

		£
Net profit		30,050
Add:	Depreciation	2,350
	Private accommodation (£1,980 + £5,920) × 30%	2,370
	Motor expenses (£4,700 × 12,000/20,000)	2,820
	Lease costs – high emission car (£3,000 × 15%)	450
	Fine (Note 1)	220
	Theft by employee (Note 2)	0
	Donation to political party	100
	Trade subscription (Note 3)	0
	Excessive salary (Note 4) (£14,000 – £10,500)	3,500
	Own consumption (Note 5) (52 × £45)	2,340
		44,200
Less:	Patent royalties (£150 × 4) (Note 6)	(600)
	Capital allowances (W)	(1,200)
	Tax adjusted trading profit	42,400

Key answer tips

In the adjustment to profits calculation it is important to list all the major items indicated in the question requirement, showing a zero (0) for expenditure that is allowable. This is because credit will be given for showing no adjustment where none is needed.

If required, also add notes to show why you have not adjusted for an item, or why you have added it back. However, lengthy explanations are not required where the requirement is just to 'calculate' the adjusted profits, rather than to explain them.

Always show your workings if the figure you are adjusting for is not clear from the question.

Tutorial note:

1.   *Fines are not allowable except for parking fines incurred by an employee.*

2.   *Defalcations are allowable provided they are by an employee rather than the business owner.*

3.   *Trade subscriptions are allowable as they have been incurred wholly and exclusively for the purposes of the trade.*

4.   *A salary to a family member must not be excessive. Since Olive's daughter is paid £3,500 more than the other sales assistants, this amount is not allowable.*

5.   *Goods for own consumption are valued at selling price.*

6.   *The patent royalties have been paid wholly and exclusively for the purposes of the trade and are therefore deductible from trading profits.*

Key answer tips

Patent royalties are allowable deductions from trading profit if they are for the purposes of the trade. As they have not yet been deducted in arriving at the profit, a deduction is required.

Read the question carefully as normally they have already been accounted for and therefore no adjustment is required.

Working: Capital allowances

	Expensive car £	Business use	Allowances £
TWDV b/f	15,800		
WDA – restricted	(3,000)	× (8,000/20,000)	1,200
	————		————
TWDV c/f	12,800		
	————		

Key answer tips

A familiar full blown capital allowances computation is given in the workings to this answer to show how the allowances are calculated.

However, where there are not many transactions it is perfectly acceptable to do one or two lines and just calculate the allowances available on each asset acquired rather than a full computation.

If you do this however, be careful and make sure you explain your calculations clearly.

(b)   **Income tax computation – 2009/10**

	Total £	Other £	Savings £	Dividends £
Trading income	42,400	42,400		
Employment income	6,000	6,000		
Building society interest				
(£1,440 × 100/80)	1,800		1,800	
Dividends (£1,080 × 100/90)	1,200			1,200
	————	————	————	————
Total income	51,400	48,400	1,800	1,200
Less Reliefs:				
Loan interest (Note)	(220)	(220)		
	————	————	————	————
Net income	51,180	48,180	1,800	1,200
Less Personal allowance	(6,475)	(6,475)		
	————	————	————	————
Taxable income	44,705	41,705	1,800	1,200
	————	————	————	————

Income tax	£	£
40,000 at 20% (Other income) (W)		8,000
1,705 at 40% (Other income)		682
41,705		
1,800 at 40% (Savings)		720
1,200 at 32.5% (Dividends)		390
44,705		
Income tax liability		9,792
Less Tax suffered at source		
Dividends (£1,200 at 10%)		(120)
PAYE		(1,320)
Building society interest (£1,800 at 20%)		(360)
Income tax payable		7,992

Tutorial note:

The loan interest qualifies as a relief deductible from total income since the loan was used by Olive to finance expenditure for a qualifying purpose. Note that the interest is quoted and is paid gross.

Working: Extension of basic rate band

	£
Basic rate band	37,400
Plus Gross pension contributions	2,600
Extended basic rate band	40,000

Capital gains tax liability – 2009/10

	£
Capital gain	12,300
Less Annual exemption	(10,100)
Taxable gain	2,200
Capital gains tax (£2,200 x 18%)	396

Balancing payment for 2009/10 – due on 31 January 2011

	£
Total income tax and CGT (£7,992 + £396)	8,388
Less Payments on account	(4,900)
Balancing payment	3,488

Payments on account – 2010/11

Payments on account are not required for capital gains tax, so the payments on account for 2010/11 will be £3,996 (£7,992 × 50%).

These will be due on 31 January and 31 July 2011.

(c) **Consequences of paying balancing payment late**

- Interest is charged where a balancing payment is paid late. This will run from 31 January 2011 to 30 April 2011.

- The interest charge will be: (£3,488 × 2.5% × 3/12) = £22

- In addition, a 5% surcharge of £174 (£3,488 at 5%) will be imposed as the balancing payment is not made within 28 days of the due date.

13   SUE MACKER

Key answer tips

Part 1 (a) required a general discussion of the meaning of the badges of trade. This is often examined and so the factors and their meaning must be learnt. Part 1 (b) then required you to specifically apply that knowledge to Sue's circumstances.

A basic income tax computation was then required assuming a trading activity exists. Watch out for the treatment of assets bought and sold in the year for capital allowance purposes.

An explanation of the treatment required if not trading should have been easy marks to gain.

Part 2 was completely independent of the first part and tested the VAT registration rules and the calculation of VAT payable.

Don't forget to take into account the recoverability of pre-registration input VAT on expenses.

(1)   (a)   **Badges of trade**

- Trading is indicated where property (the subject matter) does not yield an ongoing income or give personal enjoyment to its owner.

- The sale of property within a short time of its acquisition is an indication of trading.

- Trading is indicated by repeated transactions in the same subject matter.

- A trading motive is indicated where work is carried out to property to make it more marketable, or where steps are taken to find purchasers.

- A forced sale to raise cash for an emergency indicates that the transaction is not trading in nature.

- If a transaction is undertaken with the motive of realising a profit, this is a strong indication of trading.

(b)   **Trading activities**

Although vintage motor cars are commonly owned for personal enjoyment, trading is indicated by the number of transactions and the short period of time before the motor cars were sold.

In addition, Sue carried out a substantial amount of work on the motor cars, and there is no indication that their disposal was a forced sale.

The use of a bank loan, the rental of business premises, and the purchase of equipment are other factors that all indicate the carrying on of a trade.

(c)   **Income tax liability – 2009/10**

	£	£
Income		200,000
Cost of motor cars (£8,000 × 4)	32,000	
Restoration costs (£12,000 × 4)	48,000	
Loan interest (£75,000 × 10%)	7,500	
Rent of workshop (£400 × 12)	4,800	
Capital allowances		
(£13,500 – £5,800) (Note)	7,700	
		(100,000)
Trading profit		100,000
Less Personal allowance		(6,475)
Taxable income		93,525

Income tax

£		£
37,400 at 20%		7,480
56,125 at 40%		22,450
─────		
93,525		
─────		
Income tax liability		29,930

Tutorial note:

As Sue acquired and sold the equipment in the same tax year, she will be eligible for capital allowances on the net cost of the equipment (i.e. difference between cost and sale proceeds).

Class 2 NICs – 2009/10	£
(£2.40 for 52 weeks)	125
	───
Class 4 NIC – 2009/10	
(£43,875 – £5,715) × 8%	3,053
(£100,000 – £43,875) × 1%	561
	─────
	3,614

(d) **If not treated as trading activity**

If Sue is treated as not carrying on a trade, the disposal of the vintage motor cars will be dealt with as a capital transaction, subject to capital gains tax rather than income tax.

However, motor cars, including vintage motor cars, are exempt from CGT, so Sue will not have any tax liability for 2009/10.

(2) **Mr Moeraki**

(a) **Compulsory registration**

HM Revenue & Customs (HMRC) must be notified in either of the following situations:

(i) Where taxable supplies in the last 12 months exceed £68,000, HMRC should be notified within 30 days of the end of the month and registration is effective from the beginning of the following month.

(ii) Where taxable supplies in the next 30 days are expected to exceed £68,000, HMRC should be notified by the end of that 30 day period and registration is effective from the start of the 30 day period.

(b) **Mr Moeraki's notification date and effective registration date**

Mr Moeraki's turnover exceeds £68,000 in April 2010 (£68,100).

Accordingly he should notify HMRC by 30 May 2010.

His registration will be effective from 1 June 2010.

(c) **VAT Return – Period ended 30 June 2010**

	£	£
Output VAT		
Sales (£15,700 × 17.5%)		2,747
Input VAT		
Expenses ((£14,200 – (6 × £400)) × 17.5%	2,065	
Computer	2,900	
	———	(4,965)
VAT repayable		(2,218)

Tutorial note:

1. *VAT is charged on outputs once registration is effective (i.e. from 1 June 2010).*

2. *Mr Moeraki can recover input tax in respect of services purchased during the six months and goods purchased in the three years prior to registration.*

3. *Input tax in respect of entertaining cannot be reclaimed.*

4. *The car is not used wholly for business purposes. Accordingly the input tax cannot be reclaimed.*

14 TONY NOTE

Key answer tips

A classic question requiring a familiar adjustment of profit and capital allowances computation before leading on to calculate an income tax and capital gains tax liability, with some self-assessment at the end.

The tricky point was the calculation of the private use proportion of Tony's car. Once calculated, you then need to remember to adjust both the profit and the capital allowances computation accordingly.

Also watch out for any capital expenditure that is added back in the adjustment of profit computation as it may be eligible for plant and machinery capital allowances.

Rollover relief featured in part (b) and was a straightforward calculation.

Easy marks were available for explaining the retention of records rules. This part could have been answered first to ensure the easy marks are in the bag as soon as possible.

(a)   **Tax adjusted trading profit – year ended 5 April 2010**

		£
Net profit		19,430
Add:	Depreciation	2,640
	Motor expenses (£9,800 × 30%) (W1)	2,940
	Accountancy (Note 1)	0
	Personal financial planning advice	620
	Debt collection (Note 1)	0
	Fees for planning permission	2,600
	Replacement hard drive (Note 2)	0
	New printer (Note 3)	400
	Business travelling (Note 1)	0
	Entertaining suppliers (Note 4)	480
	Entertaining employees (Note 4)	0
	Excessive salary (£16,000 – £12,000) (Note 5)	4,000
	Wedding present for employee (Note 6)	0
	Health club subscription	710
	Donation to political party	60
	Trade subscription (Note 1)	0
	Own consumption (Note 7)	950
		———
		34,830
Less:	Use of office (£4,140 × 1/6)	(690)
	Private telephone (£680 × 25%)	(170)
	Capital allowances (W2)	(3,980)
		———
Tax adjusted trading profit		29,990
		———

Key answer tips

In the adjustment to profits calculation it is important to list all the major items indicated in the question requirement, showing a zero (0) for expenditure that is allowable. This is because credit will be given for showing no adjustment where none is needed.

If required, also add notes to show why you have not adjusted for an item, or why you have added it back. However, lengthy explanations are not required where the requirement is just to 'calculate' the adjusted profits, rather than to explain them.

Always show your workings if the figure you are adjusting for is not clear from the question.

Tutorial note:

1.   *Accountancy, debt collection fees, business travelling and trade subscription are allowable as incurred wholly and exclusively for the purposes of the trade.*

2.   *The replacement hard drive is allowable as it is replacing part of a computer system and treated as "repair and maintenance" expenditure; the whole computer is not being replaced.*

3.   *The new printer is not allowable, being capital in nature.*

4.   *The only exception to the non-deductibility of entertainment expenditure is when it is in respect of employees.*

5.   *A salary to a family member must not be excessive. Since Tony's wife is paid £4,000 more than the other sales assistants, this amount is not allowable.*

6.   *The one-off wedding present for an employee is allowable.*

7.   *Goods for own consumption are valued at selling price.*

Workings

(W1) **Private mileage**

	Total	Private	Business
Total miles	20,000		
Holiday in Europe	(2,500)	2,500	
Allocate (20:80)	17,500	3,500	14,000
		6,000	14,000
(6,000/20,000)		30%	
(14,000/20,000)			70%

(W2) **Capital allowances**

	Pool	Expensive car	Allowances
	£	£	£
	£	£	£
TWDV b/f	7,400	16,200	
Additions (with AIA)			
Printer	400		
Less AIA	(400)		400
	Nil		
WDA (20%)	(1,480)		1,480
WDA (Restricted)(W1)		(3,000) × 70%	2,100
TWDV c/f	5,920	13,200	
Total allowances			3,980

Tutorial note:

There is no temporary 40% FYA in this case as all of the expenditure is covered by the AIA.

(b) **Income tax computation – 2009/10**

	£
Trading income	29,990
Less Personal allowance	(6,475)
Taxable income	23,515
Income tax liability (£23,515 x 20%)	4,703

Capital gains tax – 2009/10

	£
Sale proceeds	320,000
Less Cost	(188,000)
Capital gain	132,000
Less Rollover relief (W)	(22,000)
Chargeable gain	110,000
Less Annual exemption	(10,100)
Taxable gain	99,900
Capital gains tax (£99,900 x 18%)	17,982

Working: Rollover relief

The sale proceeds from the disposal of the shop are not fully reinvested, and so £110,000 (£320,000 – £210,000) of the capital gain cannot be rolled over.

Rollover relief will therefore be £22,000 (£132,000 – £100,000).

(c) **Retention of business records**

- The business records for 2009/10 must be retained until 31 January 2016, being five years after the filing date of 31 January 2011.

- As Tony is in business during 2009/10, he must retain the records relating to the capital gain until the same date.

- A failure to retain records can result in a penalty of up to £3,000. However, the maximum penalty will only be charged in serious cases.

15 FOO DEE (ADAPTED)

Key answer tips

Part (a) requires a simple adjustment of profit and capital allowances computation which should not have caused any problems if you remembered that it is a 9 month accounting period and therefore the WDAs are time apportioned.

In part (b) the opening year basis of assessment rules have to be applied to calculate the trading income assessment for 2009/10 for inclusion in the income tax computation.

The employment income computation was complicated in working out the business mileage claim allowance to be deducted. Knowledge of the ordinary commuting rules and temporary workplace rules are tested.

Otherwise the income tax, capital gains tax and self-assessment parts were straightforward.

This style of question is often examined, so you need to make sure you know the approach and techniques required.

(a) **Trading profit – period ended 30 September 2010**

	£
Net profit	88,780
Add: Depreciation	3,500
Motor expenses (£4,200 × 2,000/6,000)	1,400
Private accommodation (£12,800 × 1/4)	3,200
	96,880
Less: Capital allowances (W)	(40,440)
Trading profit	56,440

Working: Capital allowances

	Pool £	Private use car £		Allowances £
Additions (no AIA or FYA)				
Car (111 – 160 g/km)		14,600		
Additions (with AIA and FYA)				
Equipment	41,200			
Less AIA (Note)	(37,500)			37,500
	3,700			
WDA (20% x 9/12)(Note)		(2,190)	× 4/6	1,460
FYA (40%)	(1,480)			1,480
	2,220			
TWDV c/f	2,220	12,410		
Total allowances				40,440

Tutorial note:

Capital allowances on new car purchases are now calculated based on the CO_2 emissions of the car.

As the car purchased in this question has CO_2 emissions of between 111 – 160 g/km, it is eligible for a writing down allowance (WDA) at 20%. The WDA then needs to be adjusted for the short accounting period and for the private use by Foo Dee, as only the business use proportion of the allowance can be claimed.

The business mileage is 4,000 out of 6,000 miles.

Note that both the WDA and the AIA are time apportioned by 9/12 as the accounting period is only 9 months long. The maximum AIA available is therefore £37,500 (£50,000 x 9/12).

The excess is eligible for the temporary FYA of 40%.

(b)   **Income tax computation – 2009/10**

	Total £	Other £	Savings £	Dividends £
Salary	38,000			
Less Pension contributions				
(£38,000 × 6%)	(2,280)			
	35,720			
Relocation costs (Note)	4,900			
	40,620			
Expense claim (W1)	(1,820)			
Employment income	38,800	38,800		
Trading profit (W2)	18,813	18,813		
Building society interest				
(£640 × 100/80)	800		800	
Dividends (£360 × 100/90)	400			400
Total income	58,813	57,613	800	400
Less Personal allowance	(6,475)	(6,475)		
Taxable income	52,338	51,138	800	400

Income tax

£		
39,400	at 20% (Other income) (W3)	7,880
11,738	at 40% (Other income)	4,695
51,138		
800	at 40% (Savings income)	320
400	at 32·5% (Dividend income)	130
52,338		

Income tax liability	13,025
Less Tax suffered at source	
Dividends (£400 at 10%)	(40)
PAYE	(8,609)
Building society interest (£800 at 20%)	(160)
Income tax payable	4,216

Tutorial note:

Only £8,000 of relocation costs are exempt, and so the taxable benefit is £4,900 (£12,900 – £8,000).

Workings

(W1) Expense claim

Ordinary commuting (travel between home and the permanent workplace, including journeys to turn off the fire alarm) and private travel do not qualify for relief.

The travel to a temporary workplace qualifies as it is for a period lasting less than 24 months.

Business mileage is therefore 4,550 miles (750 + 3,800)

Expenses claim = (4,550 miles x 40p) = £1,820

(W2) Trading income assessment – 2009/10

9 months ended 30 September 2010	
Trading profit	£56,440

Tax year	Basis of assessment	
2009/10	Opening year rules apply	
	Actual basis (1.1.2010 – 5.4.2010)	
	(£56,440 x 3/9)	£18,813

(W3) Extension of basic rate band

	£
Basic rate band threshold	37,400
Plus Personal pension contribution (£1,600 x 100/80)	2,000
Extended basic rate band	39,400

Capital gains tax liability – 2009/10

	£
Capital gain	17,100
Less Annual exemption	(10,100)
Taxable gain	7,000
Capital gains tax (£7,000 x 18%)	1,260

Balancing payment and payments on account

- No payments on account have been made, so the balancing payment for 2009/10 due on 31 January 2011 is £5,476 (£4,216 + £1,260).

- Payments on account are not required for CGT, so the payments on account for 2010/11 will be £2,108 (£4,216 × 50%).

- These will be due on 31 January and 31 July 2011.

(c) **Consequences of not paying the balancing payment**

- Interest is charged where a balancing payment is paid late. This will run from 31 January 2011 to 31 May 2011.

- The interest charge will be £46 (£5,476 × 2·5% × 4/12).

- In addition, a 5% surcharge of £274 (£5,476 × 5%) will be imposed as the balancing payment is not made within 28 days of the due date.

16   SAM AND KIM WHITE   *Walk in the footsteps of a top tutor*

Key answer tips

A classic husband and wife scenario; one employed, the other self-employed and some joint income.

The adjustment of profits was straightforward, except that some may not have known what to do with the patent royalties. In fact, if you did nothing – that was the right thing to do!

Be careful with the calculation of the private use / business use proportion of the car and remember the impact private use has on both the adjustment of profits computation and capital allowances.

Part (c) requires some thought about tax planning advice for a husband and wife; investing in ISAs and transferring assets generating income from the higher rate taxpayer to the lower rate taxpayer.

The highlighted words in the written sections are key phrases that markers are looking for.

Tutor's top tip:

The key to success when you are doing an adjustment of profits is to think about what, if anything, has already been included in the profit and loss account.

If an expense is disallowable and it has been deducted, you need to add it back. If it hasn't been deducted you do nothing.

Conversely, if an expense is allowable and it has been deducted, you include it with a zero adjustment. If it hasn't been deducted, you need to deduct it.

Read the question carefully here!

As the question just asks you to 'calculate', you do not need to explain why you are making adjustments, although you do need to make sure you label your answers so that the marker can see which expenses you are adding back or deducting.

It is also important to include all the major items of expenditure in the question, showing a zero for the adjustment figure where the expenditure is allowable.

Always show your workings if the adjustment figure is not clear from the question.

(a)   **Sam White**

Trading profit for the year ended 5 April 2010

		£
Net profit		50,000
Add:	Depreciation	7,600
	Motor expenses (£8,800 × 20%) (W1)	1,760
	Patent royalties (Note 1)	0
	Breach of contract fees (Note 2)	0
	Accountancy fees (Note 2)	0
	Personal capital gains tax advice	320
	Gifts to customers (£560 + £420) (Note 3)	980
	Own consumption	1,480
		62,140
Less:	Use of office (£5,120 × 1/8)	(640)
	Private telephone (£1,600 × 25%)	(400)
	Capital allowances (W2)	(5,360)
Trading profit		55,740

Tutorial note:

1. Patent royalties are allowed as a deduction when calculating the trading profit, because they are for the purposes of the trade. As they have already been deducted in arriving at the profit, no adjustment is required.

2. The fees incurred for accountancy and the breach of contract defence are allowable as incurred wholly and exclusively for the purporses of the trade.

3. Gifts to customers are an allowable deduction if they cost less than £50 per recipient per year, are not of food, drink, tobacco or vouchers exchangeable for goods and carry a conspicuous advertisement for the company making the gift.

Workings

(W1) **Private / business mileage**

	Total	Private	Business
Total miles	25,000		
Visiting suppliers	(5,000)		5,000
Allocate (25:75)	20,000	5,000	15,000
		5,000	20,000
(5,000/25,000)		20%	
(20,000/25,000)			80%

Tutor's top tip:

A familiar full blown capital allowances computation is given in the workings to this answer to show clearly how the allowances are calculated.

However, where there are not many transactions it is perfectly acceptable to do one or two lines and just calculate the allowances available on each asset acquired rather than a full computation.

If you do this however, be careful and make sure you explain your calculations clearly.

(W2) **Capital allowances**

	Pool £	Expensive car £	Allowances £
TWDV b/f	14,800	20,200	
WDA (20%)	(2,960)		2,960
WDA (Restricted)(W1)		(3,000) × 80%	2,400
TWDV c/f	11,840	17,200	
Total allowances			5,360

(b) **Sam White**

Income tax computation – 2009/10

Tutor's top tip:

As long as your calculation of Sam's income tax is based on your trading profit from part (a), you can still score full marks here in this part.

However, it is very important that you show your workings clearly so that the marker can see that you have applied the correct rates to each type of income.

	Total £	Other income £	Savings income £
Trading profit	55,740	55,740	
Interest received (£1,200 × 100/80) × 1/2	750		750
Total income	56,490	55,740	750
Less Personal Allowance	(6,475)	(6,475)	
Taxable income	50,015	49,265	750

	£		£
Income tax:			
On Other income	37,400	@ 20%	7,480
On Other income	11,865	@ 40%	4,746
	49,265		
On Savings income	750	@ 40%	300
	50,015		
Income tax liability			12,526

Kim White
Income tax computation – 2009/10

Tutor's top tip:

Watch the dates very carefully here!

Where a benefit has only been available for part of the tax year, it must be time apportioned.

However, if you forget to do this, you will only be penalised once and could still score full marks for the calculation of tax, as explained above.

	Total	Other income	Savings income
	£	£	£
Salary	21,600		
Beneficial loan (£12,000 x 4.75% x 10/12)	475		
	22,075		
Less Expense claim (W)	(4,625)		
Employment income	17,450	17,450	
Interest received (£1,200 × 100/80) x 1/2	750		750
Total income	18,200	17,450	750
Less Interest paid (Note)	(140)	(140)	
	18,060	17,310	750
Less Personal Allowance	(6,475)	(6,475)	
Taxable income	11,585	10,835	750

	£		£
Income tax:			
On Other income	10,835	@ 20%	2,167
On Savings income	750	@ 20%	150
	11,585		
Income tax liability			2,317

Tutorial note:

The loan interest paid of £140 is eligible for relief since the loan was used by Kim to finance expenditure for a relevant purpose. The interest is quoted and is paid gross.

Working: Expense claim

Ordinary commuting (travel between home and the permanent workplace) does not qualify for relief. The travel to a temporary workplace qualifies as it is for a period lasting less than 24 months.

Business mileage is therefore 12,500 miles (11,200 + 1,300)

Expense claim is therefore:

	£
10,000 miles at 40p	4,000
2,500 miles at 25p	625
	4,625

(c)   **Husband and wife tax planning suggestions**

Tutor's top tip:

It should be clear from your answer to part (a) that Sam is a higher rate taxpayer and Kim is a basic rate taxpayer.

Make sure you set out the rates of tax that each will be subject to, and have a go at calculating the tax saving that could be achieved here.

Individual savings accounts

- Sam can invest up to a maximum of £3,600 each tax year into a cash ISA.

- Kim is aged over 50 and can therefore invest up to a maximum of £5,100 into a cash ISA.

- Interest received from ISAs is exempt from income tax, so Sam will save tax at the rate of 40%. Kim will save tax at the rate of 20%.

- They received a 6% gross interest rate of return on their investment in the building society, calculated as:

  Gross interest = £1,200 x 100/80 = £1,500

  Gross rate of interest = £1,500/£25,000 = 6%

- Sam will therefore save tax on gross interest of £216 (£3,600 x 6%) and Kim on £306 (£5,100 × 6%) if they invested in ISAs.

  This is assuming that the interest that will be received on the ISA will be the same rate of interest as their existing investment.

Transfer to Kim's sole name

- Sam pays income tax at the rate of 40%, whilst Kim's basic rate tax band is not fully utilised.

- Transferring the building society deposit account into Kim's sole name would therefore save tax of £150 (£750 × (40% – 20%)).

Examiner's report

This question was very well answered by the majority of candidates.

In part (a) the adjustments for use of office, business use of a private telephone and own consumption caused the most problems, with a number of candidates being unsure as to whether adjustments should be added or subtracted in order to arrive at the tax adjusted trading profit.

Part (b) was also well answered, with only the expense claim for the business mileage causing any difficulty. This was often treated as a benefit rather than as an expense.

Part (c) was answered reasonably well, especially the transfer into the spouse's sole name. Many candidates correctly calculated the amount of income tax saving.

ACCA marking scheme			
			Marks
(a)	Net profit		0.5
	Depreciation		0.5
	Motor expenses		1.5
	Patent royalties		1.0
	Professional fees		1.5
	Gifts to customers		1.0
	Use of office		1.0
	Private telephone		1.0
	Own consumption		1.0
	Capital allowances	– Pool	1.0
		– Motor car	1.0
			——
			11.0
			——

		Marks
(b)	Sam White	
	Trading profit	0.5
	Building society interest	1.0
	Personal allowance	0.5
	Income tax	1.0
	Kim White	
	Salary	0.5
	Beneficial loan	1.0
	Expense claim	2.0
	Building society interest	0.5
	Loan interest	1.0
	Personal allowance	0.5
	Income tax	1.5
		———
		10.0
		———
(c)	Individual savings accounts	
	Limit	1.0
	Tax saving	1.0
		———
		2.0
		———
	Transfer to Kim's sole name	
	Tax rates	1.0
	Tax saving	1.0
		———
		2.0
		———
Total		25.0
		———

17 DOMINGO, ERIGO AND FARGO *Walk in the footsteps of a top tutor*

Key answer tips

This question involved preparing three separate income tax computations which covered a broad spectrum of income tax topics, tested compliance knowledge of self assessment and due dates of payment of tax.

The requirements and mark allocation are very clear.

Although there is a wide coverage of the syllabus, all the topics are covered at a basic level and should therefore have been manageable.

Tutor's top tips:

For part (a) a systematic approach is needed, taking one individual at a time, and therefore breaking up the information given into smaller, manageable chunks.

As you read the question it is useful to highlight all the information you will need for the income tax computations, and then as you use this information tick each item, so you can easily check you have included everything.

Remember not to ignore exempt income, as credit is given for stating that it is exempt, even though you do NOT include the figure in your computation. Remember not to get held up on any one calculation.

Always ensure that you read the question carefully. The requirement is to calculate income tax liability. Therefore do not waste time calculating income tax payable as this will not gain you any additional marks.

Make the marker your friend, if you keep your calculations clear and easy to read you will score much higher marks. Always ensure your workings are clearly labelled.

(a) (i) Domingo Gomez

Income tax computation – 2009/10

	£
Pensions (£4,500 + £2,300)	6,800
Building society interest (£15,200 x 100/80)	19,000
Interest from savings certificate (exempt)	Nil
	———
Total income	25,800
Less Personal allowance (W)	(8,040)
	———
Taxable income	17,760
	———

Tutorial note:

Interest from savings certificates is always exempt from tax.

This income is not the same as interest from a National Savings and Investment Bank account, which is taxable and would be received gross.

Make sure you read the question closely and have identified the income correctly.

Income tax

£		£
2,440 at 10% (Note)		244
15,320 at 20%		3,064
———		
17,760		
———		———
Income tax liability		3,308
		———

Tutorial note:

1. *The non-savings income is fully covered by the personal allowance, so the first £2,440 of savings income is taxed at the starting rate of 10%.*

2. *No tax relief is available in respect of the donations as they were not made under the Gift Aid scheme.*

    Making charitable donations without using the Gift Aid scheme is only beneficial to non-taxpayers. In this situation it would have enabled the charity to claim an additional £75 (£300 x 20/80) with no additional cost to Domingo.

Working: Personal age allowance

	£	£
PAA (aged 67)		9,490
Less Abatement: Total income	25,800	
Income limit	(22,900)	
Excess	2,900 x ½	(1,450)
Reduced PAA		8,040

(ii)   Erigo Gomez
Income tax computation – 2009/10

	£
Salary	36,000
Relocation costs (W1)	3,400
Pension contributions (£36,000 x 6%)	(2,160)
Charitable payroll deductions (£12 x 100)	(1,200)
Mileage allowance (W2)	(2,400)
Employment income	33,640
Less Personal allowance	(6,475)
Taxable income	27,165
Income tax liability (£27,165 at 20%)	5,433

Workings

(W1) Relocation costs

Only £8,000 of relocation costs are exempt, and so the taxable benefit is £3,400 (£11,400 – £8,000).

(W2) **Mileage allowance**

The mileage allowance received will be tax-free, and Erigo can make the following expense claim:

	£
10,000 miles at 40p	4,000
8,000 miles at 25p	2,000
	6,000
Mileage allowance (18,000 at 20p)	(3,600)
	2,400

Tutorial note:

Charitable donations via a payroll deduction scheme receive full tax relief at source as they are deducted from employment income before it is taxed.

This is exactly the same treatment as pension contributions into an employer's scheme.

(iii) **Fargo Gomez**
Income tax computation – 2009/10

	£
Trading profit (£64,800 – £2,600)	62,200
Less Capital allowances (W1)	(1,100)
Total income	61,100
Less Personal allowance	(6,475)
Taxable income	54,625

Tutorial note:

Although Fargo's business had commenced during the year, there is no adjustment required under the opening year rules.

This is because Fargo has selected a year end of 5 April, which is the only date which will avoid any overlap profits arising.

Income tax

£			£
45,600	at 20% (W2)		9,120
9,025	at 40%		3,610
54,625			
Income tax liability			12,730

Workings:

(W1) **Capital allowances**

Fargo's period of account is nine months' long so the capital allowances in respect of his motor car are:

(£11,000 x 20% x 9/12) = £1,650 x (16,000/24,000) = £1,100

(W2) **Extension of basic rate band**

	£
Basic rate band threshold	37,400
Plus Personal pension contribution (gross)	5,200
Gross Gift Aid donation (£2,400 x 100/80)	3,000
	———
Extended basic rate band	45,600
	———

Tutorial note:

1. *The advertising expenditure incurred during May 2008 is pre-trading, and is treated as incurred on 6 July 2008. An adjustment is therefore required.*

2. *Capital allowances on new purchases of cars are calculated based on their CO_2 emissions. As Fargo's car has CO_2 emissions of between 111 – 160g/km the car is eligible for a writing down allowance at 20%. This then needs to be adjusted for the short accounting period and for the private use by Fargo.*

3. *Charitable donations under Gift Aid are grossed up before being used to extend the basic rate band. This is exactly the same treatment as pension contributions to a private pension scheme.*

(b)   Self assessment deadlines

Tutor's top tips:

There are easy marks to be had in part (b), provided you have learnt the filing deadlines.

It is very important that you learn the self assessment rules and key dates for filing and payments of tax, as these are very often examined.

- Unless the return is issued late, the latest date that Domingo and Erigo can file paper self-assessment tax returns for 2009/10 is 31 October 2010.

- If Domingo completes a paper tax return by 31 October 2010 then HM Revenue and Customs will prepare a self-assessment tax computation on his behalf.

- Fargo has until 31 January 2011 to file his self-assessment tax return for 2009/10 online.

(c)   Retention of records

Tutor's top tips:

Again these are easy marks if you have learnt the rules.

As there are three marks available, it is clear that 3 separate points must be made, which gives you a clue that the filing deadlines are not the same for all three brothers.

- Domingo and Erigo were not in business during 2009/10, so their records must be retained until one year after 31 January following the tax year, which is 31 January 2012.

- Fargo was in business during 2009/10, so all of his records (both business and non-business) must be retained until five years after 31 January following the tax year, which is 31 January 2016.

- A failure to retain records for 2009/10 could result in a penalty of up to £3,000. However, the maximum penalty will only be charged in serious cases.

Examiner's report

This question was very well answered by the majority of candidates.

In part (a) many candidates did not appreciate that donations to charity not made under gift aid are simply ignored, and some candidates missed the income limit for the age-related personal allowance. The expense claim in respect of the business mileage driven by the employed brother often caused problems. Either it was incorrectly calculated, or it was treated as a benefit.

Part (b) was well answered.

In part (c) few candidates appreciated that the period of retention differs between taxpayers in business and those not in business. However, virtually all candidates were aware of the £3,000 penalty.

ACCA marking scheme		Marks
(a)(i)	**Domingo Gomez**	
	Pensions	1.0
	Building society interest	1.0
	Interest from savings certificates	0.5
	Donations	0.5
	Personal allowance	2.0
	Income tax	1.0
		———
		6.0
		———
(ii)	**Erigo Gomez**	
	Salary	0.5
	Pension contributions	1.0
	Charitable payroll deductions	1.0
	Relocation costs	1.0
	Mileage allowance	1.5
	Personal allowance	0.5
	Income tax	0.5
		———
		6.0
		———

		Marks
(iii)	**Fargo Gomez**	
	Trading profit	0.5
	Pre-trading expenditure	1.0
	Capital allowances	2.0
	Personal allowance	0.5
	Extension of basic rate band	2.0
	Income tax	1.0
		7.0
(b)	Paper returns	2.0
	Return filed online	1.0
		3.0
(c)	Domingo and Erigo	1.0
	Fargo	1.0
	Penalty	1.0
		3.0
Total		25.0

18   ANDREW ZOOM   *Walk in the footsteps of a top tutor*

Key answer tips

A classic tax exam question on self-employed versus employed which was not difficult, but presented in a scenario requiring the application of knowledge to the particular situation given.

This is a newer style of question for F6 students, but is useful preparation for those planning to move on to P6.

Tutor's top tips:

It is important to learn the rules for determining whether an individual is self employed.

However, it is not enough here to simply state those rules, instead they must be applied to the situation given.

Even without detailed knowledge of the rules here, common sense suggestions should enable students to pick up some marks.

(a)   **Factors indicating employment**

- Andrew is under the control of Slick-Productions Ltd.
- Andrew is not taking any financial risk.
- Andrew works a set number of hours, is paid by the hour and is paid for overtime.
- Andrew cannot profit from sound management.
- Andrew is required to do the work personally.
- There is an obligation to accept work that is offered.
- Andrew does not provide his own equipment.

(b)   (i)   **Treated as an employee**

Tutor's top tips:

Part (b) involves straightforward income tax and NIC calculations, which you should be able to score well on, regardless of your answer to part (a).

Don't miss the opportunity to gain these easy marks by being put off by the first part of the question, or by running out of time.

Andrew's income tax liability for 2009/10 will be:

	£
Employment income	50,000
Less Personal allowance	(6,475)
Taxable income	43,525

Income tax	£	£
37,400	at 20% (W2)	7,480
6,125	at 40%	2,450
43,525		
Income tax liability		9,930

Class 1 NIC for 2009/10 will be:		
(£43,875 – £5,715) x 11%	4,198	
(£50,000 – £43,875) x 1%	61	
		4,259
		14,189

(ii)   **Treated as self-employed**

		£
Income tax liability:		
Andrew's trading profit for 2009/10 will be £50,000, so his income tax liability will be unchanged (as above)		9,930
Class 2 NIC for 2009/10 will be (52 weeks x £2.40)		125
Class 4 NIC for 2009/10 will be:		
(£43,875 – £5,715) x 8%	3,053	
(£50,000 – £43,875) x 1%	61	
		3,114
		13,169

Examiner's report

This question was very well answered by the majority of candidates.

However, in part (a) only a few candidates pointed out that the taxpayer did not take any financial risk or profit from sound management.

The only common mistake in part (b) was that candidates often based their NIC calculations on the taxable income figure rather than on employment income or trading profit.

ACCA marking scheme		
		Marks
(a)	Control	0.5
	Financial risk	0.5
	Basis of remuneration	1.0
	Sound management	0.5
	Required to do the work personally	0.5
	Obligation to accept work offered	0.5
	Equipment	0.5
		4.0
(b)(i)	**Treated as an employee**	
	Employment income	0.5
	Personal allowance	0.5
	Income tax liability	0.5
	Class 1 NIC	1.5
		3.0
(ii)	**Treated as self employed**	
	Income tax liability	0.5
	Class 2 NIC	1.0
	Class 4 NIC	1.5
		3.0
Total		10.0

TRADING LOSSES

19   NORMA

Key answer tips

The first part required the computation of taxable income for five tax years before considering loss relief. Easy marks should have been gained here in laying out proforma computations and filling in the easy numbers before applying the opening and closing year rules to establish the trading income assessments. A loss arises in the final tax year and so the trading income assessment in that year will be £Nil.

The second part involved consideration of the options available for loss relief, including a terminal loss.

It is important to communicate to the examiner that you know the loss relief rules, however you must apply the knowledge to the specific facts of the question.

Norma's taxable income before loss relief

	2005/06 £	2006/07 £	2007/08 £	2008/09 £	2009/10 £
Trading income (W)	25,250	17,000	14,000	5,000	Nil
Employment income (£8,000 × 10/12)					6,667
Interest income	2,000	2,000	2,000	2,000	2,000
Total income	27,250	19,000	16,000	7,000	8,667
Personal allowance	(6,475)	(6,475)	(6,475)	(6,475)	(6,475)
Taxable income	20,775	12,525	9,525	525	2,192
Chargeable gain				40,000	

Working: Trading income

Tax year	Basis of assessment	£	£
2005/06	Actual basis (1.5.05 – 5.4.06)		
	Period to 31.12.05	21,000	
	1.1.06 – 5.4.06 (£17,000 × 3/12)	4,250	
			25,250
2006/07	Year ended 31.12.06		17,000
2007/08	Year ended 31.12.07		14,000
2008/09	Year ended 31.12.08		5,000
2009/10	Year of cessation		
	Period to 31 May 2009	(10,000)	
	Less: Overlap profits (1.1.06 – 5.4.06)		
	(£17,000 × 3/12)	(4,250)	
	Trading loss / Trading assessment	(14,250)	Nil

Options available to utilise loss arising in period ended 31 May 2009

(1)   **Relief against total income**

The loss arising in 2009/10 can be set against total income in 2009/10 and/or 2008/09.

(i)   Setting the loss against total income of 2009/10 would reduce total income to £Nil, would waste the personal allowance and save tax at 10% and 20%.

The remaining loss of £5,583 (£14,250 – £8,667) could be offset against total income of 2008/09, wasting most of the personal allowance and saving tax at 10% (see Tutorial Note).

(ii)   Setting the loss against total income of 2008/09 would reduce total income to £Nil, would waste the personal allowance and save tax at 10%.

The remaining loss of £7,250 (£14,250 – £7,000) could be offset against total income of 2009/10, which would waste part of the personal allowance and save tax at 10% and 20%.

Tutorial note:

The rate of tax saving in 2008/09 is 10% because Norma's taxable income consists entirely of savings income. As the question says you should assume that the 2009/10 rates and allowances apply throughout, savings income is taxed at 10% where it falls in the first £2,440 of taxable income.

In 2009/10 Norma also has savings income falling in the first £2,440 of taxable income.

Once a claim has been made to offset trading losses against total income, a further claim can be made to offset any remaining losses against chargeable gains.

Accordingly, the loss remaining in 2008/09 could be set against the chargeable gain arising in that year, but this only saves tax at 18%.

Tutorial note:

*An extended three year carry back claim against **trading income** could be made **after** considering a normal claim against **total income**.*

However, in the closing years, a terminal loss relief claim is preferable as it gives the same relief as the extended carry back relief, but there is no £50,000 restriction.

(2)   **Terminal loss relief**

The loss arising in the final 12 months of trading can be set against:
- available trading profits
- in the year of cessation, and
- the three preceding tax years
- on a last-in-first-out (LIFO) basis.

Calculation of terminal loss

£

(1)   6 April before cessation to date of cessation

6.4.09 – 31.5.09   ($\frac{2}{5} \times £10,000$)   4,000

(2)   12 months before cessation to 5 April before cessation

£

1.6.08 – 31.12.08 ($\frac{7}{12} \times £5,000$)   2,917   Profit

1.1.09 – 5.4.09   ($\frac{3}{5} \times £10,000$)   (6,000)   Loss

                                             (3,083)   Net Loss   3,083

(3)   Overlap relief

1.1.06 – 5.4.06   ($\frac{3}{12} \times £17,000$)   4,250

                                                                      ———

Terminal loss   11,333

                                                                      ———

Utilisation of terminal loss

Norma has no trading profits in 2009/10, the year of cessation.

The terminal loss can therefore be carried back against the trading profits arising in the preceding three years, on a LIFO basis, as follows:

	2007/08	2008/09
	£	£
Trading income	14,000	5,000
Less: Terminal loss relief	(6,333)	(5,000)
	———	———
	7,667	Nil
Interest income	2,000	2,000
	———	———
Net income	9,667	2,000
Less: Personal allowance	(6,475)	(6,475)
	———	———
Taxable income	3,192	Nil
	———	———

The terminal loss reduces taxable income in 2008/09 to £Nil, wasting the personal allowance and saving tax at 10%.

The remaining loss of £6,333 (£11,333 – £5,000) is then offset against the taxable income in 2007/08, saving tax at 20%.

Tutorial note:

If the trader does not have a 31 March (or 5 April) year end you should be looking for overlap relief. The overlap relief increases the loss of the final year and is included in the calculation of the terminal loss.

20 MALCOLM (ADAPTED)

Key answer tips

A loss question with limited other income such that the utilisation of the loss ends up wasting personal allowances and saves little tax under any option.

The calculation of the available losses in the opening years may have given some problems. However, remember that the calculation of the actual amount of the loss is not as important as making sure that you always consider and explain all options available for utilising the loss.

Calculation of loss relief

2008/09 – opening year	£	£
Actual basis (1.8.08 to 5.4.09)		
Period ended 30.11.08	(17,000)	
Period ended 5.4.09 (1.12.08 – 5.4.09) (4/12 × £30,000)	(10,000)	
	———	(27,000)

2009/10 – second year		
Year ended 30.11.09 (CYB)	(30,000)	
Less Loss in period 1.12.08 – 5.4.09 (cannot overlap losses)	10,000	
	———	(20,000)

Allocation of loss relief – to give the best tax saving

	2007/08 £	2008/09 £	2009/10 £	2010/11 £
Trading income		Nil	Nil	24,000
Less Loss relief b/f – 2009/10 Loss		–	–	(20,000)
		———	———	———
		Nil	Nil	4,000
Employment income	18,000	15,000	–	–
Interest income (£3,000 x 100/80)	3,750	3,750	3,750	3,750
	———	———	———	———
Total income	21,750	18,750	3,750	7,750
Less Loss relief – 2008/09 Loss	(21,750)	(5,250)		
	———	———	———	———
Net income	Nil	13,500	3,750	7,750
	———	———	———	———

Loss memorandum	2008/09 Loss £	2009/10 Loss £
Trading loss (see above)	27,000	20,000
Less Relief against total income		
In 2007/08	(21,750)	
In 2008/09	(5,250)	
	———	———
Loss carried forward	Nil	20,000
	———	———

Rationale for utilisation of losses

2008/09 Loss

Relief against total income in 2007/08

Although there is wastage of personal allowances in 2007/08, a claim against total income in this year is considered worthwhile because:

- it results in a tax saving of £3,055 ((£21,750 – £6,475) x 20%)

- there will be a repayment of income tax already paid, with interest, and

- the absence of a preferable alternative.

Relief against total income in 2008/09

The utilisation of the balance of the 2008/09 loss of £5,250 leaves in charge £13,500 which will absorb the year's personal allowance and the excess is taxed at 20%.

The tax saving is £1,050 (£5,250 x 20%).

2009/10 Loss

Carry forward of loss against trading income

The whole of the 2009/10 loss of £20,000 has been carried forward against the 2010/11 trading income. The remaining £4,000 trading income plus the interest income will absorb the year's personal allowances and the balance of £1,275 (£7,750 – £6,475) will be taxed at 10% (see Tutorial note).

The overall tax saving will be:

	£
Trading income not taxed (£20,000 x 20%)	4,000
Savings income taxed at 10% rather than 20% (£1,275 x 10%) (Note)	128
	4,128

For 2009/10, the income left in charge will be interest income of £3,750, which will absorb part of the year's personal allowance.

No tax will be payable and therefore there is no advantage in making a claim in that year.

Tutorial note:

The personal allowance will be matched firstly against the trading income, leaving the savings income to be taxed last.

Any 'savings income' falling into the first £2,440 of taxable income is taxed at 10%.

Therefore, if £1,275 of taxable income remains after a loss relief claim and the deduction of the personal allowance, it must be Savings income and will be taxed at 10%.

If the loss relief claim is not made, all of the savings income would have been taxed at 20%, therefore as a result of the claim, a 10% additional tax saving is made.

Alternative utilisation of the 2009/10 Loss

The alternative utilisation of the 2009/10 loss would have been to claim relief of £13,500 against the remaining income of the previous year, 2008/09.

This would have wasted the personal allowance in that year and only saved tax of £1,405 ((£13,500 – £6,475) x 20%).

However, it would have facilitated a claim against the capital gain of £10,000 for the remaining loss of £6,500 (£20,000 – £13,500) in 2008/09 as follows.

	£
Capital gain in year	12,000
Less Trading loss relief – remaining 2009/10 loss	(6,500)
Net gain	5,500
Less Annual exemption (restricted)	(5,500)
Taxable gain	Nil

As a result, the 2009/10 loss of £20,000 would have been utilised to save total tax of £1,747, comprising of the income tax saving of £1,405 (see above) and capital gains tax saving of £342 ((£12,000 – £10,100) x 18%).

The higher tax saving of £4,128 achieved by carrying the loss forward to the next year is therefore preferable.

Tutorial note:

*An extended three year carry back relief against **trading income** and special opening year loss relief against **total income** is available.*

However, the question avoided this extra complication by excluding information about earlier years.

21   LEONARDO

Key answer tips

An opening year loss relief question, requiring a calculation of the first few tax year assessments and consideration of loss claims available.

Part (b) should have provided easy marks in stating due dates for making elections.

You need to be aware that some of the time limits have changed in FA2009, making this area more potentially examinable in the 2010 exam sittings.

(a)   **Assessments**

Tax year	Basis period		£
2006/07	Actual basis		
	(1.9.06 – 5.4.07)	7/9 × £40,500	31,500
2007/08	First 12 months		
	(1.9.06 – 31.8.07)	£40,500 – (3/12 × £54,000)	27,000
2008/09	CYB (1.6.07 – 31.5.08)	Loss	Nil
2009/10	CYB (1.6.08 – 31.5.09)	Loss	Nil
2010/11	CYB (1.6.09 – 31.5.10)		9,000

Key answer tips

As Leonardo will not be making any significant profits in the foreseeable future there is no point in carrying losses forward, therefore offset the losses as soon as possible.

Loss memoranda

	£
Loss in 2008/09	
Loss in y/e 31.5.2008	54,000
Less Relief in 2007/08 – applying opening year rules (£54,000 x 3/12)	(13,500)
	40,500
Less Relief against total income in 2007/08	(27,000)
Less Special opening year loss relief in 2006/07	(13,500)
	Nil

	£
Loss in 2009/10	
Loss in y/e 31.5.2009	27,000
Less Special opening year loss relief in 2006/07 (£31,500 – £13,500)	(18,000)
Loss carried forward to 2010/11	9,000

Assessments after loss relief claims

	2006/07	2007/08	2008/09	2009/10	2010/11
	£	£	£	£	£
Trading income	31,500	27,000	Nil	Nil	9,000
Less Loss relief b/f	–	–	–	–	(9,000)
	31,500	27,000	Nil	Nil	Nil
Less Loss relief against total income					
– 2008/09 Loss		(27,000)			
Less Special opening year loss relief					
– 2008/09 Loss	(13,500)				
– 2009/10 Loss	(18,000)				
Net income	Nil	Nil	Nil	Nil	Nil

Tutorial note:

*Under special opening year loss provisions, losses that arise in the **first four tax years** of a trade may be set off against:*

- *the total income*
- *of the three years preceding the tax year of loss*
- *on a first-in-first-out (FIFO) basis.*

(b)   **Loss relief time limits**

(i)   **Special opening year loss relief and 'normal' loss relief against total income**

For claims to carry back losses in the first four years of a trade against income of the three preceding years, and claims to set-off losses against income of the year of the loss and income of the preceding year, the claim must be made:

−   within 12 months from 31 January next following the year of assessment in which the loss was sustained.

In the case of the loss sustained in the year ended 31 May 2008 (i.e. the loss in 2008/09), the claim must be made:

−   by 31 January 2011.

In the case of the loss sustained in the year ended 31 May 2009 (i.e. the loss in 2009/10), the claim must be made:

−   by 31 January 2012.

(ii)   Carry forward of losses

There is no specific statutory time limit on claims to carry forward losses against future trading income.

However, a claim to establish the amount of the loss to be carried forward must be made:

−   within four years from the end of the tax year in which the loss was sustained

In the case of the loss sustained in the year ended 31 May 2009 (i.e. the loss in 2009/10)

−   by 31 January 2014.

22   DEE ZYNE *Walk in the footsteps of a top tutor*

Key answer tips

An individual that is employed for part of the year, then sets up a business which is initially loss-making, is a common scenario in examination questions.

The calculation of the adjusted loss was straight forward provided you remember to time apportion WDAs in the opening period of account.

The employment income computation tested classic benefit rules and you were instructed to utilise the loss against the employment income.

Part (c) required consideration of alternative claims and it was fairly obvious why they would be more beneficial than a current year claim.

The highlighted words in the written sections are key phrases that markers are looking for.

Tutor's top tips:

In this question, Dee has 5 April as her year end, so the capital allowances are calculated for the period ended 5 April 2010.

However, where a sole trader chooses a different year end, remember that the capital allowances are always calculated for the accounting period before matching profits or losses to tax years.

(a)   **Tax adjusted trading loss – 2009/10**

	£
Trading loss	(11,440)
Patent royalties (Note)	(500)
Capital allowances (W)	(6,060)
	(18,000)

Tutorial note:

The patent royalties were incurred for the purposes of the trade and are therefore deductible in computing the tax adjusted trading loss. As they have not been accounted for in arriving at the loss, they must be adjusted for and will increase the loss.

Working – Capital allowances

	Pool £	Private use car £	Allowances £
	£	£	£	£
Additions (no AIA or FYA)			
Car (between 111 – 160 g/km)	10,400		
Car (> 160 g/km) (Note 1)		17,800	
Additions (with AIA and FYA)			
Computer	1,257		
Office furniture	2,175		
	———		
	3,432		
Less AIA (Note 2)	(3,432)		3,432
	———		
	Nil		
Less WDA (20% × $^9/_{12}$)	(1,560)		1,560
Less WDA (10% × $^9/_{12}$) (Note 3)		(1,335) × 80%	1,068
Less FYA (40%) (Note 4)	(Nil)		
	———	Nil	
TWDV c/f	8,840	16,465	
	———	———	
Total allowances			6,060
			———

Tutorial note:

1. Capital allowances on new purchases of cars are calculated based on their CO_2 emissions.

   The car with CO_2 emissions of between 111 – 160g/km is put in the main pool and is eligible for a writing down allowance at 20%.

   The car with CO_2 emissions of > 160 g/km is a private use car, has its own column and is eligible for a writing down allowance at 10%.

2. The maximum AIA and the WDAs are time apportioned because Dee's period of account is only nine months' long.

   However, the maximum AIA of £37,500 (£50,000 x 9/12) exceeds the total qualifying expenditure and therefore all of the expenditure is eligible for relief.

3. Only private use by the owner restricts capital allowances. Private use of the employee's motor car therefore does not affect the capital allowance claim, but will instead result in a benefit for the employee.

4. There is no temporary 40% FYA in this case as all of the expenditure is covered by the AIA.

(b)   **Income tax computation – 2009/10**

Tutor's top tips:

Watch the dates carefully here! Where a benefit has only been available for part of the tax year, it must be time apportioned.

If you are leaving out a benefit because it is exempt, it is always a good idea to say so, as there will often be a mark available for this.

Don't worry if your loss calculation in part (a) was not completely right. You could still score full marks in this section if your calculations are correct, based on your figures. Make sure you show your workings, so that the marker can see what rates you have used.

		£
Salary		26,000
Car benefit (W1)		940
Fuel benefit (W1)		1,310
Beneficial loan (W2)		356
Staff canteen (exempt) (Note 1)		Nil
		———
Employment income		28,606
Less Reliefs:		
Loan interest (Note 2)		(110)
Loss relief – current year		(18,000)
		———
Net income		10,496
Less Personal allowance		(6,475)
		———
Taxable income		4,021
		———
Income tax liability (£4,021 x 20%)		804
Less Tax suffered at source – PAYE		(8,530)
		———
Income tax repayable		(7,726)
		———

Tutorial note:

1.   The provision of meals in a staff canteen does not give rise to a taxable benefit.

2.   The loan interest qualifies as a deduction against total income since the loan was used by Dee to finance expenditure for a qualifying purpose.

      The qualifying interest is deducted from total income in priority to the loss relief.

Workings

(W1) **Car and fuel benefits**

CO_2 emissions = 218 g/km, available 3 months

	%
Petrol	15
Plus (215 – 135) × $^1/_5$	16
	—
Appropriate percentage	31
	—

	£
List price	17,500
Less Capital contribution	(1,500)
	——
	16,000
	——
Car benefit (£16,000 x 31% x 3/12)	1,240
Less Contribution for provision of car (£100 x 3)	(300)
	——
	940
Fuel benefit (£16,900 x 31% 3/12)	1,310
	——

(W2) **Beneficial loan**

Tutor's top tips:

Where the amount of the loan has changed during the year, you should always show both calculations of the benefit: the average and the precise method.

	£	£
Average method		
Loan at start of year	60,000	
Loan at end of year	15,000	
	——	
	75,000	
	——	
Average loan (£75,000 ÷ 2)	37,500	
	——	
Assessable benefit (£37,500 × 4.75% × 3/12)		445
		—
Precise method		
(£60,000 x 4.75% x 1/12)	237	
(£15,000 x 4.75% x 2/12)	119	
	——	
		356
		—

Dee will elect for the precise method to apply and the benefit will therefore be £356.

Tutorial note:

Remember that if the average method gives the lower benefit, the taxpayer can use the average method.

However, HMRC can insist that the precise method be used, if the difference is material.

(c)   **Alternative use of trading loss**

Tutor's top tips:

When you are describing use of losses, you must be very specific about exactly what the loss can be set against, and when. For example, don't just say "the loss can be set off in the current year", specify which tax year that is, and state that the loss can be set against total income.

The examiner has said that the use of section numbers is not required and is not encouraged at the expense of explaining the relief.

- The loss could have been claimed against total income for 2008/09.

- The loss is incurred within the first four years of trading, so a claim for special opening year loss relief could have been made against total income for the three years 2006/07 to 2008/09, earliest first.

- By claiming loss relief against her total income for 2009/10, Dee has relieved the loss entirely at the basic rate of 20% and reduced her income tax liability by £3,600 (£18,000 at 20%).

- As Dee's total income in the years 2003/04 to 2008/09 was £80,000, either of the alternative loss relief claims would have relieved the loss entirely at the higher rate of 40%, and resulted in an income tax refund of £7,200 (£18,000 at 40%).

Tutorial note:

The extended three year carry back relief introduced in FA2009 is not possible in the first year of the business as the relief is to carry back against trading profits and there will not have not been any prior to the first year!

23 SAMANTHA FABRIQUE (ADAPTED)

Key answer tips

A losses question requiring you to choose the best use of the loss.

Given the information about gains it should be fairly obvious that you need to consider a claim against capital gains. However, remember that this only saves tax at 18% and can only happen after a claim against total income has been made first in that year.

Part (a) should have provided easy marks listing the factors a taxpayer takes into account when deciding what to do with a loss.

(a) **Factors influencing choice of loss relief claims**

- The rate of income tax or capital gains tax at which relief will be obtained, with preference being given to income charged at the higher rate of 40%.
- The timing of the relief obtained, with a claim against total income/capital gains of the current year or preceding year resulting in earlier relief than a claim against future trading profits.
- The extent to which personal allowances and the capital gains annual exemption may be wasted.

Key answer tips

As long as you addressed the factors influencing the choice of relief, not what the relief options are, you should have scored well here.

(b) **Taxable income and gains**

	2006/07	2007/08	2008/09	2009/10	2010/11
	£	£	£	£	£
Trading income	21,400	40,100	21,600	Nil	10,500
Less Extended carry back relief	(9,900)	(40,100)	(Nil)	–	–
Less Loss relief b/f	–	–	–	–	(Nil)
	11,500	Nil	21,600	Nil	10,500
Interest	2,400	4,600	2,100	3,800	1,500
	13,900	4,600	23,700	3,800	12,000
Less Loss relief	–	–	(23,700)	(Nil)	–
	13,900	4,600	Nil	3,800	12,000
Less PA	(6,475)	(6,475)	(wasted)	(6,475)	(6,475)
Taxable income	7,425	Nil	Nil	Nil	5,525

	2006/07 £	2007/08 £	2008/09 £	2009/10 £	2010/11 £
Capital gains	10,400	18,800	23,300	Nil	11,000
Less Trading loss relief	–	–	(10,300)	–	–
	10,400	18,800	13,000	Nil	11,000
Less AE	(10,100)	(10,100)	(10,100)	(wasted)	(10,100)
	300	8,700	2,900	Nil	900

Loss memorandum

	£
Loss in 2009/10	84,000
Less Relief against total income:	
2009/10 (no claim as covered by PA)	(Nil)
2008/09	(23,700)
	60,300
Less Extended carry back relief:	
2007/08	(40,100)
2006/07 (£50,000 Max – £40,100)	(9,900)
Loss remaining	10,300
Less Relief against capital gains:	
2008/09	(10,300)
Loss carried forward	Nil

Utilisation of losses

Trading loss

Loss relief has been claimed:

- against total income for 2008/09,

- then an extended carry back claim against trading income, and

- then against the capital gains of 2008/09.

This gives relief at the earliest date and at the highest rates of tax.

Capital loss

The capital loss for 2009/10 is carried forward and set against the chargeable gains for 2010/11 (£11,000 – £900 = £10,100).

The brought forward loss is restricted and only needs to reduce gains down to equal the annual exempt amount.

The balance of the loss £2,500 (£3,400 – £900) is carried forward against future gains.

Tutorial note:

For 2008/09, if relief is claimed, the personal allowance is wasted in that year and the tax saving will be at 20% for income tax and 18% for capital gains.

Offsetting losses in 2009/10 however would utilise £3,800 of the loss, would waste the personal allowance and would not save any tax.

A claim against total income must be made before an extended carry back claim or relief against capital gains can be considered.

A carry back claim will save tax at 40% and 20% in 2007/08 and at 20% in 2006/07.

Carrying all of the loss forward would use £10,500 of loss, would waste the personal allowance and would only save tax of £1,105 (20% × £5,525).The remaining loss would not be relieved until subsequent years.

The optimum relief is therefore to claim against total income for 2008/09, then carry back against trading profits and then against the capital gains of 2008/09, since this gives relief at the earliest date and at the highest rates of tax.

Examiner's report

(Note that with FA2009 changes to the loss relief rules this question has been adapted and the mark allocation increased. It is now a more demanding question and not as short and straightforward as the original question to which this report refers.)

This question was generally not answered well.

Although it was technically the most demanding question on the paper, requiring a bit more thought than the other four questions, it was quite short and should not have presented too many difficulties for reasonably well prepared candidates.

In part (a) many candidates explained the loss reliefs that were available rather than the factors that must be taken into account when deciding which loss reliefs to actually claim.

In part (b) it was extremely disappointing to see the vast majority of candidates include the capital gains in their computation of taxable income. The capital gains annual exemption was often then deducted against the combined figure of taxable income and taxable gains.

Many candidates claimed loss relief against the total income for the year of the loss despite this income clearly being covered by the personal allowance.

Very few candidates, even if they showed the capital gains separately, claimed loss relief against capital gains.

	ACCA marking scheme	
		Marks
(a)	Rate of tax	1.0
	Timing of relief	1.0
	Personal allowance and annual exemption	1.0
		3.0
(b)	Trading income	0.5
	Loss relief – carry forward	1.0
	Building society interest	0.5
	Loss relief against total income	1.5
	Extended carry back relief	1.5
	Personal allowance	0.5
	Capital gains	1.5
	Loss relief against capital gains	1.0
	Explanation of most beneficial route	4.0
		12.0
Total		15.0

PARTNERSHIPS

24   PETER, QUINTON AND ROGER (ADAPTED)

Key answer tips

A loss making partnership presents a tricky problem and it is important to approach the computation in part (b) with care.

Firstly, profits / (losses) need to be allocated to each partner and then the opening year rules applied for each partner according to the date they joined the firm.

There are many loss relief options available. A brief mention of each is all you have time for in the exam. Be careful not to go into too much detail and there is no need to discuss the relative merits of each option in this question.

It is much better to mention all the reliefs available and applicable to the question succinctly than to talk about any one relief in great detail.

Part (2) concentrates on VAT topics. The VAT rules are not hard, they are however extensive and they will be examined. Emphasis in your revision must therefore be put into learning the VAT rules as there is a guaranteed 10% of the exam on VAT each sitting.

(1)   (a)   **Basis of assessment – Joining partners**

- Each partner is treated as a sole trader running a business.

- The commencement rules therefore apply when a partner joins the partnership, with the first year of assessment being on an actual basis (i.e. date of commencement to the following 5 April).

(b)   **Trading income assessments**

	Peter £	Quinton £	Roger £
2006/07			
Peter and Quinton			
Actual basis (1 January to 5 April 2007)			
(£40,000 × 1/2 × 3/12)	5,000	5,000	
2007/08			
Peter and Quinton			
CYB (y/e 31 December 2007)			
(£40,000 × 1/2)	20,000	20,000	
Roger			
Actual basis (1 January to 5 April 2008)			
(£90,000 × 1/3 × 3/12)			7,500
2008/09			
All partners – CYB (y/e 31 December 2008)			
(£90,000 × 1/3)	30,000	30,000	30,000

Tutorial note:

The commencement rules apply to:

- Peter and Quinton from 2006/07, as the partnership started on 1 January 2007.

- Roger from 2007/08, since he joined as a partner on 1 January 2008.

(c)   **Possible methods of relieving trading loss for 2009/10**

- Peter, Quinton and Roger each have a tax adjusted trading loss of £10,000 (£30,000 × 1/3) for 2009/10.

- Peter resigned as a partner on 31 December 2009. His unrelieved overlap profits of £5,000 (1 January to 5 April 2007) will therefore increase his loss to £15,000 (£10,000 + £5,000).

- Carry forward relief:

   Quinton and Roger can carry their share of the loss forward against their first available future trading profits arising in the same trade.

- Relief against total income:

   Peter, Quinton and Roger can claim relief against their total income for 2009/10 and/or 2008/09.

- Extended carry back relief:

   Peter, Quinton and Roger can carry back their share of the loss and claim relief against trading profits of 2006/07, 2007/08 and 2008/09, latest year first.

This claim can only be made after relief against total income has been considered.

- Special opening year loss relief:

  Peter, Quinton and Roger can carry back their share of the loss against their total income for 2006/07 to 2008/09, earliest year first.

- Terminal loss relief:

  Peter can carry back his share of the loss of the last 12 months trading against his trading profits for 2008/09.

  He has insufficient losses to carry back the loss any further. If he had more losses, he could carry back the loss and make a claim in respect of 2007/08 and 2006/07, in that order.

Key answer tips

The requirement is to "State the possible ways to relieve the losses". Therefore there will be no marks for discussing in detail the relative merits of each claim and which would be the most beneficial.

Remember that it is much better to mention all the reliefs available and applicable to the question succinctly than to talk about any one relief in great detail.

(2)   VAT interest and penalties

(a)   Default surcharge

A 'default surcharge' arises when a VAT return is submitted late, or a late payment of VAT due is made.

The 'surcharge default period' will initially be for 12 months and will only come to an end when no further defaults have occurred for a continuous 12-month period.

(b)   Default interest

HM Revenue & Customs may assess taxpayers to VAT where:

(i)   no returns have been submitted;

(ii)   evidence to back up the returns is deficient;

(iii)   the returns and/or information are considered to be incorrect.

Such assessments bear 'default interest' which runs from the original due date of payment of the VAT until the payment is made.

(c)   Errors on a VAT return

If Quentin discovers an error on a previous partnership VAT return, he must disclose the error to HM Revenue & Customs.

How he should notify them depends on the amount of the error.

If the error is up to the de minimus limit, it is acceptable to notify by making the necessary correction of the error on the next VAT return.

However, if the error exceeds the de minimus limit, separate notification is required.

The deminimus limit of error is the greater of:

(i)   £10,000, and

(ii)   1% of turnover

subject to an upper limit of £50,000.

If the error is not notified, the standard penalty for the submission of an incorrect VAT return may be levied. A penalty can also be levied even if disclosure is made, but it will be a lower amount and is likely to be reduced to Nil for an error below the deminimus limit.

Key answer tips

In each part, particularly part 2 (a) your study text contains more detail on the topic of the question. For example, for part 2 (a) you probably know the rates of surcharge (2%, 5% etc).

But these were not asked for.

The examiner has clearly spelt out his requirements and they should be followed to the letter. Avoid answering questions with all you know about a topic and make sure you address the specific requirements of each question.

25   XIO, YANA AND ZOE *Walk in the footsteps of a top tutor*

Key answer tips

A partnership question requiring an adjustment to profit computation and a capital allowances computation before allocating the profits between the partners and applying the basis of assessment rules.

In part (c), straight forward income tax computations were required

Tutor's top tips:

When you are calculating taxable profits for a partnership, remember to complete the steps in the right order:

Step 1:   Adjust the profits for the accounting period, for the whole partnership;

Step 2:   Calculate and deduct capital allowances for the accounting period, for the whole partnership;

> Step 3: Split the adjusted profit for the accounting period between the partners, based on the partnership agreement;
>
> Step 4: Assess each partner on his/her share of the profit, using the current year basis rules to match the profit to the correct tax year.
>
> This question was broken down into sections to encourage you to do this, and was made easier by the partnership using 5 April as the year end.
>
> Don't forget that the partners are all owners of the business, so any partners' private expenses will be disallowed, and capital allowances will be restricted for private use by the partners.
>
> Partners' salaries are not allowable business expenses, but just a way of allocating profits.

(a) Partnership's tax adjusted trading profit – year ended 5 April 2010

Tutor's top tips:

In the adjustment to profits calculation it is important to list all the major items of expenditure in the question, showing a zero for the adjustment figure where the expenditure is allowable.

If required, also add notes to show why you have not adjusted for an item, or why you have added it back. However, lengthy explanations are not required where the requirement is just to 'calculate' the adjusted profits, rather than to explain them.

		£
Net profit		36,000
Add:	Depreciation	11,750
	Impaired debts – loan to supplier written off (Note 1)	4,000
	Increase in allowance for trade debtors	0
	Motor expenses (£19,000 × 40%)	7,600
	Accountancy	0
	Legal fees in connection with defence of name (Note 2)	0
	Legal fees in connection with the grant of a new lease (Note 2)	2,100
	Decorating offices	0
	Construction of new wall (Note 3)	4,700
	Entertaining customers (Note 4)	1,060
	Entertaining staff (Note 4)	0
	Gifts to customers (Note 5)	600
		67,810
Less	Capital allowances	(7,810)
Tax adjusted trading profit		60,000

Tutorial note:

1. The loan to a supplier is not made for the purposes of the trade. The write off of the loan is therefore not an allowable deduction against trading income.

2. The costs of defending the right to an asset (the internet domain name) are allowable, whilst the costs of the grant of a new lease are capital in nature and therefore not allowable.

3. The cost of the new wall is not allowable, being capital in nature.

4. The only exception to the non-deductibility of entertainment expenditure is when it is in respect of employees.

5. Gifts to customers are only an allowable deduction if they cost less than £50 per recipient per year, are not of food, drink, tobacco, or vouchers exchangeable for goods, and carry a conspicuous advertisement for the company making the gift.

Workings: Capital allowances

	Pool £	Xio's car £	Yana's car £	Zoe's car £	B.U %	Allowances £
TWDV b/f	17,000	16,500	8,750	15,000		
Proceeds				(12,400)		
Balancing allowance				2,600	x 60%	1,560
WDA (20%)	(3,400)					3,400
WDA (20%)			(1,750)		x 60%	1,050
WDA (restricted)		(3,000)			x 60%	1,800
TWDV c/f	13,600	13,500	7,000			
Total allowances						7,810

Tutor's top tip

A familiar full blown capital allowances computation is given in the workings to this answer to show how the allowances are calculated.

However, where there are not many transactions it is acceptable to calculate the allowances available on each asset acquired as shown below rather than a full computation:

Pool (£17,000 × 20%)	£3,400
Xio's motor car (£3,000 × 60%)	£1,800
Yana's motor car (£8,750 × 20% × 60%)	£1,050
Zoe's motor car ((£15,000 – £12,400) × 60%)	£1,560

If you do this however, be careful and make sure you explain your calculations clearly.

(b)   **Trading income assessments – 2009/10**

Tutor's top tips:

Where the partnership agreement has changed during the year, you must time apportion the adjusted profits and split them using the agreement in force for each period. Don't forget to time apportion the annual salary for the first three months.

If you have made mistakes in part (a), you could still get full marks here as long as you have split your adjusted profit figure correctly. You must make sure that your workings are clear so that the marker can see how you arrived at your answer.

Year ended 5 April 2010

	Total £	Xio £	Yana £	Zoe £
3 months to 30 June 2009				
Salary (£6,000 × 3/12)	1,500	1,500		
Balance (50%/30%/20%)	13,500	6,750	4,050	2,700
	15,000	8,250	4,050	2,700
9 months to 5 April 2010				
Balance (50%/50%)	45,000	22,500	22,500	Nil
Total assessment	60,000	30,750	26,550	2,700

(c)   **Income tax computations – 2009/10**

Tutor's top tips:

As long as your income tax computations are based on your trading profits from part (b), you could still score full marks here. However, it is very important that you show your workings clearly so that the marker can see that you have applied the correct rates to each type of income.

To save time, set out the income tax computations side by side so that you don't have to write out all of the headings three times!

	Xio £	Yana £	Zoe £
Trading income	30,750	26,550	2,700
Employment income			26,000
Building society interest (£800 × 100/80)	1,000		
Dividends (£10,800 × 100/90)			12,000
Total income	31,750	26,550	40,700
Less Personal allowance	(6,475)	(6,475)	(6,475)
Taxable income	25,275	20,075	34,225

Income tax	Xio	Yana	Zoe
£	£	£	£
24,275 at 20% (Other income)	4,855		
1,000 at 20% (Savings income)	200		
20,075 at 20% (Other income)		4,015	
22,225 at 20% (Other income)			4,445
12,000 at 10% (Dividend income)			1,200
Income tax liability	5,055	4,015	5,645

Tutorial note:

Do not forget to analsye the make up of each partner's taxable income before calculating the tax, as different rates of tax apply to different sources of income.

Yana

Capital gains tax computation – 2009/10

	£
Capital gain	32,800
Less Annual exemption	(10,100)
Taxable gain	22,700
Capital gains tax (£22,700 x 18%)	4,086

26 AMY BWALYA

Key answer tips

Three independent parts to this question: an easy opening year's computation, a straight forward partnership allocation of profits, but then a difficult closing year's computation with a change of accounting date.

Even so, some easy marks were available in the last part, and the question as a whole can easily be passed without getting bogged down in the change of accounting date aspect.

(a) **Assessable trading profits**

Tax year	Basis of assessment	£
2007/08	Actual basis (1.8.07 – 5.4.08)	
	£38,500 × 8/10	30,800
2008/09	First 12 months (1.8.07 – 31.7.08)	
	£38,500 + (£52,800 × 2/12)	47,300
2009/10	CYB (y/e 31.5.09)	52,800

In 2008/09 there are overlap profits of £30,800 in respect of the eight-month period 1 August 2007 to 5 April 2008.

In 2009/10 there are overlap profits of £8,800 (£52,800 x 3/12) in respect of the two-month period 1 June 2008 to 31 July 2008.

Total overlap profits = (£30,800 + £8,800) = £39,600.

Tutorial note:

The assessment for 2008/09 is the first twelve months of trading as the accounting date falling in that year is less than twelve months from the commencement of trading.

(b) **Trading income assessments – 2009/10**

Year ended 5 April 2010	Total £	Cedric £	Eli £	Gordon £
9 months to 31 December 2009				
Salary (£6,000 × 9/12)	4,500		4,500	
Interest on capital (W)	8,250	3,000	5,250	
Balance (60%/40%)	54,750	32,850	21,900	
(£90,000 × 9/12)	67,500	35,850	31,650	
3 months to 5 April 2010				
Salary (£6,000 × 3/12)	1,500		1,500	
Interest on capital (W)	2,250		1,750	500
Balance (70%/30%)	18,750		13,125	5,625
(£90,000 × 3/12)	22,500		16,375	6,125
Total assessment	90,000	35,850	48,025	6,125

Workings: Interest on capital

For the nine-month period to 31 December 2009:

Cedric = (£40,000 × 10% × 9/12) = £3,000

Eli = (£70,000 × 10% × 9/12) = £5,250

For the three-month period to 5 April 2010:

Eli = (£70,000 × 10% × 3/12) = £1,750

Gordon = (£20,000 × 10% × 3/12) = £500

Key answer tips

The trading income assessments must be calculated by splitting the accounting period into two parts and applying the different agreements acordingly as Cedric resigned part way through the year.

Even though Eli is in the partnership for the whole accounting period, the salary agreement ended on 31 December 2009. You must therefore remember to time apportion the annual salary quoted for Eli. If not, you will apply the profit sharing ratios to an incorrect 'balance' figure.

(c)   **Assessable trading profits**

Tax year	Basis of assessment	£
2007/08	CYB (y/e 30 September 2007)	36,000
2008/09	Change of accounting date (Note)	
	(1 July 2007 to 30 June 2007)	
	(£36,000 × 3/12) + £23,400	32,400
2009/10	Year of cessation	
	(1 July 2007 to 31 December 2009)	
	Year ended 30 June 2009	28,800
	Period ended 31 December 2009	10,800
		39,600
	Less Relief for overlap profits (£4,500 + £9,000) (Note)	(13,500)
		26,100

Tutorial note:

On the change of accounting date, as the new accounting date falls earlier in the tax year (i.e. 30 June rather than 30 September), the assessment for 2008/09 (i.e. the tax year of change) is the twelve months to the new accounting date of 30 June.

As a result, in 2008/09 there are further overlap profits generated of £9,000 (£36,000 × 3/12) in respect of the three-month period 1 July 2007 to 30 September 2007.

These are deducted, along with the opening year overlap profits, in the final year of assessment.

Key answer tips

To score well in a question of this type, it is important to show the appropriate tax years to which the accounting profits relate.

It is also important to reference any workings you have performed to support your answer to your main answer clearly.

27 AE, BEE, CAE, DEE & EUE (ADAPTED) *Walk in the footsteps of a top tutor*

Key answer tips

This question tests the basis of assessment rules, but the application of the rules to partnerships, and includes the opening year rules, overlap profits and the cessation rules.

A well prepared student should have been able to secure good marks on this question and each part is independent.

Part (c) of this question has been adapted to take account of the change in rules for capital allowances.

Tutor's top tips:

Part (a) deals with both the partnership profit sharing rules together with straightforward opening year rules. This part should not have caused any problems.

(a) **Ae, Bee & Cae**

Tax year	Basis of assessment	Ae £	Bee £	Cae £
2007/08	Actual basis 1 July 2007 to 5 April 2008 £54,000 × 9/12 × 1/2	20,250	20,250	
2008/09	CYB (y/e 30 June 2008) £54,000 × 1/2	27,000	27,000	
2009/10	CYB (y/e 30 June 2009) £66,000 × 1/2	33,000	33,000	
	Actual basis 1 July 2009 to 5 April 2010 £87,000 × 9/12 × 1/3			21,750

Tutorial note:

The commencement rules apply for Ae & Bee in the tax year 2007/08 and for Cae in the tax year 2009/10, as this is the tax year in which each partner started to trade.

In the case of Cae, the fact that the partnership had been trading in the years before is not relevant.

(b)   (i)   **Dee – Assessable trading profits**

Tutor's top tips:

Part (b) deals with a change in accounting date. This was straightforward as long as you remember that 12 months trading profits needs to be taxed in each tax year.

Tax year	Basis of assessment	£
2007/08	CYB (y/e 5 April 2008)	32,880
2008/09	Change of accounting date (Note) (1 August 2007 to 31 July 2008) (£32,880 × 8/12) + £16,240	38,160
2009/10	CYB (y/e 31 July 2009)	54,120

Tutorial note:

The tax year of change is 2008/09. The tax years before and after are assessed on a normal CYB basis (i.e. assess the 12 months accounts ending in that year).

As the new accounting date falls earlier in the tax year (i.e. 31 July rather than 5 April, which is the last day of the tax year!), the assessment for 2008/09 is the 12 months to the new accounting date of 31 July.

As a result, further overlap profits are created.

(ii)   **Unrelieved overlap profits**

There are no overlap profits created on the commencement of trade as the business has a 5 April accounting date.

However, in 2008/09 there are overlap profits of £21,920 (£32,880 x 8/12) created in respect of the eight-month period 1 August 2007 to 5 April 2008.

Tutorial note:

The complication with this question arises not from the commencement of trade, which due to the date of the year-end does not cause overlap, but from the change in accounting date occurring after April 2008.

In order to tax 12 months of trade, the year to 5 April 2008 is pro-rated to 8 months and added to the short 4 month trading period, thus making a total of 12 months. As this 8 month period has already been taxed in the 2007/08 year, overlap profits arise.

(c)   **Eue**

Tutor's top tips:

Part (c) deals with the cessation of trade. The key rule to remember for cessation is that all profits not yet assessed need to be taxed, before deducting any overlap profits.

Tax year	Basis of assessment	£
2009/10	CYB (y/e 30 June 2009)	61,200
	Capital allowances (given)	(2,100)
		59,100
2010/11	Period ended 30 September 2010	72,000
	Balancing allowance (W)	(4,400)
		67,600
	Less Overlap profits	(19,800)
		47,800

Working: Capital allowances

	Pool	Allowances
Period ended 30 September 2010	£	£
TWDV b/f	6,300	
Addition		
Car (CO$_2$ between 111 – 160 g/km)	2,400	
	8,700	
Disposal	(4,300)	
Balancing allowance	4,400	4,400

Tutorial note:

Note that there is no AIA and no WDA in the final period of trade.

As all of the items in the pool are disposed of for less than the TWDV, there is a balancing allowance arising.

A common error is to give an AIA and calculate a WDA in the final period of trade, then calculate a balancing allowance/charge. The net effect on the total allowances is the same, but the principle is incorrect.

Examiner's report

This question was extremely well answered by the majority of candidates, many of whom scored maximum marks.

One of the main problems in the answers of poorer candidates was not showing the appropriate tax years, thus losing a lot of marks throughout.

The only common mistake was that in part (b) for the year of change, candidates often used an actual basis rather than the 12 months to the new accounting date.

ACCA marking scheme	Marks
Ae, Bee & Cae	
2007/08	1.5
2008/09	1.0
2009/10 Ae & Bee	1.0
2009/10 Cae	1.5
	——
	5.0
	——
Dee	
2007/08	1.0
2008/09	2.0
2009/10	1.0
Overlap profits	1.0
	——
	5.0
	——
Eue	
2009/10 Assessment	1.5
2010/11 Assessment	1.0
2010/11 Capital allowances	1.5
Relief for overlap profits	1.0
	——
	5.0
	——
Total	15.0
	——

PENSIONS AND NIC

28   DUKE AND EARL UPPER-CRUST (ADAPTED)

Key answer tips

Part (a) involves a couple of straight forward income tax computations; one for a higher rate taxpayer requiring the extension of the basic rate band for pension relief, the other a basic rate taxpayer requiring no entries in the income tax computation in respect of pensions.

Parts (b) and (c) are wholly written, covering the rules on additional pension contributions and the significance of the annual allowance.

(a)   **Duke Upper-Crust**

   Income tax computation – 2009/10

	£
Employment income (£120,000 + £40,000)	160,000
Less Personal allowance	(6,475)
Taxable income	153,525

Income tax

£	
122,400 at 20% (W)	24,480
31,125 at 40%	12,450
153,525	
Income tax liability	36,930

Net amount paid to pension company

All of Duke's pension contribution of £85,000 qualifies for tax relief as it is less than 100% of his earnings.

He will therefore have paid £68,000 (£85,000 less 20%) to his personal pension company.

Working: Extension of basic rate band

	£
Basic rate band threshold	37,400
Plus Personal pension contribution (gross)	85,000
Extended basic rate band	122,400

Earl Upper-Crust

Income tax computation – 2009/10

	£
Trading profit	34,000
Less Personal allowance	(6,475)
Taxable income	27,525
Income tax liability (£27,525 at 20%)	5,505

Tutorial note:

As Earl is a basic rate taxpayer there is no need to extend his basic rate band for the pension contribution. Relief for allowable contributions is given at source.

Net amount paid to pension company

Only £34,000 of Earl's pension contribution of £40,000 qualifies for tax relief, since relief is only available up to the amount of earnings.

The amount of tax relief is £6,800 (£34,000 at 20%), so Earl will have paid £33,200 (£40,000 – £6,800) to his personal pension company.

(b) **Maximum additional contributions**

- There is no restriction regarding the amounts that Duke and Earl could have contributed into a personal pension scheme for 2009/10.

- However, Duke would only receive tax relief on additional contributions of up to £75,000 (£160,000 – £85,000).

- Earl has already made a pension contribution in excess of his earnings for 2009/10, and so any additional pension contribution would not have qualified for any tax relief.

- Pension contributions for 2009/10 would have had to have been paid between 6 April 2009 and 5 April 2010, as it is not possible to carry back contributions.

(c) **Effect of annual allowance**

- Although there is no limit as to the amount of pension contributions that can qualify for tax relief, the annual allowance limit of £245,000 acts as an effective limit.

- Any tax relieved contributions in excess of the annual allowance are taxed at the rate of 40%, with the tax being paid under the self assessment system.

- The annual allowance charge therefore cancels out the tax relief that would have been given.

- There is no charge where contributions have not qualified for tax relief.

29 VANESSA SERVE AND SERENE VOLLEY *Walk in the footsteps of a top tutor*

Key answer tips

This question is really like two separate questions.

Part (a) is fairly straightforward, and asks for income tax and national insurance computations for a sole trader and an employee, with advice regarding payments under self assessment.

Part (b) is all about VAT and the flat rate scheme.

The highlighted words in the written sections are key phrases that markers are looking for.

Tutor's top tips:

You should be able to score highly on part (a)(i), although there were a few tricky points.

Where a sole trader has just purchased a single asset, there is no need to do a full capital allowances computation, as long as you show your workings. Remember that only the business proportion of the allowances can be claimed.

The question specifically says that the company did not provide Serene with any fuel for private journeys, so don't waste time calculating a fuel benefit! (See examiner's comments)

Watch out for the pension contributions:

- *the contribution to the personal pension is paid net, and extra relief is given by extending the basic rate band by the gross amount*

- *the occupational pension is paid gross, and is simply deducted from employment income*

Try not to get these confused.

Remember that you will score full marks for the calculation of tax if you use the correct rates, even if your taxable income figure is wrong.

(a)   (i)   **Vanessa Serve**

Income tax computation – 2009/10

	Total £	Other income £	Savings income £
Trading income	52,400		
Less Capital allowances			
(£10,400 × 20%)			
= £2,080 × 14,000/20,000	(1,456)		
	50,944	50,944	
Interest received (Note)	1,100		1,100
Total income	52,044	50,944	1,100
Less Personal Allowance	(6,475)	(6,475)	
Taxable income	45,569	44,469	1,100
Income tax:			
On Other income (W)	43,800	@ 20%	8,760
On Other income	669	@ 40%	268
	44,469		
On Savings income	1,100	@ 40%	440
	45,569		
Income tax payable			9,468

Tutorial note:

Interest from investment accounts at the National Savings & Investments Bank is received gross.

Working: Extension of basic rate band

	£
Basic rate band threshold	37,400
Plus Personal pension contribution (gross)	6,400
Extended basic rate band	43,800

Serene Volley

Income tax computation – 2009/10

	£
Salary	26,400
Less Pension contributions (£26,400 × 5%)	(1,320)
	25,080
Car benefit (W)	4,264
Employment income	29,344
Interest from savings certificate (exempt)	Nil
Total income	29,344
Less Personal allowance	(6,475)
Taxable income	22,869
Income tax liability (£22,869 at 20%)	4,574
Less Tax suffered at source – PAYE	(4,400)
Income tax payable	174

Working: Car benefit

CO_2 emissions = 192 g/km, available all year

	%
Petrol	15
Plus (190 – 135) × $\frac{1}{5}$	11
Appropriate percentage	26

Car benefit (£16,400 x 26%)	£4,264

There is no fuel benefit as private petrol is not provided by the company.

(ii)   **National insurance**

Tutor's top tip:

Remember that sole traders pay Class 2 and 4 national insurance, whereas employees pay Class 1 primary contributions.

As long as you calculate Vanessa's Class 4 contributions correctly based on your adjusted trading income figure from part (a)(i), you will be awarded full marks.

Vanessa Serve

Class 2 NICs	£
(£2.40 for 52 weeks)	125

Class 4 NICs	£
(£43,875 – £5,715) × 8%	3,053
(£50,944 – £43,875) × 1%	71
	3,124

Serene Volley

Class 1 NICs	
(£26,400 – £5,715) × 11%	2,275

Tutorial note:

Class 1 NICs are based on cash earnings, without any allowable deductions. Therefore, pension contributions are ignored, and benefits are not subject to employee Class 1 NIC.

Benefits are assessed to Class 1A NICs which are payable by the employer only, not the employee. However, the requirement is to calculate the NICs payable by the employee only, not the employer.

(iii)　**Payment of tax**

Tutor's top tip:

You must learn the rules and key dates for payment of tax under self assessment, as these are very often examined, and the examiner is repeatedly disappointed when students do not seem to learn these important rules. (See examiner's comments to this question, and others).

Don't forget that Vanessa's balancing payment due under self assessment covers both income tax and Class 4 NICs.

As long as this payment and the instalments for 2010/11 are calculated correctly based on your figures, you will be given full marks.

Vanessa Serve

Balancing payment for 2009/10 due on 31 January 2011

	£
Income tax liability	9,468
Class 4 NIC	3,124
Less: Paid on account	(8,705)
	3,887

Payments on account for 2010/11 will be

	£
(£9,468 + £3,124) = £12,592 × 50%	6,296

These will be due on 31 January 2011 and 31 July 2011.

Serene Volley

No payments on account have been made, so the balancing payment for 2009/10 due on 31 January 2011 is £174.

Payments on account for 2010/11 are not required because Serene's income tax payable for 2009/10 was less than £1,000.

Also, more than 80% of her income tax liability (£4,574 × 80% = £3,659) was met by deduction at source.

(b) (i) **VAT Return – Quarter ended 30 June 2010**

Tutor's top tip:

Part (b) is a stand alone part about VAT which could have been attempted before part (a) if you are confident with your VAT knowledge.

A standard VAT return is required, but be careful to read the question carefully to see:

- *the dates of the transactions so that the appropriate rate of VAT is used, and*

- *whether the figures in the question include or exclude VAT.*

In this case, the appropriate rate is as follows:

- *If the figure excludes VAT, the VAT is 17.5%*

- *If the figure includes VAT, the VAT is 17.5/117.5 or 7/47.*

The requirement is to 'calculate' and therefore the explanatory notes are not required as part of the answer.

	£	£
Output VAT		
Sales (£18,000 × 17.5%)		3,150
Input VAT		
Telephone (£600 × 60% × 17.5%) (Note 1)	63	
Motor car (Note 2)	Nil	
Motor repairs (£987 × 17.5/117.5) (Note 3)	147	
Equipment (£1,760 × 17.5) (Note 4)	308	
Other expenses (£2,200 – £400) × 17.5%	315	
		(833)
VAT payable		2,317

Tutorial note:

1. *An apportionment is made where a service such as the use of a telephone is partly for business purposes and partly for private purposes.*

2. *Input VAT cannot be recovered in respect of the motor car as this was not exclusively for business purposes.*

3.   *No apportionment is necessary for motor expenses provided there is some business use.*

4.   *Vanessa can recover the input VAT in respect of the equipment in the quarter ended 30 June 2010 because the actual tax point was the date that the equipment was paid for.*

(ii)   **Flat rate scheme**

Tutor's top tip:

You need to learn the key rules and features of the VAT schemes, but then you must make sure that you apply them to the specific question.

There was an easy mark available for calculating the VAT saving compared to your VAT payable from part (b)(i).

Conditions

- Vanessa can use the flat rate scheme if her expected taxable turnover for the next 12 months does not exceed £150,000.

Advantages

- The main advantage of the scheme is the simplified VAT administration. Vanessa's customers are not VAT registered, so there will be no need to issue VAT invoices.

- If Vanessa had used the flat rate scheme for the quarter ended 30 June 2010 then she would have paid VAT of £1,269 (£18,000 + £3,150) × 6%).

- This is a saving of £1,048 (£2,317 − £1,269) for the quarter.

Tutorial note:

The flat rate % is applied to the VAT inclusive taxable supplies for the quarter.

Examiner's comments

This question was generally very well answered.

In part (a) many candidates did not appreciate that it was not necessary to gross up the interest received from an investment account at the National Savings & Investment Bank, or that interest from savings certificates is exempt from tax.

The contribution to the occupational pension scheme was often used to extend the basic rate tax band rather than being deducted in calculating employment income.

Many candidates wasted time in calculating a fuel benefit despite the question clearly stating that no fuel was provided for private journeys.

The one aspect of the question that consistently caused problems was the calculation of the balancing payments and the payments on account, and this section was often not answered at all. It was disappointing that many candidates were not aware of the relevant due dates.

The VAT aspects in part (b) were well answered, although far too many candidates incorrectly deducted input VAT when calculating the amount of VAT payable using the flat rate scheme.

		ACCA marking scheme	
			Marks
(a)	(i)	**Vanessa Serve**	
		Trading profit	0.5
		Capital allowances	1.5
		Interest from NSI Bank	1.0
		Personal allowance	0.5
		Extension of basic rate band	1.0
		Income tax	1.0
		Serene Volley	
		Salary	0.5
		Pension contributions	1.0
		Car benefit	1.5
		Interest from savings certificate	0.5
		Personal allowance	0.5
		Income tax	1.0
		Tax suffered at source – PAYE	0.5
			11.0
	(ii)	**Vanessa Serve**	
		Class 2 NIC	1.0
		Class 4 NIC	1.5
		Serene Volley	
		Class 1 NIC	1.5
			4.0
	(iii)	**Vanessa Serve**	
		Balancing payment	1.5
		Payments on account	1.5
		Serene Volley	
		Balancing payment	1.0
		Payments on account not required	1.0
			5.0
(b)	(i)	Sales	0.5
		Telephone	1.0
		Motor car	0.5
		Motor repairs	1.0
		Equipment	1.0
		Other expenses	1.0
			5.0
	(ii)	Limit	1.0
		Simplified administration	2.0
		VAT saving	2.0
			5.0
	Total		30.0

30   ANN, BASIL & CHLOE *Walk in the footsteps of a top tutor*

Key answer tips

A question covering the pension relief available to three different individuals. This should be a straightforward question provided the rules had been learnt.

Relief for pension contributions is a key area of the syllabus that is tested regularly.

Tutor's top tips:

This question is classic in style with individuals in different situations contributing to a personal pension scheme.

The key is to:

- *Remember the definition of "relevant earnings"*

- *Compare the gross contributions paid with the "relevant earnings" (or £3,600 if this is higher) to decide the maximum tax allowable amount*

- *Identify, and know how to deal with, any excess contributions above the annual allowance.*

Note that the annual allowance (£245,000) and the maximum contributions allowable for a person without any relevant earnings in the tax year (£3,600) are given in the exam.

Anne Peach

Amount of pension contributions qualifying for relief

Anne can obtain relief for the lower of:

(1)   Gross contributions of £52,000

(2)   Higher of:

   (i)   £3,600

   (ii)   Relevant earnings of £48,000

Therefore, £48,000 will qualify for tax relief and her basic rate is extended to £85,400 (W).

Her taxable income falls into the extended basic rate band and is therefore taxed at 20%.

Income tax liability

	£
Trading profit	48,000
Less Personal allowances	(6,475)
Taxable income	41,525
Income tax liability (£41,525 x 20%) (W)	8,305

Working: Extension of basic rate band

	£
Basic rate band	37,400
Plus Gross allowable pension contributions	48,000
Extended basic rate band	85,400

Basil Plum

Amount of pension contributions qualifying for relief

Basil can obtain relief for the lower of:

(1)   Gross contributions of £260,000

(2)   Higher of:

      (i)   £3,600

      (ii)   Relevant earnings of £320,000

Therefore, £260,000 will qualify for tax relief and his basic rate band is extended to £297,400 (W).

However, this exceeds the annual allowance of £245,000 and therefore an excess contribution charge effectively restricts relief to £245,000.

Tutorial note:

Note that this scenario differs from the treatment for Anne (above) as Anne had contributed more than 100% of her relevant earnings into a scheme, whereas Basil has contributed less than 100% of his relevant earnings into the scheme.

Income tax liability

	£
Employment income	320,000
Less Personal allowances	(6,475)
Taxable income	313,525

Income tax

£		£
297,400 x 20% (W)		59,480
16,125 x 40%		6,450
———		
313,525		
———		
		65,930
Plus Excess contribution charge (£260,000 – £245,000) x 40%		6,000
		———
Income tax liability		71,930
		———

Working: Extension of basic rate band

	£
Basic rate band	37,400
Plus Gross allowable pension contributions	260,000
	———
Extended basic rate band	297,400

Chloe Pear

Amount of pension contributions qualifying for relief

Property income does not qualify as relevant earnings.

Therefore, as Chloe has no relevant earnings, she will only receive tax relief on £3,600 of her pension contributions.

Her taxable income falls below the basic rate band even before extension due to pension contributions, therefore her income is taxed at 20%.

Income tax liability

	£
Property income	23,900
Less Personal allowances	(6,475)
	———
Taxable income	17,425
	———
Income tax (£17,425 x 20%) (W)	3,485
	———

Examiner's report

This question was reasonably well answered, although there were few first-rate answers.

For the first taxpayer the most common mistake was to extend the basic rate tax band by the amount of contributions rather than earnings.

For the second taxpayer the basic rate band was often extended by the amount of annual allowance rather than the contributions. Many candidates did not appreciate that there would be an excess contribution charge.

Very few candidates stated that the third taxpayer would have received tax relief up to £3,600 of her contributions.

ACCA marking scheme	
	Marks
Ann Peach	
Taxable income	0.5
Extension of basic rate band	1.0
Income tax	0.5
Amount qualifying for tax relief	1.0
	3.0
Basil Plum	
Taxable income	0.5
Extension of basic rate band	1.0
Income tax	1.0
Excess contribution charge	1.5
Amount qualifying for tax relief	1.0
	5.0
Eue	
Taxable income	0.5
Income tax	0.5
Amount qualifying for tax relief	1.0
	2.0
Total	10.0

SELF ASSESSMENT

31 NICOLA (ADAPTED)

Key answer tips

A very detailed question on self-assessment which is straight forward if you have learnt the rules, very difficult if you have not!

(1) (a) **Penalties due in respect of 2009/10**

Late submission of 2009/10 Return:

– Electronic return due 31 January 2011

– Submitted 28 February 2011

– Therefore = 28 days late.

Penalty = £100

(b) **Surcharge due in respect of 2009/10**

2009/10 income tax outstanding on 31 March 2011:

(£8,000 – (2 × £2,500)) = £3,000

Surcharge = (£3,000 × 5%) = £150

(c)   **Interest due in respect of 2009/10**

    (i)   2009/10 payment on account due on 31 July 2010 and made on 31 October 2010

        Interest = (£2,500 × 2.5% × 3/12) = £16

    (ii)   Excessive claim to reduce payments on account for 2009/10

        Interest from 1.2.10 – 31.1.11 = (£1,250 × 2.5%) = £31

        Interest from 1.8.10 – 31.1.11 = (£1,250 × 2.5% × 6/12) = £16

Tutorial note:

If no claim is made, Nicola would have paid £3,750 payment on account. She claimed to only pay £2,500.

It finally turns out that she has a current year liability in excess of the previous year and so she should have paid the original payments on account of £3,750, and should not have reduced the payments at all.

Therefore, the excess claim which will be subject to interest charges will be £1,250 (£3,750 – £2,500).

Note that she is not required to have paid payments on account of £4,000, being half of the final liability of £8,000, only the amounts she would have paid had she never made the claim to reduce the payments.

    (iii) Balancing payment of 2009/10

        Due on 31 January 2011 paid on 31 May 2011

        Interest = (£3,000 × 2.5% × 4/12) = £25

    (iv)   Interest on surcharge for 2009/10 from 1 May 2011 to 31 May 2011

        (£150 × 2.5% × 1/12) = 30p (£Nil to the nearest £)

(d)   **Interest due in respect of 2010/11**

    2010/11 payment on account due on 31 January 2011 and made on 31 May 2011

    Interest = (£4,000 × 2.5% × 4/12) = £33.

Key answer tips

In practice, interest accrues on a daily basis, however in exams the calculations should be performed on a monthly basis unless the question says otherwise.

---

(2) **Tax avoidance and tax evasion**

Tax avoidance

Tax avoidance is using the taxation regime to one's own advantage by arranging your affairs to minimise your tax liability.

It is legal and does not entail misleading HM Revenue & Customs (HMRC).

Tax evasion

Tax evasion is any action taken to evade taxes by illegal means.

The main forms of tax evasion are:

- suppressing information e.g. failing to declare taxable income to HMRC
- submitting false information e.g. claiming expenses that have not been incurred

Tax evasion is an illegal activity and carries a risk of criminal prosecution (fines and/or imprisonment).

Suggestions to Nicola

- Investing in a tax efficient investment such as an Individual Savings account is an example of tax avoidance.
- If Nicola claims, as tax deductible, expenses which she has not incurred for business purposes this would be tax evasion.

Note that this is different from simply reviewing her expenses to ensure that she is claiming all business related expenditure.

For example, it is good business practice to claim for a percentage of her household expenses if she has an office in her home which she uses for business purposes.

32   PI CASSO

Key answer tips

The first part of this question involves detailed calculations to work out the income tax, Class 4 NICs and capital gains tax payable under on self-assessment and when the payments are due.

The remaining three parts require wholly written answers on three common self-assessment topics.

These are marks which are easy to gain if you have done your work, but easy to lose if you do not invest the time in learning the self-assessment rules.

(a) **Due dates of payment of tax under self-assessment**

Due date	Tax year	Payment	£
31 July 2009	2008/09	Second payment on account (W1)	2,240
31 January 2010	2008/09	Balancing payment (W2)	5,980
31 January 2010	2009/10	First payment on account (W3)	1,860
31 July 2010	2009/10	Second payment on account (W3)	1,860
31 January 2011	2009/10	Balancing payment (W4)	Nil
31 January 2011	2010/11	First payment on account (W5)	1,860

Workings

(W1) Second payment on account – 2008/09

The second payment on account for 2008/09 is based on Pi's income tax and Class 4 NIC liability for 2007/08 as follows:

	£
Income tax	3,240
Class 4 NICs	1,240
	4,480
Payments on account (50%)	2,240

(W2) Balancing payment – 2008/09

	£
Income tax	4,100
Class 4 NICs	1,480
Capital gains tax (see Tutorial Note)	4,880
	10,460
Less POAs (£2,240 x 2)	(4,480)
Balancing payment	5,980

(W3) Payments on account – 2009/10

Pi will make a claim to reduce her total payments on account for 2009/10 as follows:

	£
Income tax	2,730
Class 4 NICs	990
	3,720
Payments on account (50%)	1,860

(W4) Balancing payment – 2009/10

	£
Income tax and Class 4 NICs	3,720
Capital gains tax	Nil
	3,720
Less POAs (£1,860 x 2)	(3,720)
Balancing payment	Nil

(W5) First payments on account – 2010/11

The first payment on account for 2010/11 is based on Pi's income tax and Class 4 NIC liability for 2009/10.

	£
Income tax	2,730
Class 4 NICs	990
	3,720
Payments on account (50%)	1,860

Tutorial note:

Class 2 NICs are payable by monthly direct debit, or quarterly invoicing. They are not paid via the self-assessment system.

Capital gains tax is collected via self-assessment and is payable all in one payment on 31 January following the end of the tax year along with the balancing payment for income tax and Class 4 NICs.

Payments on account are not required for CGT.

(b) Reduction of payments on account to £Nil

- If Pi's payments on account for 2009/10 were reduced to £Nil, then she would be charged interest on the payments due of £1,860 from the relevant due date to the date of payment.

- A penalty will be charged if the claim to reduce the payments on account to £Nil was made fraudulently or negligently.

(c) Latest submission date

- Unless the return is issued late, the latest date that Pi can submit a paper based self-assessment tax return for 2009/10 is 31 October 2010.

- If Pi completes a paper based tax return by 31 October 2010 then HMRC will prepare a self-assessment tax computation on her behalf.

- Alternatively, Pi has until 31 January 2011 to file her self-assessment tax return for 2009/10 online.

- A self-assessment tax computation is then automatically provided as part of the filing process.

(d) HMRC enquiry

- If HMRC intend to enquire into Pi's 2009/10 tax return they will have to notify her within twelve months of the date that they receive the return.

- HMRC has the right to enquire into the completeness and accuracy of any return and such an enquiry may be made on a completely random basis.

- However, enquiries are generally made because of a suspicion that income has been undeclared or because deductions have been incorrectly claimed.

Examiner's report

This question was generally not well answered, and the impression given was that candidates had struggled with time management and had a lack of time remaining for this question.

Part (a) caused the most problems, with the vast majority of candidates not being able to demonstrate how payments are calculated and paid under the self-assessment system.

Class 2 national insurance contributions were often incorrectly included, whilst few candidates appreciated that a claim to reduce payments on account was possible.

In part (b) most candidates appreciated that interest would be due, but very few mentioned the potential penalty that could be charged.

It was disappointing that the self-assessment tax return submission dates were often not know in part (c), despite these being covered in the Finance Act article.

The same comment applies to part (d). Candidates often gave a long list of reasons why HMRC could enquire into a return, but failed to mention that an enquiry might be on a completely random basis.

	ACCA marking scheme	
		Marks
(a)	Second payment on account for 2008/09	1.5
	Balancing payment for 2008/09	2.0
	Claim to reduce payments on account	1.0
	Payments on account for 2009/10	1.0
	Balancing payment for 2009/10	0.5
	First payment on account for 2010/11	1.0
		——
		7.0
		——
(b)	Interest	1.0
	Penalty	1.0
		——
		2.0
		——
(c)	Paper based return	2.0
	Return filed online	1.0
		——
		3.0
		——
(d)	Notification date	1.0
	Random basis	1.0
	Income/Deductions	1.0
		——
		3.0
		——
Total		15.0
		——

CHARGEABLE GAINS

INDIVIDUALS – CAPITAL GAINS TAX

33   CHANDRA KHAN (ADAPTED)

Key answer tips

This question focuses on the capital gains reliefs available to individuals.

One unusual feature is the factory in part (b) which has been used partly for non business purposes. The rest of the question covers common situations and should not cause problems.

(a)   **Universal Ltd shares – sale at undervaluation**

	£
Deemed proceeds (Note)	110,000
Less Cost	(38,000)
	72,000
Less Gift relief (Balancing figure)	(35,000)
Chargeable gain after gift relief (W)	37,000

Tutorial note:

Chandra and her daughter are connected persons, and therefore the market value of the shares sold is used as consideration. The actual sale proceeds received are ignored.

Working: Chargeable gain after gift relief

Where there is a sale at undervaluation, a chargeable gain will arise if the actual consideration received exceeds the allowable cost:

	£
Actual proceeds	75,000
Less Cost	(38,000)
Chargeable gain after gift relief	37,000

Gift relief will be the remaining gain of £35,000 (£72,000 – £37,000)

Tutorial note:

If available, Entrepreneurs' relief is given after gift relief if there is a remaining gain to be charged. However, in this case Entrepreneurs' relief is not available as Chandra is not employed by Universal Ltd.

Furthermore, the question tells you to ignore Entrepreneurs' relief. This is because the examiner has stated that he will not examine the interaction of Entrepreneurs' relief with the other reliefs. Where relevant, a question will simply state that a particular relief is not available.

(b)   **Freehold factory**

	£
Disposal proceeds	146,000
Less Cost	(72,000)
	74,000
Less Rollover relief (W)	(55,500)
Chargeable gain	18,500

Working: Rollover relief

The proportion of the gain relating to non-business use is £18,500 (£74,000 × 25%), and this amount does not qualify for rollover relief.

The remaining gain of £55,500 (£74,000 – £18,500) can be rolled over provided:

- the business proportion of the sale proceeds is fully reinvested

- within the relevant time period between 8.11.2008 to 7.11.2012.

The business portion of sale proceeds = (£146,000 × 75%) = £109,500

Amount reinvested in qualifying business assets = £156,000

Reinvested on 10.11.09

Therefore, rollover relief is available for all of the remaining gain of £55,500.

Tutorial note:

Per the question, Entrepreneurs' relief is to be ignored. However, it is not available on this disposal anyway as the disposal of a factory is not a qualifying disposal.

The whole or substantial part of a business must be disposed of. There is no relief for the disposal of individual assets out of a business.

(c) **Goodwill**

	£
Proceeds	100,000
Less Cost	Nil
	100,000
Less Incorporation relief (W)	(80,000)
Chargeable gain (See Tutorial note)	20,000

Working: Incorporation relief

Where a business is incorporated and cash consideration is received, the proportion of the gain relating to the cash consideration cannot be deferred.

Therefore, the gain relating to the cash consideration is immediately chargeable.

Total consideration = (£200,000 + £50,000) = £250,000

Proportion of the gain relating to the cash consideration

= (£100,000 × £50,000/£250,000) = £20,000

Incorporation relief is therefore the remaining gain as it relates to the share consideration

= (£100,000 − ££20,000) = £80,000

or can be calculated as

= (£100,000 × £200,000/£250,000) = £80,000

Tutorial note:

Per the question, Entrepreneurs' relief is to be ignored.

However, for tutorial purposes, note that provided the business has been owned for at least one year, Entrepreneurs' relief will be available on the incorporation of a business. This is because there is a disposal of a qualifying business.

Entrepreneurs' relief:

- *is given after incorporation relief*

- *is applied to the remaining gain left in charge to tax, and*

- *would be £8,889 (£20,000 x 4/9) in this case, leaving a chargeable gain of £11,111 (£20,000 − £8,889).*

Chandra could elect to disapply the incorporation relief to increase the gain eligible for Entrepreneurs' relief now if she wants to.

This would be beneficial if Chandra was not employed by the new company or if she planned to sell her shares within 12 months, as in both of these cases her subsequent disposal of the shares would not qualify for Entrepreneurs' relief.

(d) **Private residence**

	£
Disposal proceeds	350,000
Less: Cost	(75,000)
	275,000
Less: Principal private residence (PPR) exemption (W1)	(240,625)
	34,375
Less: Letting relief (W2)	(34,375)
Chargeable gain	Nil

Workings

(W1) **PPR relief**

Chargeable and exempt periods of ownership

		Chargeable months	Exempt months
1.4.02 – 31.3.06	(actual occupation)		48
1.4.06 – 31.3.07	(absent – let out)	12	
1.4.07 – 1.4.10	(final 36 months)		36
		12	84

Total period of ownership (12 + 84) = 96 months.

PPR relief = (£275,000 × 84/96) = £240,625

Tutorial note:

After Chandra left her residence to live with a friend she never returned. Consequently the exemption for absence for any reason up to 3 years is not available as there is no actual occupation both before and after the period of absence.

In contrast the exemption for the final 36 months of ownership has no such restriction and is therefore still available.

(W2) **Letting relief**

Letting relief = lowest of:

(1)   £40,000

(2)   PPR = £240,625

(3)   Gain on letting = (£275,000 × 12/96) = £34,375

34 ALICE LIM (ADAPTED)

Key answer tips

This question tests reliefs available for the individual on the disposal of business assets. There are some common exam traps to watch out for.

In part (a), not all the proceeds of sale of the warehouse are reinvested, so not all of the gain can be rolled over.

In part (b), Alice receives some cash on the incorporation of her business, so she cannot roll over all the gains on incorporation.

In part (c), even though Alice buys the shares from her mother, you still use the market value as the proceeds as they are connected persons.

In part (d) it is important not to give letting relief because that relief is only available for the letting of your principal private residence.

(a) **Freehold office building**

	£	£
Disposal proceeds		152,000
Less Cost	134,000	
Rolled over gain (W)	(41,000)	
		(93,000)
Chargeable gain		59,000

Working: Rollover relief

The sale proceeds of the warehouse disposed of in April 2008 were not fully reinvested.

Accordingly, a capital gain of £15,000 (£149,000 − £134,000) would have been chargeable at the time.

The amount of gain rolled over must therefore have been £41,000 (£56,000 − £15,000).

Tutorial note:

Entrepreneurs' relief is not available as the disposal of the office building is not a qualifying disposal of the whole or part of a business. There is no relief for the disposal of individual assets out of a business.

(b)   **Incorporation of the business**

	£
Total gains before reliefs	120,000
Less Incorporation relief (W)	(80,000)
Chargeable gain (see Tutorial note)	40,000

The base cost of the 200,000 £1 shares received will be:

	£
MV of shares	200,000
Less Incorporation relief	(80,000)
Base cost	120,000

Disposal of 150,000 shares in Alilim Ltd

	£
Disposal proceeds	275,000
Less Base cost (£120,000 × 150,000/200,000)	(90,000)
Chargeable gain	185,000

Tutorial note:

Per the question, Entrepreneurs' relief is to be ignored. This is because the examiner has stated that he will not examine the interaction of Entrepreneurs' relief with the other reliefs. Where relevant, a question will simply state that a particular relief is not available.

However, for tutorial purposes, Entrepreneurs' relief is available on incorporation as it is the disposal of a qualifying business provided it has been owned for more than one year.

Entrepreneurs' relief is given after incorporation relief and is applied to the remaining gain left in charge to tax.

In this case, Entrepreneurs' relief would be £17,778 (£40,000 x 4/9), leaving a chargeable gain of £22,222 (£40,000 – £17,778).

Note that Alice could elect to disapply the incorporation relief to increase the gain eligible for Entrepreneurs' relief now if she wants to.

Advice to Alice

Alice will not be entitled to Entrepreneurs' relief on the disposal of her shares in Alilim Ltd as she has not held the shares for at least one year.

Therefore she should disclaim the incorporation relief on the transfer of her business to the company and claim Entrepreneurs' relief on the whole of the gain arising in incorporation instead.

This would save CGT at 18%.

Alternatively she could delay the sale of the shares until she has held them for 12 months and then she will qualify for Entrepreneurs' relief on their disposal.

Tutorial note:

Calculations were not required in this advice part of the question. However, for tutorial purposes, if incorporation relief is disapplied the following chargeable gains would arise:

Incorporation of the business (see working below) = £66,667

Disposal of 150,000 shares in Alilim Ltd (see working below) = £125,000

Her total gains would be £191,667 (£66,667 + £125,000) compared to £207,222 (£22,222 per Tutorial note above + £185,000).

Therefore the tax saving would be £2,800 (18% x (£207,222 – £191,667)).

Working for tutorial note:

Incorporation of the business

	£
Total gains	120,000
Less Entrepreneurs' relief (£120,000 x 4/9)	(53,333)
Chargeable gain	66,667

The base cost of her shares will then be £200,000.

Disposal of 150,000 shares in Alilim Ltd

The gain on the disposal of the shares would be:

	£
Disposal proceeds	275,000
Less Base cost (£200,000 × 150,000/200,000)	(150,000)
Chargeable gain	125,000

(c) **Family Ltd**

	£	£
Disposal Proceeds (Note)		230,000
Less Cost	168,000	
Held over gain (W)	(40,000)	
		(128,000)
Chargeable gain		102,000

Tutorial note:

Alice and her mother are connected persons, and therefore the market value would have been used when the shares were sold on 21 May 2009.

Working: Gift relief

The consideration paid for the shares did not exceed the allowable cost therefore full gift relief is available at the time of the gift.

The total gain of £40,000 (£168,000 – £128,000) was therefore held over.

Tutorial note:

Per the question, Entrepreneurs' relief is to be ignored. However, it is not available on this gift anyway as Alice does not work for Family Ltd.

(d)   **Property**

		£
Disposal proceeds		180,000
Less:	Deemed acquisition cost (Note)	(50,000)
Chargeable gain		130,000

Tutorial note:

Alice's husband is deemed to have transferred the asset at its acquisition cost (i.e. £50,000), such that no gain or loss arises on the transfer

Alice's deemed acquisition cost is the same as her husband's deemed proceeds (i.e. £50,000).

As the property has never been occupied as the principal private residence the property does not qualify for either principal private residence relief or letting relief.

35   **MICHAEL CHIN (ADAPTED)** *Online question assistance*

Key answer tips

A typical exam question on capital gains tax with a series of disposals covering a variety of topics.

All the disposals are gifts and so you must use the market value as the proceeds in the computation of the gains.

Be careful to distinguish disposals (1) and (2), which do qualify for gift relief, from the remaining disposals which do not.

Capital gains tax liability – 2009/10

Disposal of business (Note 1)

	£	£
Goodwill		
Deemed proceeds	60,000	
Less Cost	Nil	
	60,000	
Less Gift relief	(60,000)	
		Nil
Freehold property		
Deemed proceeds	150,000	
Less Cost	(86,000)	
	64,000	
Less Gift relief (W1)	(48,000)	
		16,000
Net current assets		Nil
Total chargeable gains on the disposal of the business		16,000

Ordinary shares in Minnow Ltd (Note 2)

	£	£
Deemed proceeds	180,000	
Less Cost	(87,500)	
	92,500	
Less Gift relief (W2)	(74,000)	
		18,500

Ordinary shares in Whale plc (Note 3)

	£	£
Deemed proceeds (18,000 × £6·40) (W3)	115,200	
Less Cost (W4)	(59,600)	
		55,600

Painting (Notes 4 and 5)

	£	£
Deemed proceeds	7,500	
Less Cost	(4,000)	
Gain	3,500	
Chargeable gain restricted to maximum of:		
5/3 × (£7,500 − £6,000)	2,500	2,500

Land (Notes 4 and 6)

	£	£
Deemed proceeds	50,000	
Less Cost (£50,000 / (£50,000 + £600,000)) × £500,000	(38,462)	
		11,538

Clock (Note 5)

	£	£
Non-wasting chattel bought and sold for < £6,000 = exempt		Nil
Total chargeable gains		104,138

	£
Total chargeable gains	104,138
Less Capital loss brought forward (W5)	(15,600)
Net chargeable gains	88,538
Less Annual exemption	(10,100)
Taxable gains	78,438
Capital gains tax (£78,438 x 18%)	14,119

Tutorial note:

1.   *Disposal of the business*

   The disposal of a business is treated as separate disposals of each chargeable asset in the business. A gain must be calculated on each chargeable asset.

   However, the net current assets are not chargeable assets for capital gains tax purposes.

   Gift relief is available on any gain relating to qualify business assets disposed of.

   Per the question, Entrepreneurs' relief is to be ignored. This is because the examiner has stated that he will not examine the interaction of Entrepreneurs' relief with the other reliefs.

   Where relevant, a question will simply state that a particular relief is not available.

   However, for tutorial purposes, where the full gain is not covered by gift relief, Entrepreneurs' relief may be available.

   It will be available on the gift of a qualifying business. Entrepreneurs' relief is given after gift relief.

2.   *Minnow Ltd shares*

   Gift relief is available as ordinary shares in an unquoted trading company are qualifying assets for gift relief purposes. However full relief is not available as the company holds investments.

   Per the question, Entrepreneurs' relief is to be ignored.

   However, for tutorial purposes, where the full gain is not covered by gift relief, Entrepreneurs' relief may be available.

   It will be available on the gift of shares in a personal trading company (i.e. donor owns at least 5% interest), provided the donor works for for the company and has owned the shares for at least one year. Entrepreneurs' relief is given after gift relief.

3.   *Whale plc shares*

   Gift relief is only available on shares in a quoted company if the donor owns at least 5% of the shares in the company and the company is a trading company. As Michael owns less than 1% in Whale plc, gift relief is not available.

   For the same reason, Entrepreneurs' relief would not be available.

> 4. **Painting and Investment land**
>
> A painting and investment land are not qualifying assets for gift relief purposes.
>
> 5. **Chattels**
>
> It is important to be able to recognise when an asset is a chattel (i.e. tangible and moveable) and therefore that the disposal is subject to special rules. The painting and antique clock are both chattels.
>
> 6. **Part disposal**
>
> On a part disposal the cost of the part disposed of is calculated using A/(A+B) where A is the value of the part disposed of and B is the value of the part retained.

Workings

(W1) Freehold property

The proportion of the freehold property gain relating to non-business use is £16,000 (£64,000 × 25%), and this amount does not qualify for gift relief.

The remaining gain of £48,000 (£64,000 − £16,000) can be held over (i.e. deferred) with a gift relief claim.

(W2) Minnow Ltd

The gift relief in respect of the ordinary shares in Minnow Ltd is restricted because the company has investment assets.

The proportion of gain eligible for gift relief is the proportion of chargeable business assets to chargeable assets, calculated as follows:

Gift relief = (£92,500 × £200,000/£250,000) = £74,000

(W3) Valuation of the Whale plc shares

Quarter up method = (£6.36 + $^1/_4$ × (£6.52 − £6.36)) = £6.40 per share

(W4) Share pool – Whale plc shares

		Number of shares	Cost £
December 2008	Purchase	15,000	63,000
August 2009	Purchase	12,000	26,400
		27,000	89,400
February 2010	Disposal (£89,400 x 18,000/27,000)	(18,000)	(59,600)
Balance c/f		9,000	29,800

(W5) **Capital loss brought forward**

2008/09	£
Capital gain	11,800
Less Capital loss b/f from 2007/08 – Used (Note)	(1,700)
Net chargeable gains	10,100
Less Annual exemption	(10,100)
Taxable gains	Nil

Tutorial note:

The capital loss brought forward is used in 2008/09 but the offset is restricted to preserve the annual exemption.

Loss left to c/f to 2009/10

	£
Capital loss	17,300
Less Used in 2008/09 (above)	(1,700)
Los c/f to 2009/10	15,600

36   SOPHIA TANG (ADAPTED)

Key answer tips

A straightforward computation of gains on the disposal of a business, followed by consideration of some tax planning.

Questions about capital gains are not always computational and you must be prepared to give written explanations as in parts (b) (i) and (ii).

There are usually some 'easier' marks to pick up on these written sections so make sure you attempt them.

The last part was a standard disposal of a principal private residence with relief.

(1)   (a)   **Capital gains tax liability – 2009/10**

	£	£
Freehold shop		
Deemed proceeds (Note 1)	260,000	
Less Cost	(113,000)	
	147,000	
Less Gift relief (£147,000 – £47,000) (W)	(100,000)	
Chargeable gain (Note 2)		47,000

	£	£
Chargeable gain brought forward		47,000

Freehold warehouse

	£	£
Deemed proceeds	225,000	
Less Cost	(70,000)	
Chargeable gain (Note 3)		155,000
Total chargeable gains		202,000
Less Annual exemption		(10,100)
Taxable gains		191,900
Capital gains tax (£191,900 at 18 %)		34,542

Working: Chargeable gain after gift relief

Where there is a sale at undervaluation, a chargeable gain will arise if the actual consideration received exceeds the allowable cost:

	£
Actual proceeds	160,000
Less Cost	(113,000)
Chargeable gain after gift relief	47,000

The chargeable amount of £47,000 is immediately chargeable to capital gains tax (see Tutorial note).

As a qualifying business asset the remaining gain can be held over under the gift relief provisions, provided both Sophia and Wong sign a gift relief election.

Gift relief will be the remaining gain of £100,000 (£147,000 − £47,000)

Tutorial note:

1. *Sophia and her daughter are connected persons, and therefore the market values of the assets sold are used as consideration.*

2. *Per the question, Entrepreneurs' relief is to be ignored.*

    However, for tutorial purposes, where the full gain is not covered by gift relief, Entrepreneurs' relief may be available.

    Entrepreneurs' relief is available on the freehold shop as Sophia is transferring the whole of her unincorporated business to her daughter and she has had the business for more than 12 months.

3. *The warehouse is not a business asset, and therefore does not qualify for gift relief nor Entrepreneurs' relief.*

(b) (i) **Postponement until 6 April 2010**

The gains would have been assessed in 2010/11, so the payment of the CGT liability would have been due on 31 January 2012 instead of 31 January 2011.

(ii) **Retention until death**

- The transfer of assets on death is an exempt disposal so there would not have been any CGT liability.

- Wong would have inherited the shop and warehouse with base costs of £260,000 and £225,000 respectively (i.e. the MV at the date of death).

(2) **Sale of house in 2010/11**

	£
Disposal proceeds	400,000
Less: Cost	(250,000)
	150,000
Less: Principal private residence (PPR) exemption (W)	(131,250)
Chargeable gain	18,750

Working: Principal private residence relief

Sophia used 1/8th of the house (one of the eight rooms) exclusively for business purposes.

PPR is available for the part of the house not used for business purposes:

(£150,000 × 7/8) = £131,250

Tutorial note:

Note that Sophia cannot benefit from the rules of deemed occupation for any part of the property used for business purposes.

In addition, the exemption for the last 36 months does not apply to any part of the property used wholly for business purposes throughout the period of ownership.

37   DAVID AND ANGELA BROOK *Walk in the footsteps of a top tutor*

Key answer tips

A classic question involving the calculation of capital gains tax liabilities of both a husband and his wife, with joint assets and assets held personally.

Tutor's top tips:

Be careful to spot the exempt assets. You don't need to do any calculations for these – just say that they are exempt!

Predictably a husband and wife nil gain/nil loss transfer is included, with the subsequent disposal by the recipient spouse.

Remember also to consider Entrepreneurs' relief on the disposal of shares and gift relief if they have been gifted.

David Brook

Capital gains tax liability – 2009/10

	£
Motor car (exempt)	Nil
House (W1)	20,343
Antique table (W3)	Nil
Shares in Bend Ltd (W4)	Nil
Shares in Galactico plc (W5)	14,850
Total chargeable gains	35,193
Less Annual exemption	(10,100)
Taxable gains	25,093
Capital gains tax (£25,093 at 18%)	4,517

Angela Brook

Capital gains tax liability – 2009/10

	£
House (W1)	20,343
Antique clock (W8)	2,000
Ordinary shares in Bend Ltd (W9)	26,400
Chargeable gains	48,743
Less Annual exemption	(10,100)
Taxable gains	38,643
Capital gains tax (£38,643 at 18%)	6,956

Workings

(W1) House

Tutor's top tip:

If an asset is jointly owned by husband and wife, all you need to do is to calculate the gain as usual and then split it 50:50.

Make sure you show your working for the calculation of principal private residence relief. Even if you can't count months, you will still be given marks for applying the correct principles!

	£
Disposal proceeds	381,900
Less Cost	(86,000)
	295,900
Less Principal private residence exemption (W2)	(255,214)
Chargeable gain	40,686

David and Angela will each be assessed on 50% of the chargeable gain, i.e. £20,343 (£40,686 × 50%).

(W2) Occupation of the house

The total period of ownership of the house is 240 months (207 + 33), of which 207 months qualify for exemption as follows:

	Exempt months	Chargeable months
1 October 1989 to 31 March 1993 (occupied)	42	
1 April 1993 to 31 December 1996 (working in UK)	45	
1 January 1997 to 31 December 2003 (occupied)	84	
1 January 2004 to 30 September 2006 (unoccupied)		33
1 October 2006 to 30 September 2009 (final 36 months)	36	
	207	33

PPR relief = (207/240 × £295,900) = £255,214

(W3) Antique table

Tutor's top tip:

As soon as you see the word 'antique', think about the special chattels rules.

This is a chattel bought and sold for no more than £6,000 and hence is exempt.

(W4) Shares in Bend Ltd – gift by David

Tutor's top tip:

Remember that the market value at the time of the inter-spouse gift is a red herring and irrelevant. The transfer will be at nil gain/nil loss.

Transfers between husband and wife are no gain-no loss transfers.

David makes no gain and Angela takes over David's cost of £48,000.

(W5) Shares in Galactico plc

	£
Proceeds (Market value for a gift) (15,000 × £2.95) (W6)	44,250
Less Cost (W7)	(29,400)
	———
Chargeable gain	14,850
	———

Tutorial note:

There is no gift relief and no Entrepreneurs' relief available on these shares as Galatico plc is a quoted company and David has a less than 5% interest and does not work for the company.

(W6) Value of Shares in Galactico plc shares

Quarter up method = 2.90 + ¼ (3.10 – 2.90) = £2.95

(W7) Share pool

		Number of shares	Cost £
15.6.08	Purchase	8,000	17,600
24.8.08	Purchase	12,000	21,600
		———	———
		20,000	39,200
14.2.10	Gift (£39,200 x 15,000/20,000)	(15,000)	(29,400)
		———	———
Balance c/f		5,000	9,800
		———	———

(W8) Antique clock

	£
Disposal proceeds	7,200
Less Cost	(3,700)
	———
Gain	3,500
	———

Chargeable gain cannot exceed: 5/3 x (£7,200 – £6,000) = £2,000

Tutorial note:

The clock is a chattel sold at a marginal gain, therefore in the answer the gain is compared with the 5/3^{rds} rule.

In fact, HMRC accept that antique clocks are a form of machinery, and are therefore wasting chattels, which will be exempt (if not used in a business). However, the examiner did not expect you to know this.

(W9) Shares in Bend Ltd – Sale by Angela

	£
Disposal proceeds	62,400
Less Cost (£48,000 × 15,000/20,000)	(36,000)
Chargeable gain	26,400

Tutorial note:

It is not clear what percentage interest Angela has in Bend Ltd and whether it is her personal trading company (i.e. she holds 5% interest or more). However, even if she does, Entrepreneurs' relief is not available as Angela does not work for the company.

Examiner's report

Although there were some very good answers to this question from well prepared candidates, it caused problems for many and was often the reason that they failed to achieve a pass mark.

One particular problem was that a lot of time was often spent performing unnecessary calculations for the exempt assets, and then not having sufficient time to deal with the chargeable assets. Many candidates therefore did a lot of work for this question but scored few marks.

The jointly owned property caused particular difficulty. Only a few candidates correctly calculated the principal private residence exemption.

Some candidates did not allocate the resulting chargeable gain between the couple but instead deducted an annual exemption and calculated a separate tax liability.

ACCA marking scheme		
		Marks
Jointly owned property		
Motor car		0.5
House – Proceeds		0.5
	– Cost	0.5
	– Period of exemption	2.5
	– Exemption	1.0
	– Division of gain	1.0
David Brook		
Antique table		1.0
Bend Ltd		0.5
Galatico plc	– Deemed proceeds	1.0
	– Cost	2.0
	– No gift relief	1.0
	– No Entrepreneurs' relief	1.0
Annual exemption		0.5
Capital gains tax		1.0
Angela Brook		
Antique clock		2.0
Bend Ltd	– Proceeds	0.5
	– Cost	1.0
	– No Entrepreneurs' relief	1.0
Annual exemption		0.5
Capital gains tax		1.0
Total		20.0

38 WILSON BIAZMA (ADAPTED)

Key answer tips

In part (a) easy marks were available for defining two key terms, namely residence and ordinary residence. However, don't forget to read all the requirements and state the consequences of the residence on the liability of an individual to capital gains tax.

Part (b) involved a series of disposals testing the various reliefs available, part disposals and incorporation. This style of question is a regular feature in the Paper F6 exam.

This was, however, the first time the compensation rules for damaged assets were tested.

(a) **Residence**

- A person will be resident in the UK during a tax year if they are present in the UK for 183 days or more.

- A person will also be treated as resident if they visit the UK regularly, with visits averaging 91 days or more a tax year over a period of four or more consecutive tax years.

Ordinary residence

- Ordinary residence is not precisely defined, but a person will normally be ordinarily resident in the UK if this is where they habitually reside.

Liability to capital gains tax

- A person is liable to capital gains tax (CGT) on the disposal of assets during any tax year in which they are either resident or ordinarily resident in the UK.

(b)   **Chargeable gains – 2009/10**

	£
Office building (W1)	110,000
Goodwill (W3)	66,667
Ordinary shares in Gandua Ltd (W4)	8,000
Antique vase (W6)	–
Land (W7)	17,000
Total chargeable gains	201,667

Workings

(W1) **Office building**

	£
Disposal proceeds	246,000
Less Cost	(104,000)
Capital gain before reliefs	142,000
Less Rollover relief (W2)	(32,000)
Chargeable gain	110,000

Tutorial note:

Entrepreneurs' relief is not available as this is the disposal of a single asset, not the whole or part of a business.

(W2) **Rollover relief**

Rollover relief is not available in full because not all the proceeds are reinvested.

The gain remaining chargeable is the lower of:

(i)   Total gain of £142,000, or

(ii)   Proceeds not reinvested (£246,000 – £136,000) = £110,000

Rollover relief is therefore £32,000 (£142,000 – £110,000).

(W3) **Goodwill**

	£
Disposal proceeds	120,000
Less Cost	Nil
	120,000
Less Entrepreneurs' relief (£120,000 × 4/9) (Tutorial Note)	(53,333)
Chargeable gain (Tutorial Note)	66,667

Tutorial note:

Entrepreneurs' relief is available as Wilson has disposed of a complete business which he has owned for at least one year.

Wilson has chosen to disapply incorporation relief, therefore the mixed consideration received is irrelevant.

*However, had Wilson **not** elected to disapply the incorporation relief, there would be a gain arising now due to the mixed consideration received.*

Incorporation relief would only apply to the proportion of the gain relating to the share consideration leaving a gain relating to the cash consideration as follows:

Total consideration = £200,000

Proportion of the gain relating to the cash consideration

= (£120,000 × £60,000/£200,000) = £36,000

Incorporation relief is therefore the remaining gain relating to the share consideration

= (£120,000 − £36,000) = £84,000

or can be calculated as= (£120,000 × £140,000/£200,000) = £84,000

Entrepreneurs' relief would then be:

- *given after incorporation relief*

- *applied to the remaining gain left in charge to tax (i.e. £36,000), and*

- *would be £16,000 (£36,000 x 4/9) in this case, leaving a chargeable gain of £20,000 (£36,000 − £16,000).*

The £84,000 gain relating to the share consideration would not crystallise until the shares are sold in the future.

(W4) **Ordinary shares in Gandua Ltd**

	£
Deemed proceeds (Market value)	160,000
Less Cost	(112,000)
	48,000
Less Gift relief (W5)	(40,000)
Chargeable gain	8,000

Tutorial note:

Although Gandua Ltd qualifies as Wilson's personal company, Entrepreneurs' relief is not available unless he also works for the company.

(W5) Gift relief on shares in Gandua Ltd

The gift relief in respect of the ordinary shares in Gandau Ltd is restricted because the company has investment assets.

The proportion of gain eligible for gift relief is the proportion of chargeable business assets to chargeable assets, calculated as follows:

Gift relief = (£48,000 × £150,000/£180,000) = £40,000

(W6) Antique vase

The insurance proceeds of £68,000 received by Wilson have been fully reinvested in a replacement antique vase.

The disposal is therefore on a no gain no loss basis.

The capital gain of £19,000 (insurance proceeds of £68,000 less original cost of £49,000) is set against the cost of the replacement antique vase.

(W7) Land – part disposal

	£
Disposal proceeds	85,000
Less Deemed cost (see below)	(68,000)
	———
Chargeable gain	17,000
	———

Cost of part disposed of = £120,000 × £85,000 / (£85,000 + £65,000) = £68,000.

Tutorial note:

The cost relating to the ten acres of land sold is calculated as A / (A + B) where:

A = Market value of part disposed of

B = Market value of the remainder

Examiner's report

Part (a) was reasonably well answered, although only a few candidates appreciated that ordinary residence is a matter of where a person habitually resides.

Many candidates missed an easy mark by not stating that people who are resident or ordinarily resident will be liable to capital gains tax.

Part (b) was also reasonably well answered. The disposal that caused the most problems was the incorporation of the business, with many candidates not appreciating that the gain was simply based on the value of the goodwill transferred.

ACCA marking scheme		
		Marks
(a)	183 day rule	1.0
	91 day rule	1.0
	Ordinary residence	1.0
	Liability to CGT	1.0
		───
		4.0
		───
(b)	**Office building**	
	Proceeds	0.5
	Cost	0.5
	Rollover relief	1.5
	No Entrepreneurs' relief	1.0
	Goodwill	
	Proceeds	0.5
	Cost	0.5
	No incorporation relief	1.0
	Entrepreneurs' relief	2.0
	Ordinary shares in Gandua Ltd	
	Proceeds	0.5
	Cost	0.5
	Gift relief	1.5
	No Entrepreneurs' relief	1.0
	Antique vase	
	Proceeds fully reinvested	1.0
	No gain no loss	1.0
	Gain reduces base cost	0.5
	Land	
	Proceeds	0.5
	Cost	2.0
		───
		16.0
		───
Total		20.0
		───

39 NIM AND MAE LOM *Walk in the footsteps of a top tutor*

Key answer tips

A typical capital gains tax question, requiring the calculation of capital gains tax liabilities for a husband and wife.

This is the first exam testing the new capital gains tax rules, and as such is quite different in the level of detail from previous years.

Although there is only one requirement, the question can be broken down between the two individuals and then into the different assets sold by each.

Tutor's top tips:

Nim's assets are mostly straightforward. As with any capital gains question, be careful to spot the exempt assets (gilts). You don't need to do any calculations for these – simply state that they are exempt.

There is a classic husband to wife transfer, which from Nim's perspective is simply a nil gain/nil loss disposal.

When dealing with shares, make sure you consider the matching rules first. There is a purchase within 30 days of the disposal, so this will need to be matched before the shares bought earlier, and these shares will NOT go into the share pool.

Nim Lom

Capital gains tax liability – 2009/10

	£
Ordinary shares in Kapook plc (W1)	13,600
Ordinary shares in Jooba Ltd (no gain, no loss)	Nil
Antique table (W4)	3,500
UK Government securities (exempt)	Nil
Total chargeable gains	17,100
Less Capital loss brought forward (W5)	(7,000)
Net chargeable gains	10,100
Less Annual exemption	(10,100)
Taxable gains	Nil
Capital gains tax	Nil

Workings

(W1) Ordinary shares in Kapook plc

The disposal is first matched against the purchase on 24 May 2009 of 2,000 shares (this is within the following 30 days), and then against the shares in the share pool.

	£	£
Matched with purchases in next 30 days:		
Deemed proceeds (2,000 x £3.70) (W2)	7,400	
Less Cost	(5,800)	
		1,600
Matched with share pool:		
Deemed proceeds (8,000 × £3.70) (W2)	29,600	
Less Cost (W3)	(17,600)	
		12,000
		13,600

(W2) **Valuation of ordinary shares in Kapook plc**

The shares in Kapook plc are valued at the lower of:

(i)   Quarter up method = £3·70 + ¼ x (£3·90 – £3·70) = £3.75

(ii)   Average of highest and lowest marked bargains = (£3·60 + £3·80)/2 = £3.70

(W3) **Share pool**

The cost of the shares in the share pool is calculated as:

		Number of shares	Cost £
Purchase	19 February 2001	8,000	16,200
Purchase	6 June 2006	6,000	14,600
		14,000	30,800
Disposal	20 May 2009 (£30,800 x 8,000/14,000)	(8,000)	(17,600)
Balance carried forward		6,000	13,200

(W4) **Antique table**

The antique table is a non-wasting chattel.

	£
Sale proceeds	8,700
Less Cost	(5,200)
Chargeable gain	3,500

Chargeable gain is not restricted as the maximum gain is:
5/3 × (£8,700 – £6,000)   4,500

(W5) **Capital losses brought forward**

The set off of the brought forward capital losses is restricted to £7,000 so that chargeable gains are reduced to the amount of the annual exemption.

Nim therefore has capital losses carried forward of £9,700 (£16,700 – £7,000).

Tutorial note:

The transfer of the 5,000 £1 ordinary shares in Jooba Ltd to Mae does not give rise to any gain or loss, because it is a transfer between spouses.

The disposal of UK Government securities is exempt from CGT.

Whenever you see the word 'antique' in a question, you should immediately be thinking about the chattel rules.

It is important to be familiar with the rules for the use of capital losses, which are very regularly tested. Brought forward losses are restricted to utilise the annual exemption, but current year losses must be used in full.

Mae Lom

Capital gains tax liability – 2009/10

Tutor's top tips:

Mae has disposed of the shares that she received from her husband. Remember this was a nil gain nil loss transfer, and in order for Nim to have a gain of nil, he is deemed to have transferred the asset to Mae at original cost.

The house has been Nim and Mae's main residence throughout the period of ownership, so there is no need to consider the absence rules here, however as one room was used exclusively for business purposes, principle private residence relief cannot be given in respect of that part of the gain.

When dealing with business assets make sure you consider their eligibility for Entrepreneurs' relief.

The hardest asset to deal with is the copyright, as this kind of disposal has not been seen in exam questions before. The asset is wasting (it has a useful life of less than 50 years), however it is not a chattel so the £6,000 rules do not apply. Instead the cost must be reduced for the period of time that the asset has been held by Mae.

	£	£
Ordinary shares in Jooba Ltd		
Disposal proceeds	30,400	
Less Cost (£16,000 x 2,000/5,000) (Note 1)	(6,400)	
	———	
		24,000
Principal private residence		
Disposal proceeds	186,000	
Less Cost	(122,000)	
	———	
	64,000	
Less PPR relief (W)	(56,000)	
	———	
		8,000
Business		
Goodwill	80,000	
Freehold office building	136,000	
	———	
	216,000	
Less Entrepreneurs' relief (£216,000 x 4/9)	(96,000)	
	———	
		120,000
Investment property (Note 2)		34,000
Copyright		
Disposal proceeds	9,600	
Less Cost (£10,000 x 15/20) (Note 3)	(7,500)	
	———	
		2,100
		———
Total chargeable gains		188,100
		———

	£
Total chargeable gains	188,100
Less Capital loss brought forward	(8,500)
Net chargeable gains	179,600
Less Annual exemption	(10,100)
Taxable gains	169,500
Capital gains tax (£169,500 x 18%)	30,510

Working: Principal private residence relief

One of the eight rooms in Mae's house was always used exclusively for business purposes, so the principal private residence exemption is restricted to £56,000 (£64,000 x 7/8).

Tutorial note:

1. *Nim's original cost is used in calculating the gain on the disposal of the shares in Jooba Ltd.*

2. *The investment property does not qualify for Entrepreneurs' relief because it was never used for business purposes.*

3. *The copyright is a wasting asset. The cost of £10,000 must therefore be depreciated based on an unexpired life of 20 years at the date of acquisition and an unexpired life of 15 years at the date of disposal.*

Examiner's report

Despite being the first test of the new CGT rules, this question was generally well answered.

For the husband, quite a few candidates surprisingly had problems with the valuation rules for quoted shares.

It was also not always appreciated that the transfer between spouses and the sale of the UK Government securities were respectively at no gain, no loss, and exempt. Candidates thus wasted time performing unnecessary calculations.

Many candidates had difficulty with the cost of the quoted shares disposed of, and they incorrectly included the purchase within the following 30 days as part of the share pool.

The restriction of the brought forward capital losses so that chargeable gains were reduced to the amount of the annual exemption was often missed.

For the wife, many candidates treated the private portion of the principal private residence as taxable rather than the business portion.

The investment property included within the disposal of the business was sometimes treated as exempt from CGT, and sometimes Entrepreneurs' relief was claimed in respect of it.

Only a minority of candidates correctly calculate the cost of the wasting asset.

ACCA marking scheme		Marks
Nim Lom		
Kapook plc – Deemed proceeds		2.0
– Cost		1.0
– Share pool		2.0
Jooba Ltd		1.0
Antique table		1.5
UK Government securities		0.5
Capital losses brought forward		1.0
Annual exemption		0.5
Capital losses carried forward		0.5
Mae Lom		
Jooba Ltd – Proceeds		0.5
– Cost		1.0
House – Proceeds		0.5
– Cost		0.5
– Exemption		1.0
Business – Goodwill		0.5
– Office building		0.5
– Entrepreneurs' relief		1.0
– Investment property		1.0
Copyright – Proceeds		0.5
– Cost		1.5
Capital losses brought forward		0.5
Annual exemption		0.5
Capital gains tax		0.5
		———
Total		20.0
		———

COMPANIES – CHARGEABLE GAINS

40 SHREWD LTD (ADAPTED)

Key answer tips

A question involving capital gains for a company will always require some indexation calculations.

You should be prepared to calculate indexation factors from the underlying retail price index figures as the indexation factor is not always given.

Part (1) of the question covers rollover relief which is often examined in company gains questions as it is the only relief available to single companies.

Part (2) covers the less frequently tested rules on compensation proceeds for a damaged asset. This part has been added to the original question to reflect the new syllabus.

(1) (a) **Conditions for rollover relief**

To qualify for rollover relief

- The reinvestment must take place between one year before and three years after the date of disposal.

- The old and new assets must both be qualifying assets and be used for business purposes.

- The new asset must be brought into business use at the time that it is acquired.

(b) **Chargeable gain – disposal of factory**

	£	£
Disposal proceeds (February 2010)		320,000
Less Incidental costs of disposal		(6,200)
		———
Net sale proceeds		313,800
Less Cost (October 1998)	164,000	
Incidental costs of acquisition	3,600	
	———	(167,600)
Enhancement expenditure (March 2000)		(37,000)
		———
Unindexed gain		109,200
Indexation allowance		
– Cost (£167,600 × 0.298)		(49,945)
– Enhancement (£37,000 × 0.268)		(9,916)
		———
Chargeable gain		49,339
		———

Tutorial note:

The factory extension is enhancement expenditure and therefore an allowable deduction as it has added to the value of the factory.

However, the replacement of the roof is not enhancement expenditure, being in the nature of a repair.

(c) **Rollover relief claims**

Freehold warehouse

- The sale proceeds are fully reinvested, and so the whole of the gain can be rolled over.

- The base cost of the freehold warehouse will be £290,661 (£340,000 – £49,339).

Freehold office building

- The sale proceeds are not fully reinvested, and so £40,000 (£320,000 – £280,000) of the chargeable gain cannot be rolled over and will be taxed immediately.

- The remaining gain of £9,339 (£49,339 – £40,000) can be rolled over.

- The base cost of the office building will be £270,661 (£280,000 – £9,339).

Leasehold factory

- The sale proceeds are fully reinvested, and so the whole of the gain can be deferred.

- The factory is a depreciating asset, and so the base cost of the factory is not adjusted.

- The base cost of the replacement factory will therefore be its cost of £350,000.

- The gain is held over until the earlier of ten years from the date of acquisition or the date the leasehold factory is disposed of.

Tutorial note:

Strictly full roll over requires the gross proceeds (i.e. £320,000) to be reinvested and this is the interpretation used in the examiner's answer.

However, in practice HM Revenue & Customs allow disposal costs to be taken into account so in this case full roll over would be given by reinvesting £313,800.

(2) **Painting**

- Where an asset is lost or destroyed there is a deemed disposal for capital gains purposes

- The date of disposal is 1 September 2009 (i.e. the date that the insurance proceeds are received), not 30 June 2009 (i.e. when the painting was destroyed).

- As the insurance proceeds have been used to buy a new painting within 12 months, Shrewd Ltd can claim that the destruction of the painting be treated as a no gain/no loss disposal as follows.

No gain/no loss disposal

- Since the disposal of the old asset is assumed to be on a no gain/no loss basis, the disposal proceeds are the allowable cost plus indexation allowance.

	£
Allowable cost	20,000
Indexation allowance (to September 2009)	
(212.5 − 149.8)/149.8 = 0.419 × £20,000	8,380
Deemed disposal proceeds = deemed acquisition cost	28,380

Base cost of new painting

	£	£
Cost of replacement painting		35,000
Less: Insurance proceeds	30,000	
Deemed acquisition cost	(28,380)	
		(1,620)
Replacement painting base cost		33,380

41 FORWARD LTD (ADAPTED)

Key answer tips

This question requires the corporation tax liability of a company, however before that can be calculated several chargeable gains need to be calculated.

Remember that disposals by a company are entitled to an indexation allowance and rollover relief for replacement of business assets is a key relief available for companies. No other reliefs are available. Note that the effect of reinvesting in a depreciating asset as in part (b) must be understood as this is an area that is often tested.

(a)   **Corporation tax liability – year ended 31 March 2010**

	£
Trading profit	75,000
Chargeable gains (£30,000 (W1) + £38,435 (W3) + £11,307 (W5))	79,742
PCTCT	154,742
Corporation tax liability (£154,742 × 21%)	32,496
Due date	1 January 2011

Workings

(W1) **Freehold office building**

	£
Disposal proceeds	290,000
Less Cost	(148,000)
Unindexed gain	142,000
Less Indexation allowance	
(211.7 – 133.8)/133.8 = 0.582 x £148,000	(86,136)
Capital gain before reliefs	55,864
Less Rolled over gain (W2)	(25,864)
Chargeable gain	30,000

(W2) **Rollover relief**

The sale proceeds of the office building are not fully reinvested, and so £30,000 (£290,000 – £260,000) of the capital gain cannot be rolled over.

The remaining gain of £25,864 can be deferred with a rollover relief claim.

(W3) Ordinary Shares in Backward plc

The disposal is matched against shares in the share pool:

	£
Disposal proceeds	62,500
Less Cost (W4)	(12,895)
Unindexed gain	49,605
Less Indexation allowance (£24,065 – £12,895) (W4)	(11,170)
Chargeable gain	38,435

Tutorial note:

The gain cannot be rolled over into the acquisition of the shares in Sideways plc as shares are not qualifying assets for the purpose of rollover relief.

(W4) Share pool

	Number	Cost £	Indexed cost £
April 1986 Purchase	9,000	18,000	18,000
Indexation to November 2009			
£18,000 × (212.9 – 97.7)/97.7			21,224
(do not round indexation factor)			
			39,224
November 2009 Purchase	500	6,500	6,500
	9,500	24,500	45,724
November 2009 Disposal			
Cost × 5,000/9,500	(5,000)	(12,895)	(24,065)
Balance c/f	4,500	11,605	21,659

(W5) Painting

	£
Deemed proceeds	22,000
Less: Deemed cost (see Tutorial Note)	
£15,000 × (£22,000 / (£22,000 + £20,000))	(7,857)
Unindexed gain	14,143
Less : Indexation to February 2010	
(213.5 – 156.9)/156.9 = 0.361 x £7,857	(2,836)
Chargeable gain	11,307

Tutorial note:

Where an asset is damaged, compensation is received and the proceeds are not used to restore the asset, there is a part disposal of the asset for capital gains purposes.

The deemed cost is calculated using A/(A+B) where:

A = Insurance proceeds received

B = Value of asset after damage

The date of disposal is the date that the compensation is received not the date that the asset is damaged.

(b) **Reinvestment in leasehold office building**

- The freehold office building's sale proceeds of £290,000 will be fully reinvested, and so the whole of the gain of £55,864 is eligible for rollover relief.

- The leasehold office building is a depreciating asset, so its base cost will not be adjusted.

- The base cost of the 15 year lease will therefore be its actual cost of £300,000.

- The gain will be deferred until the earliest of ten years from the date of acquisition of the leasehold building, the date that it is disposed of, or the date that it ceases to be used for trading purposes.

42 HAWK LTD *Walk in the footsteps of a top tutor*

Key answer tips

This question requires the computation of a corporation tax liability for a company, however several chargeable gains need to be calculated before the corporation tax liability computation can be performed.

You need to remember that disposals made by a company will usually have some element of indexation allowance, so you need to be aware of the rules regarding the rounding of the indexation factor.

The only capital gains relief available to companies is rollover relief and therefore it is not surprising to see it here in this question and it is often tested in corporation tax questions.

Tutor's top tips:

Part (a) consisted of a number of reasonably straightforward disposals made by a company. As long as the gains are calculated individually, a good mark can be achieved in this question.

It is important not to get bogged down with any particular computation. If you cannot remember how to deal with a disposal, move on! You will pick up far more marks by moving forward, and if you have time you can revisit the problem area again later.

Part (b) covers rollover relief and requires you to apply your knowledge of the relief.

(a)   Hawk Ltd

Corporation tax computation – year ended 31 March 2010

	£
Trading profit	125,000
Chargeable gains (W)	94,114
PCTCT	219,114
Corporation tax liability (£219,114 × 21%)	46,014

Tutorial note:

Hawk Ltd has no associated companies, therefore the PCTCT of £219,114 is taxed at 21% as profits fall below the lower limit of £300,000.

Workings: Chargeable gains

	£	£
Office Building		
Proceeds (April 2009)	260,000	
Less Costs of disposal	(3,840)	
Net disposal proceeds	256,160	
Less Cost and legal fees (July 1990)		
(£81,000 + £3,200)	(84,200)	
Enhancement (May 2002)	(43,000)	
Unindexed gain	128,960	
Less Indexation allowance		
On cost:		
(211.5 – 126.8)/126.8 = 0.668 x £84,200	(56,246)	
On enhancement		
(211.5 – 176.2)/176.2 = 0.200 x £43,000	(8,600)	
		64,114

	£	£
Chargeable gain b/f		64,114
Shares in Albatross (5,000 shares)		
Proceeds (August 2009)	42,500	
Less Cost (below) (Note 1)	(17,500)	
		25,000

Share pool	*Number*	*Cost* £
1 August 2009 Purchase	6,000	18,600
17 August 2009 Purchase	2,000	9,400
	8,000	28,000
29 August 2009 Disposal (£28,000 x 5,000/8,000)	(5,000)	(17,500)
	3,000	10,500

	£	£
Shares in Cuckoo (10,000 preference shares)		
Proceeds (October 2009)	32,000	
Less Cost (below)	(15,000)	
		17,000

Consideration received at time of takeover:		
Ordinary shares	(5,000 x 3 x £4.50)	67,500
Preference shares	(5,000 x 2 x £2.25)	22,500
		90,000

Therefore cost of shares disposed of in October 2009:	
£60,000 x (£22,500/£90,000)	15,000

	£	£
Land		
Proceeds (March 2010)	120,000	
Less Cost of part disposed of (Note 2) £203,500 x (£120,000 / (£120,000 + £65,000))	(132,000)	
Allowable loss		(12,000)
Net chargeable gains		94,114

Tutorial note:

1.   There is no indexation allowance available on either of the share disposals, as the purchase and sale occur in the same month.

2.   There is no indexation allowance available on the disposal of the land, as indexation cannot create or increase a loss.

> *The disposal of the land is a part disposal and therefore the allowable cost is calculated by apportioning the original cost to the part disposed of as follows:*
>
> *Original cost x A / (A + B)   where: A = MV of the element disposed of*
>
> *B = MV of the element retained*

(b)   **Rollover relief**

(i)   **Minimum amount of reinvestment**

- The only disposal that qualifies for rollover relief is the sale of the freehold office building.

- The office building was sold for £256,160 (net of disposal expenses) and this is therefore the amount that Hawk Ltd will have to reinvest in order to claim the maximum possible amount of rollover relief.

Tutorial note:

HMRC allow full rollover relief provided the net sale proceeds are reinvested in qualifying assets within the qualifying time period.

It is not necessary to reinvest the gross sale proceeds. However, the examiner gave credit if the gross sale proceeds were used in this part.

(ii)   **Period of reinvestment**

- The reinvestment will have to take place between 1 May 2008 and 30 April 2012, being one year before and three years after the date of disposal.

(iii)   **Amount of corporation tax deferred**

- Corporation tax of £13,464 (£64,114 at 21%) will be saved if the maximum possible amount of rollover relief is claimed.

Examiner's report

Part (a) was reasonably well answered.

As regards the freehold office building, many candidates did not appreciate that indexation would also be available for the incidental costs of acquisition.

For the quoted shares many candidates based their answers on the rules applicable to individuals rather than the pooling rules. The allocation of cost following the reorganization also caused problems.

Part (b) was also reasonably well answered, with a number of candidates providing perfect answers.

ACCA marking scheme		Marks
(a) **Office building**		
Disposal proceeds		0.5
Costs of disposal		0.5
Cost		0.5
Costs of acquisition		0.5
Enhancement expenditure		0.5
Indexation – Cost		1.0
– Enhancement		1.0
Albatross plc		
Proceeds		0.5
Cost		2.0
Cuckoo Ltd		
Proceeds		0.5
Value of shares – Ordinary shares		1.0
– Preference shares		1.0
Cost		1.5
Land		
Proceeds		0.5
Cost		2.0
Corporation tax liability		
Net chargeable gains		1.0
Calculation		1.5
		────
		16.0
(b) Qualifying disposal		1.0
Amount of reinvestment		1.0
Period of reinvestment		1.0
Corporation tax saving		1.0
		────
		4.0
Total		────
		20.0

CORPORATION TAX

CORPORATION TAX BASICS AND ADMINISTRATION

43   ELONGATED LTD (ADAPTED)

Key answer tips

The first part of this question is testing 'text book' knowledge. Some easy marks are available here; and note that for four marks you need to give four points.

Part (a) (ii) covers the treatment of long periods of account which is a popular exam topic. You must remember to split the period into the first 12 months and then the remaining short period.

The rules for splitting profits must be learnt. A columnar presentation of the two accounting periods is usual and makes your answer easier to mark.

> Part (b) includes a capital allowance computation and deals with property income which you should find straight forward.
>
> Finally easy marks available for some corporation tax self assessment knowledge if you have learnt it.

(a)   (i)   **Accounting periods**

Start of an accounting period

- An accounting period will normally start immediately after the end of the preceding accounting period.

- An accounting period will also start when a company commences to trade, or when its profits otherwise become liable to corporation tax.

End of an accounting period

- An accounting period will normally finish 12 months after the beginning of the accounting period or at the end of a company's period of account.

- An accounting period will also finish when a company ceases to trade, or when its profits otherwise cease being liable to corporation tax.

(ii)   **Corporation tax computations**

	Year ended 31.12.08 £	Period ended 31.3.09 £
Trading profit (12/15 : 3/15)	233,600	58,400
Property business income (12/15 : 3/15)	56,200	14,050
Chargeable gain	–	44,075
	289,800	116,525
Less: Gift Aid	(1,200)	–
PCTCT	288,600	116,525
Plus: Franked investment income	–	40,000
Profits	288,600	156,525
Corporation tax (W)		
(£288,600 × 20% × 3/12)	14,430	
(£288,600 × 21% × 9/12))	45,454	
(£116,525 × 28%)		32,627
Less Marginal relief		
7/400 × (£375,000 − £156,525) × £116,525/£156,525		(2,846)
Corporation tax liability	59,884	29,781
Due dates	1.10.09	1.1.10

Tutorial notes:

1. *Trading profits and property business profits are allocated on a time basis: 12/15 to the year ended 31 December 2008 and 3/15 to the period ended 31 March 2009.*

2. *Chargeable gains are allocated to the accounting period in which the disposal takes place.*

3. *Gift Aid payments are deducted from the profits of the accounting period in which it is paid.*

Working: Corporation tax rate

		y/e 31.12.08	3 m/e 31.3.09
		£	£
Upper limit	(Full / 3/12)	1,500,000	375,000
Lower limit	(Full / 3/12)	300,000	75,000
Profits		288,600	156,525
		Small	Marginal relief applies

The accounting period ended 31 December 2008 straddles FY2007 and FY2008.

The small companies limits were the same in both financial years but the rates of tax changed.

The tax is therefore payable at 20% for FY2007 and at 21% for FY2008.

(b)   (i)   **Corporation tax computation for the year ended 31 March 2009**

	£
Trading profit	704,228
Less: Capital allowances (W1)	(67,930)
	636,298
Property business income (W2)	102,600
PCTCT	738,898
Corporation tax (£738,898 × 28%)	206,891
Less Marginal relief	
7/400 × (£1,500,000 − £738,898)	(13,319)
Corporation tax liability	193,572

Workings

(W1) Plant and machinery

	Pool	Special rate pool	Allowances
	£	£	£	£
Year ended 31 March 2010				
Additions (no AIA or FYA) (Note 1)				
Car (CO$_2$ between 111 – 160 g/km)		11,400		
Car (CO$_2$ > 160 g/km)			15,800	
Additions (with AIA)				
Office furniture	51,425			
Less AIA (Max)	(50,000)			50,000
	———			
	1,425			
WDA (20%)		(2,280)		2,280
WDA (10%)			(1,580)	1,580
FYA (40%) (Note 2)	(570)			570
	———	855		
Additions with FYA				
Car (CO$_2$ < 111 g/km)	13,500			
Less FYA (100%) (Note 1)	(13,500)			13,500
	———	Nil		
TWDV c/f		9,975	14,220	
		———	———	
Total allowances				67,930
				———

Tutorial note:

1. *Capital allowances on new car purchases are now calculated based on the CO$_2$ emissions of the car as follows:*

    CO$_2$ emissions of < 111 g/km: eligible for a FYA of 100%. CO$_2$ emissions of between 111 – 160 g/km: put in main pool, eligible for a WDA at 20%. CO$_2$ emissions of > 160 g/km: put in special rate pool, eligible for a WDA at 10%.

    The appropriate rates are given in the tax rates and allowances.

2. *Any excess of expenditure on plant and machinery over the AIA maximum is eligible for the temporary FYA of 40%.*

(W2) **Property business income**

	£	£
Premium received	70,000	
Less: 70,000 × 2% × (10 – 1)	(12,600)	
		57,400
Rent receivable – Office 1 (£50,000 × 9/12)		37,500
– Office 2 (£34,000 × 9/12)		25,500
		120,400
Less Allowable deductions:		
Decorating		(9,600)
Advertisements		(8,200)
Property business income		102,600

(ii) **Self-assessment tax return**

- Elongated Ltd's self-assessment corporation tax return for the year ended 31 March 2010 must be submitted by 31 March 2011.

- If the company fails to submit its self-assessment tax return by 31 March 2011 then there will be an automatic fixed penalty of £100.

- The penalty increases to £200 if the self-assessment tax return is more than three months late.

- There will be an additional corporation tax related penalty of 10% of the tax unpaid if the self-assessment tax return is more than six months late, or 20% if more than 12 months late.

44   ARABLE LTD

Key answer tips

This question deals with the calculation of corporation tax for a short accounting period. You should remember that the length of the period affects the calculation of the maximum AIA and the WDA for capital allowances, and the limits for determining the rate of corporation tax to apply.

Other things to watch out for in this question are the effect of the short period on the lease premium deduction and the fact that the company has associated companies, which also affects the small company limits for calculating corporation tax.

Make sure you attempt the administration points in part (b) which should be easy marks to obtain.

(a) **Corporation tax computation – 9 months ended 31 December 2009**

	£	£
Trading profit		288,900
Capital allowances – Plant and machinery (W2)	64,210	
– IBA (W1)	3,090	
Deduction for lease premium (W3)	2,700	
		(70,000)
		218,900
Property business income (W4)		31,700
Interest income – Loan interest (£6,000 + £3,000)		9,000
Chargeable gain (W5)		25,890
PCTCT		285,490
Plus: Franked investment income (£18,000 × 100/90)		20,000
Profits		305,490
Corporation tax (W6)		
(£285,490 at 28%)		79,937
Less: Marginal relief		
7/400 × (£375,000 – £305,490) × £285,490/£305,490		(1,137)
Corporation tax liability		78,800

Workings

(W1) **Industrial buildings allowance**

	£
Site preparation	14,000
Professional fees	6,000
Drawing office	40,000
Factory	146,000
Eligible expenditure (Note 1)	206,000
IBAs (£206,000 x 2% x 9/12) (Note 2)	3,090

Tutorial note:

1. *The cost of the land does not qualify. The showroom does not qualify as it cost more than 25% of the total potentially qualifying cost*

    Total potential qualifying cost = (£400,000 – £120,000) = £280,000

    25% of potential qualifying cost = (£280,000 × 25%) = £70,000.

    Cost of showroom = £74,000

    Therefore the showroom will not be eligible for relief.

> *In practice some of the other costs may be treated as relating to the showroom and would therefore not qualify. This approach would be awarded equivalent marks*
>
> 2. *The accounting period is nine months long, so the WDA is time apportioned.*

Workings

(W2) Plant and machinery

	Pool	Special rate pool	Allowances
	£	£ £	£
Additions (no AIA or FYA) (Note 1)			
Car (CO$_2$ between 111 – 160 g/km)	11,200		
Car (CO$_2$ > 160 g/km)		14,600	
Additions (with AIA but no FYA) (Note 2)			
Machinery	31,000		
Alterations	3,700		
	———		
	34,700		
Less AIA (£50,000 × 9/12) (Note 3)	(34,700)		34,700
	———	Nil	
Additions (with AIA and FYA)			
Lorry	22,000		
Computer	5,400		
	———		
	27,400		
Less AIA (£37,500 Max – £34,700)	(2,800)		2,800
	———		
	24,600		
WDA (20% × 9/12) (Note 4)	(1,680)		1,680
WDA (20% × 9/12) (Note 4)		(2,190)	2,190
FYA (40%) (Note 3)	(9,840)		9,840
	———	14,760	
Car (CO$_2$ < 111 g/km) (Note 1)	13,000		
Less FYA (100%)	(13,000)		13,000
	———	Nil	
WDV c/f	24,280	12,410	
	———	———	
Total allowances			64,210
			———

Tutorial notes:

1. *Capital allowances on new car purchases are now calculated based on the CO$_2$ emissions of the car as follows:*

   CO$_2$ emissions of < 111 g/km: eligible for a FYA of 100%. CO$_2$ emissions of between 111 – 160 g/km: put in main pool, eligible for a WDA at 20%. CO$_2$ emissions of > 160 g/km: put in special rate pool, eligible for a WDA at 10%.

   The appropriate rates are given in the tax rates and allowances.

> 2. The machinery purchased on 15 February 2009 and the related building alterations are incurred pre-trading, but are eligible for capital allowances and are treated as if incurred on 1 April 2009. They are therefore brought into the first capital allowances computation.
>
> However, the pre-trading additions would not qualify for the 40% FYA as they were acquired before 1 April 2009, and the FYA is based on the date the expenditure was actually incurred.
>
> 3. The AIA will be set first against the pre-trading expenditure as it is not eligible for the FYA. Any excess maximum AIA is then set against the other qualifying expenditure. Any excess expenditure over the AIA is eligible for the temporary FYA of 40%.
>
> 4. The maximum AIA and WDAs are time apportioned because Arable Ltd's accounting period is nine months long.

(W3) Deduction for lease premium

The first office building has been used for business purposes, and so a proportion of the lease premium assessed on the landlord can be deducted.

	£
Premium received	75,000
Less: 75,000 × 2% × (15 − 1)	(21,000)
Amount assessed on the landlord	54,000

Allowable deduction for 9 month period = (£54,000 ÷ 15 x 9/12) = £2,700

(W4) Property business income

	£
Premium received for sub-lease	50,000
Less: £50,000 × 2% × (5 − 1)	(4,000)
	46,000
Less: Relief for premium paid for head lease (£54,000 × 5 /15) i.e. (duration of sub-lease)/(duration of head lease)	(18,000)
	28,000
Rent receivable (£14,800 × 3/12)	3,700
Property business income	31,700

(W5) Chargeable gain

	£
Disposal proceeds	37,576
Less Cost (see below)	(11,625)
Unindexed gain	25,951
Less Indexation (£11,686 − £11,625) (see below)	(61)
Chargeable gain	25,890

Share Pool	Number	Cost £	Indexed cost £
Purchase (May 2009)	15,000	12,000	12,000
Indexation to August 2009			
£12,000 × (212.3 – 211.7)/211.7			34
			12,034
Purchase (August 2009)	5,000	11,250	11,250
	20,000	23,250	23,284
Indexation to December 2009			
£23,284 × (213.1 – 212.3)/212.3			88
			23,372
Disposal (December 2009)			
Cost × 10,000/20,000	(10,000)	(11,625)	(11,686)
Balance carried forward	10,000	11,625	11,686

Tutorial note:

The indexation allowance in the share pool is not rounded to three decimal places.

(W6) **Corporation tax rates**

		£
Upper limit	(£1,500,000 x 1/3 x 9/12)	375,000
Lower limit	(£300,000 x 1/3 x 9/12)	75,000
Profits		305,490
		Marginal relief applies

The limits are reduced for a nine month period and there are three associated companies.

The accounting period falls entirely within FY2009.

(b) **Self assessment corporation tax return**

- Arable Ltd's self-assessment corporation tax return for the period ended 31 December 2009 must be submitted by 31 December 2010.

- It will be possible for Arable Ltd to amend its return at any time before 31 December 2011, being 12 months after the filing date.

- If an error or mistake in a return is subsequently discovered, then Arable Ltd can make a claim for relief before 31 December 2013, being four years from the end of the chargeable accounting period.

Tutorial note:

Some of the time limits for making claims has changed in FA2009, for example, the error and mistake claim date. As a result, time limits may be more potentially examinable in 2010 than in previous years.

45   ZOOM PLC (ADAPTED)   *Online question assistance*

Key answer tips

This question has many of the usual features of corporation tax questions with marks for computing capital allowances and corporation tax.

One unusual aspect however is part (a)(ii) where the examiner gives you the figure of profits chargeable to corporation tax and asks for a reconciliation between that and the profit before tax.

Do not waste time trying to make your reconciliation agree if it doesn't on your first attempt.

Since you are given the PCTCT you can use that figure in part (c) to calculate corporation tax even if your reconciliation does not quite balance.

Knowledge of the quarterly instalment rules is often tested and should give some easy marks if you know the rules.

Tutorial note:

1.   *Capital allowances on new car purchases are now calculated based on the CO_2 emissions of the car as follows:*

  CO_2 emissions of < 111 g/km: eligible for a FYA of 100%. CO_2 emissions of between 111 – 160 g/km: put in main pool, eligible for a WDA at 20%. CO_2 emissions of > 160 g/km: put in special rate pool, eligible for a WDA at 10%.

  The appropriate rates are given in the tax rates and allowances.

2.   *Purchases pre 1 April 2009 are eligible for the AIA, but not the temporary FYA of 40%. The AIA will be allocated to these purchases first as the balance on these items is only eligible for a WDA of 20%.*

  However, purchases on or after 1 April 2009 qualify for the AIA and the balance is eligible for the temporary FYA of 40%.

3. It is assumed that the election to treat the computer as a short life asset has not been made. If it had been made, a separate column would be set up, but the AIA would not be allocated to it in preference to the pre 1 April purchase. Therefore, the allowances in this year would be identical whether or not the election is made.

4. The sale proceeds for the expensive motor car sold are restricted to original cost. The sale proceeds for the lorry and the equipment are deducted from the main pool as they are less than the original cost of the lorry.

(a) **Capital allowances for plant and machinery**

y/e 31 December 2009	Pool	Motor car	Special rate pool	Allowances
	£	£	£	£
TWDV b/f	19,600	20,200		
Additions (no AIA or FYA) (Note 1)				
Car (CO_2 > 160 g/km)			16,600	
Car (CO_2 between 111 – 160 g/km)	11,850			
Additions (with AIA but not FYA)				
Equipment (Note 2)	54,600			
Less AIA	(50,000)			50,000
	———			
	4,600			
Additions (with AIA and FYA)				
Computer (Note 3)	12,300			
Less AIA (Max already given)	(Nil)			
	———			
	12,300			
Proceeds (Note 4)		(23,200)		
(£9,800 + £1,000)	(10,800)			
	———	———		
	25,250	(3,000)		
Balancing charge		3,000		(3,000)
		———		
WDA (20%)	(5,050)			5,050
WDA (10%)			(1,660)	1,660
FYA (40%)	(4,920)			4,920
	———			
	7,380			
Addition (with 100% FYA)				
Car (CO_2 < 111 g/km)	14,200			
Less FYA (100%)	(14,200)			14,200
	———			
	Nil			
	———		———	
TWDV c/f	27,580		14,940	
	———		———	
Total allowances				72,830
				———

(ii)   **Reconciliation of profits – year ended 31 December 2009**

	£
Profit before taxation	910,000
Add: Depreciation	48,100
Patent royalties (Note 1)	0
Interest payable (Note 2)	0
	958,100
Less: Income from investments	(127,100)
Capital allowances – Plant and machinery	(72,830)
Trading profit	758,170
Interest income – Bank interest	10,420
– Loan interest	22,500
Property business profit (W)	29,750
Profits chargeable to corporation tax	820,840

Tutorial note:

1.   *The patent royalties received are included as part of the trading profit, so no adjustment is required.*

2.   *The interest on a loan used for trading purposes is deductible in calculating the trading profit and has already been deducted, so no adjustment is required.*

Working – Property business profit

	£	£
Rent receivable – Office 1 (£3,200 × 10 months)		32,000
– Office 2 (£26,400 × 8/12)		17,600
		49,600
Irrecoverable rent (£3,200 × 2)	6,400	
Advertising	4,800	
Decorating	5,200	
Insurance ((£3,360 × 9/12) + (£3,720 × 3/12))	3,450	
		(19,850)
Property business profit		29,750

(b)   **Quarterly instalment payments – y/e 31 December 2009**

- Large companies have to make quarterly instalment payments in respect of their corporation tax liability. A large company is one paying corporation tax at the full rate.

- Zoom plc has three associated companies, so the upper limit is reduced to £375,000 (£1,500,000/4). Corporation tax will therefore be at the full rate for the year ended 31 December 2009.

- The exceptions for quarterly instalments do not apply because Zoom plc was also a large company for the year ended 31 December 2008.

(c)   **Corporation tax liability – y/e 31 December 2009**

- Zoom plc's corporation tax liability for the year ended 31 December 2009 is £229,835 (£820,840 at 28%).

- The company will have paid this in four quarterly instalments of £57,459 (£229,835 x 1/4) as follows:

	£
14.07.2009	57,459
14.10.2009	57,459
14.01.2010	57,459
14.04.2010	57,459
	229,835

Tutorial note:

The year ended 31 December 2009 straddles 31 March 2009, therefore 3 months of the year falls into FY 2008 and 9 months into FY 2009.

However, there is no change in rate between the two years and so the liability can be calculated in one computation.

(d)   **If Zoom plc had no associated companies**

- Zoom plc's 'profits' for corporation tax purposes for the year ended 31 December 2009 is:

	£
PCTCT	820,840
Plus FII (£49,500 x 100/90)	55,000
Profits	875,840

- Zoom plc is no longer a large company since its profits are below the upper limit of £1,500,000.

- The corporation tax liability will therefore be due in one amount on 1 October 2010.

- The corporation tax liability will be:

	£
Corporation tax (£820,840 at 28%)	229,835
Less: Marginal relief	
7/400 × (£1,500,000 − £875,840) × £820,840/£875,840	(10,237)
Corporation tax liability	219,598

46   ALPHABETIC LTD (ADAPTED)

Key answer tips

A tricky little question covering corporation tax administration rules.

In part (a) it is important to read the question carefully and work out the interest in days rather than months as requested.

Part (b) asks for the payments the company would actually make during the year before they are sure of the correct tax bill for the accounting period. This is an everyday practical problem in tax departments as companies always have to make their first three quarterly payments before they are sure of the final liability.

Be careful to calculate each instalment based on the expected liability at that date.

(a)   (i)   **Interest already paid on overdue tax, now repayable**

The tax was due nine months after the end of the accounting period (i.e. 1 May 2010).

Actually paid on 1 June 2010.

Overpaid tax = (£100,000 − £90,000) = £10,000

Interest = £10,000 at 2.5% for 31 Days = £10,000 × 2.5% × 31/365 = £21

Tutorial note:

Interest on overdue tax runs from the due date until the day before the payment.

So for a payment due on 1 May which was actually paid on 1 June, the interest runs from 1 May to 31 May (i.e. 31 days).

(ii)   **Interest on overpaid tax payable**

Interest accrues for the period 1 June to 27 September 2009 (i.e. for 119 days)

Tutorial note:

In addition to recovering the interest on overdue tax paid, HMRC will give a repayment supplement on overpaid tax from the date the tax is paid (or due date if later) to the date of repayment.

The original question asked for a calculation of interest in this part. However, the current rate of interest is 0%, therefore the requirement has been amended to just ask for the dates!

(b)   **Betamatic Ltd – Pay days**

		£
14 October 2009	(First quarterly instalment): (28% × £2,300,000 × ¼)	161,000
14 January 2010	(Second instalment):	161,000
14 April 2010	(Third instalment): Total due to date: (28% × £2,120,000 × ¾) Paid already (£161,000 + £161,000)	445,200 (322,000)
		123,200
14 July 2010	(Final instalment): (28% × £2,080,000) Less Paid already (£322,000 + £123,200)	582,400 (445,200)
		137,200

Tutorial note:

You were only asked to show the amounts of tax payable, you were not asked to calculate the interest that would be paid to Betamatic Ltd on the overpaid instalments.

47   REALITY LTD

Key answer tips

This is a detailed question on property business profit for a company. There are four properties involved, however it is important to appreciate that a calculation of profit for each property separately is not necessary. The company is assessed on the net profits from all properties.

The trickiest part of the question is dealing with the lease premiums for Property 3. However, a comfortable pass mark can be obtained in this question even if this part is answered incorrectly.

It is also important to get the easy mark for bringing in the rent received for Property 3 for the 7 months of letting even if you struggled with the lease element.

(a)   **Basis of assessment – property income**

- A company's income from land and buildings is computed on the basis that the company is carrying on a business, with the profit or loss calculated on the accruals basis.

- Where a company has more than one rental property, the income and expenses are aggregated in order to arrive at the property business profit or loss.

(b)   **Property business profit – year ended 31 March 2010**

	£	£
Rent receivable – Property 1 (£750 × 9 months)		6,750
– Property 2 (£625 × 12 months)		7,500
– Property 3 (£6,600 × 7/12)		3,850
– Property 4 (£800 × 3 months)		2,400
Premium received for sub-lease – Property 3	20,000	
Less: 20,000 × 2% × (5 – 1)	(1,600)	
	———	
	18,400	
Less: Relief for premium paid for head lease (W)	(7,750)	
	———	10,650
Less : Allowable deductions		
Irrecoverable rent (£750 × 2)	1,500	
Repairs	6,800	
Advertising	1,100	
Wear and tear allowance – Property 2		
(£7,500 × 10%)	750	
Decorating (Note 4)	3,900	
Insurance ((£5,040 × 9/12) + (£5,280 × 3/12))	5,100	
	———	(19,150)
		———
Property business profit		12,000
		———

Tutorial note:

1.   *There are several properties to deal with in this question. However, only one computation is required. There is no need to do separate computations to calculate a profit or loss for each property. The company will be assessed on the net property income for the year.*

2.   *No deduction is available for replacement furniture where the 10% wear and tear allowance is claimed.*

3.   *Interest paid in respect of a loan used to purchase property is set off under the loan relationship rules against interest income, not against property income.*

4.   *Decorating costs for Property 4, incurred in the period from purchase of the property up until first letting, are allowable. However, if a property is bought in a dilapidated state such that it cannot be let, the costs of making it useable are treated as capital and added to the cost of the property.*

Working: Relief for premiums paid on head lease

The amount of the head lease assessed on the landlord of Property 3 is calculated as:

	£
Premium received	50,000
Less: 50,000 × 2% × (20 – 1)	(19,000)
Amount assessed on the landlord	31,000

Allowable deduction from premium on sub-lease:

Amount assessed on the landlord x (duration of sub-lease / duration of head lease)

= (£31,000 × 5 years (duration of sub-lease) / 20 years (duration of head lease)

= £7,750

Corporation tax computation – year ended 31 March 2010

	£
Trading profit	84,000
Property business profit	12,000
Interest (£9,600 – £5,600)	4,000
PCTCT	100,000
Corporation tax (£100,000 × 21%)	21,000

48 BALLPOINT LTD (ADAPTED) *Walk in the footsteps of a top tutor*

Key answer tips

This is a wide ranging corporation tax question involving adjustment of profits, capital allowances and a chargeable gain to calculate.

The highlighted words in the written sections are key phrases that markers are looking for.

Tutor's top tips:

It is important when answering questions as long as this, that you have a good technique for dealing with all the information.

You should read the question carefully and highlight key pieces of information as you go through.

Part (a) should have been a very quick and easy way to earn 3 marks, as long as you broke your answer down into 3 separately identifiable points.

(a)   **Residency status**

- Companies that are incorporated overseas are only treated as being resident in the UK if their central management and control is exercised in the UK.

- Since the directors are UK based and hold their board meetings in the UK, this would indicate that Ballpoint Ltd is managed and controlled from the UK, and therefore it is resident in the UK.

- If the directors were to be based overseas and to hold their board meetings overseas, the company would probably be treated as resident overseas since the central management and control would then be exercised outside the UK.

(b)   **Trading profit for the year ended 31 December 2009**

	£
Profit before taxation	520,000
Add: Depreciation	59,900
Gifts to customers – pens (Note 1)	0
Gifts to customers – food hampers (Note 1)	770
Gifts to employees (Note 2)	0
Gift aid donation (Note 3)	600
Donation to local charity (Note 4)	0
Donation to political party (Note 4)	300
Accountancy and audit (Note 5)	0
Legal fees – issue of share capital (Note 6)	3,100
Legal fees – issue of debentures (Note 6)	0
Legal fees – defence of internet domain name (Note 7)	0
Replacement roof (Note 8)	0
Initial repairs to office building (Note 9)	13,900
Car lease costs (Note 10)	0
Entertaining customers (Note 11)	3,700
Entertaining employees (Note 11)	0
Counselling services for employees (Note 12)	0
Fine	2,600
Interest payable (Note 13)	0
	————
	604,870
Less: Dividends	(45,000)
Disposal of industrial building	(60,000)
Capital allowances – plant and machinery (W)	(68,310)
Capital allowances – IBAs (Note 14)	0
	————
Trading profit	431,560
	————

Tutor's top tips:

In the adjustment to profits calculation it is important to list all the major items indicated in the question requirement, showing a zero (0) for expenditure that is allowable. This is because credit will be given for showing no adjustment where none is needed.

If required, also add notes to show why you have not adjusted for an item, or why you have added it back. However, lengthy explanations are not required where the requirement is just to 'calculate' the adjusted profits, rather than to explain them.

Always show your workings if the figure you are adjusting for is not clear from the question.

Tutorial note:

1. *Gifts to customers are an allowable deduction if they cost less than £50 per recipient per year, are not of food, drink, tobacco, or vouchers for exchangeable goods, and carry a conspicuous advertisement for the company making the gift.*

2. *Gifts to employees are allowable, although the gift might result in a taxable benefit as regards the employee.*

3. *The Gift Aid donation is allowable but is deducted from total profits in the PCTCT computation, it is not an allowable deduction in the adjustment ofprofits and therefore needs to be aded back.*

4. *Small donations to a local charity are allowable but political donations are not.*

5. *Accountancy and audit fees are allowable as incurred wholly and exclusively for the purposes of the trade.*

6. *Legal fees in connection with the issue of share capital are not allowable, being capital in nature.*

    However, under the loan relationship rules all costs associated with loans related to the trade (i.e. debentures) are deductible in calculating trading profits. The costs of obtaining loan finance (even if abortive) are therefore allowable.

7. *The costs of defending the right to an asset (the internet domain name) are also an allowable trading deduction.*

8. *The replacement of the roof is allowable since the whole structure is not being replaced.*

9. *The repairs to the office building are not allowable, being capital in nature, as the building was not in a usable state when purchased and this was reflected in the purchase price.*

10. *All of the car leasing costs are allowable as the car has CO_2 emissions of less than 160 g/km. If the CO_2 emissions had exceeded 160 g/km, 15% of the lease costs would be disallowable.*

11. The only exception to the non-deductibility of entertainment expenditure is when it is in respect of employees.

12. The costs of counselling services for redundant employees are allowable, whilst fines are generally not allowable.

13. Interest on a loan used for trading purposes is deductible in calculating the trading profit on an accruals basis.

14. In the year of disposal of the factory, no WDA is available and no IBA balancing adjustments arise.

Working: Plant and machinery

	£	Pool £	Exp car £	Special rate pool £	Allowances £
TWDV b/f		8,200	9,800		
Additions (no AIA or FYA) (Note 1)					
Car ($CO_2 > 160$ g/km)				18,200	
Car (CO_2 between 111 – 160 g/km)		11,400			
		19,600			
Additions (with AIA but no FYA)					
Equipment (Note 2)	61,260				
Less AIA (Max)					
(Note 3)	(50,000)				50,000
		11,260			
Additions (with AIA and FYA)					
Equipment (Note 2)	4,300				
Less AIA (used)	(Nil)				
	4,300				
Proceeds					
– Equipment		(2,700)			
– Car (2)		(10,110)			
		18,050			
WDA (20%)		(3,610)			3,610
WDA (20%)			(1,960)		1,960
WDA (10%)				(1,820)	1,820
FYA (40%)	(1,720)				1,720
		2,580			
Addition with FYA					
Car ($CO_2 < 111$ g/km)	9,200				
FYA (100%)	(9,200)	Nil			9,200
TWDV c/f		17,020	7,840	16,380	
Total allowances					68,310

Tutor's top tips:

Ballpoint Ltd has a year end 31 December 2009, which straddles 31 March 2009, therefore it is important to identify the additions of plant and machinery before and after 31 March 2009. This is because the temporary FYA is only available for purchases from 1 April 2009 to 31 March 2010.

It is also important to look carefully at the CO_2 emissions for the cars. There are three categories, all treated differently. Remember that the appropriate rates of allowances are given to you in the tax rates and allowances in the examination.

Tutorial note:

1. *Capital allowances on new car purchases are now calculated based on the CO2 emissions of the car as follows:*

    CO2 emissions of < 111 g/km: eligible for a FYA of 100%. CO2 emissions of between 111 – 160 g/km: put in main pool, eligible for a WDA at 20%. CO2 emissions of > 160 g/km: put in special rate pool, eligible for a WDA at 10%.

    The appropriate rates are given in the tax rates and allowances.

2. *Purchases pre 1 April 2009 are eligible for the AIA, but not the temporary FYA of 40%. The AIA will be allocated to these purchases first as the balance on these items are only eligible for a WDA of 20%.*

    However, purchases on or after 1 April 2009 qualify for the AIA and the balance is eligible for the temporary FYA of 40%.

3. *There is only one AIA of £50,000 for Ballpoint Ltd and its 100% subsidiary, and this AIA can be shared between the two companies in any way they choose. However, this aspect of capital allowances is not examinable, so you should assume that the maximum AIA is claimed by Ballpoint Ltd.*

(c)   **Corporation tax computation – year ended 31 December 2009**

Tutor's top tip:

Don't worry if you made some mistakes in part (b) as you can still score full marks here for calculating the tax correctly based on your figures.

You must make sure you set out your workings clearly so that the marker can see what you have done.

	£
Trading profit	431,560
Chargeable gain (W1)	20,160
	451,720
Less Gift Aid donation	(600)
	451,120
Less Group relief (Note 1)	(42,000)
Profits chargeable to corporation tax	409,120
Plus Franked investment income (£27,000 × 100/90) (Note 2)	30,000
Profits	439,120
Corporation tax (W2) (£409,120 at 28%)	114,554
Less: Marginal relief	
7/400 × (£750,000 − £439,120) × £409,120/£439,120	(5,069)
Corporation tax liability	109,485

Tutorial note:

1. *Remember that group relief is set off after Gift Aid, whereas if a company claims relief for its own loss, the loss is set off before Gift Aid.*

2. *Group dividends are not included as franked investment income.*

Workings

(W1) Chargeable gain

	£
Disposal proceeds	300,000
Less: Cost	(240,000)
Unindexed gain	60,000
Less: Indexation allowance	(39,840)
Chargeable gain	20,160

(W2) Corporation tax rates

		£
Upper limit	(£1,500,000 x ½)	750,000
Lower limit	(£300,000 x ½)	150,000
Profits		484,250

Therefore marginal relief applies

The year end straddles 31 March 2009, but there is no change in rate and therefore only one computation is required to calculate the corporation tax liability.

49 DO-NOT-PANIC LTD (ADAPTED)

Key answer tips

A short question involving a long period of account which requires knowledge of the rules of how to split income and gains between two chargeable accounting periods.

When the question was set, the capital allowance rules were different and more was involved in the calculation than under the current rules.

The old capital allowances rules do apply to part of this 15 month period, however the examiner has stated that he will not test the old rules in the 2009 exam sittings.

The question has therefore been adapted to apply the new rules only throughout the whole 15 month period

Corporation tax liabilities – fifteen-month period ended 31 March 2010

	Year ended 31 December 2009 £	Period ended 31 March 2010 £
Trading profit (12/15 : 3/15) (Note 1)	252,000	63,000
Less Capital allowances (W1)	(24,000)	Nil
	228,000	63,000
Chargeable gains (£42,000 – £4,250) (Note 2)	–	37,750
Profits chargeable to corporation tax	228,000	100,750
Plus Franked investment income	–	25,000
Profits	228,000	125,750
Corporation tax (W2)		
(£228,000 × 21%)	47,880	
(£100,750 × 28%)		28,210
Less Marginal relief		
7/400 × (£375,000 – £125,750) × £100,000/£125,750		(3,469)
	47,880	24,741
Due dates	1 October 2010	1 January 2011

Tutorial note:

1. *Trading profits are allocated on a time basis: 12/15 to the year ended 31 December 2009 and 3/15 to the period ended 31 March 2010.*

2. *The capital loss of £4,250 for the year ended 31 December 2009 is carried forward and set against the first available future gains in 3 months ended 31 March 2010.*

Workings

(W1) Capital allowances

		Pool	Allowances
	£	£	£
Year ended 31 December 2009			
Additions (with AIA)			
Equipment	24,000		
Less AIA (100%)	(24,000)		24,000
		Nil	
TWDV c/f		Nil	
Period ended 31 March 2010			
WDA		Nil	Nil
TWDV c/f		Nil	

(W2) Corporation tax rate

		y/e 31.12.09	p/e 31.3.10
		£	£
Upper limit	(Full / 3/12)	1,500,000	375,000
Lower limit	(Full / 3/12)	300,000	75,000
Profits		228,000	125,750
		Small	Marginal relief applies

The accounting period ended 31 December 2009 falls partly into FY2008 (3 months) and partly into FY2009 (9 months). However, there is no change in rate of tax and therefore the liability can be calculated for the whole year in one computation.

Examiner's report

Depending on whether candidates appreciated that the period of account needed to be split into a twelve-month period and a three-month period, this question was either answered very well or quite badly.

Invariably many of the less well prepared candidates calculated corporation tax based on a fifteen-month period.

Even when the correct approach was taken, many candidates did not appreciate that the first twelve month period spanned two financial years, however the rates of corporation tax did not change.

The due dates were often omitted or incorrect.

ACCA marking scheme	
	Marks
Trading profit	1.0
Capital allowances	1.0
– Year ended 31 December 2009	0.5
– Period ended 31 March 2010	0.5
Capital gains	1.5
Franked investment income	1.0
Corporation tax	
– Year ended 31 December 2009	1.5
– Period ended 31 March 2010	2.0
Due dates	1.0
	———
Total	10.0
	———

50 GASTRON LTD *Walk in the footsteps of a top tutor*

Key answer tips

This was a classic corporation tax computational question, requiring an adjustment of profits and capital allowances computation, corporation tax computation, and some self assessment.

All these areas are highly likely to be tested and should be well practiced.

Parts (d) and (e) involve capital gains groups, which may be seen as tricky, but most of the marks can be won by simply stating the rules, rather than needing application to the question.

Tutor's top tips:

This question has clear mark allocations, which should be used to allocate the time spent on each section. You need to adopt a logical approach, using the requirements to break down the information and plan your answer.

It is possible to score very well on this sort of question, which is not technically difficult, as long as you do not panic over the quantity of information.

Part (a) gives you clear guidance on the approach that is needed, and you should follow this – starting with the profit before tax and then making the necessary adjustments.

Work through the notes in order, and ensure you have dealt with every single item, as credit is given for showing an adjustment of nil where one is not necessary, as stated in the requirement.

If you are not sure of how to deal with an item, make a sensible assumption and move on, but do not ignore it, or waste unnecessary time.

Note that as the question has asked you to 'calculate' the adjusted profits you do not need to explain each adjustment that you make, but you should show any workings.

Make sure you do a separate capital allowances working, which is clearly referenced, as there are a number of purchases and disposals in the period, and a full working is required.

(a)　**Trading profit – year ended 31 March 2010**

	£	£
Profit before taxation	640,000	
Depreciation	85,660	
Amortisation of leasehold property (Note 1)	6,000	
Deduction for lease premium (W2)		4,920
Gifts of pens to customers (Note 2)	1,200	
Gifts of hampers to customers (Note 2)	1,100	
Donation (Note 3)	0	
Legal fees re renewal of lease (Note 4)	0	
Legal fees re issue of debentures (Note 4)	0	
Entertaining suppliers (Note 5)	1,300	
Entertaining employees (Note 5)	0	
Income from investments		87,000
Profit on disposal of shares		80,700
Interest payable (Note 6)	0	
Capital allowances (W1)		62,640
	————	————
	735,260	235,260
Allowable deductions	(235,260)	————
	————	
Tax adjusted trading profit	500,000	
	————	

Tutorial note:

1.　The amortisation of a lease is disallowable (just like depreciation), but there is relief for the 'revenue' element of the premium spread over the life of the lease (like capital allowances).

　　The revenue element is calculated using the $P - (P \times 2\% \times (n - 1))$ formula and then divided by the life of the lease to calculate the annual deduction.

2.　Gifts to customers are only an allowable deduction if they cost less than £50 per recipient per year, are not of food, drink, tobacco, or vouchers for exchangeable goods, and carry a conspicuous advertisement for the company making the gift.

　　The pens caost £60 and the hampers contain food, therefore neither are allowable.

3.　Small donations to a local charity are allowable.

4.　The costs of renewing a short-lease (less than 50 years) and of obtaining loan finance are specifically allowable.

5.   The only exception to the non-deductibility of entertainment expenditure is when it is in respect of employees.

6.   Interest on a loan used for trading purposes is deductible in calculating the trading loss on an accruals basis.

Workings

(W1) Plant and machinery

	Pool	Expensive car	Allowances
	£	£	£
TWDV b/f	16,700	18,400	
Additions (no AIA or FYA)			
Car (CO$_2$ between 111 – 160 g/km)	9,800		
Additions (with AIA and FYA) (Note 1)			
Equipment	21,600		
Lorry	17,200		
	———		
	38,800		
Less AIA (100%)	(38,800)		38,800
	———		
	Nil		
Proceeds – equipment	(3,300)		
	———	———	
	23,200	18,400	
WDA (20%)	(4,640)		4,640
WDA (Restricted) (Note 1)		(3,000)	3,000
FYA (40%) (Note 2)	(Nil)		
	———	Nil	
Addition qualifying for FYA			
Car (CO$_2$ < 111 g/km)	16,200		
Less: FYA (100%)	(16,200)		16,200
	———	Nil	
TWDV c/f	18,560	15,400	
	———	———	———
Total allowances			62,640
			———

Tutorial note:

1.   Brought forward 'expensive' cars are dealt with under the old rules. A WDA of 20% is available regardless of the car's CO$_2$ emissions, however, the total WDA for a 12 month period is restricted to £3,000

Capital allowances on new car purchases are now calculated based on the CO$_2$ emissions of the car as follows:

> CO_2 emissions of < 111 g/km: eligible for a FYA of 100%. CO_2 emissions of between 111 – 160 g/km: put in main pool, eligible for a WDA at 20%. CO_2 emissions of > 160 g/km: put in special rate pool, eligible for a WDA at 10%.
>
> The appropriate rates are given in the tax rates and allowances.
>
> 2.   The temporary FYA is not available as the expenditure is already covered by the AIA.

(W2) **Deduction for lease premium**

The office building has been used for business purposes, and so the proportion of the lease premium assessed on the landlord can be deducted, spread over the life of the lease.

	£
Premium received	60,000
Less: £60,000 x 2% x (10 – 1)	(10,800)
Amount assessed on the landlord	49,200

This is deductible over the life of the lease, so the deduction for the year ended 31 March 2010 is £4,920 (£49,200/10).

Tutor's top tips:

Many students find dealing with lease premiums tricky, however, it is simply a case of learning the formula and applying it to the figures in the question.

There is no other way to attempt to deal with this question if you haven't learnt the formula! See W2 for the computation of the allowable deduction.

(b)   **Gastron Ltd – Corporation tax computation for the year ended 31 March 2010**

Tutor's top tips:

Part (b) requires a corporation tax computation, which will incorporate the figure calculated in part (a).

As long as you use the adjusted trading profit figure you have calculated correctly you can score full marks here, even if you have made errors earlier in the question.

	£
Trading profit	500,000
Property business profit (W1)	12,800
Bank interest	12,400
Chargeable gain	74,800
Profits chargeable to corporation tax	600,000
Plus Franked investment income (£36,000 x 100/90) (Note)	40,000
'Profits'	640,000
Corporation tax (£600,000 at 28%) (W2)	168,000
Less Marginal relief	
7/400 x (£750,000 – £640,000) x £600,000/£640,000	(1,805)
	166,195

Tutorial note:

Group dividends are not included as franked investment income. Therefore only the dividends received from Tasteless plc, the unconnected company will be grossed up and added to the PCTCT to calculate profits.

Workings:

(W1) **Property business profit**

	£	£
Rent receivable – First tenant (£1,800 x 9)		16,200
– Second tenant (£1,950 x 2)		3,900
		20,100
Irrecoverable rents (£1,800 x 2) (Note)	3,600	
Decorating	3,700	
		(7,300)
Property business profit		12,800

Tutorial note:

The rent is taxable on an accruals basis, and therefore all 9 months of rent for the first tenant are included. However, as the tenant left owing two months' rent, the irrecoverable rent is an allowable deduction.

(W2) **Corporation tax rate**

Gastron Ltd has one associated company, so the upper limit is reduced to £750,000 (£1,500,000 x ½) and the lower limit £150,000 (£300,000 x ½).

Profits fall in between the limits, therefore marginal relief applies.

(c) **Corporation tax due dates and interest**

Tutor's top tips:

Part (c) requires the due date for payments of corporation tax and the interest that will be charged if the tax is paid late.

It is important to actually calculate the interest here, rather than simply stating the way it will be calculated.

Note that the rates of interest on underpaid and overpaid tax are given in the tax tables.

- Gastron Ltd's corporation tax liability for the year ended 31 March 2010 must be paid by 1 January 2011.

- If the company does not pay its corporation tax until 31 August 2011, then interest of £2,770 (£166,195 at 2.5% = £4,155 x 8/12) will be charged by HM Revenue and Customs for the period 1 January 2011 to 31 August 2011.

(d) **Definition of a capital gains group**

Tutor's top tips:

This part requires only a definition of a capital gains group for 2 marks.

It is useful to learn this definition, as this is a common requirement in a question involving groups.

- Companies form a capital gains group if at each level in the group structure there is a 75% shareholding.

- However, the parent company must also have an effective interest of over 50% in each group company.

(e) **Gains group election**

Tutor's top tips:

Knowledge of time limits and deadlines is very useful for obtaining easy marks.

The most common deadline for claims and elections is two years from the end of the accounting period, and if you don't know the deadline, this can be a good guess to make!

> However, it is important to state the actual date, not just the general rule, so you must apply the rule to the dates in the question.

- Gastron Ltd and Culinary Ltd must make the election by 31 March 2012 (within two years of the end of the accounting period in which the disposal outside of the group occurred).

- Culinary Ltd's otherwise unused capital loss of £66,000 can be set against Gastron Ltd's chargeable gain of £74,800.

- It is beneficial for the balance of the chargeable gain of £8,800 (£74,800 − £66,000) to arise in Culinary Ltd as it will only be taxed at the rate of 21%, instead of at the marginal rate (29·75%) in Gastron Ltd.

Tutorial note:

It is not necessary to do a further corporation tax computation in order to calculate the most beneficial way of making this election.

The question states that Culinary is paying tax at 21%, and in part (b) you have calculated that Gastron Ltd is paying tax at 28% less marginal relief. This is an effective rate of tax of 29.75%.

It can be useful to learn the effective rate of tax in the margin, as this will help you to quickly calculate the benefit of any tax or loss relief.

Examiner's report

This question was very well answered, with only part (e) consistently causing problems.

In part (a) candidates were instructed to list all of the items referred to in the notes, and to indicate by the use of zero any items that did not require adjustment. This method should be quicker for candidates than writing separate explanatory notes, and shows that they have considered any non-taxable and non-deductible items, rather than simply forgetting about them.

Candidates are advised that this will be a standard approach in future and they should ensure they follow this instruction to be able to score full marks.

Despite the instruction some candidates did not list those items not requiring any adjustment.

Parts (a) and (b) were kept separate for a very good reason – namely to help candidates. Therefore those candidates who attempted to combine both parts into one calculation not surprisingly often had problems.

Given the new capital allowances rules, it was pleasing to see many candidates correctly calculate the correct figure for capital allowances. Although I can applaud candidate's attempts to save paper, it is not good examination technique to try and squeeze a capital allowances computation of this size into 5 or 6 lines at the end of a page.

In part (c) a disappointing number of candidates gave 31 January as the payment date.

Only a few candidates appreciated that interest would be due, and fewer still correctly calculated the actual amount payable.

In part (d) most candidates appreciated that a 75% shareholding was necessary, but were then often unsure where the 50% limit fitted in. The holding company must have an effective interest of 50%.

In part (e) many candidates simply stated that losses could be set against profits, without making any attempt to use the information given in the question.

	ACCA marking scheme	
		Marks
(a)	Profit before taxation	0.5
	Depreciation	0.5
	Amortisation of leasehold property	0.5
	Lease premium – assessable amount	1.5
	Lease premium – deduction	1.0
	Gifts of pens to customers	0.5
	Gifts of hampers to customers	0.5
	Donation	0.5
	Legal fees re renewal of lease	0.5
	Legal fees re issue of debentures	0.5
	Entertaining suppliers	0.5
	Entertaining employees	0.5
	Income from investments	1.0
	Disposal of shares	0.5
	Interest payable	0.5
	Plant and machinery – Main pool	2.0
	– AIA	1.5
	– Expensive car	1.0
	– FYA	1.0
		15.0
(b)	Trading profit	0.5
	Property business profit	2.0
	Bank interest	0.5
	Chargeable gain	0.5
	Franked investment income	1.0
	Group dividends	0.5
	Corporation tax	2.0
		7.0
(c)	Due date	1.0
	Interest	2.0
		3.0
(d)	75% shareholding	1.0
	50% effective interest	1.0
		2.0
(e)	Time limit	1.0
	Set off of capital losses	1.0
	Tax rate	1.0
		3.0
Total		30.0

WITH OVERSEAS ASPECTS

51   ALBERT LTD

Key answer tips

This is a question with two distinct parts that can be answered independently.

The first part of this question is a standard computation of corporation tax. This should not cause you any particular difficulty but watch out for the trade losses brought forward.

The second part is a more testing requirement to calculate corporation tax if either a foreign branch or a subsidiary is set up. However, with FA2009 changes to the treatment of overseas dividends, this part is now much simpler than the original question.

It is advisable to deal with the branch and the subsidiary separately rather than try to do side by side computations.

(a)   **Albert Ltd**
       Corporation tax liability – year ended 31 March 2010

		£
Trading profit (W1)		902,689
Less: Trading losses brought forward		(25,000)
		———————
		877,689
Interest income		12,000
Chargeable gain		120,000
		———————
		1,009,689
Less Gift Aid		(15,500)
		———————
Profits chargeable to corporation tax		994,189
		———————
Corporation tax (W4)		
(£994,189 x 28%)		278,373
Less Marginal relief		
7/400 × (£1,500,000 – £994,189)		(8,852)
		———————
Corporation tax liability		269,521
		———————

Workings

(W1) Trading profit

	£
Operating profit	876,429
Add: Depreciation	82,000
Gift Aid	15,500
Political donation	48,000
Legal fees for the collection of trade debts	0
	1,021,929
Less: Capital allowances – Plant and machinery (W2)	(113,240)
– IBAs (W3)	(6,000)
Tax adjusted trading profit	902,689

(W2) Plant and machinery – capital allowances computation

	Pool	Expensive car	Special rate pool	Allowances
	£	£	£	£
TWDV b/f	45,200	22,400	198,000	
Additions				
(with AIA and FYA)				
Machine	63,000			
Less AIA	(50,000)			50,000
	13,000			
Proceeds		(18,200)		
	45,200	4,200		
Balancing allowance		(4,200)		4,200
WDA (20%)	(9,040)			9,040
WDA (10%)			(19,800)	19,800
FYA (40%)	(5,200)			5,200
	7,800			
Addition: Car				
(CO$_2$ < 111 g/km)	25,000			
Less FYAs (100%)	(25,000)			25,000
	Nil			
TWDV c/f	43,960		178,200	
Total allowances				113,240

Tutorial note:

1. Private use of the expensive motor car by the finance director is irrelevant for companies, full allowances are available. The director will be assessed to income tax on the private use of the a car as an employment benefit.

2. A car purchased with CO_2 emissions of < 111 g/km is eligible for a FYA of 100%.

(W3) **Industrial buildings allowances**

Eligible cost = (£380,000 – £80,000) = £300,000

IBAs = (2% × £300,000) = £6,000

(W4) **Corporation tax rates**

Albert Ltd has no associated companies and therefore its profits are compared to the full limits.

As profits fall between £300,000 and £1,500,000; marginal relief applies.

(b) **Corporation tax liabilities with an overseas operation in 2011**

(i) **Overseas branch**

Albert Ltd – Corporation tax liability – year ending 31 March 2011

	£
Trading profit – UK	1,200,000
Trading profit – Branch (Note)	180,000
Profits chargeable to corporation tax	1,380,000
Corporation tax (W1)	
(£1,380,000 x 28%)	386,400
Less Marginal relief	
7/400 × (£1,500,000 – £1,380,000)	(2,100)
	384,300
Less: Double tax relief (W2)	(45,000)
Corporation tax liability	339,300

(ii) **Overseas subsidiary**

Albert Ltd – Corporation tax liability for the year ending 31 March 2011

	£
Trading profit – UK	1,200,000
Overseas dividend income (Note)	Nil
Profits chargeable to corporation tax	1,200,000

		£
Corporation tax (W1) (£1,200,000 x 28%)		336,000
Less: Double tax relief (Note)		(Nil)
Corporation tax liability		336,000

Tutorial note:

With a branch, the UK company is taxable on the whole of the profits and DTR is available for withholding tax. However, with a foreign subsidiary the UK company is no longer taxed on the profits as dividends received from the subsidiary are exempt from UK corporation tax. DTR is therefore no longer a consideration as overseas dividends are not taxed twice.

Remember that the subsidiary will count as an associated company, but a branch operation will not. Therefore, an overseas subsidiary (but not a branch) will affect the UK company's corporation tax rate as the limits are divided by the number of associated companies.

Albert Ltd's 'profits' are compared to the appropriate limits to determine the rate of tax, but remember that the overseas dividends of a subsidiary are group income and as such are not treated as Franked Investment Income in the calculation of 'Profits'.

Workings:

(W1) Corporation tax rate

		Branch	Subsidiary
		£	£
Upper limit	(Full / x 1/2)	1,500,000	750,000
Lower limit	(Full / x 1/2)	300,000	150,000
Profits		1,380,000	1,200,000
		Marginal relief applies	*Full rate applies*

An overseas subsidiary is an associated company and therefore the limits are divided by two.

(W2) Double taxation relief – Branch income

DTR = lower of:

(i)	Overseas tax suffered on branch income	£45,000
(ii)	UK tax on overseas income (£384,300/£1,380,000 × £180,000)	£50,126

Therefore DTR is £45,000

52 HELIUM LTD (ADAPTED)

Key answer tips

This is a standard corporation tax question with the added complication of some overseas income to deal with.

Think carefully about the treatment of the overseas income in (b), and note that the stakes in the overseas companies are carefully chosen. One investment is an investment of more than 50%, and therefore a subsidiary. The other is an investment of less than 50% and is therefore not a subsidiary.

As well as the overseas income, there are the usual capital allowances computations and lease premium to deal with, which are very common in this type of question.

There are also some easy marks to pick up for the due dates in part (c).

(a)   **Tax adjusted trading profit – year ended 31 March 2010**

	£
Adjusted trading profit	175,810
Capital allowances – IBAs (W1)	(4,700)
– Plant and Machinery (W2)	(68,020)
Rent (£500 × 4 × 8/12)	(1,333)
Lease premium deduction (W3)	(1,757)
	———
Tax adjusted trading profit	100,000
	———

Workings

(W1) **Industrial buildings allowance**

	£
Car park	15,000
Factory	220,000
	———
Qualifying expenditure	235,000
	———
IBAs (£235,000 x 2%)	4,700
	———

Tutorial note:

1.   *The cost of the land does not qualify. The air-conditioning unit qualifies as plant and machinery in the special rate pool. The office does not qualify as it cost more than 25% of the total potentially qualifying cost.*

Total potential qualifying cost = (£450,000 − £95,000 − £40,000) = £315,000

25% of potential qualifying cost = (£315,000 × 25%) = £78,750.

Cost of offices = £80,000, therefore the office is not eligible for relief.

2.   *Although purchased just one month before the year end, the length of ownership is irrelevant, it is the length of the accounting period that is important. As the computation is for the year ended 31 March 2010, the full 2% WDA is available.*

(W2) Plant and machinery – capital allowances computation

		Pool	Expensive car	Special rate pool	Short-life asset	Allowances
	£	£	£	£	£	£
TWDV b/f		13,100	25,400		5,000	
Addition (no AIA or FYA)						
Car (CO$_2$ > 160 g/km) (Note 1)				26,000		
Additions						
(with AIA but not FYA)						
Air-conditioning unit	40,000					
Less AIA (Notes 2 & 3)	(40,000)					40,000
	———			Nil		
Additions						
(with AIA and FYA)						
Computer (Note 4)	21,000					
Less AIA (remaining)	(10,000)					10,000
	———					
	11,000					
Proceeds						
(lower of cost or SP)		(4,000)	(17,200)			
		———	———	———		
		9,100	8,200	26,000		
Balancing allowance			(8,200)			8,200
			———			
WDA (20%)		(1,820)				1,820
WDA (20%)					(1,000)	1,000
WDA (10%)				(2,600)		2,600
FYA (40%)	(4,400)					4,400
	———	———				
		6,600				
		———				
TWDV c/f		13,880		23,400	4,000	
		———		———	———	
Total allowances						68,020
						———

Tutorial note:

1.   *A car purchased with CO$_2$ emissions of > 160 g/km is put into the special rate pool and is eligible for a WDA of 10%.*

2.   *Helium Ltd has a subsidiary. Where there is a group, only one AIA is available and can be shared between the companies in whatever proprtion they choose. However, the subsidiary in this case is an overseas company which cannot have UK capital allowances, therefore all of the AIA will go to Helium Ltd.*

3. The air-conditioning unit is an integral feature in a building and hence is included in the special rate pool. As the rate of WDA in this pool is only 10%, the AIA should be allocated against this pool in preference to the main pool.

4. The computer is eligible for the remaining £10,000 of the maximum AIA (£50,000 – £40,000) and the balance is eligible for the temporary FYA of 40% as it was purchased between 1 April 2009 and 31 March 2010.

(W3) Lease premium deduction

	£
Premium	85,000
Less: £85,000 × 2% × (20 – 1)	(32,300)
Amount assessed on landlord	52,700
Allowable deduction for the year: (£52,700/20 × 8/12)	1,757

Tutorial note:

The office building is used for business purposes and so a proportion of the premium assessed on the landlord can be deducted. The deduction is the assessment on the landlord spread over the life of the lease.

However, note that Helium Ltd has only had the lease for 8 months of the accounting period and therefore the deduction must be time apportioned.

(b) Corporation tax liability – year ended 31 March 2010

	Total	UK income	Overseas rental
	£	£	£
Trading profit	100,000	100,000	
Overseas rental (W1) (Note 1)	130,000		130,000
Overseas dividends (Note 2)	Nil		
	230,000	100,000	130,000
Less Gift Aid (Note 3)	(30,000)	(30,000)	
PCTCT	200,000	70,000	130,000
Corporation tax (28%) (W2)	56,000		
Less Marginal relief 7/400 x (£750,000 – £210,000) x £200,000/£210,000	(9,000)		
Corporation tax (Note 4) (W3)	47,000	16,450	30,550
Less DTR (W4) (Note 1 and 2)	(19,500)		(19,500)
Corporation tax liability	27,500	16,450	11,050

Tutorial note:

1. *The overseas rental income is taxable and DTR is available for withholding tax.*

2. *However, overseas dividends are exempt from UK corporation tax. DTR is therefore no longer a consideration as overseas dividends are not taxed twice.*

    Remember that Argon Ltd is a subsidiary and will count as an associated company, but Boron Ltd is not a subsidiary and therefore is not associated.

    Helium Ltd's 'profits' are compared to the appropriate limits to determine the rate of tax. Don't forget that the overseas dividend of a subsidiary(i.e. Argon Ltd) is group income and as such is not treated as Franked Investment Income (FII) in the calculation of 'Profits'. Boron Ltd's dividends are however treated as FII.

3. *The Gift Aid is set against the UK trading profit in order to maximise the amount of double taxation relief.*

4. *The effective rate of corporation tax is used to allocate the liability to the different sources of income.*

Workings

(W1) Overseas rental income

		£
Net rental income		110,500
Plus Withholding tax (£110,500 x 15/85)		19,500
Gross rental income to include in PCTCT		130,000

(W2) Corporation tax rates

		£
PCTCT		200,000
Plus Franked Investment Income (FII) (Note) (£9,000 x 100/90)		10,000
Profits		210,000

Upper limit	(£1,500,000 x 1/2)	750,000
Lower limit	(£300,000 x 1/2)	150,000
		Marginal relief applies

Argon Ltd is a subsidiary and is therefore an associated company, therefore the limits are divided by two.

Tutorial note:

1. *The definition of an associated company includes overseas subsidiaries.*

> 2. Franked Investment Income includes overseas dividends, but excludes group income (i.e. dividends from subsidiaries). Therefore Boron Ltd's dividend is included as FII, but Argon Ltd's is not. The net cash dividend is grossed up by 100/90 in exactly the same way as a UK dividend.

(W3) Effective rate of corporation tax

The effective rate of corporation tax is: (£47,000 / £200,000) x 100 = 23.5%

Therefore, the UK corporation tax relating to the different sources of income is as follows:

UK income: (£70,000 x 23.5%) = £16,450

Overseas rental income (£130,000 x 23.5%) = £30,550

(W4) Double tax relief – rental income

DTR = lower of:

(i)	Overseas tax suffered (W1)	£19,500
(ii)	UK tax on overseas rental income (W3)	£30,550

DTR is therefore £19,500

(c) Payment date and filing date

Helium Ltd is not a large company for the purposes of paying corporation tax as it does not pay corporation tax at the full rate.

Its corporation tax liability is therefore due 9 months and 1 day after the end of the accounting period, which is 1 January 2011 for the year ended 31 March 2010.

Helium Ltd is required to file its corporation tax return for the year ended 31 March 2010 by 31 March 2011, being 12 months after the end of the accounting period.

WITH VAT ASPECTS

53   STRETCHED LTD

Key answer tips

This question deals with the rules for a 15 month period of account which must be split into two accounting periods of 12 months and 3 months. For ease, use a columnar layout to do the corporation tax computations side by side. Don't forget to pick up the easy marks for stating the due dates of payment.

At least 10 marks of VAT will be included in the examination and it is most likely to appear as part of question 1 or 2. In this case it appears as an independent part (b) to the question.

It is important not to neglect VAT. The points tested in this question are all commonly examined.

(1)   (a)   **Corporation tax computations**

	Year ended 31.12.09 £	Period ended 31.3.10 £
Trading profit (12/15 : 3/15) (Note 1)	264,000	66,000
Less Capital allowances (W1)	Nil	(14,300)
	264,000	51,700
Less Loss relief b/f	(23,000)	–
	241,000	51,700
Property business profit (12/15 : 3/15) (Note 1)	36,000	9,000
Chargeable gains (£44,000 – £3,000) (Note 2)	41,000	–
	318,000	60,700
Less Gift Aid donation	–	(5,000)
Profits chargeable to corporation tax	318,000	55,700
Plus Franked investment income	30,000	–
Profit	348,000	55,700
Corporation tax (W2)		
(£318,000 × 28%)	89,040	
(£55,700 × 21%)		11,697
Less Marginal relief		
7/400 × (£1,500,000 – £348,000) × £318,000/£348,000	(18,422)	
	70,618	11,697
Due dates	1 Oct 2010	1 Jan 2011

Tutorial note:

1. *Trading profits and property business profits are allocated on a time basis: $^{12}/_{15}$ to the year ended 31 December 2009 and $^{3}/_{15}$ to the period ended 31 March 2010.*

2. *The capital loss of £6,700 for the period ended 31 March 2010 is carried forward, it cannot be carried back and set off against previous gains.*

Workings

(W1) Capital allowances

A capital allowance computation is only required for the short 3 month period as follows:

	£	Pool £	Allowances £
Period ended 31 March 2010			
Additions (with AIA)			
Office equipment	17,000		
Less AIA (£50,000 × $^3/_{12}$)	(12,500)		12,500
	──────		
	4,500		
FYA (40%)	(1,800)		1,800
	──────	2,700	
		──────	
TWDV c/f		2,700	
		──────	──────
Total allowances			14,300
			──────

Tutorial note:

The AIA must be time apportioned as it is only a 3 month accounting period, however the FYA is never time apportioned.

(W2) Corporation tax rates

		y/e 31.12.09 £	p/e 31.3.10 £
Upper limit	(Full / x 3/12)	1,500,000	375,000
Lower limit	(Full / x 3/12)	300,000	75,000
Profits		348,000	55,700
		Marginal relief	Small

The accounting period ended 31 December 2009 falls partly into FY2008 (3 months) and partly into FY2009 (9 months).

However, there has not been a change in rate of tax and therefore the corporation tax liability can be calculated in one computation for the while year.

(b) Advantages of 31 March year end

- Being aligned with the financial year will make it easier for a company to calculate its corporation tax liability, since the same rates, reliefs and legislation will apply throughout the accounting period.

- For owner-managed companies, alignment with the income tax year (the odd five days can be ignored) will make it easier as regards calculating the most tax efficient method of extracting profits from the company.

(2)   (a)   **VAT return for quarter to 30 June 2010**

Tutorial note:

The appropriate rate of VAT for the quarter to 30 June 2010 is as follows:

- *If the figure excludes VAT, the VAT is 17.5%*
- *If the figure includes VAT, the VAT is 17.5/117.5 or 7/47.*

(i)   **Goods**

The basic tax point for sale of the goods is the date of despatch (i.e. 20 June 2010).

Deposit received

Where payment is received before the basic tax point this becomes the actual tax point.

Output VAT of £745 (£5,000 × 7/47) should therefore be accounted for in respect of the deposit in the quarter to 30 June 2010.

Balance of invoice

Where an invoice is issued within 14 days of the basic tax point, the invoice date will become the actual tax point.

The actual tax point in respect of the invoice for the balance due of £25,000 is therefore 1 July 2010.

Output VAT will therefore not be due in respect of the invoice until the quarter ended 30 September 2010.

(ii)   **Sales director's cars**

Purchase and sale of cars

As the sale director's new car is to be used partly for private purposes, input VAT is not recoverable in respect of the purchase of this car.

VAT would not have been reclaimed on the purchase of the sales director's old car, as this was also used for private purposes.

No output VAT is therefore charged on the sale of this car.

Fuel costs

The company can reclaim input VAT on the full cost of the fuel.

Input VAT of £89 (£600 × 7/47) should be reclaimed in the quarter to 30 June 2010.

As there is some private use of the cars output VAT, in respect of the private fuel, based on a prescribed scale charge, is payable in the quarter to 30 June 2010.

(iii) **Entertaining costs**

Input VAT of £149 (£1,000 × 7/47) is recoverable in respect of staff entertaining.

Input VAT of £74 (£500 × 7/47) in respect of entertaining customers is not recoverable.

(b) **Implications of submitting and paying VAT late**

The late submission of the VAT return for the quarter ended 30 September 2009 will have resulted in HM Revenue & Customs issuing a surcharge liability notice specifying a surcharge period running to 30 September 2010.

The late payment of VAT for the quarter ended 30 June 2010 will be the first default in the surcharge period. A surcharge of 2% of the VAT due will be charged.

In addition, the surcharge period will be extended to 30 June 2011.

54 WIRELESS LTD *Walk in the footsteps of a top tutor*

Key answer tips

This question has two independent parts.

Part (a) involved a classic corporation tax computation with the standard need to compute capital allowances. There was a small amount of overseas income to deal with in the computation but otherwise it is straightforward.

Part (b) covers various aspects of VAT, and is mainly written.

The highlighted words in the written sections are key phrases that markers are looking for.

Tutor's top tips:

Part (a) (i) should be an easy 2 marks, although you must make sure that you have two separately identifiable points in your answer.

Note that the requirement is only for the definition of when an accounting period starts, not when it ends. Try not to waste time giving information which is not mark earning.

Part (b) on VAT could have been answered next to obtain some more relatively easy marks very quickly.

(a) (i) **Start of an accounting period for corporation tax purposes**

- An accounting period will normally start immediately after the end of the preceding accounting period.

- An accounting period will also start when a company commences to trade or when its profits otherwise become liable to corporation tax.

(ii) **Wireless Ltd**

Tutor's top tip:

Most important in this part was the need to read the question carefully and only produce the PCTCT for the company.

There is no requirement to calculate the tax liability and you should not waste time producing unnecessary computations that will waste time and earn no marks.

There were a few tricky bits, notably the director's remuneration: remember that the employer's NIC is deductible too.

Profits chargeable to corporation tax – period ended 31 March 2010

	£
Trading profit	68,400
Less Director's remuneration (W1)	(25,212)
Capital allowances – Plant and machinery (W2)	(26,180)
– IBA (W3)	(980)
	16,028
Loan interest	1,110
Overseas income (W4)	7,500
	24,638
Less Gift aid donation	(1,800)
Profits chargeable to corporation tax	22,838

Workings

(W1) **Director's remuneration**

The director's remuneration can be deducted as it was paid within nine months of the end of the period of account.

The employer's Class 1 NIC will be:

(£23,000 – £5,715) x 12·8% = £2,212

Total allowable deduction for employing director

(£23,000 salary + £2,212 employer's NIC) = £25,212

(W2) Capital allowances – plant and machinery

	Pool	Allowances
	£	£	£
Additions (no AIA or FYA) (Note 1)			
Car (CO_2 between 111 – 160 g/km)		10,600	
Additions (with AIA and FYA)			
Office equipment	10,400		
Machinery	10,200		
Alterations	4,700		
	———		
	25,300		
Less AIA (Note 2)	(25,000)		25,000
	———		
	300		
Less WDA (20% × 6/12) (Note 2)		(1,060)	1,060
Less FYA (40%) (Note 2)	(120)		120
	———	———	
		180	
		———	
TWDV c/f		9,720	
		———	
Total allowances			26,180
			———

Tutorial note:

1. Cars purchased with CO_2 emissions of between 111 – 160 g/km are put in main pool, and are eligible for WDA of 20%.

2. The maximum AIA must be time apportioned for a six month period, the maximum AIA is therefore £25,000 (£50,000 x 6/12).

   WDAs are also restricted to 6/12 because of Wireless Ltd's short accounting period.

   However, FYAs are given in full and are never time apportioned.

3. The private use of the car is irrelevant, full allowances are available. The director will be assessed to income tax on the private use of the a car as an employment benefit.

4. The office equipment purchased on 20 September 2009 is pre-trading and is treated as incurred on 1 October 2009.

(W3) Industrial buildings allowance

Tutor's top tip:

You should show the application of the 25% test for the general offices, as there are usually marks available for doing this.

	£
Site preparation	8,000
Canteen for employees	22,000
Factory	68,000
Eligible expenditure	98,000
IBAs (2% x £98,000 x 6/12)	980

Tutorial note:

The cost of the land does not qualify.

The office does not qualify as it cost more than 25% of the total potentially qualifying cost.

Total potential qualifying cost = (£200,000 – £60,000) = £140,000

25% of potential qualifying cost = (£140,000 × 25%) = £35,000.

Cost of offices = £42,000

Therefore the office is not eligible for relief.

In practice some of the site preparation costs may be treated as relating to the general offices and would therefore not qualify. This approach would be awarded equivalent marks.

(W4) **Overseas income**

Overseas dividends

Overseas dividends are exempt from UK corporation tax.

As the dividends are received from an overseas subsidiary, they are group income and are not treated as Franked Investment Income.

Overseas branch profits

Overseas branch profits are taxable and DTR is available for withholding tax.

The gross amount of the branch profits must included in the PCTCT calculation and is calculated as follows:

	£
Net branch profits	6,750
Plus Withholding tax (£6,750 × 10/90)	750
Gross branch profits	7,500

Tutor's top tip:

There is no need to calculate the Double Taxation Relief on branch profits as the corporation tax liability has not been asked for – only PCTCT is required.

(b)   **VAT issues**

Tutor's top tip:

The examiner was disappointed with the candidates' lack of VAT knowledge.

The VAT rules are not hard, they are however extensive but they will be examined. Emphasis in your revision must therefore be put into learning the VAT rules as there is a guaranteed 10% of the exam on VAT each sitting.

It is useful to use bullet points for this type of written answer. Try to at least match the number of bullet points with the number of marks available.

(i)   **Compulsory registration**

- Wireless Ltd would have been liable to compulsory VAT registration when its taxable supplies during any 12-month period exceeded £68,000.

- This happened on 28 February 2010 when taxable supplies amounted to £87,100 (£9,700 + £18,200 + £21,100 + £14,800 + £23,300).

- Wireless Ltd would have had to notify HMRC by 30 March 2010, being 30 days after the end of the period.

- The company will have been registered from 1 April 2010 or from an agreed earlier date.

(ii)   **Input VAT on goods purchased prior to registration**

- The goods must have been acquired for business purposes and not be sold or consumed prior to registration.

- The goods were acquired in the three years prior to VAT registration.

Input VAT on services supplied prior to registration

- The services must have been supplied for business purposes.

- The services were supplied in the six months prior to VAT registration.

(iii) **Advantage of voluntary registration**

- Wireless Ltd's sales are all to VAT registered businesses, so output VAT can be passed on to customers.

- The company's revenue would therefore not have altered if it had registered for VAT on 1 October 2009.

- However, registering for VAT on 1 October 2009 would have allowed all input VAT incurred from that date to be recovered.

(iv) **Additional information for a valid VAT invoice**

The following information is required:

(1) An identifying number (invoice number).

(2) Wireless Ltd's VAT registration number.

(3) The name and address of the customer.

(4) The type of supply.

(5) The rate of VAT for each supply.

(6) The quantity and a description of the goods supplied.

Examiner's report

Although fairly well answered, most candidates scored less marks on this question than on question one, despite it being potentially worth five marks more.

The first section of part (a) caused no problems for well prepared candidates.

The second section was also well answered, although many candidates were unsure as to what adjustment was necessary for the director's remuneration, and the related national insurance contributions, that had not been taken into account when preparing the draft accounts.

However, the VAT aspects in part (b) were not so well answered.

Few candidates appreciated when VAT registration would have been necessary, with many candidates basing their answer on the future test rather than the historical test.

As regards voluntary VAT registration, few candidates appreciated that the company's revenue would not have altered given that all its customers were VAT businesses.

Very few candidates could provide more than two or three of the six pieces of additional information that the company needed to show on its sales invoices in order for them to be valid for VAT purposes.

		ACCA marking scheme	
			Marks
(a) (i)		End of preceding accounting period	1.0
		Commencement of trading	1.0
			——
			2.0
			——
(ii)		Trading profit	0.5
		Director's remuneration	1.0
		Employer's Class 1 NIC	1.0
	P & M	– WDA	1.5
		– AIA	2.5
		– FYA	0.5
	IBA	– Land	0.5
		– General offices	1.0
		– Eligible expenditure	1.0
		– Allowance	1.0
		Loan interest	0.5
		Overseas income	2.0
		Gift aid donation	1.0
			——
			14.0
			——

			Marks
(b)	(i)	Registration limit	1.0
		February 2010	1.0
		Notification	1.0
		Date of registration	1.0
			───
			4.0
			───
	(ii)	Goods	
		Business purposes/Not sold or consumed	1.5
		Three year limit	1.0
		Services	
		Business purposes	0.5
		Six month limit	1.0
			───
			4.0
			───
	(iii)	Output VAT	1.0
		Revenue	1.0
		Input VAT	1.0
			───
			3.0
			───
	(iv)	An identifying number	0.5
		Wireless Ltd's VAT registration number	0.5
		The name and address of the customer	0.5
		The type of supply	0.5
		The rate of VAT for each supply	0.5
		Quantity and description	0.5
			───
			3.0
			───
Total			30.0
			───

RELIEF FOR TRADING LOSSES

55   HALF-LIFE LTD (ADAPTED)

Key answer tips

A loss question which is largely computational but it involves the use of a normal ongoing trading loss, an extended carry back loss and a terminal loss.

There are two consecutive losses, the first arising from a short nine month period. The second is the terminal loss of the last twelve months trading.

Make sure you give get the easy marks and give the dates required in part (b).

For ease, use a columnar format to present the loss offset in part (a) and remember to show your record of the losses and their usage.

Remember that information about the new extended carry back relief is given in the tax rates and allowances in the examination.

(a)   **Profits chargeable to corporation tax**

	y/e 31 March 2007 £	y/e 31 March 2008 £	y/e 31 March 2009 £	p/e 30 June 2009 £	y/e 30 June 2010 £
Trading profit	224,000	67,400	38,200	Nil	Nil
Property income	8,200	12,200	6,500	4,400	–
Chargeable gains	–	–	5,600	–	23,700
	232,200	79,600	50,300	4,400	23,700
Loss relief					
– Loss for p/e 30.6.09 (W1)		(7,000)	(50,300)	(4,400)	
– Loss for y/e 30.6.10 (W2)	(174,150)	(72,600)			(23,700)
	58,050	Nil	Nil	Nil	Nil
Less Gift Aid	(1,200)	(1,000) wasted	–	–	(700) wasted
PCTCT	56,850	Nil	Nil	Nil	Nil

Unrelieved Gift Aid Donations

Gift Aid of £1,000 and £700 for respectively the year ended 31 March 2008 and the year ended 30 June 2010 are unrelieved.

Loss Memorandum

	£	£
Loss for the period ended 30 June 2009	61,700	
Loss for the year ended 30 June 2010		308,800
Losses utilised:		
Current period claim		
– Period ended 30 June 2009	(4,400)	
12 month carry back claim		
– y/e 31 March 2009	(50,300)	
36 month extended carry back claim		
– y/e 31.3.08 (W1)	(7,000)	
Current year claim		
– y/e 30 June 2010		(23,700)
36 month terminal loss carry back claim		
– y/e 31 March 2008		(72,600)
– y/e 31 March 2007 (W2)		(174,150)
Losses unrelieved	Nil	38,350

Workings

(W1) **Extended carry back claim – set off in y/e 31.3.08**

Normally the length of the loss making period is not relevant, however with the extended carry back relief the maximum £50,000 that can be carried back must be time apportioned where there is a short loss making period.

Set off in y/e 31.3.08 is therefore the lower of:

(i)   Total profits in y/e 31.3.08 = £79,600

(ii)   Maximum carry back = (£50,000 x 3/12) = £12,500

(iii) Remaining loss = £7,000

The set off is therefore £7,000.

(W2) **Terminal loss – set off in y/e 31.3.07**

For the year ended 31 March 2007, loss relief is restricted to £174,150 (£232,200 × 9/12) as only 9 months of the year falls into the 36 months carry back period from the start of the final loss making accounting period.

Tutorial note:

The trading loss for the period ended 30 June 2009 can be relieved against total profits of the current period and the previous 12 months.

The trading loss for the year ended 30 June 2010 can be relieved against total profits of the current year and the previous 36 months because it is a terminal loss.

The extended carry back relief is not applicable as the terminal loss provisions give the same relief but there is no restriction in carry back.

(b)   **Due date for loss relief claims**

- The loss relief claims against total profits in respect of the loss for the period ended 30 June 2009 must be made by 30 June 2011.

- The loss relief claims against total profits in respect of the loss for the year ended 30 June 2010 must be made by 30 June 2012.

(c)   **Corporation tax repayments**

Year ended 31 March 2007

- Corporation tax of £34,830 (£174,150 at 20%) will be repaid in respect of the year ended 31 March 2007, since the relevant tax rate both before and after the loss relief claim is 20%.

Year ended 31 March 2008

- PCTCT for the year ended 31 March 2008 were originally £78,600 (£79,600 – £1,000 Gift Aid)

- PCTCT after loss relief is £Nil

- Corporation tax of £15,720 (£78,600 at 20%) will be repaid.

Year ended 31 March 2009

- PCTCT for the year ended 31 March 2009 were originally £50,300

- PCTCT after loss relief is £Nil

- Corporation tax of £10,563 (£50,300 at 21%) will be repaid.

56   SOFA LTD (ADAPTED)  *Online question assistance*

Key answer tips

The first part of this question involves a standard adjustment of profit computation where the company is loss making. A detailed capital allowances computation is required and care should be taken as there are many places where this computation could go wrong.

The second part is more difficult and requires detailed group relief knowledge and the calculation of the maximum surrender possible to three subsidiaries including one with a non-coterminous year end and another which only joined the group part way through the year.

The part is independent and could be answered first, before part (a), as the question tells you to assume a loss of £200,000.

(a)   **Trading loss – year ended 31 March 2010**

		£
Loss before taxation		(240,000)
Add: Depreciation		87,100
	Audit and accountancy (Note 1)	0
	Legal fees – issue of share capital (Note 2)	7,800
	Legal fees – renewal of 10 year lease (Note 3)	0
	Legal fees – issue of debentures (Note 2)	0
	Construction of new wall (Note 4)	9,700
	Repairing wall (Note 4)	0
	Entertaining suppliers (Note 5)	1,360
	Entertaining employees (Note 5)	0
	Counselling employees (Note 6)	0
	Health and safety fine	420
	Interest payable (Note 7)	0
		————
		(133,620)
Less: Profit on disposal of shares		(4,300)
	Bank interest received	(8,400)
		————
		(146,320)
Less: Capital allowances – Plant and machinery (W1)		(69,340)
		————
Trading loss		(215,660)
		————

Tutorial note:

1. Audit and accountancy is allowable, as incurred wholly and exclusively for the purposes of the trade.

2. Legal fees in connection with the issue of share capital are not allowable, being capital in nature. However, the cost of obtaining loan finance is allowable as a trading expense under the loan relationship rules as the loan was used for trading purposes.

3. The cost of renewing a short-lease (less than 50 years) is specifically allowable as a trading expense.

4. The new wall is not allowable, being capital in nature. However, repairing a wall is allowable.

5. The only exception to the non-deductibility of entertainment expenditure is when it is in respect of employees.

6. The costs of counselling services for redundant employees are specifically allowable.

7. Interest on a loan used for trading purposes is deductible in calculating the trading loss on an accruals basis.

Workings

(W1) Plant and machinery – Capital allowances computation

Tutorial note:

1. Capital allowances on new car purchases are now calculated based on the CO_2 emissions of the car as follows:

    CO_2 emissions of < 111 g/km: eligible for a FYA of 100%. CO_2 emissions of between 111 – 160 g/km: put in main pool, eligible for a WDA at 20%. CO_2 emissions of > 160 g/km: put in special rate pool, eligible for a WDA at 10%.

    The appropriate rates are given in the tax rates and allowances.

2. Remember to include the expenditure on the fixtures and fittings in the second hand building which are not eligible for IBAs, as they are eligible for plant and machinery allowances.

3. The excess over the qualifying expenditure above the AIA is eligible for the temporary FYA of 40%.

	£	Pool £	Expensive Car £	Special rate pool £	Allow-ances £
TWDV b/f		16,700	16,400		
Additions (No AIA or FYA) (Note 1):					
Car (CO$_2$ > 160 g/km)				22,200	
Car (CO$_2$ between 111 – 160 g/km)		10,900			
Additions (with AIA and FYA):					
Equipment	11,400				
Fixtures (Note 2)	44,800				
	56,200				
Less AIA (Max)	(50,000)				50,000
	6,200				
Disposal proceeds:					
Expensive car			(17,800)		
Car (2)		(8,800)			
Lorry		(7,600)			
		11,200	(1,400)	22,200	
Balancing charge			1,400		(1,400)
WDA (20%)		(2,240)			2,240
WDA (10%)				(2,220)	2,220
FYA (40%) (Note 3)	(2,480)				2,480
		3,720			
Additions with FYA					
Car (CO$_2$ < 111 g/km)	13,800				
Less FYA (100%)	(13,800)				13,800
		Nil			
TWDV c/f		12,680		19,980	
Total allowances					69,340

(b) **Maximum group relief**

Settee Ltd

The accounting periods of Settee Ltd and Sofa Ltd are not coterminous. Therefore, Settee Ltd's profits chargeable to corporation tax and Sofa Ltd's trading loss must be apportioned on a time basis.

Year ended 31 March 2010 and year ended 30 June 2009

The corresponding accounting period is 1 April 2009 to 30 June 2009 (3 months)

Year ended 31 March 2010 and year ended 30 June 2010

The corresponding accounting period is 1 July 2009 to 31 March 2010 (9 months)

Settee Ltd can therefore claim the following group relief

CAP to 30 June 2009

Sofa Ltd can surrender (3/12 × £200,000)	£50,000
Settee Ltd can accept (3/12 × £240,000)	£60,000
Therefore maximum loss claim is £50,000	

CAP to 30 June 2010

Sofa Ltd can surrender (9/12 × £200,000)	£150,000
Settee Ltd can claim (9/12 × £90,000)	£67,500
Therefore maximum loss claim is £67,500	

Couch Ltd

Couch Ltd is not a 75% subsidiary of Sofa Ltd, so no group relief claim is possible.

Futon Ltd

Futon Ltd did not commence trading until 1 January 2010, so the corresponding accounting period is the 3 months from 1 January 2010 to 31 March 2010.

Sofa Ltd can surrender (3/12 × £200,000)	£50,000
Futon Ltd can claim	£60,000
Therefore maximum loss claim is £50,000	

Examiner's report

Part (a) of this question was very well answered.

A certain amount of bad examination technique was evident as regards the adjustments in computing the trading loss.

Some candidates went into far too much detail explaining the adjustments made, thus wasting time, whilst others produced figures without any workings at all. This was fine for correct answers, but not so for incorrect ones.

Where no adjustment was necessary, such as for the interest payable, then this fact should have been clearly shown or stated.

Most candidates did not answer part (b) very well.

Many candidates wasted a lot time by performing detailed calculations showing the amount of group relief that should have been claimed rather than the amount that actually could be claimed.

ACCA marking scheme

		Marks
(a)	Loss before taxation	0.5
	Depreciation	0.5
	Professional fees	2.0
	Repairs and renewals	1.0
	Other expenses	2.0
	Profit on disposal of shares	0.5
	Bank interest received	0.5
	Interest payable	1.0
	P & M – Pool	3.5
	– Expensive motor car sold	1.5
	– Expensive motor car acquired	1.0
	– Fixtures	1.0
	– AIA and WDA	2.0
	– Balancing charge	1.0
	– Pool items sold	0.5
	– FYA	1.5
		――――
		20.0
		――――
(b)	Settee Ltd	2.5
	Couch Ltd	1.0
	Futon Ltd	1.5
		――――
		5.0
		――――
Total		25.0
		――――

57 JOGGER LTD (ADAPTED) *Walk in the footsteps of a top tutor*

Key answer tips

This question was difficult in that it included several topics that students are traditionally uncomfortable with, namely: losses; IBAs; lease premiums; and associated companies.

However, the question still contained some straight forward marks which should have been obtained.

Tutor's top tips:

As with many F6 questions, at first sight the question may seem daunting. However, if you approach it with care, you should be able to score well. It is easy to see a question such as this and panic. However, there is no need. A good layout and calm approach is necessary.

Part (i) is straight forward, once you see past the loss.

Part (ii) requires a little manipulation to account for the lease premium and the associated companies. Once these areas are dealt with the computational side of the question is not difficult.

Part (iii) deals with the implications of missing filing deadlines, and is a straightforward test of knowledge retention.

(a)　(i)　**Jogger Ltd – Trading loss for the year ended 31 March 2010**

	£
Operating loss	(56,400)
Add: Depreciation	12,340
Less: Capital allowances – Plant and machinery (W1)	(2,060)
– Industrial buildings (W2)	(5,000)
Tax adjusted trading loss	**(51,120)**

Tutorial note:

As requested in the question, the model answer starts with the operating loss and therefore only depreciation and capital allowances need to be adjusted for.

However, the original question did not specify which figure to start with.

The normal start point is the profit before tax. The examiner could have asked you to start the computation with the profit before tax of £268,000. You would then have needed to deduct all of the sources of income from investments of £222,060 and the profit on the disposal of shares of £102,340 to give a loss of £56,400.

In this instance, starting with the operating loss of £56,400 is therefore an acceptable short cut which saves time in the exam.

However, since setting this question, the examiner has stated in an article that he will in future always give the starting point. He will also ask you to list all of the items referred to in the question which may impact on the adjustment of profits computation, and to indicate with the use of a zero (0) any items that do not require adjustment.

(W1) **Capital Allowances**

	Pool	Expensive car	Allowances
	£	£	£
TWDV b/f	21,600	8,800	
Additions (no AIA or FYA) (Note 1)			
CO$_2$ (between 111 – 160 g/km)	11,800		
	33,400		
Disposal proceeds (Note 2)	(8,600)	(11,700)	
	24,800	(2,900)	
Balancing charge		2,900	(2,900)
Less WDA (20%)	(4,960)		4,960
TWDV c/f	19,840		
Total allowances			**2,060**

Tutorial note:

1. A car purchased with CO_2 emissions of between 111 – 160 g/km is put into the main rate pool and is eligible for a WDA of 20%. Cars are not eligible for the AIA.

2. The proceeds of both disposals were less than the original cost of the asset, therefore the disposal proceeds are deducted.

(W2) **Industrial Building Allowances**

	£
Total Cost (excluding land)	340,000
Less: General offices (Note)	(90,000)
Total eligible cost	250,000

IBAs = (£250,000 x 2%) = £5,000

Tutorial note:

The general office does not qualify as it cost more than 25% of the total potentially qualifying cost of £340,000

25% of potential qualifying cost = (£340,000 ×25%) = £85,000.

Cost of offices = £90,000

Therefore the general office is not eligible for relief.

However, the cost of the canteen is eligible.

(ii)   **Corporation tax computation – year ended 31 March 2010**

	£
Trading profits	Nil
Property income (W1)	126,000
Bank interest	8,460
Loan interest (£16,400 + £8,200)	24,600
Chargeable gain	98,300
Total profits	257,360
Less Loss relief – Current year claim	(51,120)
PCTCT	206,240
Plus FII (£45,000 × 100/90)	50,000
Profits	256,240

		£
Corporation tax (£206,240 × 28%) (W2)		57,747
Less Marginal relief		
7/400 x (£500,000 − £256,240) × £206,240/£256,240		(3,433)
Corporation tax liability		54,314

Workings

(W1) Property income

	£
Premium received	100,000
Less (£100,000 x 2%) x (10 − 1)	(18,000)
Assessable as income	82,000
Rent receivable	44,000
Property income	126,000

(W2) Corporation tax rates

Jogger Ltd has two associated companies, therefore the lower and upper limits are:

Lower limit = £100,000 (£300,000 x 1/3)

Upper limit = £500,000 (£1,500,000 x 1/3)

As 'Profits' are £256,240, marginal relief applies.

(iii) **Implications of late filing and payment**

- Jogger Ltd's self-assessment tax return for the year ended 31 March 2010 must be submitted by 31 March 2011.

- If the company submits its self-assessment tax return eight months late, then there will be an automatic fixed penalty of £200, since the return is more than three months late.

- There will also be an additional corporation tax related penalty of £5,431 being 10% of the tax unpaid, since the self-assessment tax return is more than six months late.

Tutorial note:

The tax geared penalty starts when 18 months or more have passed after the end of the return period (i.e. this is the same as saying 6 months or more after the filing date).

(b)   **VAT**

Tutor's top tips:

Part (b) was quite difficult, as it required students to recall a large amount of knowledge regarding various different VAT issues which is not difficult if learnt, but extremely difficult if neglected in revision.

VAT is an important area, and students should take care to ensure that all areas of the syllabus are covered as the 11 marks available for this particular part of the question were challenging.

When answering written elements in the exam, keep your comments short and to the point. One mark will be available for a well explained point. Don't take the opportunity to write everything you know about VAT. Keep your comments relevant to the question.

(i)   **Implications of late filing and payment of VAT returns**

- The late submission of the VAT return for the quarter ended 30 September 2008 will have resulted in HM Revenue and Customs (HMRC) issuing a surcharge liability notice specifying a surcharge period running to 30 September 2009.

- The late payment of VAT for the quarter ended 31 March 2009 will have resulted in a surcharge of £778 (£38,900 × 2%).

- The surcharge period will also have been extended to 31 March 2010.

- Although Jogger Ltd then submitted three consecutive VAT returns during this surcharge period on time, this was insufficient to revert to a clean default surcharge record.

- The late payment of VAT for the quarter ended 31 March 2010 will therefore have resulted in a surcharge of £4,455 (£89,100 × 5%).

- The surcharge period will also have been extended to 31 March 2011.

(ii)   **Benefits and conditions of using the Annual Accounting Scheme**

- The reduced administration from only having to submit one VAT return each year should mean that default surcharges are avoided in respect of the late submission of VAT returns.

- In addition, making payments on account based on the previous year's VAT liability will improve both budgeting and possibly cash flow where a business is expanding.

- Jogger Ltd can apply to use the annual accounting scheme if its expected taxable turnover for the next 12 months does not exceed £1,350,000 exclusive of VAT.

- In addition, the company must be up to date with its VAT returns.

Examiner's report

This question was generally well answered, and it was pleasing to see many very good answers for the VAT aspects in part (b).

When calculating the trading loss a number of candidates made this far more complicated than necessary by commencing with the profit before taxation figure rather than the operating loss figure.

Those candidates who attempted to combine the first two aspects of part (a) into one computation generally had difficulty, and can only be advised to deal with each requirement separately.

Those few candidates who treated the dividend income as part of the profits chargeable to corporation tax cannot expect to pass this examination.

In part (b) surprisingly few candidates knew the turnover limit applicable to the annual accounting scheme.

ACCA marking scheme			Marks
(a)	(i)	Operating loss	0.5
		Depreciation	0.5
		P&M – Pool	2.0
		P&M – Expensive car	1.5
		IBA – Qualifying Expenditure	2.0
		IBA – WDA	0.5
			–––
			7.0
			–––
	(ii)	Property income	2.0
		Bank interest	0.5
		Loan interest	1.0
		Chargeable gain	0.5
		Loss relief	1.0
		Franked investment income	1.0
		Corporation tax	2.0
			–––
			8.0
			–––
	(iii)	Due date	1.0
		Fixed penalty	1.5
		Corporation tax related penalty	1.5
			–––
			4.0
			–––
(b)	(i)	Q/e 30.09.08	2.0
		Q/e 31.03.09	2.0
		Q/e 31.03.10	2.0
			–––
			6.0
			–––
	(ii)	One VAT return	1.5
		Payments on account	1.5
		Limit	1.0
		VAT returns	1.0
			–––
			5.0
			–––
Total			30.0

WITH GROUP ASPECTS

58 STRAIGHT PLC

Key answer tips

This question starts with a diagram of a group but most of the marks in the question can be obtained without having to think about the group aspects at all. However, be careful to answer the question set, so that in part (a) you are asked simply to calculate the trading profit.

When writing an explanation of why the companies form a gains group, it is important to give enough detail in your answer and to apply your knowledge to the facts of the question. A calculation of the effective interest of Straight in each of the companies is necessary to illustrate your answer.

(a) **Tax adjusted trading profit – year ended 31 March 2010**

		£
Operating profit		173,915
Add:	Depreciation	21,200
	Car lease costs(15% x £8,500) (Note 1)	1,275
	Entertaining customers (Note 2)	10,000
	Entertaining staff (Note 2)	0
	Fine (Note 3)	1,250
		207,640
Less:	Capital allowances (W)	(22,640)
Tax adjusted trading profit		185,000

Tutorial note:

1. *A flat rate disallowance of 15% of the leasing costs applies to cars with CO_2 emissions exceeding 160 g/km. Note that there is no disallowance for cars with CO_2 emissions 160 g/km or less.*

2. *The only exception to the non-deductibility of entertainment expenditure is when it is in respect of employees.*

    The £150 limit per head for staff entertaining is only relevant in determining whether the party represents a taxable benefit on the employees, all of the cost is an allowable deduction for the company.

3. *Fines for breach of regulations are disallowable.*

Working: Plant and machinery capital allowances

	Pool	Expensive car	Short-life asset	Allowances
	£	£	£	£
TWDV b/f	31,200	18,400	4,000	
SLA transfer (Note 1)	4,000		(4,000)	
			———	
Addition (with AIA and FYA)	12,400			
Less AIA	(12,400)			12,400
	———			
	Nil			
Proceeds		(15,200)		
	———	———		
	35,200	3,200		
Balancing allowance		(3,200)		3,200
WDA (20%)	(7,040)			7,040
FYA (40%) (Note 2)	Nil			
	———	Nil		
		———		
TWDV c/f	28,160			
	———			
Total allowances				22,640
				———

Tutorial note:

1. *The SLA has not been disposed of within 4 years of the end of the accounting period in which it was acquired and the balance on the SLA pool is therefore transferred to the general pool on 1 April 2009.*

2. *Thre is no temporary FYA of 40% as the expenditure on plant and machinery is covered by the AIA.*

(b) (i) **Capital gains group**

- Companies form a capital gains group if at each level in the group structure there is a 75% shareholding.

- The parent company must have an effective interest of over 50% in each group company.

- Arc Ltd, Bend Ltd and Curve Ltd are all 75% subsidiaries, and Straight plc has an effective interest of 100% in Arc Ltd, 80% in Bend Ltd and 60% (80% × 75%) in Curve Ltd.

- If Straight plc's holding in Arc Ltd were only 80% then it would have an effective interest of less than 50% in Curve Ltd (80% × 80% × 75% = 48%).

(ii) **Corporation tax computation – year ended 31 March 2010**

	£
Trading profit (part (a))	185,000
Less Loss relief b/f	(15,000)
	170,000
Net chargeable gains (W1)	70,000
PCTCT	240,000
Plus FII (£9,000 x 100/90) (Note)	10,000
Profits	250,000
Corporation tax (W2)	
(£240,000 at 28%)	67,200
Less Marginal relief	
7/400 × (£375,000 – £250,000) × £240,000/£250,000	(2,100)
Corporation tax payable	65,100

Tutorial note:

Group dividends are not included as franked investment income. Therefore only the dividend from Triangle plc is included.

Workings

(W1) **Net chargeable gain**

	£
Chargeable gain	140,000
Less Rollover relief (see below)	(60,000)
Chargeable gains after rollover relief	80,000
Less Capital loss b/f	(10,000)
Net chargeable gain	70,000

The sale proceeds of £80,000 (£350,000 – £270,000) is not reinvested in qualifying business assets.

Therefore £80,000 of the £140,000 gain will be chargeable in the year ended 31 March 2010.

A rollover relief claim can be made to defer the balance of the gain of £60,000 (£140,000 – £80,000). The gain is rolled over against the base cost of the replacement asset.

(W2) Corporation tax rates

		£
Upper limit	(£1,500,000 x 1/4)	375,000
Lower limit	(£300,000 x 1/4)	75,000
Profits		250,000
		Marginal
		relief applies

There are four associated companies in the group

(iii) Joint election for capital gains

- Straight plc and Arc Ltd must make the election by 31 March 2012 (i.e. within two years of the end of the accounting period of the company making the disposal outside of the group).

- Arc Ltd's otherwise unused capital loss of £40,000 can be set against Straight plc's gain of £70,000, leaving £30,000 chargeable.

- This is beneficial as relief for the capital loss is obtained at the highest marginal rate of corporation tax in FY2009 of 29.75%.

59 MEADOW LTD (ADAPTED)

Key answer tips

The first part of the question is a 'standard' PCTCT computation but watch the treatment of the central heating in the factory. It is not eligible for IBAs but is eligible for capital allowances in the special rate pool.

Remember not to waste time calculating any tax, the question only asks for PCTCT.

For the group part of the question, it is essential to draw a diagram of the group to help you determine the relationships. This can be included as one of the workings to your answer.

In a loss relief group, when the phrase 'the most favourable manner' is used it means that where possible you must use losses in the group companies paying at the marginal rate, then the full rate then the small company rate.

(a) Profits chargeable to corporation tax – year ended 31 March 2010

	£
Trading profit (W1)	529,850
Property business income (W4)	12,950
Interest income (Note)	700
Chargeable gain (W5)	34,715
	578,215
Less Gift Aid	(6,500)
Profits chargeable to corporation tax	571,715

Tutorial note:

The loan to the ex-employee is for a non-trade purpose. The interest is assessed as interest income on an accruals basis.

Workings

(W1) **Trading profit**

		£
Operating profit		579,110
Add: Depreciation		32,200
Gift Aid		6,500
Gifts to customers (Note 1)		1,600
Legal fees – acquisition of factory (Note 2)		5,500
Interest payable (Note 3)		0
		624,910
Capital allowances	– IBAs (W2)	(4,600)
	– Plant and machinery (W3)	(90,460)
Tax adjusted trading profit		529,850

Tutorial note:

1. *Alcoholic drinks are disallowed.*

2. *Legal fees in connection with the acquisition of the factory are not allowable, being capital in nature.*

3. *The loan to acquire the factory is a loan relationship made for the purposes of the trade. The interest is therefore deductible from trading profits.*

(W2) **Industrial buildings allowances**

	£
Total cost	280,000
Less: Land	(50,000)
Eligible expenditure	230,000
IBAs (2% x £230,000)	4,600

(W3) Plant and machinery – capital allowances computation

	Pool £	Special rate pool £	Expensive car £	Allowances £
	£			
TWDV b/f	25,300		11,600	
Additions (no AIA or FYA)				
Car (CO$_2$ between 111 – 160 g/km)	14,400			
Additions (with AIA but no FYA)				
Central heating (Note 2)	40,000			
Less AIA	(40,000)			40,000
	———	Nil		
Additions (with AIA and FYA)				
Lorry	23,000			
Less AIA (max £50,000)	(10,000)			10,000
	13,000	39,700	Nil	11,600
WDA (20%)		(7,940)		7,940
WDA (20%)			(2,320)	2,320
FYA (40%)	(5,200)			5,200
	———	7,800		
Addition (with FYA)				
Car (CO$_2$ < 111 g/km)	25,000			
Less FYAs (100%)	(25,000)			25,000
	———	Nil		
TWDV c/f	39,560	Nil	9,280	
Total allowances				90,460

Tutorial note:

1. *Private use of the car by the quality control manager is irrelevant. He will be assessed to income tax on the private use as a benefit in his employment income computation. Full capital allowances are available from the company's point of view.*

2. *The central heating system is classed as an integral feature in a building and must be placed in the special rate pool. As this pool only receives a 10% writing down allowance, the AIA should be allocated against expenditure in this pool in priority to the main pool.*

3. *Any remaining AIA will be set against the main pool additions. Excess expenditure above the AIA will be eligible for the temporary FYA of 40%.*

4. *Low-emission cars (i.e. CO$_2$ emissions of less than 111 g/km) always qualify for 100% FYAs.*

(W4) **Property business income**

	£	£
Rent (£5,000 × 9/12)		3,750
Lease premium:		
Premium	10,000	
Less: £10,000 × 2% × (5 – 1)	(800)	
		9,200
Property business income		12,950

(W5) **Chargeable gain – Shares in Grassland plc**

	£
Proceeds	45,000
Less Cost (W6)	(8,571)
Unindexed gain	36,429
Less Indexation allowance (£8,571 × 0.200)	(1,714)
Chargeable gain	34,715

(W6) **Cost of Grassland plc shares**

	£
Consideration received for Lawn Ltd shares:	
Ordinary shares (5,000 × £5)	25,000
Preference shares (5,000 × £2)	10,000
	35,000

On the takeover the base cost of the shares in Lawn Ltd is allocated to the shares in Grassland plc by reference to the value of the consideration received as follows:

	Cost £
5,000 ordinary shares (12,000 × 25,000/35,000)	8,571
5,000 preference shares (12,000 × 10,000/35,000)	3,429
	12,000

Tutorial note:

Technically the indexation up to the date of the takeover should be calculated and both the cost and indexed cost at that date are allocated to the ordinary shares and preference shares.

When the shares are disposed of at a later date, further indexation is available on the indexed cost allocated to those shares, from the date of the takeover up to the date of disposal.

> However, the examiner only gave a single indexation factor in the question, and therefore did not expect a two part indexation allowance computation. Calculating the indexation from purchase to disposal in one computation is an acceptable shortcut.

(b)   **Group companies**

(i)   **Associated companies in Meadow Ltd group**

- Poppy Ltd, Cornflower Ltd, Bluebell Ltd and Cowslip Ltd are all under the common control (shareholding of over 50%) of Meadow Ltd, and are therefore associated companies.

- Daisy Ltd is a dormant company and therefore does not count as an associated company.

- Trefoil Ltd is not an associated company as Meadow Ltd only has a 40% interest in it.

(ii)   **Group relief group**

- To be part of a group relief group one company must be a 75% subsidiary of the other, or both companies must be 75% subsidiaries of a third company.

- The holding company must have an effective interest of at least 75% of the subsidiary's ordinary share capital also have the right to receive at least 75% of the subsidiary's distributable profits and net assets on a winding up.

- As an overseas resident company Poppy Inc is included in the group for the purposes of determining group ownership but it cannot itself benefit from group relief.

- The group relief group therefore consists of Meadow Ltd, Cornflower Ltd, Bluebell Ltd and Cowslip Ltd.

(iii)   **Profits chargeable to corporation tax**

	Meadow Ltd	Bluebell Ltd	Cowslip Ltd	Trefoil Ltd
	£	£	£	£
PCTCT before group relief	571,715	50,000	190,000	350,000
Less Group relief (W)	(70,000)		(130,000)	
PCTCT	501,715	50,000	60,000	350,000

Working: Group relief

The relevant lower and upper limits for corporation tax purposes in respect of the 5 associated companies (does not include Trefoil Ltd) are:

		£
Upper limit	(£1,500,000 x 1/5)	300,000
Lower limit	(£300,000 x 1/5)	60,000

Given the PCTCTs of all of the group companies before loss relief, the companies pay tax at the following rates:

Meadow Ltd   28%

Bluebell Ltd   21%

Cowslip Ltd   Marginal relief applies
                   (i.e. profits in the margin are taxed at 29.75%)

Trefoil Ltd   21%

Meadow Ltd, Bluebell Ltd and Cowslip Ltd can benefit from a group relief claim as they are part of the group relief group (see part (b)(ii)).

Trefoil Ltd is not part of the group relief group and so cannot benefit from Cowslip Ltd's loss.

Poppy Inc is an overseas resident company and is therefore not subject to UK corporation tax.

Cornflower Ltd's trading loss is therefore most effectively relieved as follows:

- bring the profits of Cowslip Ltd down to the small company rate limit of £60,000. This saves corporation tax at the highest marginal rate of 29.75%.

- the balance of Cornflower Ltd's trading loss of £70,000 (£200,000 – £130,000) is surrendered to Meadow Ltd. This saves corporation tax at the full rate of 28%.

60   TOCK-TICK LTD

Key answer tips

A long question requiring a computation of corporation tax with some group aspects included as a separate requirement.

It is important to have a methodical way of working through the question so you do not miss any important information. Use the standard pro-formas for adjustment of profit and for capital allowances.

When considering the group aspects in part (c), don't forget that a subsidiary is counted as an associate, so reducing the small company limits for calculating corporation tax.

(a) **Tax adjusted trading profit – year ended 31 March 2010**

		£
Profit before taxation		186,960
Add:	Impaired debts (Note 1)	0
	Depreciation	99,890
	Gifts to customers – pens (Note 2)	0
	Gifts to customers – food hampers (Note 2)	720
	Donation to political party	6,200
	Long service awards (Note 3)	0
	Gift Aid donation (Note 4)	600
	Donation to national charity (Note 4)	250
	Donation to local charity (Note 4)	0
	Audit and accountancy (Note 5)	0
	Legal fees – issue of share capital (Note 6)	2,900
	Costs of registering a trademark (Note 5)	0
	Legal fees – renewal of a short lease (Note 6)	0
	Legal fees – debt collection (Note 5)	0
	Legal fees – court action	900
	Replacing roof (Note 7)	0
	Office extension (Note 7)	53,300
	Entertaining suppliers (Note 8)	2,160
	Counselling services for staff (Note 9)	0
	Secondment of staff to a charity (Note 9)	0
	Interest payable (Note 10)	0
		353,880
Less:	Disposal of office building	(78,100)
	Loan interest received	(12,330)
	Capital allowances (W)	(13,380)
Tax adjusted trading profit		250,070

Tutorial note:

1. *Impaired debts charged in accordance with Financial accounting guidelines by a company are allowable for tax purposes, as they will be specific in nature.*

2. *Gifts to customers are an allowable deduction if they cost less than £50 per recipient per year, are not of food, drink, tobacco, or vouchers exchangeable for goods, and carry a conspicuous advertisement for the company making the gift.*

   Therefore the gift of the pens is allowable, but the gift of hampers of food is not allowable.

3. *The long service award is deductible in calculating the trading profit.*

4. *The Gift Aid donation is allowable as a deduction from total profits in the company's PCTCT computation. It is not also allowable in the adjustment of profits computation, therefore it must be added back in this computation.*

> *Gifts to national charity that are **not** made under the Gift Aid scheme are **not** allowable against the adjustment of profits, nor are they allowable against PCTCT in the main corporation tax computaton.*
>
> *The exception to the rule is that small gifts to local charities are an allowable deduction from the adjustment of profits.*
>
> 5. *Audit and accountancy fees, costs of registering a trademark and debt collection fees are all allowable as incurred wholly and exclusively for the purposes of the trade.*
>
> 6. *Legal fees in connection with the issue of share capital are not allowable, being capital in nature. However, legal fees in connection with the **re**newal of a **short** lease (i.e. life of 50 years or less) are specifically allowable.*
>
> 7. *The replacement of the roof is allowable since the whole structure is not being replaced. The office extension is not allowable, being capital in nature.*
>
> 8. *The only exception to the non-deductibility of entertainment expenditure is when it is in respect of employees.*
>
> 9. *The costs of counselling services for redundant employees and of seconding an employee to charity are allowable.*
>
> 10. *Interest on a loan used for trading purposes is deductible in calculating the trading profit on an accruals basis.*

Working – Plant and machinery

	Pool £	Expensive car £	Short-life asset £	Allowances £
TWDV b/f		12,200	21,600	2,300	
Additions (with AIA and FYA)				
Equipment	6,700			
Less AIA	(6,700)			6,700
	Nil			
Proceeds (Note 2)			(33,600)	(460)	
		12,200	(12,000)	1,840
Balancing charge			12,000		(12,000)
			12,000		
Balancing allowance				(1,840)	1,840
WDA (20%)		(2,440)			2,440
FYA (40%)(Note 1)	(Nil)				
		Nil			
Additions (with FYA)					
Car (CO$_2$ < 111 g/km)	14,400				
Less FYA (100%)	(14,400)				14,400
	Nil				
TWDV c/f		9,760			
Total allowances					13,380

Tutorial note:

1. There is no temporary FYA as all of the expenditure is covered by the AIA.

2. The sale proceeds for the expensive motor car sold are restricted to original cost.

(b) **Profits chargeable to corporation tax – y/e 31 March 2010**

	£
Trading profit	250,070
Interest income – Loan interest	12,330
Chargeable gain (W)	11,200
	273,600
Gift aid donation	(600)
Profit chargeable to corporation tax	273,000

Working: Chargeable gain

	£
Sale proceeds	276,000
Less: Cost	(197,900)
Less: Indexation allowance (given)	(66,900)
Chargeable gain	11,200

(c) **Effect on PCTCT**

(i) **Group relief**

- Tock-Tick Ltd owns more than 75% of the share capital of Clock Ltd. They therefore form a group for group relief purposes.

- The accounting periods are not coterminous, so the claim for group relief would be restricted to the lower of:

  (i) Available loss of Clock Ltd
  (1 April 2009 – 31 December 2009) (£62,400 × $^9/_{12}$) = £46,800

  (ii) Available profits of Tock-Tick Ltd
  (1 April 2009 – 31 December 2009) (£273,000 × $^9/_{12}$) = £204,750

- Tock-Tick Ltd's profits chargeable to corporation tax would therefore have been reduced by £46,800.

Group rollover relief

- Tock-Tick Ltd owns more than 75% of the share capital of Clock Ltd. They therefore form a gains group. In a gains group, gains realised by one group company can be rolled over into assets acquired by another group company.

- The sale proceeds from the disposal of the office building are not fully reinvested, and so £6,000 (£276,000 – £270,000) of the capital gain cannot be rolled over.

- Tock-Tick Ltd's profits chargeable to corporation tax would therefore have been reduced by £5,200 (£11,200 – £6,000).

(ii) **Corporation tax liability – year ended 31 March 2010**

	£
Original PCTCT	273,000
Less: Group relief	(46,800)
Gain rolled over	(5,200)
Revised PCTCT	221,000
Corporation tax (£221,000 at 28%) (W)	61,880
Less Marginal relief	
7/400 × (£750,000 – £221,000)	(9,258)
Corporation tax liability	52,622

Working: Corporation tax rates

Tock-Tick Ltd has one associated company.

The small companies rate limits are therefore £750,000 (£1,500,000 x 1/2) and £150,000 (£300,000 x 1/2).

The company is therefore a marginal relief company.

61 MUSIC PLC

Key answer tips

In this question there are 9 marks for written explanations of the gains group and associated company rules. It is important to state the basic rule and then apply to the facts of the question. Be careful with the overseas company, which is included but unable to enjoy the benefits of gains group status.

When calculating property business profit, always watch out for furnished lettings which will need a calculation of wear and tear allowance. Property 3 has lease premiums paid and received which is a tricky area but is examined and so you should learn the proforma calculation.

(a) **Capital gains group**

- Companies form a capital gains group if at each level in the group structure there is a 75% shareholding, provided the parent company has an effective interest of at least 50%.

- Alto Ltd, Bass Ltd, Cello Ltd, Echo Inc and Flute Ltd are all 75% subsidiaries, and Music plc has an effective interest of 60% (80% × 75%) in Flute Ltd. All of these companies therefore form a capital gains group.

- However, Bass Ltd and Cello Ltd will only be included in respect of assets acquired or disposed of whilst they were members of the group.

- Drum Ltd and Gong Ltd are not included since Drum Ltd is not a 75% subsidiary, and Music plc's effective interest in Gong Ltd is only 48% (80% × 75% × 80%).

- Although Echo Inc is included, companies that are resident overseas are not able to take advantage of the provisions applicable to a capital gains group.

(b) **Associated companies**

- Alto Ltd, Bass Ltd, Cello Ltd, Echo Inc, Flute Ltd and Gong Ltd are all under the common control of Music plc, and are therefore associated companies.

- For associated company purposes, it does not matter where a company is resident. Echo Inc is therefore included despite being resident overseas.

- Companies that are only associated for part of the accounting period, such as Bass Ltd and Cello Ltd, count as associated companies for the whole of the period.

- Drum Ltd is not included as an associated company since Music plc's effective interest in this company is only 45%.

(c) **Property business income – year ended 31 March 2010**

	£	£
Rent – Property 1 (£2,500 × 4 × 7/12)		5,833
– Property 2 (£650 × 9) + £700 (Note)		6,550
– Property 3 (£2,000 × 9/12)		1,500
– Property 4 (£500 × 9)		4,500
		18,383
Lease premium – Property 3 (W1)		28,500
		46,883
Allowable deductions:		
Irrecoverable debt – Property 2	650	
Decoration – Property 1	2,500	
Advertising/fees (£1,500 + £250)	1,750	
Council tax/water rates (£1,200 + £600)	1,800	
Repairs – Property 2	500	
Wear and tear allowance – Property 1		
(£5,833 – £1,800) × 10% (Note)	403	
		(7,603)
Property business income		39,280

Key answer tips

The company is assessed on the net profits from all properties.

It is therefore not necessary to compute profits / losses for each property separately and one combined computation is all that is needed.

Tutorial note:

Property 1

The replacement dishwasher is disallowed as it is an item of capital as Music plc claims the wear and tear allowance. The wear and tear allowance is calculated on rent received less council tax and water rates paid by the landlord.

Property 2

Property business income is calculated on the accruals basis. The date that rent is received is irrelevant.

Relief is available for irrecoverable debts.

Similarly the invoice received in April for work carried out in March 2010 should be accrued for in the accounts to 31 March 2010.

Property 3

The premium paid for the head lease is deductible over the duration of the sublease divided by the duration of the head lease (see W2).

Property 4

Expenditure incurred on making the property inhabitable is capital and is therefore not deductible.

Workings

(W1) **Lease premium**

	£
Premium received	45,000
Less: £45,000 × 2% × (10 − 1)	(8,100)
	36,900
Deduction for premium paid (W2)	(8,400)
	28,500

(W2) **Deduction for premium paid on head lease**

	£
Premium	60,000
Less: £60,000 × 2% × (30 − 1)	(34,800)
Amount assessed on landlord	25,200

Allowable deduction
= Amount assessed x (duration of sub-lease / duration of head lease)
= £25,200 x 10/30 = £8,400

(d) **Corporation tax liability – year ended 31 March 2010**

	£
Trading profit	92,000
Interest income	12,000
Property business income (part (c))	39,280
Net chargeable gains (W1)	23,000
PCTCT	166,280
Plus Franked investment income	15,000
Profit	181,280
Corporation tax (W2)	
(£166,280 × 28%)	46,558
Less: Marginal relief	
7/400 × (£214,286 − £181,280) × £166,280/£181,280	(530)
Corporation tax liability	46,028

Tutorial note:

1. The capital gain of £120,000 is included in Music plc's profits chargeable to corporation tax since an appropriate election has been made with Alto Ltd. Capital losses may be set against this gain.

2. Group dividends are not included as franked investment income.

Workings

(W1) **Net chargeable gain**

	£
Net chargeable gain in the year (by election)	120,000
Less Capital losses in the year	(65,000)
	55,000
Less Capital losses b/f	(32,000)
Net chargeable gain	23,000

(W2) **Corporation tax rates**

		£
Upper limit	(£1,500,000 x 1/7)	214,286
Lower limit	(£300,000 x 1/7)	42,857
Profits		181,280
		Marginal
		relief applies

There are seven associated companies in the group

(e) Bank loan

All costs incurred in connection with the loan will be taxed in accordance with the loan relationship rules. Therefore the tax treatment of the loan interest and the arrangement fee will be the same.

Under the loan relationship rules costs incurred in relation to loans used for the purposes of the trade are deductible as trading expenses. If the loan was therefore used to acquire plant and machinery, the interest and arrangement fee would be deducted from the company's trading profit.

Costs incurred in relation to loans used for non-trade purposes are deductible from interest income. If the loan was used to acquire a property which was to be rented out, the interest and fees would therefore be deducted not from trading income, and not from property business income (as for individuals), but from the company's interest income.

VALUE ADDED TAX

62 CONFUSED LTD

Key answer tips

A more difficult question than usual testing less mainstream topics in VAT.

The first part requires clear explanation of the differences between standard rated, zero rated and exempt supplies. Do not worry if you missed the point that traders making wholly zero rated supplies need not register.

The last part has some tricky points on sale of a business and the difference between selling assets individually or as a complete business.

(a) Standard rated supplies

- Confused Ltd will be required to register for VAT as it is making taxable supplies in excess of the registration limit of £68,000.

- Output VAT of £13,125 (£75,000 × 17.5%) per month will be due, and input VAT of £1,489 (£10,000 × 17.5/117.5) per month will be recoverable.

Zero-rated supplies

- Confused Ltd will be required to register for VAT as it is making taxable supplies in excess of the registration limit of £68,000.

- However, as it is making zero-rated supplies, when it is required to register it can apply for an exemption from registration if it wishes.

- Output VAT will not be due, but input VAT of £1,489 per month will be recoverable if it registers for VAT.

Exempt supplies

- Confused Ltd will not be required or permitted to register for VAT as it will not be making taxable supplies.

- Output VAT will not be due and no input VAT will be recoverable.

(b) Disclosure of errors

- If the net errors total less than the greater of £10,000 or 1% of turnover, then they can be voluntarily disclosed by simply entering them on the next VAT return.

- If the net errors total more than this limit then they can be voluntarily disclosed, but disclosure must be made separately to HM Revenue & Customs (HMRC).

- Default interest will be charged if the net errors total more than the limit.

(c) Sale of assets on a piecemeal basis

- Perplexed Ltd will cease to make taxable supplies so its VAT registration will be cancelled on 31 December 2010 or an agreed later date.

- The company will have to notify HMRC by 30 January 2011, being 30 days after the date of cessation.

- Output VAT will be due in respect of fixed assets on which VAT has been claimed (although output VAT is not due if it totals less than £1,000).

Sale of business as a going concern

- If the purchaser is already registered for VAT then Perplexed Ltd's VAT registration will be cancelled as above.

- If the purchaser is not registered for VAT then it can take over Perplexed Ltd's VAT registration.

- A sale of a business as a going concern is outside the scope of VAT, and therefore output VAT is not due.

63 ASTUTE LTD

Key answer tips

A straight forward question on the three special accounting schemes available to small businesses.

Make sure you illustrate your answer by referring to the numbers in the question and do not just write about the schemes in general.

(a) **Annual accounting scheme**

- Astute Ltd can apply to use the annual accounting scheme if its expected taxable turnover for the next 12 months does not exceed £1,350,000 exclusive of VAT.

- In addition the company must be up to date with its VAT returns.

- The reduced administration from only having to submit one VAT return each year should mean that default surcharges are avoided in respect of the late submission of VAT returns.

- In addition, making payments on account based on the previous year's VAT liability will improve both budgeting and possibly cash flow where a business is expanding.

(b) **Flat rate scheme**

- Bright Ltd can use the flat rate scheme if its expected taxable turnover for the next 12 months does not exceed £150,000.

- The main advantage of the scheme is the simplified VAT administration. Bright Ltd's customers are not VAT registered, so there will be no need to issue VAT invoices.

- Using the normal basis of calculating the VAT liability, Bright Ltd will have to pay annual VAT of £8,478 (£75,000 − £10,000 = £65,000 × 15/115).

- If Bright Ltd uses the flat rate scheme then it will pay VAT of £6,750 (£75,000 × 9%), which is an annual saving of £1,728 (£8,478 − £6,750).

(c) **Cash accounting scheme**

- Clever Ltd can use the cash accounting scheme if its expected taxable turnover for the next 12 months does not exceed £1,350,000 exclusive of VAT.

- In addition, the company must be up to date with its VAT returns and VAT payments.

- Output VAT will be accounted for three months later than at present since the scheme will result in the tax point becoming the date that payment is received from customers.

- The recovery of input VAT on expenses will not be affected as these are paid in cash.

- The scheme will also provide automatic bad debt relief should a customer default on the payment of a debt.

64 ROCKING-HORSE LTD (ADAPTED)

Key answer tips

Another question on registration issues; covering the futures test, pre registration VAT and voluntary registration. These are all areas that are often examined and should not have caused too much trouble.

Be careful with the dates so that you apply the appropriate rate of VAT.

(a) **Compulsory registration**

- Traders must register for VAT if at any time they expect their taxable supplies for the following 30-day period to exceed £68,000.

- Rocking-Horse Ltd realised that its taxable supplies for November 2009 were going to be at least £69,000. The company was therefore liable to register from 1 November 2009, being the start of the 30-day period.

- Rocking-Horse Ltd had to notify HM Revenue & Customs (HMRC) by 30 November 2009, being the end of the 30-day period.

(b) **Recovery of input VAT**

- Input VAT of £2,040 (£13,600 × 15%) can be recovered on the stock of goods held at 1 November 2009.

  The stock was not acquired more than three years prior to registration, nor was it sold or consumed prior to registration.

- The same principle applies to fixed assets, so input VAT of £9,300 (£62,000 × 15%) can be recovered on the fixed assets purchased during August 2009.

- Input VAT of £1,290 ((£2,400 + £2,800 + £3,400) = (£8,600 × 15%)) can be recovered on the services incurred from 1 August to 31 October 2009.

  This is because the services were not supplied more than six months prior to registration.

- The total input VAT recovery is therefore £12,630 (£2,040 + £9,300 + £1,290).

(c) **Voluntary registration**

- Rocking-Horse Ltd's sales are all to VAT registered businesses, so output VAT can be passed on to customers.

- The company's revenue would therefore not have altered if it had registered for VAT on 1 August 2009.

- However, additional input VAT of £4,740 ((£3,600 + £13,200 + £28,400 − £13,600) = (£31,600 × 15%)) would have been recovered in respect of goods purchased.

(d) **HMRC Information and inspection powers**

- Previously, the separate parts of HMRC had different powers for inspecting business premises and records. This meant that a business might receive several visits to look at records.

- HMRC now have unified powers to undertake compliance checks with one set of powers to inspect business records, assets and premises. The new regime covers income tax, capital gains tax, corporation tax, VAT and PAYE.

- HMRC have the power to ask taxpayers for supplementary information, provided formal information notices are issued with a right of appeal.

- They can also request information from third parties provided either the taxpayer or the new First-tier Tribunal agrees.

- The purpose of a VAT control visit is to provide an opportunity for HMRC to check the accuracy of VAT returns.

(d) **The unified appeal system**

- The taxpayer can appeal against a decision within 30 days.

- If the taxpayer is not satisfied with the outcome of the discussions, they can request a review by another HMRC officer or have their case referred to an independent Tax Tribunal.

- They must also apply to postpone all or part of the tax charged, otherwise they will have to pay the disputed amount.

- There are two tiers to the Tax Tribunal system:

  - the First-tier Tribunal deals with all but the most complex cases

  - the Upper Tribunal review and decide appeals from the First tier Tribunal on points of law, deal with complex cases requiring detailed specialist knowledge and are responsible for the enforcement of decisions made by the Tribunals.

- A decision of the Upper Tribunal may be appealed to the Court of Appeal, but only if they relate to a point of law.

65 SANDY BRICK

Key answer tips

Most of the marks in this question are available for a calculation of VAT payable in part (c).

Make sure you use a standard proforma as shown in the answer. It is normal and acceptable to do the workings on the face of the computation.

Parts (a) and (b) require straight forward statements of fact that you should have learnt!

(a) **Supply of services**

- The basic tax point for services is the date that they are completed.

- If an invoice is issued or payment received before the basic tax point, then this becomes the actual tax point.

- If an invoice is issued within 14 days of the basic tax point, the invoice date will usually replace the basic tax point date and becomes the actual tax point.

(b) **VAT invoices**

- A VAT invoice must be issued when a standard rated supply is made to a VAT registered person.

- A VAT invoice should be issued within 30 days of the date that the taxable supply of services is treated as being made.

(c) **VAT Return – Quarter ended 31 March 2010**

	£	£
Output VAT		
Sales to VAT registered customers (Note 1)		
(£44,000 × 95% × 17.5%)		7,315
Sales to non-VAT registered customers		
(£16,920 – £5,170 = £11,750 × 17.5/117.5)		1,750
Advance payment (£5,000 × 17.5/117.5)		745
		———
		9,810
Input VAT		
Materials (Note 2) (£11,200 – £800 = £10,400 × 17.5%)	1,820	
Office equipment (Note 3) (£120 × 9 = £1,080 × 17.5%)	189	
Telephone (Note 4) (£400 × 70% × 17.5%)	49	
Motor repairs (Note 5) (£920 × 17.5%)	161	
Equipment (£6,000 × 17.5)	1,050	
	———	(3,269)
VAT payable		6,541

Tutorial note:

1. *The calculation of output VAT on sales must take into account the discount for prompt payment, even if customers do not take it. VAT is therefore calculated on 95% (100% – 5%) of the sales value.*

2. *Input VAT cannot be claimed in respect of the materials used in constructing Sandy's private residence since the goods are not used for business purposes.*

3. *Input VAT can be recovered on services supplied in the six months prior to registration, so the office equipment claim can be backdated to July 2009.*

The question says assume that the rate of 17.5% applies throughout.

> *In fact, the office equipment purchased pre-registration only suffered VAT at 15%, and the business can only recover the VAT actually suffered. However, the examiner has said that he will not set a question straddling the change in rates that requires the use of both rates.*
>
> 4.   *An apportionment is made where a service such as the use of a telephone is partly for business purposes and partly for private purposes.*
>
> 5.   *However, no apportionment is necessary for motor expenses provided there is some business use.*
>
> 6.   *The tax is calculated as 17.5/117.5 for transactions quoted gross, however the use of 7/47 is also acceptable.*

66   VICTOR STYLE *Online question assistance*

Key answer tips

This is a question covering the common issues of registration and the flat rate scheme but which also asks for the effect of registration on profit. This is unusual because traders usually pass on the cost of VAT to their customers, but in this case the question clearly states that it was not possible to raise prices as a consequence of becoming registered.

Provided you work carefully through the numbers, this should be a straight forward question.

(a)   **Compulsory registration**

- A trader must register for VAT when taxable supplies during any 12-month period exceed £68,000.

- This will have happened on 30 November 2009 when taxable supplies amounted to £68,020 ((£5,300 × 10) + (£7,510 × 2)) for the previous 12 months.

- Victor was therefore liable to register from 1 January 2010, being the end of the month following the month in which the limit was exceeded.

- He had to notify HM Revenue & Customs by 30 December 2009, being 30 days after the end of the 12-month period.

(b)   **VAT payable – y/e 31 December 2010**

- Output VAT will be £13,422 (£7,510 × 12 = £90,120 × 17.5/117.5) since Victor must absorb this himself rather than pass it on to his customers.

- Input VAT will be £715 (£400 × 12 = £4,800 × 17.5/117.5).

- The total VAT payable by Victor during the year ended 31 December 2010 is therefore £12,707 (£13,422 – £715).

(c)   **Flat rate scheme**

- The main advantage of the flat rate scheme is the simplified VAT administration. Victor's customers are not registered for VAT, so there will be no need to issue VAT invoices.

- If Victor had used the flat rate scheme from 1 January 2010, then he would have paid VAT of £10,814 (£90,120 × 12%) during the year ended 31 December 2010.

- This is a saving of £1,893 (£12,707 – £10,814) for the year.

(d)   **Reduction in net profit**

- If Victor had not increased his prices, his net profit for the year ended 31 December 2010 based on the information given would have been £58,800 (£5,300 – £400 = £4,900 × 12).

- As a result of increasing his prices, Victor's net profit will be as follows:

	£
Sales (£90,120 – £13,422)	76,698
Less Expenses (£4,800 – £715)	(4,085)
Net profit	72,613

- This is a increase in net profit of £13,813 (£72,613 – £58,800).

- If the flat rate scheme had been used from 1 January 2010 there would have been an increase in net profit of £15,706 (£13,813 + £1,893).

67   RAM-ROM LTD

Key answer tips

This question required some detailed knowledge about pre registration VAT and the information required on VAT invoices. The last part required application of the rules about cash accounting to the particular circumstances of the company.

This is a tricky question to score highly on, but there are easy marks to be gained and these should be obtained as quickly as possible rather than getting bogged down with detail.

(a)   **Input VAT recovered on registration**

- Input VAT of £13,800 (£92,000 × 15%) can be recovered on the stock of goods held at 1 January 2010.

  The stock was not acquired more than three years prior to registration, nor was it sold or consumed prior to registration.

- The same principle applies to fixed assets, so input VAT of £16,290 (£42,000 + £66,600 = £108,600 × 15%) can be recovered on the fixed assets that have not been sold.

- Input VAT of £7,290 (£7,400 + £6,300 + £8,500 + £9,000 + £9,200 + £8,200 = £48,600 × 15%) can be recovered on the services incurred from 1 July 2009 to 31 December 2009.

  This is because these services were not supplied more than six months prior to registration.

- The total input VAT recovery is therefore £37,380 (£13,800 + £16,290 + £7,290).

Tutorial note:

Pre-registration expenditure suffered VAT at 15%. The business can only recover the VAT actually suffered.

(b) **VAT invoices**

The following additional information is required on the invoices:

(1) A sequential and unique identifying number (invoice number).

(2) Ram-Rom Ltd's VAT registration number.

(3) The rate of VAT for each supply.

(4) The VAT-exclusive amount for each supply.

(5) The total VAT-exclusive amount.

(6) The amount of VAT payable.

(c) **Discounts**

- Where a discount is offered for prompt payment then output VAT is calculated on the selling price less the amount of discount offered.

- There is no amendment to the amount of output VAT charged if the customer does not take the discount but instead pays the full selling price.

(d) **Cash accounting scheme**

Conditions of the scheme

- Ram-Rom Ltd can use the cash accounting scheme if its expected taxable turnover for the next 12 months does not exceed £1,350,000 exclusive of VAT.

- In addition, the company must be up to date with its VAT returns and VAT payments.

Advantages of the scheme

(1) Output VAT will be accounted up to four months later than at present since the scheme will result in the tax point becoming the date that payment is received from customers.

(2) The recovery of input VAT will only be delayed by one month.

(3) The scheme will also provide automatic bad debt relief should a customer default on the payment of a debt.

68   LITHOGRAPH LTD (ADAPTED)

Key answer tips

Monthly payments on account under the annual accounting scheme are based on the VAT payable for the previous year. This first part of the question was only worth three marks and therefore it should be clear that detailed computations are not required and that the reason for the previous year information in the question is for the purposes of this part.

Calculations based on the current year position were not required until the next part of the question, which required a VAT return and should be an expected standard requirement.

(a)   **Monthly payments on account of VAT**

- Each payment on account of VAT will be £1,020 (£10,200 × 10%), being 10% of the VAT payable for the previous year.

- Lithograph Ltd will have made nine payments on account, and these will have been paid for the months of April to December 2009, being months 4 to 12 of the annual VAT return period.

(b)   (i)   **VAT payable – year ended 31 December 2009**

	£	£
Output VAT		
Sales (£160,000 × 15%)		24,000
Motor car scale charge (£1,660 × 15/115)		217
Office equipment (£8,000 × 15%)		1,200
		–––––
		25,417
Input VAT		
Purchases (£38,000 × 15%)	5,700	
Expenses (Note 1) (£28,000 – £3,600 = £24,400 × 15%)	3,660	
Machinery (£24,000 × 15%)	3,600	
Bad debt (Note 3) (£4,800 × 15%)	720	
	–––––	
		(13,680)
		–––––
VAT payable		11,737
		–––––

Tutorial note:

1.   *Input VAT on business entertainment is not recoverable.*

2.   *Input VAT cannot be recovered in respect of the motor car as this is not exclusively for business purposes.*

> 3. *Relief for the bad debt is available because the claim is made more than six months from the time that payment was due, and the debt has been written off in the company's books.*
>
> 4. *The tax is calculated as 15/115 for transactions quoted gross, however the use of 3/23 is also acceptable.*

        (ii)   **Annual VAT return**

- Lithograph Ltd made payments on account totalling £9,180 (£1,020 × 9), so a balancing payment of £2,557 (£11,737 – £9,180) would have been due with the annual VAT return.

- The annual VAT return, along with the balancing payment, would have been due by 28 February 2010, being two months after the end of the annual VAT period.

69 DENZIL DYER

Key answer tips

A question ranging over a number of VAT issues. Make sure you consider each part and write enough for each part.

Remember also to relate your answer to the specific circumstances of the business.

Numbered points or bullet points are the best way to make your answer 'marker friendly'.

(a)   **Identification of the type of supply**

- The type of supply, whether standard rated or zero-rated, has no effect on the recovery of input VAT for Denzil.

- However, output VAT is only due in respect of standard rated supplies. Incorrectly classifying a supply as zero-rated would not remove Denzil's liability to pay the output VAT which is calculated on the actual price charged. This would then be an additional cost to the business.

(b)   **Accounting for output VAT**

- Output VAT must be accounted for according to the VAT period in which the supply is treated as being made. This is determined by the tax point.

- The printing contracts are supplies of services, so the basic tax point for each contract will be the date that it is completed.

- Where payment is received before the basic tax point, then this date becomes the actual tax point. The tax point for each 10% deposit is therefore the date that it is received.

- If an invoice is issued within 14 days of the basic tax point, the invoice date will usually replace the basic tax point date and becomes the actual tax point. This will apply to the balance of the contract price since Denzil issues invoices within three to five days of completion.

(c)   **VAT implications of discounts**

- Where a discount of 5% is given for an order of more than £500 then output VAT is simply calculated on the revised, discounted, selling price.

- As regards the 2.5% discount offered for prompt payment, output VAT is calculated on the selling price less the amount of discount offered.

- There is no amendment to the amount of output VAT charged if the customer does not take the discount but instead pays the full selling price.

(d)   **Conditions for the recovery of input VAT**

- The supply must be made to Denzil since he is the taxable person making the claim.

- The supply must be supported by evidence, and this will normally take the form of a VAT invoice. Denzil will therefore not be able to recover any input VAT in respect of the purchases of office supplies for cash, where there is no invoice.

- Denzil must use the goods or services supplied for business purposes, although an apportionment can be made where supplies are acquired partly for business purposes and partly for private purposes.

(e)   **Circumstances for issuing VAT invoices**

- Denzil must issue a VAT invoice when he makes a standard rated supply to one of his VAT registered customers.

- A VAT invoice is not required if the supply is zero-rated or if the supply is to a non-VAT registered customer.

- A VAT invoice should be issued within 30 days of the date that the supply of services is treated as being made.

70   ANNE ATTIRE *Walk in the footsteps of a top tutor*

Key answer tips

Standalone VAT questions are not as common as seeing VAT as part of a longer income tax or corporation tax question, but either way VAT will be tested (a guaranteed 10%) and there are easy marks to be had if you have learnt the rules, as they are very straightforward to apply.

It is an important area of the syllabus and you should take care to ensure you have covered all areas.

The question has three independent parts, which have clear requirements and mark allocations. If you do not have the required knowledge to deal with part (b) do not allow this to put you off attempting the other parts.

Tutor's top tips:

Part (a) is a standard VAT return, which does not have any particularly difficult items.

Cash and credit sales are both dealt with in the same way, except that the discount is only applicable to the credit sales.

Be careful to ensure you deal with the discounts correctly, in respect of both the credit sales and the bad debts.

(a)   **VAT return – Quarter ended 30 November 2009**

	£	£
Output VAT		
Cash sales (£28,000 x 15%)		4,200
Credit sales (Note 2) (£12,000 x 95% x 15%)		1,710
		———
		5,910
Input VAT		
Purchases and expenses (£11,200 x 15%)	1,680	
Impairment loss (Note 3) (£800 x 95% x 15%)	114	
	———	(1,794)
		———
VAT payable		4,116
		———

The VAT return for the quarter ended 30 November 2009 should have been submitted by 31 December 2009, being one month after the end of the VAT period.

Tutorial note:

1.   *As the VAT return is for the quarter ended 30 November 2009, all the VAT calculations are at 15%. The VAT rate increases to 17.5% from 1 January 2010.*

2.   *The calculation of output VAT on the credit sales takes into account the discount for prompt payment, even for those 10% of customers that did not take it.*

3.   *Relief for an impairment loss is not given until six months from the time that payment is due. Therefore relief can only be claimed in respect of the invoice due for payment on 10 April 2009.*

Relief is based on the amount of output VAT that would originally have been paid taking into account the discount for prompt payment.

(b)   **Cash accounting**

Tutor's top tips:

Part (b) requires students to recall a reasonable amount of knowledge regarding the cash accounting scheme, which is not difficult if learnt, but extremely difficult if neglected in revision. These are not rules that you will be able to make up in the exam, so do take the time to learn them!

When answering written elements in the exam, keep your comments short and to the point.

Bullet points or a numbered answer (one mark per well explained point), are useful both in structuring your answer and for the marker reading it. Don't take the opportunity to write everything you know about VAT. Keep your comments relevant to the question.

- Anne can use the cash accounting scheme if her expected taxable turnover for the next 12 months does not exceed £1,350,000.

- In addition, Anne must be up-to-date with her VAT returns and VAT payments.

- Output VAT on most credit sales will be accounted for up to one month later than at present since the scheme will result in the tax point becoming the date that payment is received from customers.

- However, the recovery of input VAT will be delayed by two months.

- The scheme will provide automatic bad debt relief should a credit sale customer default on the payment of a debt.

(c)   (i)   **Sale of assets on a piecemeal basis**

Tutor's top tips:

Part (c) concerns the disposal of a VAT registered business.

Again, it is important to make short, clear points, matched to the number of marks available. Therefore two points are required for each part of the answer, although here the same point can be made twice!

If you do not know all the rules, you could still potentially pick up a mark or two, with some sensible comments, such as the need to deregister when you cease trading.

- Upon the cessation of trading Anne will cease to make taxable supplies, so her VAT registration will be cancelled on the date of cessation or an agreed later date.

- Output VAT will be due in respect of the value of the fixed assets at the date of deregistration on which VAT has been claimed (although output VAT is not due if it totals less than £1,000).

(ii) **Sale of business as a going concern**

- Since the purchaser is already registered for VAT, Anne's VAT registration will be cancelled as above.

- A sale of a business as a going concern is outside the scope of VAT, and therefore output VAT will not be due.

Tutorial note:

If the purchaser was not already registered for VAT, Anne could consider transferring her VAT registration. However, that point would not be relevant to this scenario.

It is important to always make your comments relevant to the circumstances in the question.

Examiner's report

This was the first time that VAT has been examined as a separate question, and it was therefore pleasing to see many very good answers.

In part (a) candidates often did not appreciate that the calculation of output VAT on credit sales had to take account of the discount for prompt payment even if it was not taken by customers.

In part (b) the answers of many candidates lacked sufficient depth to gain full marks. For example, the turnover limit of £1,350,000 was usually known, but only a minority of candidates correctly stated that it applied for the following 12-month period.

The same comment applies to part (c). For example, candidates generally appreciated that the taxpayer's VAT registration would be cancelled, but few stated that the reason for the cancellation was the cessation of making taxable supplies.

Many candidates stated that on a sale of the business as a going concern the VAT registration could be taken over by the purchaser despite the question clearly stating that the purchaser was already registered for VAT.

ACCA marking scheme		Marks
(a)	Output VAT – Cash sales	1.0
	– Credit sales	1.5
	Input VAT – Purchases and expenses	1.0
	– Impairment loss	1.5
	Due date	1.0
		6.0
(b)	Limit	1.0
	VAT returns and VAT payments	1.0
	Output VAT	1.0
	Input VAT	1.0
	Bad debt relief	1.0
		5.0

			Marks
(c) (i)	**Sale of assets on a piecemeal basis**		
	Cancellation of VAT registration		1.0
	Output VAT		1.0
			2.0
(ii)	**Sale of business as a going concern**		
	Cancellation of VAT registration		1.0
	Output VAT not due		1.0
			2.0
Total			15.0

Section 3

PILOT PAPER EXAM QUESTIONS

All FIVE questions are compulsory and MUST be attempted.

1   On 31 December 2009 Mark Kett ceased trading as a marketing consultant. He had been self-employed since 6 April 2004, and had always prepared his accounts to 5 April. On 1 January 2010 Mark commenced employment as the marketing manager of Sleep-Easy plc. The company runs a hotel.

The following information is available for the tax year 2009/10.

Self-employment

(1)   Mark's tax adjusted trading profit for the nine-month period ended 31 December 2009 is £21,700. This figure is before taking account of capital allowances.

(2)   The tax written down values for capital allowances purposes at 6 April 2009 were:

	£
General pool	13,800
Expensive motor car	14,600

The expensive motor car was used by Mark, and 40% of the mileage was for private purposes.

(3)   On 15 June 2009 Mark had purchased office furniture for £1,900. All of the items included in the general pool were sold for £18,800 on 31 December 2009. On the cessation of trading Mark personally retained the expensive motor car. Its value on 31 December 2009 was £11,800.

Employment

(1)   Mark is paid a salary of £3,250 (gross) per month by Sleep-Easy plc, from which income tax of £620 per month has been deducted under PAYE.

(2)   During the period from 1 January 2010 to 5 April 2010 Mark used his private motor car for business purposes. He drove 2,500 miles in the performance of his duties for Sleep-Easy plc, for which the company paid an allowance of 16 pence per mile. The relevant HM Revenue & Customs authorised mileage rate to be used as the basis of an expense claim is 40 pence per mile.

(3)   On 1 January 2010 Sleep-Easy plc provided Mark with an interest free loan of £80,000 so that he could purchase a new main residence.

(4)   During the period from 1 January 2010 to 5 April 2010 Mark was provided with free meals in Sleep-Easy plc's staff canteen. The total cost of these meals to the company was £400.

Property income

(1) Mark let out a furnished property throughout the tax year 2009/10. He received gross rents of £8,600, 5% of which was paid to a letting agency. During December 2009 Mark spent £540 on replacing dilapidated furniture and furnishings.

(2) From 6 April 2009 to 31 December 2009 Mark let out a spare room in his main residence, receiving rent of £350 per month.

Investment income

(1) During the tax year 2009/10 Mark received dividends of £2,880, interest from government stocks (gilts) of £2,900, and interest of £430 from an individual savings account (ISA). These were the actual cash amounts received.

(2) On 3 May 2009 Mark received a premium bond prize of £100.

Other information

(1) On 15 December 2009 Mark made a gift aid donation of £800 (net) to a national charity.

(2) Mark's payments on account of income tax in respect of the tax year 2009/10 totalled £11,381.

Required:

(a) **Compute the income tax payable by Mark for the tax year 2009/10, and the balancing payment or repayment that will be due for the year.** **(22 marks)**

(b) **Advise Mark as to how long he must retain the records used in preparing his tax return for the tax year 2009/10, and the potential consequences of not retaining the records for the required period.** **(3 marks)**

(Total: 25 marks)

2 (a) Scuba Ltd is a manufacturer of diving equipment. The following information is relevant for the year ended 31 March 2010:

Operating profit

The operating profit is £180,300.

The expenses that have been deducted in calculating this figure include:

	£
Depreciation and amortisation of lease	45,200
Entertaining customers	7,050
Entertaining employees	2,470
Gifts to customers (diaries costing £25 each displaying Scuba Ltd's name)	1,350
Gifts to customers (food hampers costing £80 each)	1,600

Leasehold property

On 1 July 2009 Scuba Ltd acquired a leasehold office building that is used for business purposes. The company paid a premium of £80,000 for the grant of a twenty-year lease.

Purchase of industrial building

Scuba Ltd purchased a new factory from a builder on 1 July 2009 for £240,000, and this was immediately brought into use. The cost was made up as follows:

	£
Drawing office serving the factory	34,000
General offices	40,000
Factory	98,000
Land	68,000
	240,000

Plant and machinery

On 1 April 2009 the tax written down values of plant and machinery were as follows:

	£
General pool	47,200
Expensive motor car	22,400

The following transactions took place during the year ended 31 March 2010:

		Cost/(Proceeds)
		£
3 April 2009	Purchased machinery	22,800
29 May 2009	Purchased a computer	1,100
4 August 2009	Purchased a motor car	10,400
18 November 2009	Purchased machinery	7,300
15 February 2010	Sold a lorry	(12,400)

The motor car purchased on 4 August 2009 for £10,400 has CO_2 emissions of 140 grams per kilometre and is used by the factory manager, and 40% of the mileage is for private journeys. The lorry sold on 15 February 2010 for £12,400 originally cost £19,800.

Property income

Scuba Ltd lets a retail shop that is surplus to requirements. The shop was let until 31 March 2009 but was then empty from 1 April 2009 to 31 July 2009. During this period Scuba Ltd spent £6,200 on decorating the shop, and £1,430 on advertising for new tenants. The shop was let from 1 August 2009 to 31 March 2010 at a quarterly rent of £7,200, payable in advance.

Interest received

Interest of £430 was received from HM Revenue & Customs on 31 October 2009 in respect of the overpayment of corporation tax for the year ended 31 March 2008.

Other information

Scuba Ltd has no associated companies, and the company has always had an accounting date of 31 March.

Required:

(i) Compute Scuba Ltd's tax adjusted trading profit for the year ended 31 March 2010.

Your computation should commence with the operating profit of £180,300, and should list all of the items referred to that are relevant to the adjustment of profits, indicating by the use of zero (0) any items that do not require adjustment.

You should ignore value added tax (VAT). **(15 marks)**

(ii) Compute Scuba Ltd's corporation tax liability for the year ended 31 March 2010. **(4 marks)**

(b) Scuba Ltd registered for value added tax (VAT) on 1 April 2007.

The company's VAT returns have been submitted as follows:

Quarter ended	VAT paid/ (refunded) £	Submitted
30 June 2007	18,600	One month late
30 September 2007	32,200	One month late
31 December 2007	8,800	On time
31 March 2008	3,400	Two months late
30 June 2008	(6,500)	One month late
30 September 2008	42,100	On time
31 December 2008	(2,900)	On time
31 March 2009	3,900	On time
30 June 2009	18,800	On time
30 September 2009	57,300	Two months late
31 December 2009	9,600	On time

Scuba Ltd always pays any VAT that is due at the same time that the related return is submitted.

During February 2010 Scuba Ltd discovered that a number of errors had been made when completing its VAT return for the quarter ended 31 December 2009.

As a result of these errors the company will have to make an additional payment of VAT to HM Revenue & Customs.

Required:

(i) State, giving appropriate reasons, the default surcharge consequences arising from Scuba Ltd's submission of its VAT returns for the quarter ended 30 June 2007 to the quarter ended 30 September 2009 inclusive. **(8 marks)**

(ii) Explain how Scuba Ltd can voluntarily disclose the errors relating to the VAT return for the quarter ended 31 December 2009, and state whether default interest will be due. **(3 marks)**

(Total: 30 marks)

3   Paul Opus disposed of the following assets during the tax year 2009/10:

(1)   On 10 April 2009 Paul sold 5,000 £1 ordinary shares in Symphony Ltd, an unquoted trading company, for £23,600. He had originally purchased 40,000 shares in the company on 23 June 2007 for £110,400. Paul has never been employed by Symphony Ltd.

(2)   On 15 June 2009 Paul made a gift of his entire shareholding of 10,000 £1 ordinary shares in Concerto plc to his daughter. On that date the shares were quoted on the Stock Exchange at £5.10 – £5.18, with recorded bargains of £5.00, £5.15 and £5.22. Paul's shareholding had been purchased on 29 April 1994 for £14,000. The shareholding is less than 1% of Concerto plc's issued share capital, and Paul has never been employed by Concerto plc.

(3)   On 9 August 2009 Paul sold a motor car for £16,400. The motor car had been purchased on 21 January 2006 for £12,800.

(4)   On 4 October 2009 Paul sold an antique vase for £8,400. The antique vase had been purchased on 19 January 2009 for £4,150.

(5)   On 31 December 2009 Paul sold a house for £220,000. The house had been purchased on 1 April 2003 for £114,700. Paul occupied the house as his main residence from the date of purchase until 30 June 2006. The house was then unoccupied until it was sold on 31 December 2009.

(6)   On 16 February 2010 Paul sold three acres of land for £285,000. He had originally purchased four acres of land on 17 July 2008 for £220,000. The market value of the unsold acre of land as at 16 February 2010 was £90,000.

(7)   On 5 March 2010 Paul sold a freehold holiday cottage for £125,000. The cottage had originally been purchased on 28 July 2008 for £101,600 by Paul's wife. She transferred the cottage to Paul on 16 November 2009 when it was valued at £114,800.

Required:

(a)   **Compute Paul's capital gains tax liability for the tax year 2009/10, and advise him by when this should be paid.**   **(15 marks)**

(b)   **State the conditions necessary to obtain Entrepreneurs' relief on the disposal of shares.**   **(3 marks)**

(c)   **Calculate the capital gains tax reduction for Paul assuming that he did qualify for Entrepreneurs' relief on the disposal of shares in Symphony Ltd.**   **(2 marks)**

(Total: 20 marks)

4   Li Fung commenced in self-employment on 1 October 2005. She initially prepared accounts to 30 June, but changed her accounting date to 31 March by preparing accounts for the nine-month period to 31 March 2009.

Li's trading profits since she commenced self-employment have been as follows:

	£
Nine-month period ended 30 June 2006	18,600
Year ended 30 June 2007	24,900
Year ended 30 June 2008	22,200
Nine-month period ended 31 March 2009	16,800
Year ended 31 March 2010	26,400

Required:

(a) State the qualifying conditions that must be met for a change of accounting date to be valid. **(3 marks)**

(b) Compute Li's trading income assessments for each of the five tax years 2005/06, 2006/07, 2007/08, 2008/09 and 2009/10. **(9 marks)**

(c) Advise Li of the advantages and disadvantages for tax purposes of changing her accounting date from 30 June to 31 March. **(3 marks)**

(Total: 15 marks)

5   Loser Ltd 's results for the year ended 30 June 2007, the nine month period ended 31 March 2008, the year ended 31 March 2009 and the year ended 31 March 2010 are as follows:

	Year ended 30 June 2007 £	Period ended 31 March 2008 £	Year ended 31 March 2009 £	Year ended 31 March 2010 £
Trading profit/(loss)	86,600	(25,700)	27,300	(98,300)
Property business profit	–	4,500	8,100	5,600
Gift Aid payments	(1,400)	(800)	(1,200)	(1,100)

Loser Ltd does not have any associated companies.

Required:

(a) State the factors that will influence a company's choice of loss relief claims.

You are not expected to consider group relief. **(3 marks)**

(b) Assuming that Loser Ltd claims relief for its losses as early as possible, compute the company's profits chargeable to corporation tax for the year ended 30 June 2007, the nine month period ended 31 March 2008, the year ended 31 March 2009 and the year ended 31 March 2010.

Your answer should clearly identify the amount of any losses that are unrelieved. **(5 marks)**

(c) Explain how your answer to (b) above would have differed if Loser Ltd had ceased trading on 31 March 2010. **(2 marks)**

(Total: 10 marks)

Section 4

ANSWERS TO PILOT PAPER EXAM QUESTIONS

1   MARK KETT

Key answer tips

Income tax questions often test the rules for both self employment and employment together as in this question. You must be ready to prepare a detailed income tax computation and remember to state when income is exempt rather than just leave it out.

Watch out for the extension of the basic rate band for the Gift Aid payment.

As Mark is in his final year of trading the capital allowances computation merely calculates balancing allowances or charges.

Do not ignore the section on administration requirements. There are some easy marks here for stating the rules for record keeping.

(a)   **Income tax computation – 2009/10**

	Total	Other income	Savings income	Dividend income
	£	£	£	£
Trading income (W1)	23,120	23,120		
Employment income (W3)	10,100	10,100		
Property business profit (W6)	7,310	7,310		
Interest from government stocks (received gross)	2,900		2,900	
Dividends (£2,880 × 100/90)	3,200			3,200
ISA interest (exempt)	–		–	
Premium Bond prize (exempt)	–		–	
	————	————	————	————
Total income	46,630	40,530	2,900	3,200
Less Personal Allowance	(6,475)	(6,475)		
	————	————	————	————
Taxable income	40,155	34,055	2,900	3,200
	————	————	————	————

Income tax:

	£		£
On Other income	34,055	x 20%	6,811
On Savings income	2,900	x 20%	580
On Dividend income	1,445	x 10%	144
Basic rate threshold (W7)	38,400		
On Dividend income	1,755	x 32.5%	570
	40,155		

	£
Income tax liability	8,105
Less Tax suffered at source	
Dividends (£3,200 at 10%)	(320)
PAYE (£620 × 3)	(1,860)
Income tax payable for 2009/10	5,925
Less Payments on account	(11,381)
Balancing repayment	(5,456)

Tutorial note:

1. Interest from Individual Savings Accounts (ISAs) and Premium Bond prizes are exempt from income tax.

2. Interest on Government stocks is received gross.

3. The basic rate band must be extended for the gross Gift Aid donation.

Workings

(W1) Trading income

	£
Trading profit	21,700
Add Net balancing charge (W2)	1,420
Trading income	23,120

Tutorial note:

A net balancing charge (see W2) increases the trading profit assessment for the period.

(W2) **Capital allowances**

	Pool £	Motor car £		Allowances £
TWDV b/f	13,800	14,600		
Addition	1,900			
	15,700			
Disposals	(18,800)	(11,800)		
Balancing charge	(3,100)			(3,100)
Balancing allowance		2,800	× 60%	1,680
Net balancing charge (Note)				(1,420)

Tutorial note:

1. In the year of cessation, there are no AIA, FYA or WDAs. The market value of disposals is deducted and balancing charges and balancing allowances arise.

2. If an overall net balancing allowance arises, it is deducted from trading profits.

   If an overall net balancing charge arises, the net balancing charge is added to the trading profits in the final year.

(W3) **Employment income**

	£
Salary (£3,250 × 3 months)	9,750
Beneficial loan (W4)	950
Staff canteen (Note 1)	Nil
Less Expense claim (W5) (Note 2)	(600)
Employment income	10,100

Tutorial note:

1. The provision of meals in a staff canteen does not give rise to a taxable benefit.

2. When calculating the employment income, remember that Mark can deduct the difference between the mileage allowance received and the official rate of allowance.

(W4) **Beneficial loan**

The benefit is calculated as 4.75% of the average loan outstanding during the period, time apportioned if the loan has not been in existence for the whole period.

(£80,000 × 4.75% × 3/12) = £950

(W5) **Mileage allowance**

	£
Authorised mileage rate (2,500 miles at 40p)	1,000
Less Mileage allowance paid by company (2,500 at 16p)	(400)
Expense deduction	600

(W6) **Property income**

	£
Rent receivable	8,600
Less Agency fees (£8,600 at 5%)	(430)
Wear and tear allowance (£8,600 at 10%)	(860)
Property business profit	7,310

Tutorial note:

1. *There is no deduction available for the replacement of furniture and furnishings, the wear and tear allowance is claimed instead.*

2. *Mark's property income from the rent of his spare room is £3,150 (£350 x 9) which is less than £4,250, and it is therefore exempt under the rent-a-room scheme.*

(W7) **Extension of basic rate band**

	£
Basic rate band threshold	37,400
Plus Gift Aid donation (£800 x 100/80)	1,000
Extended basic rate band	38,400

(b) **Retention of records**

- The business records relating to self-employment and property income for 2009/10 must be retained until 31 January 2016 (i.e. five years after the 31 January following the end of the tax year.)

- As Mark is in business during 2009/10, all of his other records relating to employment and investment income must also be retained until the same date.

- A failure to retain records for 2009/10 can result in a penalty of up to £3,000. However, the maximum penalty will only be charged in serious cases.

ACCA marking scheme			
			Marks
(a)	Trading profit		0.5
	Capital allowances	– Pool	2.0
		– Motor car	2.0
	Employment income		1.0
	Beneficial loan		1.0
	Staff canteen		0.5
	Expense claim		1.5
	Property business profit		2.0
	Furniture and furnishings		0.5
	Rent-a-room scheme		1.0
	Interest from government stocks		1.0
	Dividends		1.0
	Individual savings account		0.5
	Premium bond prize		0.5
	Personal allowance		0.5
	Extension of basic rate band		1.0
	Income tax		2.5
	Tax suffered at source	– PAYE	1.0
		– Dividends	1.0
	Balancing repayment		1.0
			——
			22.0
			——
(b)	Business records		1.0
	Other records		1.0
	Penalty		1.0
			——
			3.0
			——
	Total		25.0
			——

2 SCUBA LTD

Key answer tips

This is a classic question testing your knowledge of corporation tax. There is a great deal of information to deal with and it is essential you have a methodical approach.

First draw up the proforma for the adjusted profit computation and insert the profit figure. Include in your computation both the items that need adjustment, with the relevant figure, **and** the items that do not need adjustment with a zero (0).

Before you can complete the adjusted profit computation you need to do workings to calculate capital allowances.

Then you can complete the calculation of PCTCT and the corporation tax liability. Note carefully the information about associated companies.

Part (b) contains 11 marks for VAT and requires detailed knowledge of the default surcharge and the treatment of errors on a VAT return.

Remember that VAT is an important area in the syllabus and will always appear in the examination for about 10 marks and can be as high as 15 marks of the paper.

(a)   (i)   Trading profit – year ended 31 March 2010

		£
Operating profit		180,300
Add	Depreciation and amortisation of lease	45,200
	Entertaining customers (Note 1)	7,050
	Entertaining employees (Note 1)	0
	Gifts to customers – diaries (Note 2)	0
	Gifts to customers – food hampers (Note 2)	1,600
		234,150
Less	Deduction for lease premium (W1)	(1,860)
	Capital allowances – IBA (W3)	(3,440)
	– Plant and machinery (W2)	(43,240)
Trading profit		185,610

Tutorial note:

1.   *The only exception to the non-deductibility of entertainment expenditure is when it is in respect of employees.*

2.   *Gifts to customers are an allowable deduction if they cost less than £50 per recipient per year, are not of food, drink, tobacco, or vouchers for exchangeable goods, and carry a conspicuous advertisement for the company making the gift.*

The gift of diaries is therefore allowable but the gift of hampers is not allowable.

Workings

(W1) Deduction for lease premium

The office building is used for business purposes, and so a proportion of the lease premium assessed on the landlord can be deducted.

	£
Premium received	80,000
Less: 80,000 × 2% × (20 – 1)	(30,400)
Amount assessed on the landlord	49,600

This is deductible over the life of the lease, starting from 1 July 2009, so the deduction for the year ended 31 March 2010:

(£49,600 ÷ 20) × 9/12 = £1,860.

(W2) Plant and machinery

	£	Pool £	Motor car £	Allowances £
TWDV b/f		47,200	22,400	
Addition (no AIA or FYA)				
(Notes 1, 2 and 3)				
Car (CO_2 between 111 – 160 g/km)		10,400		
Additions (with AIA and FYA)				
Machinery	22,800			
Computer	1,100			
Machinery	7,300			
	———			
	31,200			
Less AIA (Note 3)	(31,200)			31,200
	———			
	Nil			
Proceeds – Lorry		(12,400)		
		———		
		45,200		
WDA (20%)		(9,040)		9,040
WDA (Restricted)			(3,000)	3,000
FYA (40%) (Note 4)	(Nil)			
	———	Nil		
		———	———	
TWDV c/f		36,160	19,400	
		———	———	
Total allowances				43,240
				———

Tutorial note:

1. Brought forward 'expensive' cars are dealt with under the old rules. A WDA of 20% is available regardless of the car's CO_2 emissions, however, the total WDA for a 12 month period is restricted to £3,000.

2. New car purchases where the CO_2 emissions are between 111 – 160 g/km are put in the main pool, and are eligible for a WDA at 20%.

3. The private use of the motor car by the factory manager is irrelevant, full allowances are available. The manager will be assessed to income tax on the private use of the a car as an employment benefit.

4. The temporary FYA is not available as the expenditure is already covered by the AIA.

(W3) **Industrial buildings allowance**

	£
Drawing office	34,000
General offices	40,000
Factory	98,000
Eligible expenditure	172,000
IBAs (£172,000 × 2%)	3,440

Tutorial note:

1. *The cost of the land does not qualify.*

    The general offices does qualify as it cost less than 25% of the total potentially qualifying cost.

    Total potential qualifying cost = (£240,000 − £68,000) = £172,000

    25% of potential qualifying cost = (£172,000 × 25%) = £43,000.

    Cost of offices = £40,000

    Therefore the general offices are eligible for relief.

2. *The industrial building was purchased part way through the year, however the length of ownership is not relevant. The length of the accounting period is important.*

    As it was purchased in the year ended 31 March 2010, the full 2% allowance is available.

(a) (ii) **Corporation tax computation – year ended 31 March 2010**

	£
Trading profit	185,610
Property business profit (W1)	11,570
Interest	430
PCTCT	197,610
Corporation tax liability (W2) (£197,610 × 21%)	41,498

Workings

(W1) Property business profit

	£
Rent receivable	
(£7,200 x 1/3) = £2,400 per month × 8 months	19,200
Less: Decorating	(6,200)
Advertisements	(1,430)
Property business profit	11,570

(W2) Corporation tax rates

Scuba Ltd has no franked investment income, therefore the PCTCT = 'Profits'.

Scuba Ltd has no associated companies and therefore 'Profits' are compared to the full upper and lower limits of £1,500,000 and £300,000.

As 'Profits' are £197,610, the company is a small company and therefore the rate of corporation tax is 21%.

(b) (i) Default surcharge

- The late submission of the VAT return for the quarter ended 30 June 2007 will have resulted in HM Revenue & Customs issuing a surcharge liability notice specifying a surcharge period running to 30 June 2008.

- The late payment of VAT for the quarter ended 30 September 2007 will have resulted in a surcharge of £644 (£32,200 × 2%).

- The late payment of VAT for the quarter ended 31 March 2008 will have resulted in a surcharge of £170 (£3,400 × 5%), but this will not have been collected as it was less than £400.

- Although the VAT return for the quarter ended 30 June 2008 was submitted late, this will not have resulted in a surcharge as Scuba Ltd was due a refund for this period.

- The continued late submission of VAT returns will have resulted in the surcharge period being extended to 30 September 2008, then to 31 March 2009, and finally to 30 June 2009.

- Scuba Ltd then submitted the four consecutive VAT returns during the surcharge period running to 30 June 2009 on time, and so will have reverted to a clean default surcharge record.

- The late submission of the VAT return for the quarter ended 30 September 2009 will therefore simply have resulted in a surcharge liability notice specifying a surcharge period running to 30 September 2010.

(ii) Errors on VAT return

- If the net errors total less than the higher of £10,000 or 1% of turnover, then they can be voluntarily disclosed by simply entering them on the VAT return for the quarter ended 31 March 2010.

- If the net errors total more than this limit, then they can be voluntarily disclosed, but disclosure must be made separately to HM Revenue & Customs.

- Default interest will be charged if the net errors total more than the limit.

Tutorial note:

In either case a penalty for submitting an incorrect return can be charged.

However, it is unlikely that a penalty will be charged for an error due to a mistake, rather than a deliberate error, where the mistake is small enough to be disclosed on the next VAT return.

ACCA marking scheme

			Marks
(a)	(i)	Trading profit	
		Operating profit	0.5
		Depreciation and amortisation	0.5
		Entertaining (Staff 0.5 Customers 0.5)	1.0
		Gifts to customers (Diaries 0.5 Food hampers 0.5)	1.0
		Lease premium – Assessable amount	1.5
		– Deduction	1.5
		IBA – Land	0.5
		– General offices	1.0
		– Eligible expenditure	1.0
		– Allowance	1.0
		P & M – Pool	2.0
		– Motor car	1.0
		– AIA	2.5
			———
			15.0
			———
	(ii)	Corporation tax computation	
		Trading profit	0.5
		Property business profit	
		– Rent receivable	1.0
		– Expenses	1.0
		Interest	1.0
		Corporation tax	0.5
			———
			4.0
			———
(b)	(i)	Default surcharge	
		Quarter ended 30 June 2007	1.0
		Quarter ended 30 September 2007	1.0
		Quarter ended 31 March 2008	2.0
		Quarter ended 30 June 2009	1.0
		Extension of surcharge period	1.0
		Four consecutive VAT returns on time	1.0
		Quarter ended 30 September 2009	1.0
			———
			8.0
			———
	(ii)	Errors on VAT return	
		Net errors below limit	1.0
		Net errors above limit	1.0
		Default interest	1.0
			———
			3.0
			———
Total			30.0
			———

3   PAUL OPUS (ADAPTED)

Key answer tips

This is a capital gains computation for an individual covering the commonly tested areas of shares, chattels, principal private residence exemption, part disposals and a husband and wife transfer.

Be careful with the share valuation rules for the Concerto shares. Also remember that for part disposals, you split the cost in proportion to the values of the part disposed of and the part kept, and not their sizes.

Even if you do not manage to calculate all the gains, make sure you get the easy marks for calculating the capital gains tax liability (based on your figures) and stating the due date of payment.

Entrepreneurs' relief is an important business relief tested in parts (b) and (c).

(a)   **Capital gains tax liability – 2009/10**

	£	£
Ordinary shares in Symphony Ltd (Note 1)		
Disposal proceeds	23,600	
Less Cost (£110,400 × 5,000/40,000)	(13,800)	
	————	9,800
Ordinary shares Concerto plc (Note 2)		
Deemed proceeds (10,000 × £5.11) (W1)	51,100	
Less Cost	(14,000)	
	————	37,100
Car (exempt) (Note 3)		Nil
Antique vase (W2)		4,000
House		
Disposal proceeds	220,000	
Less Cost	(114,700)	
	————	
	105,300	
Less Principal private residence exemption (W3)	(97,500)	
	————	7,800
Land		
Disposal proceeds	285,000	
Less Cost of part disposal (W4)	(167,200)	
	————	117,800
Holiday cottage		
Disposal proceeds	125,000	
Less Cost (Note 4)	(101,600)	
	————	23,400
		————
Total chargeable gains		199,900
Less Annual exemption		(10,100)
		————
Taxable gains		189,800
		————
Capital gains tax (£189,800 × 18%)		34,164
		————
Due date		31 January 2011

Tutorial note:

1.   There is no Entrepreneurs' relief on the Symphony shares as Paul does not work for the company.

2.   There is no gift relief available on the quoted shares in Concerto plc as it is not Paul's personal trading company (i.e. Paul owns less a 5% interest in the company). For the same reason, Entrepreneurs' relief is not available.

3.   Motor cars are exempt from CGT.

4.   The transfer of the holiday cottage between Paul and his wife is a nil gain / nil loss transfer. This means that the asset is transferred to Paul at the original cost, which is then used in his computation on the subsequent disposal of the shares.

Workings

(W1)   **Value of Concerto plc shares**

The shares in Concerto plc are valued at the lower of:

(i)   Quarter up method = (£5.10 + 1/4 × (£5.18 − £5.10)) = £5.12

(ii)   Average of marked bargains = (£5.00 + £5.22) × 1/2 = £5.11

Therefore valued at £5.11 per share

(W2)   **Antique vase**

	£
Proceeds	8,400
Less Cost	(4,150)
Gain	4,250
Capital gain cannot exceed:	
5/3 × (£8,400 − £6,000)	4,000

Tutorial note:

The antique vase is a non-wasting chattel.

It is important to be able to recognise when an asset is a chattel (i.e. tangible and moveable) and therefore that the disposal is subject to special rules.

In this case the chattel cost less than £6,000 but was sold for more than £6,000 and so the 5/3 rds rule applies.

(W3) **Principal private residence relief**

The total period of ownership of the house is 81 months, of which a total of 75 months qualify for exemption (i.e. 39 months period of actual occupation from 1 April 2003 to 30 June 2006, plus final 36 months).

PPR exemption = (£105,300 × 75/81) = £97,500

(W4) **Cost of part disposal**

The cost of the three acres of land sold:

$$£220,000 \times \frac{£285,000}{£285,000 + £90,000} = £167,200$$

Tutorial note:

On a part disposal the cost of the part disposed of is calculated using A/(A + B) where:

A = the value of the part disposed of, and

B = the value of the part retained.

(b) **Conditions for obtaining Entrepreneurs' relief on shares**

- Shares must have been owned for 1 year prior to the year of disposal
- The shares must be in a trading company
- The individual disposing of the shares must be:
  - an employee of the company, **and**
  - own at least 5% of the ordinary share capital and voting rights of the company.

(c) **Tax reduction if Entrepreneurs' relief on shares in Symphony Ltd**

Entrepreneurs' relief reduces the gain on the shares by 4/9 ths.

The capital gains tax reduction would therefore be £784 (18% × 4/9 × £9,800).

Tutorial note:

Entrepreneurs' relief reduces the capital gains tax payable on certain qualifying business disposals. If applicable, the first £1 million of gains on qualifying business disposals will be reduced by 4/9ths.

The remaining 5/9ths are taxed at 18% in the normal way, resulting in an effective rate of tax of 10% on the first million of qualifying gains (18% x 5/9 = 10%).

ACCA marking scheme			
			Marks
(a)	Symphony Ltd	– Proceeds	0.5
		– Cost	1.0
	Concerto plc	– Proceeds	2.0
		– Cost	0.5
	Motor car		0.5
	Antique vase		2.0
	House	– Proceeds	0.5
		– Cost	0.5
		– Exemption	2.0
	Land	– Proceeds	0.5
		– Cost	2.0
	Holiday cottage		1.0
	Annual exemption		0.5
	Capital gains tax		1.0
	Due date		0.5
			――
			15.0
			――
(b)	1 mark per condition		3.0
(c)	Calculation		2.0
			――
Total			20.0

4   LI FUNG

Key answer tips

This question tests both the rules for opening years and for change of accounting date for a sole trader. It is important not to ignore questions like this.

It is possible to pick up some easy marks for the written parts even if you cannot do all the calculations.

(a)   **Conditions for a valid change of accounting date**

- The change of accounting date must be notified to HM Revenue & Customs by the 31 January following the tax year in which the change is made (i.e. for 2008/09 by 31 January 2011).

- The first accounts to the new accounting date must not exceed 18 months in length.

- There must not have been a change of accounting date within the preceding five tax years, although this does not apply if the present change is made for genuine commercial reasons.

(b)   **Trading income assessments**

		£
2005/06	Actual basis	
	(1 October 2005 to 5 April 2006)	
	(£18,600 × 6/9) (Note 1)	12,400

		£
2006/07	First 12 months trading (1 October 2005 to 30 September 2006) £18,600 + (£24,900 × 3/12)	24,825
2007/08	CYB (y/e 30 June 2007)	24,900
2008/09	Change of accounting date (1 July 2007 to 31 March 2009) (Note 2)	
	Year ended 30 June 2008	22,200
	Period ended 31 March 2009	16,800
		39,000
	Relief for overlap profits (W)	(18,625)
		20,375
2009/10	CYB (y/e 31 March 2010)	26,400

Working: Overlap profits

There are overlap profits of:

- £12,400 in respect of the six-month period 1 October 2005 to 5 April 2006, and

- £6,225 (£24,900 × 3/12) in respect of the three-month period 1 July 2006 to 30 September 2006.

The total overlap profits are therefore £18,625 (£12,400 + £6,225).

The overlap profits arise over a 9 month period (6 months and 3 months).

Tutorial note:

1. *The assessment for 2006/07 is the first twelve months of trading as the accounting date falling in that year is less than twelve months from the commencement of trading.*

2. *As the accounting year end is moving to a date later in the tax year (i.e. 31 March rather than 30 June), the basis period for the year of change will be the period ending with the new accounting date.*

   In this case, the period running from the end of the 2007/08 assessment to 31 March 2009. Therefore, profits for 21 months (from 1 July 2007 to 31 March 2009) are assessed.

   The normal basis of assessment is 12 months. Accordingly, 9 months (21 months – 12 months) of the overlap profits may be offset.

   Therefore, all nine months of overlap profits arising in the opening years are relieved in the year of change.

(c) **Advantages of changing from 30 June to 31 March**

- If Li changes her accounting date from 30 June to 31 March the application of the basis period rules will be simplified.

- The maximum assessment in the year of cessation will be for twelve months.

- Li's existing overlap profits are fully utilised as a result of the change. Otherwise, these overlap profits would not be relieved until the cessation of trading.

Disadvantages of changing from 30 June to 31 March

- The disadvantage is that the interval between earning profits and paying the related tax liability will be nine months shorter with an accounting date of 31 March.

ACCA marking scheme			Marks
(a)	Notification		1.0
	18 month limit		1.0
	Change within five years		1.0
			———
			3.0
			———
(b)	Assessments	– 2005/06	1.0
		– 2006/07	1.5
		– 2007/08	1.0
		– 2008/09	2.0
		– 2009/10	0.5
	Overlap profits		2.0
	Relieved in 2008/09		1.0
			———
			9.0
			———
(c)	Simplification		0.5
	Assessment in year of cessation		0.5
	Overlap profits		1.0
	Disadvantages		1.0
			———
			3.0
			———
Total			15.0
			———

5 LOSER LTD

Key answer tips

A tricky question on corporation tax loss reliefs. There are two trading losses to deal with and it is important to deal with the earlier loss first. It is also important to lay out your answer using a standard proforma.

Note that the new transitional rules introduced in FA2009 which allow an extended carry back of losses for accounting periods ended between 24 November 2008 and 23 November 2010 are tested. The losses can therefore be carried back 36 months rather than 12 months.

(a) **Factors influencing the choice of loss reliefs**

- The rate of corporation tax at which relief will be obtained, with preference being given to profits charged at the marginal rate of 29.75% in FY2008 and FY2009 (32.5% in FY2007) to the full rate of 28% in FY2008 and FY2009 (30% in FY2007).

- The timing of the relief obtained, with a claim against total profits in the current year and previous 12 (or 36) months resulting in earlier relief than a claim to carry forward the loss against future trading profits.

- The extent to which relief for Gift Aid payments will be lost, since these cannot be carried forward.

(b) **Loser Ltd – Profits chargeable to corporation tax**

	y/e 30 June 2007 £	p/e 31 March 2008 £	y/e 31 March 2009 £	y/e 31 March 2010 £
Trading profit	86,600	Nil	27,300	Nil
Property profit	–	4,500	8,100	5,600
Total profits	86,600	4,500	35,400	5,600
Loss relief				
– Current period		(4,500)		(5,600)
– 12 months c/b	(21,200)		(35,400)	
– Extended 36 months carry back	(50,000)		–	
	15,400	Nil	Nil	Nil
Less Gift Aid	(1,400)	wasted	wasted	wasted
PCTCT	14,000	Nil	Nil	Nil

Loss working	p/e 31 March 2008 £	y/e 31 March 2010 £
Trading loss	25,700	98,300
Loss against total profits		
– Current period (p/e 31.3.08)	(4,500)	
– 12 month carry back (y/e 30.6.07)	(21,200)	
– Current period (y/e 31.3.10)		(5,600)
– 12 month carry back (y/e 31.3.09)		(35,400)
– Extended 36 months carry back (p/e 31.3.08) (y/e 30.6.07)(Maximum) (Note)		(Nil) (50,000)
Loss carried forward	Nil	7,300

Tutorial note:

As the loss making accounting period ends between 24 November 2008 and 23 November 2010, up to £50,000 of the remaining loss (after the 'normal' current period and 12 month carry back claim against total profits) is available to carry back for a further 24 months.

The 24 months covers the 9 months to 31 March 2008, then the year ended 30 June 2007 and then three months of the year ended 30 June 2006. However, the maximum carry back is set off before going back to the year ended 30 June 2006.

Note that the loss making period is 12 months in length (y/e 31 March 2010) and therefore the maximum extended carry back claim is £50,000. The maximum £50,000 is only time apportioned if the loss making period is less than 12 months.

(c) **If Loser Ltd ceased to trade on 31 March 2010**

- The whole of the trading loss for the final twelve months of trading can be relieved against total profits for the previous 36 months under the terminal loss relief rules.

- There is no £50,000 maximum restriction.

- Therefore the unrelieved losses of £7,300 could have been carried back and fully set off in the year ended 30 June 2007.

ACCA marking scheme		
		Marks
(a)	Rate of corporation tax	1.0
	Timing of relief	1.0
	Gift Aid	1.0
		———
		3.0
		———
(b)	Trading profit	0.5
	Property business profit	0.5
	Loss relief – current and carry back 12 months	1.0
	Loss relief – extended carry back	1.0
	Gift Aid	1.0
	Unrelieved trading loss	1.0
		———
		5.0
		———
(c)	Terminal loss relief – not restricted	1.0
	Year ended 30 June 2007	1.0
		———
		2.0
		———
Total		10.0
		———